VOYAGE
OF
REDISCOVERY

VOYAGE
OF
REDISCOVERY

A CULTURAL ODYSSEY
THROUGH POLYNESIA

BEN FINNEY

WITH MARLENE AMONG, CHAD BAYBAYAN,
TAI CROUCH, PAUL FROST, BERNARD KILONSKY,
RICHARD RHODES, THOMAS SCHROEDER,
DIXON STROUP, NAINOA THOMPSON,
ROBERT WORTHINGTON, AND ELISA YADAO

ILLUSTRATIONS BY RICHARD RHODES

UNIVERSITY OF CALIFORNIA PRESS
BERKELEY / LOS ANGELES / LONDON

The publisher gratefully acknowledges the contribution
provided by the General Endowment Fund of the
Associates of the University of California Press.

University of California Press
Berkeley and Los Angeles, California

University of California Press
London, England

Copyright © 1994 by
The Regents of the University of California

Library of Congress Cataloging-in-Publication Data
Finney, Ben R.
    Voyage of rediscovery: a cultural odyssey through
  Polynesia. Ben Finney with Marlene Among . . . [et al.];
  illustrations by Richard Rhodes.
        p.   cm.
    Includes bibliographical references and index.
    ISBN 0-520-08002-5 (cloth: alk paper)
    1. Navigation—Polynesia.   2. Canoes and canoeing—
  Polynesia.   3. Hōkūleʻa (Canoe).   4. Polynesia—
  Description.   5. Polynesia—Social life and customs.
  I. Title.
  GN670.F56   1994
  910.4'5—dc20
                                                94–3998
                                                   CIP

Printed in the United States of America

2 3 4 5 6 7 8 9

The paper used in this publication meets the minimum re-
quirements of American National Standard for Information
Sciences—Permanence of Paper for Printed Library Materials,
ANSI Z39.48–1984 ⊚

Left endpaper: Hawaiʻi to Aotearoa 1985
Right endpaper: Aotearoa to Hawaiʻi 1986–1987

To the memory of Tommy Holmes of Hawai'i who co-founded the Polynesian Voyaging Society and sailed on the 1976 voyage; Andy Ali'i Espirito of Hawai'i and Rodo Tuko Williams of Tahiti who sailed on the 1976 voyage; Eddie Aikau of Hawai'i who sailed on the 1978 voyage; Dan Wright of Canada and Puaniho Tauotaha of Tahiti who sailed on the Voyage of Rediscovery; Ray Lanterman of Hawai'i, Board of Directors, Polynesian Voyaging Society; and the Māori leaders Sir James Henare, Tupi Puriri, and Nicky Conrad who welcomed us to Aotearoa in 1985

CONTENTS

FIGURES

PREFACE

In midsummer of 1985, *Hōkūle'a*,* a reconstruction of an ancient Polynesian voyaging canoe, set sail for the South Pacific from the fishing village of Miloli'i on the southwestern coast of the island of Hawai'i, the largest in the Hawaiian chain. Two years later this twin-hulled canoe returned from the South Pacific to the island of O'ahu, landing at Kualoa, the sandy point rich in Hawaiian history from which she had been launched in 1975. During those two years the crew, composed primarily of Hawaiians and their fellow Polynesians from islands south of the equator, sailed *Hōkūle'a* over 12,000 nautical miles through Polynesia, touching on seven archipelagos spread from Hawai'i to New Zealand.

This long voyage was the culmination of an initiative, begun in the early 1960s, to reconstruct Polynesian sailing canoes and then test both them and the traditional ways of navigating without instruments over legendary migration and voyaging routes. Our experimental effort was started primarily to challenge the dismissal of Polynesian sailing and navigational abilities, and the consequently warped portrayals of Polynesian prehistory, con-

---

*Pronounced *Hō-kū-le-'a*. The macrons over vowels indicate that they are longer than unmarked vowels and are stressed. The (') indicates a consonant called a glottal stop. It is similar to the sound between the *oh's* in the English *oh-oh*. As vowel length and glottal stops are critical to the meaning of Hawaiian and other Polynesian words, they are marked where known.

tained in the then influential books of Thor Heyerdahl and Andrew Sharp. Heyerdahl claimed that the canoes of the ancestral Polynesians were too primitive to have allowed them to sail into the Pacific from Southeast Asia against the flow of the trade winds and accompanying currents, and therefore Polynesia must have been settled from the Americas by people drifting and sailing before these dominant easterly winds and currents. Although Andrew Sharp accepted that Polynesia had been settled from the Southeast Asian side of the Pacific, he contended that because the Polynesians could not navigate accurately without instruments, and because their canoes were frail craft unsuited for long voyages, they had settled their island world "accidentally" by being randomly pushed to the various islands by the vagaries of wind and current. Since by the 1960s Polynesian voyaging canoes had disappeared and ways of navigating without instruments had been largely forgotten, those of us who objected to Heyerdahl's and Sharp's negative characterizations of Polynesian voyaging technology and skills—as well as the way these authors employed their negative characterizations to promote distorted views of how the islands had been discovered and settled—concluded that we would have to reconstruct the canoes and ways of navigating, and then test them at sea, in order to get at the truth.

After a decade of planning, of navigational trials conducted on a modern catamaran, and the reconstruction and testing of a Hawaiian double canoe, a group of us formed the Polynesian Voyaging Society for the purpose of building a deep-sea voyaging canoe and testing her and Polynesian navigational methods on the legendary voyaging route between Hawai'i and Tahiti. In 1975 we launched *Hōkūle'a*, and in 1976 sailed her from Hawai'i to Tahiti and back, a voyage that went a long way toward refuting the dismissive theories of Heyerdahl, Sharp, and others by demonstrating how a traditionally navigated canoe of ancient design was well adapted to sailing under various wind and sea conditions between islands separated by thousands of miles of blue water.

Hōkūle'a was built for more than just conducting nautical experiments, however. Without the voyaging canoe the Hawaiians, Tahitians, and other Polynesian peoples that we know today would never have existed. The far-flung islands in the middle of the Pacific were beyond the reach of humankind until some 3,500 years ago when their distant ancestors, seafarers at the western edge of the Pacific, developed the double canoe as an exploring, colonizing vessel and then started pushing eastward until finally, after many generations, their descendants found and colonized all the inhabitable islands of that oceanic realm we now call Polynesia. Yet, at the time we started our efforts, the voyaging canoes that had made this migration possible, as well as the seamanship and navigational skills employed to sail and guide them, were at best dim memories among contemporary Hawaiians and other Polynesians. Moreover, those oral traditions about their seafaring past that had been written down were under attack as wild exaggerations if not outright fictions. We therefore hoped that by enabling Hawaiians and other Polynesians to reconstruct a voyaging canoe and then sail her by traditional methods over a legendary voyaging route, they would gain a needed sense of their cultural heritage as descendants of the premier seafarers of the ancient world.

The 1976 voyage to Tahiti and return did boost the Hawaiians' consciousness about, and pride in, their voyaging heritage; however, one element was missing in that re-creation. Although *Hōkūle'a* had been captained by a Hawaiian, and largely crewed by Hawaiians, because we could not find any Hawaiians or other Polynesians who still retained the old navigational skills, we recruited a master navigator from a remote Micronesian atoll in the western Pacific to guide the canoe to Tahiti. By 1980, however, a young Hawaiian named Nainoa Thompson had learned how to navigate without instruments, and that year he and a mostly Hawaiian crew sailed the canoe to Tahiti and back once more. By using the stars, ocean swells, and other natural signs to guide the canoe both ways, Nainoa duplicated and extended the 1976 feat, demonstrating how a young Hawaiian could relearn this intellectually demanding art and apply it successfully over a long sea route sailed centuries ago by his ancestors.

The Voyage of Rediscovery was designed to extend the scientific and cultural reach of *Hōkūle'a* beyond Hawai'i and Tahiti by sailing her over a number of other voyaging routes celebrated in the ancient traditions and by getting the islanders along the way involved in our endeavor. That this last voyage was basically Polynesian in conception, and owed its success primarily to those Hawaiians, Tahitians, Marquesans, Cook Islanders, Māori, Tongans, and Samoans who sailed *Hōkūle'a* from island to island during the two-year odyssey, has made it all the more culturally significant. Those who sailed *Hōkūleʻa* enjoyed the unique experience of stepping back in time to relive their seafaring heritage, whereas those who helped the canoe get underway, greeted her along the way, or simply followed the progress of the voyage were able to vicariously experience this adventure in cultural rediscovery.

A word of caution is necessary here in interpreting the scientific meaning of our voyage, however. By sailing *Hōkūleʻa* between Hawaiʻi and Tahiti, Rarotonga and Aotearoa, and other centers of the Polynesian world, we cannot claim to have established that earlier canoe voyagers followed exactly the same routes or sailed over them just as we did. But we can say that by sailing throughout Polynesia in a canoe designed to perform like an ancient voyaging craft, and by directly testing our relearned skills in traditional navigation and seamanship over a variety of legendary voyaging routes, we have been able to gain realistic, hands-on insights into canoe sailing, noninstrument navigation, and how to use variations in wind patterns to sail where you want to go. We can further assert that these findings are revolutionizing our understanding of how the early Polynesians were able to explore and settle their vast island world as well as to what degree they were able to maintain communication over the vast expanses of open ocean separating the far-flung outposts of their nation.

In the pages that follow I have applied a perspective on Polynesian seafaring gained through developing this experimental approach to canoe voyaging, co-founding the Polynesian Voyaging Society and serving as its first president, and sailing on *Hōkūleʻa* whenever I could get leave from my duties at the University of Hawaiʻi. From the beginning, however, this has been a group project, and it has been a rare privilege to work with literally thousands of people and organizations whose ideas, labors, and contributions have made these experimental and cultural endeavors possible.

The Hawaiian concept of *laulima* literally means "many hands," or, figuratively, a group of people working cooperatively together. Both meanings apply to the multitudes of people spread across Polynesia who helped make the Voyage of Rediscovery a reality. Our effort has been built upon the base of the Polynesian Voyaging Society, a nonprofit, membership organization, and a major part of our funding for the voyage came from the people of Hawai'i through state appropriations to support the educational aspects of our program. We would also like to acknowledge support from the Hawai'i Maritime Center, the Gerbode Foundation, the Cooke Foundation, the Sam and Mary Castle Foundation, Myron Thompson and Laura Thompson, Clorinda Lucas, Edward Kawananakoa, Po'omai Kawananakoa, Abigail Kawananakoa, Jane Dunaway, Clarence Coleman, Kapi'olani Marignoli, Tom Gentry, Edward Scripps II, Bernard Kilonsky, and all the many others without whose generous contributions we never could have made our voyage. Similarly, we are indebted to Governor George Ariyoshi, Governor John Waihe'e, their staffs, and other state and local officials for their active encouragement and help, as well as to people all over Hawai'i who have lent us a hand, including, for example, the people of Miloli'i who hosted *Hōkūle'a* and her crew before departure for the South Pacific, and the citizens of Kalaupapa who gave the crew their first meal upon returning to Hawaiian soil. We would also like to acknowledge the help of Hawaiian Airlines, Bank of Hawai'i, Hawai'i Public Television, KGMB-TV, radio station KCCN, the University of Hawai'i's Peacesat organization and its Hawai'i Institute of Geophysics, the U.S. Navy, the U.S. Coast Guard, and the many other companies and organizations who pitched in to help during the voyage. In addition, we would like to register a special thanks to Dr. Charman Akina and all the other physicians who looked after the health needs of our crew members, particularly those who left their island homes to work on the project in Hawai'i.

Unfortunately, to list all the individuals and organizations in Hawai'i, on the islands along *Hōkūle'a*'s route, and elsewhere in the world that contributed to the success of this project would result in a book-length supplement. The names of key persons involved in the voyage—crew members who sailed each leg of the Voyage of Rediscovery, the officers of the Polynesian Voyaging Society that sponsored the voyage, those officials and leaders in the South Pacific who welcomed *Hōkūle'a* to their islands, and those in Hawai'i who welcomed the canoe home to Kualoa—are listed in appendixes A, B, and C. These were prepared by Marlene Among (who coordinated the project while serving as assistant to the president of the Polynesian Voyaging Society), and Robert Worthington (who handled the protocol between the canoe's crew and delegates from the Polynesian Voyaging Society and the islanders at the various island stops). We hope that those who, because of space limitations, could not be listed will accept our sincere apologies.

In addition, the cooperative nature of recording data on canoe performance, navigation, and weather and sea conditions so necessary for the detailed descriptions of separate legs of the voyage contained in the pages to follow, and the contribution of oceanographers and meteorologists to analyzing those data, are recognized in the coauthorship of chapters 5 through 7. These coauthors are: navigator Nainoa Thompson; crew members Chad Baybayan, Tai Crouch, Richard Rhodes (who also drew the charts, figures, and other illustrations for this book), and Elisa Yadao (who has produced a series of television films on the voyage); meteorologists Paul Frost, Bernard Kilonsky (who also served on the crew), and Tom Schroeder; and oceanographer Dixon Stroup (who also served on the crew). For reading and offering comments on one or more of the chapters of this book, I am particularly indebted to Roger Green, Terry Hunt, Will Kyselka, Abraham Pi'ianai'a, Gordon Pi'ianai'a, Barry Rolett, Jo-anne Kahanamoku Sterling, Leon Paoa Sterling, and Douglas Yen. For the preparations of the illustrations, Richard Rhodes and I are indebted to Ev Wingert, Thomas Schroeder, and Bernard Kilonsky who provided technical help and advice, and to Cliff Watson and Cary Sneider for loaning us photographs to be used as models for some of the drawings. Finally, I would especially like to thank Myron Thompson, president of the Polynesian Voyaging Society, Laura Thompson, and Nainoa Thompson for their warm support and wise counsel in the preparation of this book. Support for writing this book was provided by the Polynesian Voyaging Society. All royalties are assigned to the Society for its research and educational programs.

Chapter 5, "Wait for the West Wind," and chapter 6, "Voyage to Aotearoa," are adapted from articles of the same titles that previously appeared in that preeminent forum for Polynesian studies, the *Journal of the Polynesian Society.*[1]

1

WITHOUT SHIPS OR COMPASS

A Sea So Vast

How the Polynesians, sailing in canoes hewn with stone adzes and setting their course by the stars, winds, and ocean swells, were able to explore and colonize their island realm has long been one of the most intriguing questions about the spread of humankind over our planet. To begin to understand why it has been so hard to answer that question, we first need to consider the immensity of Polynesia, a vast triangular region of the Pacific defined by the archipelago of Hawai'i north of the equator, by Rapa Nui, that tiny dot on the map across the equator far to the southeast that is known to the outside world as Easter Island, and on the southwestern side of the Pacific by Aotearoa, a pair of huge continental fragments and small offshore islands that now form the country of New Zealand (fig. 1).

Particularly in this age of transoceanic jet travel, the great dimensions of Polynesia cannot truly be appreciated without sailing from island to island throughout the region. Readers from outside the Pacific can get some feel for the size of this oceanic realm by using a globe to compare it with a part of the world more familiar to them. Hold one end of a string at Kaua'i, the

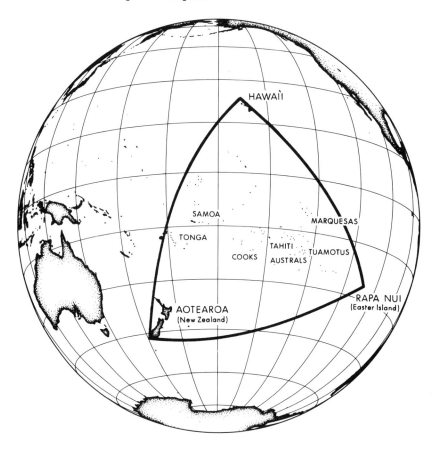

Figure 1. The Polynesian Triangle. A few small Polynesian settlements lie outside this triangle.

northernmost of the permanently inhabited islands of Hawai'i, and then extend the string to Rapa Nui. Cut the string there, and set it aside. Repeat this for the Rapa Nui to Aotearoa leg of the triangle, and then the Aotearoa to Hawai'i leg. Then reconstruct the triangle by placing these strings over a section of the globe you know better. If, for example, you start in London, you will probably be surprised to find that the first string will extend clear across Northern Europe and Siberia almost to the Pacific coast of the Russian Republic, the second from there down across China and Tibet to South India, and the third from there across Southwestern Asia and Southern Europe to London, thereby making a "Eurasian triangle" that encloses the better part of two continents.

Also basic to the problem of comprehending how the islands of the Polynesian triangle were first discovered and settled was the fundamental contrast between the oceanic view of the world held by the Polynesians, and the continental thinking of those first European visitors to Polynesia who were so surprised to learn that the islands they found in the vast stretches of the Pacific already had been discovered and settled. To the Polynesians, their ocean was a familiar, life-giving world that gave them food, provided seaways for exploration, and was strewn with fertile islands on which they could settle, plant their taro, bananas, and other crops, and raise their children. But, to those first European explorers, to sail into this largest of oceans the Pacific seemed a terrifyingly alien void. Even realization of its existence, then its great extent, was slow in coming. Columbus thought that in reaching the islands of the Caribbean he was on the threshold of Asia. Later, when in 1520 Magellan breached what geographers had finally surmised was a New World barrier to Asia by sailing through the straits at the tip of South America that now bear his name, he assumed the seas that stretched before him could be crossed in a matter of weeks. After an agonizing three months and twenty days, during which many of his starving crew died, Magellan reached the Philippines. So the outside world discovered, in the words of one of Magellan's chroniclers, "a sea so vast the human mind can scarcely grasp it."[1]

Daring as were Magellan and the succession of European navigators who followed him into the Pacific over the next two and a half centuries, these men did not really attempt to explore this newfound sea. They belonged to Europe's first age of exploration during which the primary object of risking one's life on harrowing ocean voyages was to reach Asia and its riches. A few European navigators did sail into the Pacific to search for the fabled *Terra Australis*, the Southern Continent that cosmographers of that era thought must lie in the temperate latitudes of the South Pacific. Until the late eighteenth century, however, most of those who ventured into the Pacific did so to reach ports on the other side of this wide ocean, and as quickly as possible—haste often becoming a necessity as more and more of their crew fell victim to scurvy, or just plain starvation, on the slow, poorly provisioned ships of this age. These included the famous Manila Galleons that for more than two centuries sailed, laden with Mexican silver, through Polynesian waters on the outbound leg from Mexico to the Philippines without any-one on board realizing that they were transiting one of the globe's major cultural regions. This meant that the European discovery of Polynesia and the Polynesians themselves took centuries, for there was no concerted attempt made to look for islands within this sea, much less for the people who might be living there.

People Without Skill or the Possibility of Sailing to Distant Parts

When early European explorers did happen across one of the Polynesian islands, the presence there of thriving communities of tall, handsome people puzzled these intruders from another ocean. As proud Atlantic seamen who had only recently devel-oped the technology of ocean-spanning vessels and of ways of navigating far out of sight of land, they had trouble conceiving how these seemingly primitive islanders who were without ships or compass could have preceded them into this greatest of the world's oceans. Some refused even to consider the idea that the ancestors of these Stone Age islanders could have ever sailed great distances into the Pacific to discover and settle the islands there, and they sought to explain the presence of the voyagers' descendants in the middle of the ocean by other means.

Consider, for example, the comments made in 1595 by Pedro Fernandez de Quiros, navigator of the Spanish expedition that chanced upon a collection of rugged volcanic islands some 4,000 miles west of Peru that the expedition's leader, Alvaro Mendaña, named Las Marquesas de Mendoza after his patron, the Viceroy of Peru. Although Quiros admired the physical beauty of the Marquesans, he was not at all impressed by their sailing canoes or their tales of overseas voyaging. Indeed, because they did not have large sailing vessels and navigational instruments, the navigator judged them to be a "people without skill or the possibility of sailing to distant parts." Thus, when they tried to tell Quiros how they sailed their canoes to islands lying to the south of their archipelago, Quiros refused to believe that these islands could be very far away. Although the Marquesans were probably referring to their raids on the Tuamotu atolls located several hundreds of miles south of the Marquesas, Quiros reck-oned that because of the primitive state of their maritime tech-nology these islands must lie just over the horizon. Quiros's reasoning was further shaped by his vision of a great Southern Continent. He theorized that these nearby isles must be part of a chain of closely spaced islands that led to the Southern Continent, and that this land mass and immediately offshore islands must have provided the ancestors of the Marquesans with an overland route and then island stepping stones that enabled them to move all the way from Asia into the Pacific without having to cross great stretches of open ocean.[2]

A century and a quarter later, the maverick Dutch navigator, Jacob Roggeveen, was even more perplexed as to how seemingly primitive people had come to be living on Rapa Nui—which he called Easter Island because he had chanced upon this minuscule island on Easter Sunday of 1722 while sailing across the Pacific in search of the Southern Continent or any other rich lands that he and his associates might exploit. Where the Marquesans at least had fairly good-sized double canoes, the Rapa Nui had only small, outrigger canoes that measured no longer than ten feet in length and were made by sewing a great many scraps of wood together. The islanders apparently could not make larger canoes for want of timber because generations of settlers had cleared the forests for agriculture and to obtain wood to construct houses and other structures, as well as to use for rollers, levers, and scaffolding in moving and erecting the stone images for which the island is so famous. Since the Rapa Nui had neither large oceangoing vessels, nor the compass or any other navigational devices, the Dutch navigator dismissed the idea that the ancestors of these people had settled their island by sailing there in canoes. After considering that the Spanish might have brought them, or that God might have specially created them on the island, Roggeveen gave up, declaring that "the ability of human understanding is powerless to comprehend by what means they could have been transported" to this isolated island so distant from any continental land mass.[3]

The common element in these and other attempts, during this early age of exploration, to explain the origins of the people European explorers kept finding on the oceanic islands they stumbled across, was the assumption that the slim canoes of these islanders, and whatever noninstrument methods they might have for navigating, were simply not up to the task of intentionally exploring the Pacific and colonizing the many islands there. It therefore seemed logical to the European mind of this era that the solution to the puzzle of how these islands had originally been settled must lie elsewhere than in the islanders' seemingly rudimentary sailing technology and navigational abilities.

How Shall We Account for This Nation Spreading Itself So Far over This Vast Ocean?

Not until the coming of Europe's second, scientific age of exploration did a reasonable hypothesis begin to emerge as to where the Polynesians came from and how they managed to colonize their island world. Whereas Columbus, Magellan, and other early explorers were primarily searching for oceanic routes to the riches of Asia, their successors in this second age added a new quest to Europe's maritime expansion. In the words of the French historian Fernand Braudel, they sailed the seas "to obtain new information about geography, the natural world, and the mores of different peoples."[4] To be sure, this quest for information about new places, their minerals, flora and fauna, and peoples was hardly divorced from the geopolitical designs of England, France, and the other countries that sent their ships to reconnoiter distant seas. But the approach was fundamentally different and did yield a wealth of knowledge. In the Pacific the leaders of this new approach to oceanic exploration—driven by the Enlightenment ideal of scientific investigation, and aided by better ships, more precise navigational methods, and more nutritious foods that allowed some respite from scurvy—crisscrossed the ocean, finding and charting island after island, cataloging the plants and animals found there, and investigating the islanders, their languages, and customs. Only then was the reality and extent of Polynesia realized and credence given to the idea that the ancestors of the people living there could have intentionally sailed into this great ocean to find and settle so many scattered islands.

Captain James Cook, the greatest of the explorers in this scientific phase of European global expansion, was the first to realize and document the cultural realm of Polynesia. Those earlier European navigators, such as Quiros and Roggeveen, who in traversing the Pacific had made landfall on Polynesian islands here and there in the triangle had utterly failed to recognize that they were sailing through a vast region occupied by people sharing a common cultural heritage. During his three expeditions into the Pacific from 1768 to 1779, Cook crossed Polynesia from both east to west and west to east, as well as from south to north, and was the first to discover that all the people living on islands in this vast triangular region belonged to, as he called it, the "same Nation."

Key to this recognition that all the people living in this region were so much alike was the realization that the languages they spoke were all closely related. Linguistic discoveries made during Cook's first voyage established that people speaking related languages were spread 2,000 miles across the South Pacific from Tahiti to Aotearoa. After leaving Tahiti, where Cook and his astronomers and officers had been sent to observe the transit of Venus across the face of the sun, Cook was guided south from Tahiti to the island of Rurutu in the Austral Islands by a learned Tahitian named Tupaia who was accompanying the English back to England. There, the English found that the people spoke a language practically identical with Tahitian, just as Tupaia said they would. From Rurutu, Cook sailed his ship, the *Endeavour*, farther south into temperate latitudes and then west across the South Pacific until he made landfall on the east coast of the North Island of Aotearoa. Because the people they met ashore looked so much like the Tahitians, Cook tried hailing them in his rudimentary Tahitian, but with no effect other than to make them threaten the English with their spears and a challenging dance. When, however, Tupaia tried shouting to the people, Cook noted that "they immediately understood him." The obvious closeness of the two languages, plus further inquiries by Cook and his chief scientist, Joseph Banks, that revealed that the people of Aotearoa shared the same customs and basic cosmology as the Tahitians, led the English navigator to conclude that the two peoples "had one Origin or Source."[5]

After returning to England, Cook was again sent out to the South Pacific, this time to search in the high latitudes of the ocean in order to see if the hypothesized Southern Continent might be found there. After, however, probing as far south as latitude 71°10', an impenetrable wall of ice forced Cook back to the north. Instead of returning directly to England with news that no Southern Continent existed in these frigid latitudes, Cook decided to make another sweep across the tropical South Pacific to search out islands previously visited by European explorers but "imperfectly explored." This consummate navigator wanted to fix the position of islands seen by earlier explorers but only roughly located on the map. Although his predecessors could measure their latitude by observing the height of the North Star or the noonday sun, they had no way of determining their longitude other than imprecisely estimating it by dead reckoning. Cook, however, could accurately determine longitude by using one of the first chronometers to be put into service to convert star sights into precise measurements of angular distance, and was also skilled in the difficult method of calculating longitude by observing "lunar distances."[6]

Cook started his sweep across the tropical Pacific on the eastern, South American side of the ocean by searching for the island Roggeveen had found on that Easter Sunday a half century previous. Cook first sailed his ship, the *Resolution*, north to the island's reported latitude, but well to the east of the longitude where the Dutch navigator's dead reckoning had placed it. Then he sailed her down that latitude until, to his great satisfaction, Rapa Nui finally appeared on the horizon. The English were not prepared, however, for their next discovery. Two men paddled out in a small canoe, and "immediately called out for a rope," naming it to everyone's surprise "by the same word as the Tahiteans." Then, the first islander to climb aboard the *Resolution* gave further proof of a connection between the two languages. The man was so amazed by the great size of the ship that he proceeded to measure out her length by fathoming the gunnels from bow to stern with his outstretched arms, calling out as he did so the "Numbers by the same names as they do at Otaheite [Tahiti]." The realization of this linguistic tie between the Rapa Nui people and the Tahitians, as well as their obvious similarity in appearance and customs, led Cook to proclaim in his journal that "it is extraordinary that the same Nation should have spread themselves over all the isles in this Vast Ocean from New Zealand to this Island which is almost a fourth part of the circumference of the Globe."[7]

Cook continued westward across the ocean, touching on the Marquesas and Tongan archipelagos where the English immediately recognized that the islanders spoke languages akin to those spoken on Tahiti and the other islands touched upon in this part of the Pacific. Sailing further westward, however, took the *Resolution* out of Polynesian waters and into the island region extending from New Guinea to Fiji now called Melanesia.

When Cook and his scientists encountered the dark-skinned inhabitants of the Melanesian islands that Cook named New Caledonia and the New Hebrides (now called Vanuatu), and did not recognize that any of their languages, save one, were related to those of the islands to the east, they concluded that they had left the region of the "same Nation." The one exception was a language, which they recognized to be close to Tongan, that was spoken by a fairer-skinned emigrant group in Vanuatu. This discovery led Cook to surmise, correctly as it turns out, that more such outliers of the nation he had found to the east were to be found in these western Pacific waters.[8]

The discovery that Polynesians had colonized islands across the equator in the North Pacific did not come until Cook's third voyage when he sailed north from Tahiti toward the northwest coast of North America to search for a waterway through or around that continent to the Atlantic, the long-hypothesized Northwest Passage. Cook had no reason to believe that in these North Pacific waters he might find people related to those south of the equator. The Tahitians had not told him about any islands that far north, and when he chanced upon an atoll just across the equator (which he named Christmas Island because the discovery was made the day before Christmas), Cook found it to be uninhabited. (In fact, archaeological remains since discovered there indicate that the island had previously been occupied by Polynesians.) When, after sailing another two and a half weeks to the north, Cook and his men spied first one and then another high, mountainous island, they therefore had no reason to believe that people of this "same Nation" had spread that far to the north. Indeed, Cook records in his journal that there was even "some doubt whether or no[t] the island was inhabited." Yet, when they approached the shore of Kaua'i, the second of the two islands to come into view, they saw people who looked like Tahitians coming out in canoes. Then, when the canoes came alongside, Lieutenant King records in his journal how they caught the "sound of Otaheite [Tahitian] words in their speech," and how upon asking them "for hogs, breadfruit, yams, in that Dialect, we found we were understood, & that these were in plenty on shore." To his agreeable surprise, Cook concluded that the "South Sea Islanders" had indeed spread across the equator into the Northern Hemisphere.[9]

Cook did not, however, name this region Polynesia, or call

the islanders Polynesians. Polynesia literally means "many islands." In 1756 the provincial French magistrate and scholar Charles de Brosses had combined the Greek roots for "many" and "islands" to construct the term *Polynésie* to stand for all the islands of the Pacific. Three-quarters of a century later, after the explorations of Cook and other navigators had revealed the great multiplicity and diversity of islands and peoples in the Pacific, J. S. C. Dumont-d'Urville, then France's leading Pacific explorer, delimited the term *Polynésie* so that it stood only for the islands inhabited by closely related peoples which lie mostly within the triangle formed by Hawai'i, Rapa Nui, and Aotearoa. This French construct, rendered in English as Polynesia, has since come to be regularly employed for this island world and has also been transliterated into various Polynesian languages, as, for example, *Polenekia* in Hawaiian and *Porinetia* in Tahitian.[10]

Cook's discovery that the Polynesians extended north across the equator as well as for a considerable distance across the South Pacific caused the navigator to pen in his journal the question that has occupied explorers, scholars, and students ever since: "How shall we account for this Nation spreading itself so far over this Vast ocean?"[11] Cook himself never had the opportunity to answer that question fully. Before he could return to England and reflect at leisure upon Polynesian origins, the English navigator met his end on the shores of Kealakekua Bay on the island of Hawai'i while trying to take the ruling chief of the island hostage to secure the return of a stolen boat. Nonetheless, the seeds for a theory of Polynesian settlement that takes into account both the nautical abilities of the islanders and the nature of the circulation of winds in the Pacific are to be found in earlier journal entries dating back to 1769.

That year, while on his first voyage into the Pacific, Cook stopped three months in Tahiti to prepare for, and then carry out, the observation of the transit of Venus across the face of the sun as part of an international effort to determine by trigonometric calculations the distance between the Earth and the sun. During his long stay in Tahiti Cook did something no previous European explorer to touch on a Polynesian island had ever done: he learned the basics of the local language, and then he used his rudimentary linguistic skills to inquire of the islanders how they sailed and navigated their canoes, what other islands they knew about, and where they themselves had sailed. His primary guide in local nautical matters was Tupaia, the learned Tahitian who befriended the expedition, and who was to sail for England with Cook. On Tahiti, Tupaia had told Cook and the other curious Englishmen about how his countrymen sailed their canoes and navigated by reference to the sun, moon, and stars, and furnished them with sailing directions to a multitude of islands in the seas surrounding Tahiti. Cook was impressed enough with both the practical seamanship and navigational skills of the Tahitians, and their wide geographical knowledge, to accept that which had been unthinkable to Quiros, Roggeveen, and other early explorers: that the ancestors of these islanders must have sailed into the Pacific on their own.

Unfortunately, Cook never developed his thoughts about Polynesian migration beyond a few lines in his journal. These, nonetheless, are telling. While heading south from Borabora, an island just to the west-northwest of Tahiti, Cook penned the following passage that remarkably anticipates current thinking about how the islands of Polynesia were settled. Concerning Tahitian canoes (which he calls "proes" from the Malay *prahu*, or "Pahee's" from the Tahitian *pahi*), Cook wrote:[12]

> In these Proes or Pahee's as they call them from all accounts we can learn, these people sail in those seas from Island to Island for several hundred Leagues, the Sun serving them for a compass by day and the Moon and Stars by night. When this comes to be prov'd we Shall be no longer at a loss to know how the Islands lying in those Seas came to be people'd, for if the inhabitants of Uleitea [Ra'iatea, a day and a half's sail to the west-northwest of Tahiti] have been at islands laying 2 or 300 Leagues to the westward of them it cannot be doubted but that the inhabitants of those western Islands may have been at others as far to westward of them and so we may trace them from Island to Island quite to the East Indias.

The main elements for a theory of Polynesian settlement are in this passage: an acceptance that Tahitians' canoes were seaworthy and capable of sailing at least "2 or 300 leagues" (around 600 to 900 miles), that they had a "compass" provided by the sun, moon, and stars that they used to orient themselves at sea, and that their ancestors employed this technology to move, from island to island, all the way from the "East Indias" (roughly modern Indonesia, plus adjacent islands of Malaysia and the Philippines) to the eastern Pacific.

Cook's willingness to give the islanders credit for having intentionally explored and settled their island world was not solely a product of his times. This preeminent English seaman genuinely admired the canoes of the Tahitians and believed them when they said that they navigated without instruments. In contrast, consider how the remarks of one of Cook's contemporaries, the French navigator Julien Crozet, betray a total skepticism about Polynesian seamanship. In 1772 Crozet visited Aotearoa as an officer on the ill-fated Marion de Fresne expedition. He had with him a list of Tahitian words from the Bougainville expedition that had touched on Tahiti the year before Cook had stopped there to observe the transit of Venus. In his journal Crozet relates how surprised he was to find that when he read the words to the islanders they "understood me perfectly," and goes on to write: "I soon recognized that the language of this country was absolutely the same as that of Taïty [Tahiti] more than 600 leagues distant from New Zealand." But Crozet could not imagine that either these people or the Tahitians were capable of communicating over great distances by sea. Instead, he invoked a sunken continent to explain their linguistic relationship: "People so widely separated and without a means of navigation do not speak the same language unless they were once and the same people and inhabited perhaps the same continent, of which the volcanic shocks have left us only the mountains and their savage inhabitants . . ."[13]

Cook chose the "East Indias" as the origin point for the Polynesian migration because the linguistic trail led from Tahiti to there. Sailing with Cook was Joseph Banks, a young botanist who had studied philology at Oxford and who later became president of the Royal Society. On board the ship was a collection of published accounts of previous voyages through the Pacific, in which were short vocabularies from a handful of islands scattered from Southeast Asia eastward into the Pacific as far as the western edge of Polynesia. By comparing the list of Tahitian words he had compiled with these vocabularies, Banks was able to show how Tahitian was directly related to languages spread across the Pacific to the "East Indias."

Cook saw only one obstacle to accepting a Polynesian origin in island Southeast Asia: the proposed migration trail led through tropical latitudes, and in the tropics trade winds blowing from east to west normally prevail. Whereas these would make it relatively easy for voyagers from South America to sail westward with the wind into the Pacific, steady trade winds seemingly would have presented a formidable obstacle for any voyagers originating at the western edge of the Pacific to sail eastward across the ocean. Yet, because he could see no resemblance between the islanders and the Native Americans he had seen in person and in drawings, Cook rejected the idea of an American origin to the Polynesians. To him, the trail of linguistic evidence indelibly marked the direction of migration, and he therefore sought to explain how canoe voyagers could have moved eastward into the Pacific against the direction of the trade winds.

Cook realized that Tahitian canoes sailed well with the wind and across the wind, but he had doubts that they could be forced to windward for the long distances required to move eastward across the Pacific. Tupaia supplied the intelligence needed to remove Cook's doubts. He told Cook that a series of islands extended far to the west of Tahiti, and that when his countrymen wanted to sail back to Tahiti from one of these western islands, they waited for spells of favorable westerly winds that frequently replace the trade winds during the summer:[14]

> Tupia [Tupaia] tells us that during the Months of Novr Decemb^r & January Westerly winds with rain prevail & as the inhabitants of the Islands know very well how to make proper use of the winds there will no difficulty arise in Trading or sailing from Island to Island even tho' they lay in an East & West direction.

This crucial bit of information was all the English navigator needed to envisage how people sailing in canoes could have worked their way eastward from the Asian side of the Pacific by waiting for and then exploiting seasonal westerly wind reversals to move from island to island, farther and farther into the ocean.

A Developing Theory

Over the next century, Cook's sketchy proposal was developed into a general consensus about Polynesian origins and migration by a variety of explorers, scientists, and other writers.

Linguistic studies showed, for example, that Banks and Cook were on firm ground when they traced the languages of Polynesia back to island Southeast Asia. In fact, they were not the first to identify a linguistic relationship between these regions. Sixty years earlier a Dutch scholar, Adriaan Reeland, had published a dissertation in which he compared words from vocabularies gathered by early explorers from a few islands in Melanesia and along the western edge of Polynesia to word lists from Malaya and Java and found them to belong to the same family of languages. Upon publication of the vocabularies gathered by Cook and Banks, and later Pacific explorers and scientists, linguists expanded upon Reeland's discovery to establish definitively the existence of a great language family that they called the Malayo-Polynesian family, named from the distribution of its constituent languages from Malaya to Polynesia. Now, it is more commonly called the Austronesian ("Southern Islands") language family in recognition that islands where these related languages are spoken extend beyond Malaya across the Indian Ocean to the great island of Madagascar. This span of related languages from an island immediately offshore Africa across two oceans to the easternmost Polynesian outpost of Rapa Nui (which lies farther to the east than Utah's Salt Lake City) made Austronesian the most widespread language family on the globe—until European seafarers spread Indo-European tongues around the world.[15]

During his second expedition into the Pacific, Cook sailed west from tropical Polynesia into that part of the Pacific that Dumont-d'Urville was to label as *Melanésie*, or Melanesia, because of the dark skin of the people living on the islands stretching from New Guinea to Fiji. Within this region, the expedition visited New Caledonia, some small islands adjacent to it, and the archipelago to the north that Cook called the New Hebrides, but which is now known as Vanuatu. Although Cook and his scientists did find a Polynesian population on one island in Vanuatu, the bulk of the people they encountered in Melanesia seemed to them to be very different in appearance, language, and culture than the "nation" they had left to the east. To explain this difference in island populations, Johann Reinhold Forster, the naturalist on Cook's second expedition, focused on skin color and proposed that there had been two main migrations into the Pacific: an early thrust of dark-skinned peoples followed by a later migration of brown-skinned voyagers. In terms of Dumont-d'Urville's geographical categories (which we still use today), Forster was referring to an initial migration of dark-skinned peoples into Melanesia, and a subsequent movement of brown-skinned peoples to Polynesia and to Micronesia, the island region north of Melanesia that Dumont-d'Urville had called *Micronésie* because of the small size of the islands there. Forster's formulation in turn led the eighteenth-century physical anthropologist Johann Blumenbach to add to the four races of mankind he had originally specified (Caucasian, Asiatic, American, and Ethiopian) a fifth, oceanic race that he called Malay.[16]

As for the means of migration, most writers agreed that Polynesians and their Micronesian cousins had migrated into the Pacific by canoe. In fact, when the distribution of oceangoing canoes and people speaking Austronesian languages was systematically considered, it was realized that canoe voyagers from Southeast Asia must have also expanded across the Indian Ocean to Madagascar where the national language, Malagasy, still bears witness to the Austronesian origins of the first people to occupy this great island (fig. 2).

To the early European navigators, the sailing canoes they encountered in Polynesian waters looked so different from their own ships that at first they had difficulty appreciating the merits of these highly sophisticated craft. As was eventually realized, these oceanic canoes were anything but simple dugout vessels. A craft made from a narrow dugout log is not stable enough for deep-sea sailing; if rigged with a sail of any size, it will capsize when hit by a strong wind or rolled by heavy seas. Atlantic and Mediterranean seafarers had solved the problem of achieving stability under sail by building broad-beamed plank boats to make a wide enough base to raise a sail, and by weighting their vessels with heavy ballast to further counteract the overturning force of the wind. The people of Southeast Asia and the Pacific had hit upon an entirely different solution to this stability problem. Instead of making wide and ballasted monohull vessels, they kept the narrow, unballasted canoe hull, but incorporated it into composite craft designed to provide a wide enough stance to be able to carry sail without capsizing. They

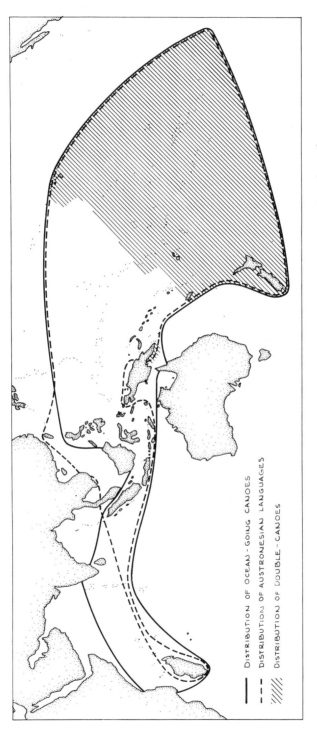

DISTRIBUTION OF OCEAN-GOING CANOES

DISTRIBUTION OF AUSTRONESIAN LANGUAGES

DISTRIBUTION OF DOUBLE-CANOES

Figure 2. The oceanic expansion of the Austronesians showing distribution of the language family and oceangoing canoes.

did this by adding an outrigger float off to one side of the hull to make a single-outrigger canoe, or by adding outrigger floats off each side of the hull to make a double-outrigger canoe. An even more stable platform for carrying sail was made by taking two hulls, placing them side by side but some distance apart, and then connecting them with cross beams and lashing the whole assembly together with coconut fiber line to make a double canoe. Although the Polynesians widely employed single-outrigger canoes for fishing and transport, because of the greater stability and carrying capacity of the double canoe, as well as its widespread distribution throughout Polynesia and eastern Melanesia (see fig. 2), this craft came to be considered by students of Polynesian migration to be the type of canoe by which most of the islands of Polynesia had been discovered and settled.

Practically all the post-Cook explorers, and the scientists who accompanied them, were well acquainted with the alternation of easterly trade winds and spells of westerly wind, and most agreed that the latter must have been crucial to the Polynesian expansion eastward against the direction of the trade winds. For example, Horatio Hale, who sailed as a philologist on the United States Exploring Expedition to the Pacific during the years 1838 to 1841, prefaced his report on Polynesian languages and migration with a refutation of what he called[17]

> the only argument of importance which has been urged against the migration of the eastern islanders [Polynesians] from the west, . . . the supposed prevalence of easterly winds within the tropics. Against this many voyagers have adduced facts serving to show that these winds are by no means constant, and that they are frequently interrupted by others from the contrary direction; and some have suggested the connection of these last with the northwest monsoon of the China and Malayan seas. The observations made during our cruise have served to confirm this opinion, and put beyond a doubt the fact that during the winter months of our hemisphere, westerly and northwesterly winds prevail in the Pacific as far east as the limit of the Paumotu Archipelago [the Tuamotu Islands], and perhaps still farther.

So, in the century after Cook, his prescient suggestions were further developed into a widely accepted theory by explorers and scientists who followed him into the Pacific. The Polynesians, it was thought, sailed by canoe, probably of the double-hulled type, into the Pacific from island Southeast Asia; then, using westerly winds to head east, they explored the ocean before them, finding and settling the many islands there. There were, of course, dissenting theories, including a number of variations on Crozet's sunken continent idea and other such unfounded speculations. Two of the dissenting theories from this period bear mention, however, because they were to be revived in earnest in the middle of the twentieth century: Martínez de Zúñiga's thesis of the South American origin of the Pacific islanders, and John Lang's counterthesis of the accidental settlement of the Pacific islands from voyagers pushed by westerly winds out into the ocean from the western, Asian side of the Pacific.

In 1803 Joaquin Martínez de Zúñiga, a Spanish priest stationed in the Philippines, published a book on the history of the Philippines in which he argued that the prevailing ideas about the settlement of the Pacific from Asia were all wrong. He was primarily interested in the origin of the Filipino people, or "Indians" as he called them, but realized that their history was linked to that of the Polynesians and other Pacific islanders because they "have the same language, the same manner and customs, and consequently the same origin as our Indians." Because he mistakenly thought that the languages of the Philippines and the Pacific islands were closely related to those of South America, Martínez de Zúñiga proposed that "the Indians of the Philippines are descended from the aborigines of Chile and Peru." Realizing, however, that he was going against the accepted idea that the migration was from west to east across the Pacific, Martínez de Zúñiga invoked the easterly trade winds to explain why the migration was actually from east to west. Because, he declared, the islanders could not sail eastward against the trade winds, they must have come from the east, from South America, and have reached the islands of the Pacific by sailing westward before the trade winds.[18]

Later in the nineteenth century, John Lang, a Presbyterian minister stationed in Australia, argued in a pair of books that although the Polynesians came from the west, they had not intentionally set out to explore eastward into the ocean and to settle any islands they found there. Lang seized upon the common realization that westerly wind shifts had enabled the Polynesians to move eastward across the ocean and converted it into a thesis that they had been involuntarily driven to distant lands by westerly gales. He hypothesized that while sailing from one closely spaced island to another

> the unskillfulness of the pilot, or the unexpected change of wind, would often carry the adventurous islanders far beyond their reckoning; and in such circumstances they would either founder at sea, or perish of hunger, or be driven they knew not whither, till they reached some unknown and previously undiscovered island. In the latter case, they would gladly settle on the new-found land; fearful of again trusting themselves to the ocean, and entirely ignorant as to what course they should steer for their native isle.

This involuntary migration proceeded, said Lang, from Southeast Asia eastward clear across the Pacific as successive generations of lost voyagers were swept before westerly gales. Sharing Martínez de Zúñiga's mistaken assumption that Pacific and South American languages were related, Lang even proposed that South America originally had been "discovered by a party of famished Polynesians who had been caught suddenly in a violent gale of westerly wind off the coast of Easter Island, and driven across the intervening tract of ocean to America."[19]

Despite these and other similarly ill-informed speculations, the theory that Polynesia had been settled by voyagers intentionally sailing from Southeast Asia generally prevailed throughout the nineteenth century. This orthodoxy was incomplete, however, for Cook's sketchy hypothesis had been only partially fleshed out. Although studies of languages, canoe types, customs, and other cultural traits might point to an origin in Southeast Asia, no one was able to specify the exact route migrants followed to Polynesia or precisely how they sailed and navigated their canoes.

In the late 1800s a major effort was mounted, primarily by Europeans resident in Hawai'i and Aotearoa, to break out of this impasse by examining the traditions of epic voyages told by the islanders themselves. Among the most prominent of these amateur scholars were Swedish-born Abraham Fornander, a judge and a newspaper editor living in the Kingdom of Hawai'i, and S. Percy Smith, a New Zealand land surveyor who founded the *Journal of the Polynesian Society* largely to provide a forum for tracing Polynesian migrations. Both started out by focusing on the legends of their respective home islands, specifically on those Māori legends that told of the discovery and colonization of Aotearoa from a land called Hawaiki and those Hawaiian tales about voyaging between an already settled Hawai'i and the distant cultural center of Kahiki. Then, using traditions from all over Polynesia as well as from Hawai'i and Aotearoa, plus free-ranging comparisons of Polynesian words with supposed counterparts in Sanskrit, Hebrew, and a variety of Eurasian languages, they traced the Polynesians back across the Pacific, through island Southeast Asia, to the Asian mainland where they attempted to connect them to the Aryans, Chaldeans, and other ancient peoples.[20]

Although Smith and Fornander may have been on an arguably defensible course when they pointed to Tahiti, Ra'iatea, and the other Society Islands as forming both the legendary Māori homeland of Hawaiki and the fabled land of Kahiki in Hawaiian legends, the methods they applied to identifying an ultimate Polynesian homeland in Asia were highly suspect. To erect their elaborate migrational histories, they and other amateur prehistorians of their time committed a number of scholarly sins—the uncritical acceptance of oral traditions that incorporated modern geographical knowledge and introduced biblical themes, the combining of separate tribal legends to develop a coherent history, and the unsystematic comparison of isolated words across a wide range of languages. What is more, these writers can also be accused of having grossly exaggerated the swiftness by which the Polynesians crossed the Pacific in great migratory waves, as well as the accuracy of their navigation. They painted the Polynesian voyagers bigger than life, to the point of declaring them to be superhuman seafarers who, to quote Smith's colleague Elsdon Best, "traversed the vast expanse of the Pacific as western peoples explored a lake."[21]

Nevertheless, despite their dubious methods of tracing migrations, and their hyperbole about Polynesian seafaring capabilities, the reconstructions of Fornander, Smith, and other such scholars were widely accepted in their day. Although the professional anthropologists who began working in Polynesia from the 1920s onward may not have believed all the details in these flawed reconstructions, they did not explicitly reject them or the migrational thinking that lay behind them. In fact, during the 1920s and 1930s it became commonplace for anthropologists to attribute such basic features of Polynesian societies as the division between chiefs and commoners to the overlayering of one migrational wave over another.[22]

Even the work of such a skilled and culturally informed anthropologist as the Māori scholar Te Rangi Hiroa—known to the outside world by his European name, Peter Buck—showed how little hard evidence about Polynesian migrations there really was. His book on these migrations, *Vikings of the Sunrise*, stands as a literary work that captures the romance and danger of voyaging as conveyed by the Polynesians in their oral traditions. If examined closely, however, for actual evidence about the Polynesian migration, the book reveals that orthodox thinking about Polynesian origins was still full of gaps and unsubstantiated assumptions. Buck, for example, argued on primarily racial grounds that the main body of ancestral Polynesians had not moved through Melanesia on their way eastward. Despite the continuous distribution from Southeast Asia and New Guinea to Polynesia of such crops as breadfruit, taro, and yams and other indications that the ancestral Polynesians had passed through Melanesia, Buck did not believe that the brown-skinned Polynesians could have sojourned among the dark-skinned Melanesians. Instead, he proposed that they must have passed to the north of New Guinea through the islands of Micronesia where the people appeared to him to be more akin to the Polynesians in race and culture. Similarly, although Buck lavishly quoted from the legends of many islands to portray the Polynesians as great seafarers, he did not fully explain how they managed to sail their canoes so far eastward into the Pacific and then to the far corners of Polynesia, or how they navigated their craft.[23]

Although not all of Buck's contemporaries agreed with the migration routes he proposed, or with his heavy reliance on oral traditions for reconstructing the migration, their objections were generally within the bounds of what might be called the orthodox theory of Polynesian migration. Specific routes and other details might be questioned, but the consensus remained that Polynesia had been settled by an intentional migration from the west. Then, at midcentury, a Norwegian adventurer, followed by a New Zealand historian, burst into the otherwise quiet waters of Polynesian studies with pronouncements that the accepted thinking about Polynesian origins and settlement was all wrong.

American Indians in the Pacific

One sunny trade-wind day in 1947 a raft made of balsa wood logs crashed upon the reef of Raroʻia atoll in the Tuamotu archipelago. The raft, the soon-to-be-famous *Kon-Tiki*, carried a Norwegian adventurer, Thor Heyerdahl, and his fellow Scandinavians on an experimental mission. They had left Peru 101 days earlier, determined to demonstrate that the sailing rafts which in pre-Columbian times had ranged along the west coast of South America could have reached Polynesia. In this specific sense, their voyage was successful, for it did show that balsa wood rafts are well suited for drifting and sailing with wind and current westward into the Pacific, a finding that a number of subsequent raft voyages from South America to Polynesia (and in some cases beyond) have reinforced.[24]

Heyerdahl needed this demonstration to lend credence to a theory he had developed some years earlier after a visit to the Marquesas Islands. Impressed by the east-to-west flow of the trade winds past these high, volcanic islands and the seemingly incessant pounding of wind-driven waves rolling in from the east, Heyerdahl formulated, in apparent ignorance of Martínez de Zúñiga's writings, what he thought was a new and daring theory—that the first people to reach the Marquesas and other islands of Polynesia must have come from South America, pushed by wind and current. Like the Spanish priest a century and a half before him, Heyerdahl thought it impossible for early canoe voyagers to have sailed directly eastward from island Southeast Asia to Polynesia against the easterly trade winds and accompanying ocean currents, and that therefore Polynesia must have been settled by voyagers entering the Pacific from South America, sailing and drifting before wind and current. Hence, Heyerdahl entitled the massive volume on his theory *American Indians in the Pacific*.[25]

Heyerdahl differed from Martínez de Zúñiga, however, in that he did not believe that this westward movement carried all the way across to the Philippines and the rest of island Southeast Asia. He had a much more complicated way of accounting for what even he had to admit was an obvious cultural relationship between the people of Southeast Asia and those of Polynesia by theorizing that the Polynesians actually stemmed from two separate migrations from the American mainland into the Pacific.

After raft voyagers from the Peruvian coast supposedly settled Polynesia about 500 A.D., Heyerdahl proposed that a second migration from British Columbia sailed to the islands around 1000 A.D. He imagined that these hypothetical early voyagers originated in island Southeast Asia, then rode the Kuroshio current north past Japan and out into the open waters of the North Pacific. He proposed that they then headed eastward, taking advantage of the westerly winds and currents common in the higher latitudes there, to reach British Columbia. After a pause, from there their descendants sailed with the easterly trade winds and accompanying currents to Polynesia, where they mixed with the earlier settlers from South America, introducing the Polynesian language and other traits from Southeast Asia.[26]

Accidental Voyagers

A few years after Heyerdahl published his challenging if not exactly original views, Andrew Sharp, a retired New Zealand civil servant turned historian, wrote a slim volume entitled *Ancient Voyagers in the Pacific.* Where Heyerdahl had revived Martínez de Zúñiga's theory of the American origin of the Polynesians, Sharp resuscitated Lang's thesis of the accidental settlement of Polynesia by voyagers driven eastward across the Pacific by westerly winds. Sharp accepted the orthodox view that the Polynesians had come from the western, Asian side of the Pacific, but rejected the idea that they had intentionally colonized their ocean world. To this acerbic historian, the vision of the Polynesians as great voyagers who had set out to explore and settle the Pacific was nothing but romantic nonsense. The settlement of Polynesia was simply the product of many accidental voyages, over which the Polynesians had little or no control, which had moved people slowly westward across the Pacific and then throughout the Polynesian triangle.[27]

Sharp admitted that the Polynesians were capable of intentional voyaging between adjacent islands and archipelagos. He declared, however, that beyond 300 miles all voyaging and island settlement had to be unintentional because Polynesians lacked the technology and skills for purposefully making such long voyages. He claimed that Hawai'i, the Marquesas, Rapa Nui, and other islands without close neighbors had been "accidentally" discovered and settled in two ways: (1) by the chance arrival of a drifting canoe that, while sailing along the coast of an island or between closely spaced islands, had been blown off course by adverse winds or had strayed off course through navigational error; (2) by the fortuitous landfall by a canoe load of exiles who had been driven from their home island by war, famine, or other causes and were blindly floating around the ocean in hopes of being cast upon the shores of an uninhabited island.

Sharp traced his inspiration not from Lang, but from none other than Cook, claiming that his thesis of accidental settlement was "Captain Cook's forgotten theory." On his third voyage into the Pacific, before heading north for his fateful encounter with the Hawaiians, Cook had touched on the small island of Atiu in the archipelago later to be named the Cook Islands after the English navigator. There Ma'i (whom the English called "Omai"), a Tahitian whom Cook was taking back to England, met four of his countrymen who told a tale of their drift voyage to the island. Some ten years earlier they were part of a group of twenty men and women who had set sail from Tahiti to Ra'iatea, a day and a half's sail away. For some reason, however, they missed the island and drifted for many days to the southwest until the canoe, which had by then been overturned, came within sight of Atiu, at which point the Atiuans spotted the wreckage and rescued the five survivors. After repeating this tale in his journal, Cook tersely commented: "This circumstance very well accounts for the manner the inhabited islands in this Sea have been at first peopled; especially those which lay remote from any Continent and from each other."[28]

As Cook did not elaborate on this before his death in Hawai'i, we can only guess how he might have reconciled this comment with his earlier assumption that the islands had been intentionally colonized. Cook's words may have reflected a shift in his thinking from his first voyage when he proposed that Polynesia had been settled intentionally, although it is not at all clear that he meant this remark to replace his earlier writings on the subject. As his biographer, John Beaglehole, suggests, had Cook lived through his third voyage to see England again and to reflect at leisure on this question, he might well have come to a conclusion similar to that of Anderson the surgeon on his last voyage, who considered that voyages of both "design" and "accident" accounted for the settlement of Polynesia.[29]

Despite the New Zealand historian's attempt to identify his thesis of accidental settlement with the great Cook, Sharp's argument rested ultimately upon a highly negative assessment of Polynesian voyaging capabilities, coupled with an exaggerated view of the hazards of the oceanic environment of the tropical Pacific, both of which were alien to Cook's thinking. In Sharp's mind, the islands of Polynesia were but tiny specks of land lost within an immense sea; the clouds were forever hiding the stars; the winds and currents were constantly and unpredictably shifting; the storms frequently swept the region. In this dangerous and unpredictable environment Sharp judged that the Stone Age navigator, lacking the compass or any other instruments, could never have successfully guided a canoe over long distances. Even when the night skies were clear, Sharp contended that the degree of error inherent in judging star bearings with the naked eye, plus the shifting winds and currents, would have rendered the traditional navigator's rudimentary skills useless after several hundreds of miles of sailing, if not before. What is more, to Sharp, Polynesian canoes were frail craft liable to break up in anything but light airs and calm seas and capable of sailing only with wind and current. Because of these navigational and nautical deficiencies, and the hazards of the oceanic environment, he considered that the many islands of Polynesia could only have been discovered and settled through a long series of random accidental voyages.

The Archaeologists Respond to Heyerdahl

Heyerdahl's challenge to orthodox thinking about Polynesian origins drew much more attention than that posed by Sharp, both because of the immense popularity of his book and widely shown film about the voyage, and because of the outrage expressed by orthodox scholars who charged that Heyerdahl had so utterly dismissed decades of research and multiple lines of evidence about Polynesian origins. Despite scholarly protestations, however, it soon became evident that Heyerdahl had uncovered a major weakness in orthodox thinking. The evidence for the linguistic and cultural relationship between island Southeast Asia and Polynesia was not matched by island-by-island archaeological research demonstrating that the ancestral Polynesians had indeed migrated from Southeast Asia eastward through either Melanesia, or Micronesia, or both, to their eventual mid-Pacific homes. The necessary archaeological excavations had not been conducted. Surveys of monumental structures and other surface remains in Hawai'i, Tahiti, and a number of other islands as well as a few pioneering excavations conducted here and there had yielded some clues about cultural relationships and hence possible sequences of settlement within Polynesia, but between there and Southeast Asia the archaeological map was largely blank. The picture was grossly incomplete, and Heyerdahl was not remiss in pointing this out.

The appropriate archaeological response was, therefore, to go out to the islands and dig in the ground for the evidence that might indicate by what route Polynesia had been settled. This is exactly what followed, and results of these excavations carried out over the last several decades have not supported Heyerdahl's theory. Excavations conducted in Hawai'i, the Marquesas, Rapa Nui, and other islands along the eastern frontier of Polynesia have not turned up the distinctively Native American potsherds, arrowheads, or other artifacts that should have been found had these islands been settled from either North or South America. In contrast, work in Melanesia and along the western frontier of Polynesia has confirmed that Polynesia was first settled from islands to the west. Through a type of pottery, decorated with distinctively stamped patterns and called Lapita after a site in New Caledonia where it was found in abundance, archaeologists have been able to trace the migration of seafaring peoples who were directly ancestral to the Polynesians from islands of the Bismarck Archipelago off the northeast coast of New Guinea eastward through Melanesia to Fiji, Tonga, and Samoa at the western edge of what was to become Polynesia, where they appear to have arrived between 1500 B.C. and 1000 B.C.[30]

Although archaeologists cannot yet specify the exact seaway by which these Lapita voyagers entered the Pacific, the most likely route was from the island region of northeast Indonesia and the southern Philippines eastward along the northern coast of New Guinea to the Bismarck Archipelago. Beyond this, however, the trail of people speaking Austronesian languages ancestral to these seafarers is still subject to much speculation, although a number of linguists and archaeologists propose that Austronesian speakers originated in southern China, moved first to Taiwan, and then from there migrated south into the Phil-

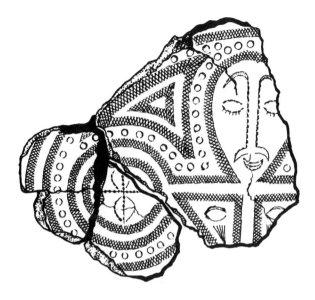

ippines and Indonesia before turning east toward the open Pacific. If this reasoning about Austronesian origins is correct, the "East Indias" of Cook and Banks, and our more contemporary term, "Southeast Asia," should perhaps be thought of as prehistorically including the southeastern part of the Chinese mainland and Taiwan, as well as the islands of the Philippines, Indonesia, and the adjacent lands around the southeastern end of the Asian mainland.

In addition to confirming two centuries of theorizing about the west-to-east direction of migration to Polynesia, archaeological research over the last several decades had also led to some unanticipated discoveries concerning the early settlement of Australia, New Guinea, and adjacent islands. Finds made in New Guinea and Australia of ancient stone tools and skeletal remains indicate that the first people to venture eastward beyond the offshore islands and archipelagos of Southeast Asia did so tens of thousands of years earlier than formerly thought. Their crossings are now estimated to have taken place some 40,000 to 60,000 years ago during the last glacial era when the huge masses of water locked in the world's glaciers greatly lowered sea levels, turning Australia, New Guinea, and adjacent continental shelves into a great continent that geologists call Sahul, and narrowing the sea channels between there and the easternmost islands of Indonesia to a point where some adventurous people, perhaps using rudimentary rafts of bamboo or logs, were able to reach the uninhabited shores of Sahul. Archaeological sites recently discovered in the Bismarcks and Northern Solomons that date from around 20,000 to 30,000 years ago indicate that some descendants of these pioneering migrants must have further developed their seafaring skills to the point where they could reach these offshore islands.[31]

Some archaeologists have even proposed that the seafaring tradition behind the Lapita expansion to Polynesia stemmed from this ancient, pre-Austronesian adaptation to the sea, not from emigrants from Southeast Asia. Yet, the results of a recent series of excavations throughout the Bismarcks organized to investigate this hypothesis indicate that at the base of the Lapita cultural horizon is an intrusion into the Bismarcks of seafaring peoples from the west. This may not necessarily mean, however, that the original inhabitants of the Bismarcks and adjacent islands contributed nothing to the colonization of islands farther to the east. Although the Lapita people may have been consummate sailors, they hardly lived off the sea alone. In fact, they might better be called seafaring farmers rather than seafarers, for their subsistence economy was based more on cultivated plants, such as taro, breadfruit, and yams, than on fish and other marine products. Indeed, they had to develop a portable agricultural system to colonize the new lands they found far to the east, as these oceanic islands did not have the rich plant and animal life of the islands of Southeast Asia and western Melanesia needed to sustain large populations. Thus, the Lapita people took with them on their canoes the seedlings, cuttings, and other planting materials needed to reproduce their food and medicinal plants, as well as breeding stock for their domesticated animals, the pig, dog, and chicken, so that they could establish their agricultural economy on the virgin islands they found in eastern seas. It therefore seems likely that these migrants would have tried to learn all they could about locally cultivated plant varieties in the Bismarcks and adjacent islands from the indigenous farmers there and may well have added some of these to their portable agricultural system.[32]

The available archaeological evidence clearly indicates that these seafaring farmers who pushed the human frontier to the western edge of the Polynesian triangle (obligingly marking their

trail with Lapita pottery) were the immediate ancestors of the Polynesians. But this does not mean that they were themselves identifiably Polynesian. Present indications are that ancestral Polynesian culture, the proto-Polynesian language, and the characteristic Polynesian physical type developed in and around the archipelagos of Fiji, Tonga, and Samoa, not on any distant archipelago or adjacent continental shores. Strictly speaking, there was no migration of Polynesians to Polynesia, only the movement of those people who were directly ancestral to the Polynesians. The current answer to the old question of where the Polynesians came from is therefore really very short and simple: although their immediate ancestors came from the western Pacific, the Polynesians came from Polynesia.

Answering Sharp's Challenge

Although Heyerdahl's theory of American origins may have found little acceptance in scholarly circles, Sharp's theory of accidental settlement had an immediate appeal to many archaeologists and historians. They saw it as a welcome correction to seemingly overblown or ill-founded accounts of Polynesian voyaging and colonizing achievements penned by earlier writers, one that offered a simple explanation of Polynesian settlement based on random processes rather than a complicated one based on feats that were difficult for them to imagine. Instead of having to accept seemingly superhuman sailing and navigational skills to account for a complicated story of intentional migration, by following Sharp's model of accidental settlement all they had to assume was that the Polynesians had enough seafaring ability to put themselves at risk of being randomly pushed around the Pacific by the vagaries of wind and current.

Unlike Cook and other explorers and scientists who traveled through the Pacific during the age of sail, few of those who accepted Sharp's ideas had ever sailed the Pacific on any kind of wind-powered craft. Consequently, they found it difficult to conceive of anyone sailing far beyond sight of land in a canoe and then trusting their life to reach land by watching the stars, the swells, and other natural signs. Furthermore, the tides of academic fashion, particularly in archaeology, were then running strongly against the study of migration. Whereas scenarios of migration had once been commonly employed by archaeologists and other prehistorians around the world to account for cultural developments, by the 1960s migration studies were considered passé, and the focus had switched to investigating internal processes of local adaptation and change.

Not all students of Polynesia embraced Sharp's theory of accidental settlement, however. A number of us thought that although Smith, Best, and other enthusiasts may have exaggerated Polynesian voyaging capabilities, Sharp had swung the pendulum too far over the other way. We felt that in labeling the process of settlement as accidental, and in denigrating the skills of Polynesian canoe builders, sailors, and navigators, Sharp had arrogantly and without foundation denied to Polynesians their rightful place in history as great voyagers and colonizers. Sharp was unmoved by his critics, however. Indeed, he immensely enjoyed the controversy that followed the publication of his book and encouraged it by vigorously replying to his critics. For example, in the preface to a revised edition of his book he boasted that, since the first edition appeared, "I have gathered upwards of a hundred published notices of the book, have had a dozen protracted and interesting exchanges of letters with experts of various sorts, and have been involved in 2,191 oral discussions of the book's theme." Later, when he sent me a letter inviting me to debate him on my plan to sail a canoe from Hawai'i to Tahiti and return, Sharp declared: "Published controversy is not only the lifeblood of scholarship but the best assurance of mounting interest and book sales! I charge no commission to the many authors whose works I have aided in this way."[33]

As all the reviews, critiques, replies, and counter-replies accumulated, it became clear that the information needed either to refute or confirm Sharp's hypothesis was simply not there. Voyaging canoes and traditional navigators had long since disappeared from Polynesian waters, victims of the wrenching transformations of Polynesian societies that had occurred over the last two centuries. The debate was therefore being conducted primarily with information on canoes, navigation methods, and voyaging accomplishments written by the explorers and other early European visitors. Since these writers typically did not have the time, language skills, or motivation to investigate these topics thoroughly, their observations were sketchy and in some cases grossly ambiguous if not downright contradictory. Disputants could therefore pick and choose from the literature whatever observations or opinions supported their case, and their opponents could do likewise, with the predictable result that the debate produced little in the way of new insights, much less any definitive answers.[34]

The famous map of Tupaia, the Tahitian who befriended the English on Cook's first voyage, provides a case in point. Tupaia carried in his mind a mental file of the many islands that surrounded Tahiti which he conveyed to the curious English by naming each island and then telling them how many days it took to sail to that island and in what direction one had to sail. From this verbal testimony, Cook drew a map that, for better legibility, is redrawn here as figure 3. After correcting for directional reversals apparently based on whether Cook interpreted a Tahitian directional term as meaning toward that direction or away from it, the map arguably indicates that Tupaia knew about the main Polynesian islands in the tropical heart of Polynesia. Starting from Tahiti, he verbally sketched out an area—bounded by the Marquesas to the northeast, the Tuamotus to the east, the Australs to the South, the Cook Islands to the southwest, and Samoa, Fiji, and Rotuma to the west—that is about as large as Australia or the contiguous United States. (Apparently Tupaia did not mention the peripheral islands of Hawai'i, Rapa

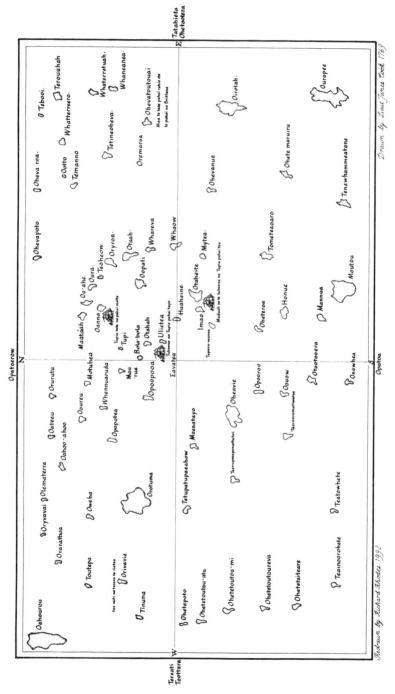

Figure 3. Redrawing of Captain James Cook's chart of the islands surrounding Tahiti from directions furnished by Tupaia (Skelton 1955, viii, chart 11).

Nui, and Aotearoa, indicating that even if the Tahitians may have vaguely known about these islands they did not necessarily include them in their geographical compilations.)[35]

As Tupaia told the English that he had been to some of these islands and that others had been visited by fellow Tahitians, his geographical knowledge was taken as evidence of considerable voyaging skills on the part of the Tahitians. Tupaia was able to demonstrate his own navigational abilities after he joined Cook's expedition to sail back to England when he guided Cook to one of the islands he had told them about, Rurutu in the Australs. Then, as the *Endeavour* sailed south from the Australs and then west across the Pacific, whenever the English asked Tupaia to point back to Tahiti, to their astonishment they found upon checking their charts that Tupaia was uncannily accurate no matter what had been the twists and turns of the ship's track. Unfortunately, however, Tupaia never reached England. After crossing the Pacific and making it as far west as the Dutch East Indies, Tupaia, along with his Tahitian servant and a number of his English shipmates, fell mortally ill while the *Endeavour* was in dry dock being repaired at the pestilential port of Batavia. During subsequent expeditions to Tahiti, neither Cook nor the other European navigators ever met another learned man so willing to share his knowledge as was this Tahitian sage, leaving us perhaps forever in the dark about the exact details of how the Tahitians knew about so many islands for a considerable distance around their own.

Nonetheless, in subsequent generations, many a student of Polynesian nautical culture came to cite Tupaia's famous chart and his navigational feats during the *Endeavour*'s traverse across the Pacific as evidence that the Tahitians must have been able to sail back and forth to islands distributed over a wide expanse of the South Pacific. Sharp dismissed all this as so much romanticizing. Quoting the opinion of Anderson, the surgeon on Cook's third voyage, he argued that Tupaia's map was based only on passive knowledge. Sharp asserted that the Tahitians never sailed back and forth between distantly separated islands and that Tupaia's mental file of islands spread over the South Pacific merely indicated that he and other Tahitians had avidly collected information on islands beyond their own voyaging range by questioning the surviving crewmen of each drifting canoe that washed up on their own islands.[36]

Since by the 1960s, the time when the debate over Sharp's book was raging, there were no indigenous Polynesian experts in geography and navigation of Tupaia's caliber left to question or to have demonstrate their skills, neither Sharp nor his opponents could win the argument over Tupaia's map, or for that matter over any of the other issues that this New Zealand historian had so tendentiously raised. New information was needed to break out of this impasse. Computer simulations designed to test Sharp's drift hypothesis were then being planned, as were expeditions to remote atolls in Micronesia to study traditional navigation practices that still survived there. What was really needed, however, was some method of learning how well Polynesian voyaging canoes sailed, and how feasible it was to navigate over the long Polynesian seaways solely by naked-eye observations of the stars, sun, and moon, as well as by the study of the winds, ocean swells, and other clues supplied by nature. If all the canoes and navigators were gone, it seemed obvious that there was a nautically appropriate way to respond to Sharp's challenge: reconstruct the canoes and ways of navigating, and then test them by sailing between distantly separated islands over which the Polynesians said their ancestors once voyaged.

2

EXPERIMENTAL VOYAGING

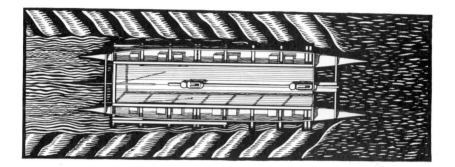

Rehu Moana

In December of 1965 the modern cruising catamaran *Rehu Moana* arrived off the North Island of Aotearoa after sailing there from Tahiti. The remarkable feature of this voyage was that the catamaran's owner, physician David Lewis, employed quasi-Polynesian methods to guide his vessel over 2,000 nautical miles* to Aotearoa, navigating all the way without a compass or sextant. He had sailed first to Rarotonga in the Cook Islands, and from there to Aotearoa's North Island, equipped only with a lifeboat chart of the Pacific Ocean, a star map, and a table of the sun's bearings (which he felt contained only information that approximated what a master Polynesian navigator would have carried in his head). Lewis made only one major error: he overshot Rarotonga and had to be corrected by a back-up navigator aboard the catamaran who was independently tracking the vessel with the aid of instruments and navigational charts. For the leg from Rarotonga to Aotearoa, however, he accurately guided the *Rehu Moana* to a landfall on the coast of the North Island only 26 miles south of where he expected to sight land.[1]

Lewis's claims for the voyage were modest: "We have here of course done nothing to prove whether the old Maoris made long

---

*Nautical miles and knots (nautical miles per hour) are used throughout this book. One nautical mile equals 1.15 statute (land) miles, and 1.85 kilometers.

deliberate voyages or indeed made any at all. What I believe we have demonstrated is that methods such as they used are accurate enough to render the major traditional voyages navigationally quite feasible." Although Andrew Sharp totally dismissed this feat as irrelevant because of the printed material carried on board the *Rehu Moana*, as well as Lewis's prior geographical knowledge, it was readily apparent that this innovative experimenter had done much to demonstrate the practicality of non-instrument methods for guiding a vessel to a distant landfall.[2]

Nālehia

While Lewis was sailing *Rehu Moana*, I was working at the University of California, Santa Barbara, with a group of my students to reconstruct a double-hull Hawaiian sailing canoe 40 feet in length (fig. 4). The reconstruction was based upon the plan of King Kamehameha III's royal canoe drawn early in the nineteenth century by a young French naval officer, François Edmond Paris.[3] My goal was to test this replica in order to develop basic information on the performance characteristics of a sailing canoe of traditional design, and then to use that information to estimate the feasibility of deliberate voyaging between distantly separated Polynesian islands.

One of the main questions I sought to answer was whether a Polynesian double canoe could sail to windward, or whether this type of craft could only be used to sail across and before the wind. A number of yachtsmen who watched us building the canoe were doubtful that she would sail to windward at all. They argued that the shallow, rounded hulls would offer little resistance to leeway, and that the Hawaiian sail, an inverted triangle with the two upper corners pulled together to give its "crab-claw" appearance, had neither the proper aerodynamic shape nor enough area to drive the canoe into the wind. Yet, within a half-hour after first raising sail, we had the answer to our question. After running a mile downwind along the Santa Barbara coast, we pointed the twin hulls of our canoe back into the wind and slowly but surely tacked back to our starting point.

After preliminary tests in Santa Barbara waters, we loaded the canoe onto a Honolulu-bound barge in order to test her in the trade winds and accompanying seas for which its inspiration, the Hawaiian *wa'a kaulua* (literally, "double canoe") had been

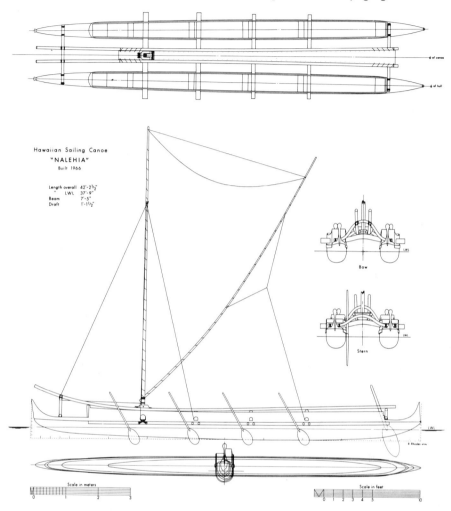

Figure 4. Nālehia: *Sail and deck plans, end views, and lines. End views omit third through fifth cross beams (Finney 1977, 1279).*

adapted. The sight of an ancient-style canoe sailing along the coast of the island of Oʻahu attracted much attention, and Mary Kawena Pukui, then Hawaiʻi's leading scholar of Hawaiian language and culture, christened our craft *Nālehia*, Hawaiian for "the skilled ones," referring to the way the two slim hulls so gracefully rode the seas.

Extensive sailing tests in the open ocean confirmed that *Nālehia* could indeed sail to windward, even in heavy trade wind seas. To determine the canoe's windward capability, we first

measured the angle at which the canoe could sail to the "true wind," that is, the wind flow independent of the canoe's movement, and not the "apparent wind" flowing over the craft which is skewed by the forward movement of the canoe. Then we estimated the leeway, expressed in degrees, made as the canoe skidded slightly sideways under the pressure of the wind by visually measuring the difference between the heading of the canoe and the wake she left in the ocean. Then we subtracted the leeway angle from the angle the canoe was heading into the true wind to arrive at an accurate measure of the canoe's windward performance. The result of repeated trials indicated that *Nālehia* could "make good" up to about 75 degrees off the true wind when sailing in light to moderate seas (fig. 5), but that attempts to make the canoe sail much closer in the wind were counterproductive, serving only to increase leeway and make the canoe's speed fall off precipitously.[4]

Most deep-sea sailing canoes elsewhere in Polynesia have deeper, more V-shaped hulls than those of *Nālehia*. These would seem to be better adapted for resisting leeway than the rounded Hawaiian ones, which appear to have been developed by the Hawaiians to make their canoes easier to handle in rough interisland channels and surf-filled coastal waters characteristic of their archipelago.[5] It was when we tried sailing *Nālehia* hard

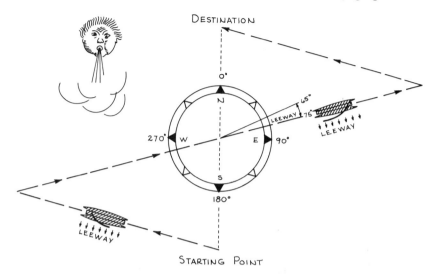

Figure 5. Nālehia *sailing to windward, making good a course of 75° after taking into account leeway.*

into the wind in heavy, trade wind seas that these rounded hulls proved disadvantageous. Whereas in light to moderate seas *Nā-lehia* could point fairly well to windward, in heavy seas the hulls tended to slide more to leeward. As hulls with a more V-shape, such as those known on voyaging canoes from some other island groups, would probably hold a heading to windward better in heavy seas, it seemed reasonable to propose that a double canoe with hulls specifically designed for open ocean voyaging would probably be able to make good at least 75 degrees off the wind in trade wind seas, a conservative estimate that subsequent tests with *Hōkūle'a* have confirmed.[6]

Although this limited windward capacity may be nothing like that of a racing yacht, I made the case that it would have enabled Polynesian canoes to sail much better than Sharp and other critics allowed. Long voyages to windward made by tacking directly against the wind may have been out of the question for Polynesian mariners, but it seemed to me that their canoes sailed well enough to windward to have cut obliquely across the wind to destinations that would have been beyond their reach if they could only sail before the wind. That was not just empty theorizing. I had a route in mind over which to test the ability of a Polynesian double canoe to sail long slants across and slightly into the trade winds: the legendary voyaging track between Hawai'i and Tahiti, which is celebrated in Hawaiian traditions about how Mo'ikeha, Pa'ao, and other heroic figures once sailed back and forth between these two centers.

To reach Tahiti from Hawai'i requires some capability of sailing to windward against the easterly trade winds that sweep across the route. A canoe could easily sail over the 2,250 miles of open ocean between Hawai'i and Tahiti if the two islands were aligned directly north and south of each other, and if there was no current across the course. But Tahiti lies south-southeast of Hawai'i, which means a vessel bound from Hawai'i to Tahiti has to sail hard into the wind to make several hundreds of miles of "easting" to reach the longitude of Tahiti. Furthermore, the westward-flowing currents that typically accompany the trades make the task of pushing to windward to reach Tahiti all the harder. Nonetheless, by plotting the windward capacity figure of 75 degrees derived from the *Nālehia* tests against average figures for wind direction and current drift derived from U.S. Navy pilot charts over the route, it looked like a canoe sailing from Hawai'i could probably make just enough easting against wind and current to reach Tahiti (fig. 6). Since the return voyage to Hawai'i would be, because of the windward position of Tahiti relative to Hawai'i, an easier sail than the leg to Tahiti, it seemed likely that the legendary voyages between Hawai'i and Tahiti probably had been within the sailing capabilities of the Polynesian double canoe. Furthermore, judging from David Lewis's experimental voyage to Aotearoa, it also seemed likely that Polynesian navigators could have successfully guided their canoes over the long sea road between these islands.

In 1967, after completing the *Nālehia* tests, I published an article outlining how a traditionally navigated voyaging canoe could be sailed from Hawai'i to Tahiti and return. Reconstructing such a craft, and then sailing her by traditional means over the thousands of miles of open ocean separating Hawai'i and Tahiti would, I proposed, directly confront Sharp's contention that "in the days before navigation instruments deliberate navigation to and from distant ocean islands was impossible in any form of sailing or paddling craft."[7]

Hōkūle'a

A stint of anthropological fieldwork in the New Guinea Highlands documenting the commercial achievements of the first gen-

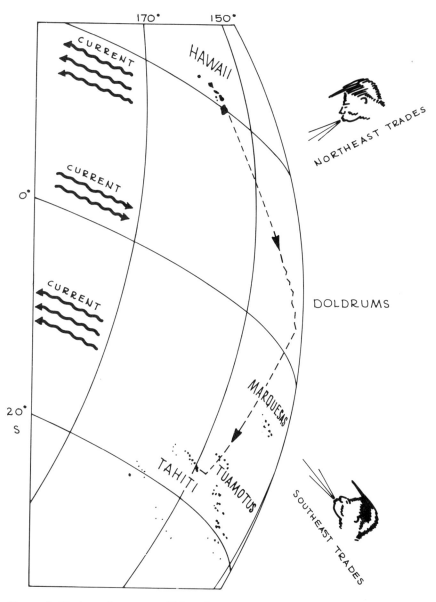

Figure 6. Projected course to Tahiti (Finney 1967, 157).

eration of indigenous businessmen there, followed by an appoint-
ment at the Australian National University (where David Lewis
and I had a chance to work together), intervened before I could
return to Hawai'i in 1970 to take up a position at the Univer-

sity of Hawai'i and get back to my canoe experiments. By then interest in Hawai'i's maritime heritage was growing, and in 1973 I joined with two other Polynesian voyaging enthusiasts, artist Herb Kawainui Kane and racing canoe paddler Charles "Tommy" Holmes, to found the Polynesian Voyaging Society. We designed the Society as a nonprofit, educational organization dedicated, in general, to conducting experimental research on Polynesian voyaging and disseminating the results of that research, and, in particular, to reconstructing a voyaging canoe, testing her over the legendary Hawai'i-Tahiti route, and then applying the results of our experiment to the debate about Polynesian migration.

The task of reconstructing an archaic Polynesian voyaging canoe presented serious problems of both design and fabrication. Our project fell within the domain of experimental archaeology, that branch of archaeology devoted to re-creating ancient artifacts and practices and then testing them under realistic conditions in order to shed light on their function and capabilities, and therefore on the conditions of life in prehistoric times. Experimental archaeologists have long been making and testing archaic artifacts, such as arrowheads, stone axes, and wooden ploughs. Ideally, the archaeologist should start with an actual example of an ancient artifact and then copy it as closely as possible using the materials and tools employed by the original makers. This can be fairly easily accomplished with a simple artifact, such as an arrowhead or an ax, for which there are abundant examples excavated from archaeological sites, as well as easily available materials that can be shaped using well-known techniques. But it is much more difficult to follow the ideal when the artifact is large and complex, such as a sailing vessel, and made up of numerous separate parts, the re-creation of which would require a detailed model as well as the revival of a wide range of lost skills.[8]

Where complete, or nearly complete, remains of ancient vessels have been recovered it has been possible to make reasonably authentic reconstructions. The Viking practice of burying a chieftain's long boat along with his remains under a massive mound of earth has meant that archaeologists have been able to recover fairly well-preserved remains of these medieval craft. In addition, the raising of several Viking ships that had been sunk in a fjord to block the channel against raiders have provided still more models for duplication. A number of replicas of these archaeologically recovered craft have been reconstructed and tested in recent years, although the most spectacular example of Norse experimental voyaging was carried out in 1893 when a reconstructed Viking long boat, modeled on the famous Gokstad Ship found in a burial mound on the shores of Oslo Fjord, was sailed from Norway to New York.[9]

In the Mediterranean, where underwater archaeologists have been particularly active, the nearly complete remains of a number of ancient vessels of various types have been recovered. One of these, a Greek cargo ship thought to have been sunk by pirates in the fourth century B.C., has recently been reconstructed by Greek shipwrights as the *Kyrenia II*, and then tested by sailing over Mediterranean trading routes once exploited by the ancient Greeks. The archaeologists were able to provide the shipwrights with detailed plans of the hull design and construction based on the recovered materials, and somewhat less precise descriptions, based upon literary passages and depictions on pottery of ships under sail, of the gunnels, masts, sails, rigging, and other parts of the vessel that had not survived submergence in the sea.[10]

Those of us seeking to reconstruct ancient Polynesian craft have not been so fortunate as to have such complete archaeological materials and other information on which to model our reconstructions. Although Hawaiians and some other Polynesians interred the bones of their dead in small canoe hulls, or sections of larger ones, and then secreted them in remote caves, they apparently did not bury entire voyaging canoes with their dead. Neither did Polynesian canoes typically sink to the bottom of coastal seas when holed or swamped. Unlike Greek ships and other Western monohull sailing ships that carried heavy ballast to counteract the lateral pressure of the wind upon their sails, Polynesian double canoes gained stability through the wide stance provided by the twin hulls and therefore did not need any ballast. This means that an unballasted Polynesian craft swamped during a storm, or holed for whatever reason, would not sink, but would drift awash in the sea. Unless such a disabled craft could be repaired and baled out, it would remain drifting until so ravaged by teredo worms that it fell apart, or until it might be thrown up onto some shore to rot or be scavenged there. Even if somehow a canoe, say one heavily loaded with rocks, did happen to sink just offshore, its remains would face much more hostile conditions, such as heavy surf surge, strong coastal currents, and a variety of marine organisms, than normally encountered in the generally calmer and less biologically active Mediterranean waters.

Perhaps the best chance for finding remains of an ancient voyaging canoe would be in a swampy area where mud, sand, and anaerobic conditions would have protected the wood and inhibited decay. Although no complete voyaging canoe has ever been found under such circumstances, bits and pieces of canoes have been found in swamps here and there around Polynesia. The most spectacular such finds have come from a swamp on the island of Huahine near Tahiti, where Bishop Museum archaeologist Yoshihiko Sinoto excavated an 18-foot-long steering sweep and a 17-foot-long plank, both apparently from a large voyaging canoe, which seem to have been washed up and then buried under sand by a tsunami that struck a thousand or so years ago.[11]

As for literary descriptions and pictorial representations of ancient voyaging canoes, again the experimental voyager working in Polynesia is greatly disadvantaged compared with his colleagues in Scandinavia and the Mediterranean. With the arguable exception of the so far minimally uninformative pictograms of the Easter Islanders, the Polynesians had no writing system and hence could leave no written records of their great voyaging canoes. These do, of course, feature prominently in their legends; but oral references to canoes do not add up to a detailed design. Furthermore, although early Polynesians had pottery, they apparently did not decorate it with detailed representations of their craft. On some islands Polynesians did sketch their canoes by chipping their outlines on the surface of large rocks or smooth lava flows. However, although some Hawaiian canoe petroglyphs have proven useful for reconstructing sail shapes, in neither they nor ones found elsewhere in Polynesia are the canoes outlined precisely enough to reveal exact design and construction details.

Given this lack of archaeological specimens of archaic voyaging canoes to copy, as well as the paucity of useful design guides to be found in the pictorial arts, we were left with one major resource to design our canoe: the drawings made by the artists and draftsmen employed by Cook and other early explorers of

Polynesian canoes from the era of first European contact. However, no single one of these contact era designs could have been copied directly to represent an ancient voyaging canoe, for each represents a local development incorporating adaptations to the island or archipelago in question and the transport needs of the people, and in some cases innovations from elsewhere in the Pacific. For example, in late prehistoric times the Māori people of Aotearoa were taking advantage of the huge trees growing there to build dugout canoes that were broad enough so as to make stable paddling vessels without having to add an outrigger float or join two of them together. Then, at the time of European contact the Tongans were adopting a double-ended hull design and movable lateen-like sail pioneered by Micronesian sailors that provided superior performance to their traditional canoe which, like *Nālehia*, had a permanent bow and stern and a fixed Polynesian sprit sail.

Instead, then, of trying to copy a particular canoe design in use in Hawai'i, Aotearoa, Tonga, or any other archipelago at the time of European contact, we studied all the drawings of canoes made by early European visitors to come up with a common-denominator design to represent a basic voyaging canoe of earlier centuries. Project co-organizer Herb Kane (a Hawaiian name, pronounced Kā-ne, not Cain), a talented Hawaiian artist with a powerful drive to reach back into Polynesia's voyaging past, developed the design of the canoe. By analyzing the wide variety of Polynesian canoe types, he arrived at the concept of a twin-hulled craft with two masts, each rigged with a Polynesian sprit sail—a design intended to sail like the canoes that, according to legend, voyaged between Hawai'i and Tahiti around the twelfth century.

In addition to resisting the temptation to copy the Micronesian-inspired lateen sail rig of late Tongan canoes, Herb avoided other features that would have enhanced the sailing performance of the craft beyond the Polynesian capabilities of some eight centuries ago. Instead, for example, of designing deep-V hulls to reduce leeway, he chose a more rounded, semi-V shape, modeled on the cross-sections of canoe types from around Polynesia that were being used primarily for deep-sea voyaging at the time of contact. Similarly, instead of spreading the hulls far apart to get increased performance, Herb followed traditional precedent in placing the hulls relatively close together. A wider spacing would have allowed the canoe to carry much larger sails, and hence sail faster. The object was not, however, to emulate a modern racing catamaran, in which aluminum torsion tubes and other exotic components are employed to achieve a wide stance and hence carry a great deal of sail. Rather, it was to reproduce a traditional double canoe that was limited by the materials at hand—wooden cross beams and sennit lashings—to a narrow spacing between hulls and therefore a relatively modest sail area. Illustrative of what might have happened to our canoe had we separated the hulls widely in order to carry more sail was the experience of a yachtsman who, just after we built our canoe, constructed a double canoe featuring widely separated hulls and a huge lateen sail of the Tongan type. In high winds and rough seas the cross beams gave way, the hulls separated and capsized, and the entire vessel was lost.

Some aspects of Herb's design did reflect specifically Hawaiian canoe features, such as the high, curving prow pieces and arched cross beams. Inclusion of these features seemed appropriate since these were adapted to the rough Hawaiian waters where we would conduct extensive sea trials before heading south for Tahiti. Hawaiian canoe builders designed the high, curving prow pieces typical of their canoes for functional reasons as well as for beauty; they are ideal for cutting through heavy seas such as those that commonly build up in the channels between the islands of the Hawaiian chain. Similarly, by making the cross beams that connect the two hulls in a distinctively arched shape, the canoe builders were able to elevate the deck (mounted between the hulls and resting atop the arched sections of the cross beams) higher above the seas funneling between the hulls than would be possible with straight cross beams.

Although the sails were cut in the typically Hawaiian crab-claw shape, which in itself seemed well adapted to the strong trades that frequently blow through the Hawaiian archipelago, the entire sail rig departed somewhat from the Hawaiian design. The Hawaiian sail, like most other sail types in East Polynesia, was laced to two spars. The thinner, curved spar served as the boom for the sail, while the thick, straight spar served as the mast. The sail could not therefore be raised or lowered independent of the two spars. The whole assembly was raised as a unit, after which the forward spar had to be stayed by running lines from it down to the ends of the cross beams where they protruded beyond the hulls to serve as shrouds, and by running another line from the spar to the forward cross beam to serve as a forestay. To lower the sail, the shrouds and forestay had to be released so that the whole rig could be lowered to the deck as a unit.

Although this arrangement worked well with *Nālehia*, there was some fear that it would be too difficult to raise and lower the larger sail rigs required for the new canoe. Accordingly, we worked out a system, based on precedents from elsewhere in Polynesia, for raising and lowering each sail rig on poles mounted on each mast step and stayed by lines running to the outer ends of the cross beams. First, the sail rigs are pulled upright by means of a line running through a U-shaped fixture mounted on the top of each pole. Then the forward spar of each sail rig is lashed to the pole so that together they form a mast, after which the sail is let out. However, although this system may make it easier to raise and lower sail, it does not necessarily enhance sailing performance. In fact, the extra disruption in air flow caused by the pole and its stays may even detract slightly from optimal performance.

Herb's design called for a canoe a little over 60 feet long, considerably shorter than the largest canoes seen in Polynesia by early European visitors—those from Hawai'i, Tonga, Samoa, and Fiji which measured in excess of a hundred feet in length, and were capable of carrying hundreds of people. Although some urged us to build a larger canoe, we knew that constructing a canoe appreciably longer than 60 feet would strain our resources and abilities. Besides, David Lewis's contention that "the preferred size of a vessel for deep sea voyaging seems to have been in the 50–75-foot range" made a lot of sense. Some of the biggest canoes from Hawai'i were apparently built for transporting soldiers on inter-island campaigns rather than for long-range voyaging. For example, the largest canoe reported from Hawai'i, a craft measured at 108 feet as it lay rotting on a beach, was almost certainly one of the fleet of huge *peleleu* canoes that Kamehameha had built to invade the island of Kaua'i to complete his conquest of the entire chain. The word *peleleu* to describe these big canoes is telling, for it means "extended." Accordingly, we settled on a more moderate-sized craft, one big enough, we felt, to represent the sailing characteristics of a traditional deep-sea voyaging canoe, yet not so large as to be beyond our means.[12]

Once Herb completed the overall design, he turned it over to Rudy Choy, a pioneering designer of catamarans, and his partner Warren Seamans, an expert catamaran builder, who then refined the plan and translated it into technical drawings with which we could begin construction. Ideally, according to the precepts of experimental archaeology, we should have built our canoe out of traditional materials, using only those tools and techniques that were available to pre-European Polynesian canoe builders.[13] In the strictest sense, this would have involved an immense undertaking. First, we would have had to trek to one of the ancient quarries where Hawaiians once mined fine-grained basalt for their adzes, such as the one located 11,000 feet up the slopes of the dormant volcano of Mauna Kea on Hawai'i Island. Using only stone tools, we would have had to chip out stone blanks, grind these by hand into serviceable adze blades, and then lash these onto wooden handles using line made from native fibers. Then, we would have had to ascend the slopes of Hawai'i's still volcanically active peak of Mauna Loa to the remaining stands of *koa* (*Acacia koa*), Hawai'i's premier tree for building canoes, that are located around the 6,000- to 7,000-foot level. There we would have had to find a pair of sound *koa* trees tall enough to be able to obtain two long hulls from them, a task that probably would have proved to be next to impossible because of the wholesale destruction of the *koa* forests that has occurred in modern times.

Assuming that we could have found the trees, felled them without damaging the wood, and then roughly shaped them on the spot, we would still have had to organize hundreds of men to haul the roughly hewn and still immensely heavy logs from the uplands across 10–15 miles of rough, lava terrain to the shore. There, using a range of stone adzes, chisels, and gouges, as well as other traditional tools such as coral rubbers and shark-skin in lieu of sandpaper, we would have had to shape the logs to make the dug-out base for each hull, cut and shape the timbers needed to build up the gunwales of each hull and to make the decking, cross beams, and other structural members of the vessel. In addition, this purist approach would also have involved weaving sails out of pandanus leaves and braiding miles of lash-

ing line from course, water-resistant fibers stripped from coconut husks.

In other words, following the ideal of using traditional materials, tools, and methods of construction would have meant a time-consuming revival of a wide range of arts and crafts (some of which have been totally lost in Hawai'i, or almost so), not to mention locating all the right materials and recruiting an army of workers. We realized that to attempt such a task would make it impossible to complete the project in any reasonable length of time, if indeed it would be feasible in this day and age to go completely back to ancient methods and materials. Regrettably, we were therefore forced to build the hulls out of modern materials and by modern techniques, although the hulls, the cross beams connecting them, and other components of the canoe were lashed together following traditional precedent and not joined by metal fasteners.

The base section of each hull was fabricated from three overlapping layers of narrow plywood strips which were fastened onto a framework made up of templates and stringers to give the hull the proper shape. The completed sections were then given a protective coating of fiberglass and resin which also served to add needed weight. Planks were then lashed to the hull base in order to raise the freeboard. The curved cross beams were made of strips of wood bent to shape and then laminated together. Although we had hoped to secure enough sennit line from Kiribati (formerly known as the Gilbert Islands) in Micronesia, and from the Polynesian outlier of Kapingamarangi also located in Micronesia, to lash at least some of the cross beams to the hulls and secure other components such as the rails and decking with this traditional material, we were only able to obtain a small amount of canoe-grade sennit. Hence, the canoe was lashed together mostly with readily obtainable synthetic line. Weavers from Kiribati and Kapingamarangi were, however, able to make for us enough long strips of pandanus matting to enable us to sew the strips together to make a traditional sail for experimental purposes.

We realized, of course, that because of the use of modern materials our sea trials could tell us nothing about the strength and durability of materials used in traditional craft. Nevertheless, because we sought to approximate the shape and weight of a traditional canoe, we felt that our vessel would be a reasonably "performance accurate" reconstruction that would sail and handle like the voyaging canoes that once sailed in Polynesian seas, and hence would tell us much about voyaging capabilities in earlier centuries (fig. 7). Furthermore, although our project might have fallen somewhat short of the ideal when it came to construction, we planned to set a new experimental standard in the actual conduct of the voyage. Previous long voyages made by reconstructed craft, such as those made by the *Kon-Tiki* and the Norse vessel that was sailed to North America in 1893, had all been one-way trips, navigated by modern methods. In contrast, we planned to make a roundtrip voyage navigated by traditional, noninstrument methods.

We named our canoe *Hōkūleʻa*, a choice meant to reflect our confidence that it would be possible to use the stars to guide our vessel to Tahiti and then back to Hawaiʻi. *Hōkūleʻa* is the Hawaiian name for the bright star known by modern astronomers as Arcturus, which now passes directly over the island of Hawaiʻi in its passage across the sky, thereby celestially marking the latitude of the island. *Hōkūleʻa* translates as "Star of Joy," a fitting name, we thought, for a star that any homesick Hawaiian sailor returning from southern latitudes would like to see arching higher and higher overhead as he sails north toward Hawaiʻi.[14]

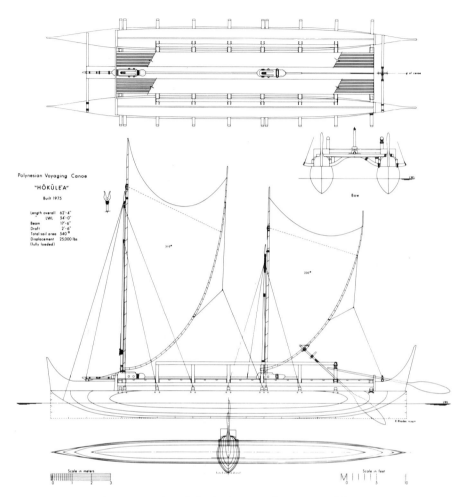

Polynesian Voyaging Canoe

"HŌKŪLE'A"

Built 1975

Length overall	62'-4"
" LWL	54'-0"
Beam	17'-6"
Draft	2'-6"
Total sail area	540
Displacement	25,000 lbs.
(fully loaded)	

Bow

Scale in meters

Scale in feet

Figure 7. Hōkūle'a: *Sail and deck plans, end views, and lines in 1976. Sleeping shelters, animal cages, and stern rails not shown. Reconstruction of the canoe in 1978–1979 altered sheer line of gunwales slightly; sail plan was altered during 1985–1987 voyage (Finney 1977, 1280).*

Navigation

Although we had every confidence that traditional navigators had once been able to guide their canoes between Hawai'i and Tahiti, we did not feel that any of us could fully re-create the ancient ways of navigating for our voyage. Because of his experimental voyage from Tahiti to Aotearoa, and the extensive study of traditional navigation he had conducted afterward, David Lewis could probably have navigated the canoe to Tahiti and return in a more or less traditional manner. But when he joined our effort in Hawai'i, David agreed with us that it would be more culturally appropriate to enlist a traditional navigator from some remote region of the Pacific where at least a vestige of the old ways of navigating still survived, and then have him adapt his methods for the long round-trip between Hawai'i and Tahiti.

We realized, however, that we probably would not be able to find such a person anywhere in Polynesia. David had in fact undertaken such a search in the late 1960s when he was sailing around the South Pacific on his yacht doing research for a book on Pacific Island navigation. At Tikopia, Tonga, and a few other Polynesian islands, he did find a few older men who still knew much about navigation, but did not discover any active navigators whom he felt could do the job of navigating *Hōkūle'a* to Tahiti and return. Since it did not look like it would be possible to find a Polynesian navigator, we decided the best alternative would be to recruit a navigator from the one region of the Pacific where traditional, long-distance navigation was still vigorously practiced: the remote atolls of the central Caroline Islands, part of a new nation now known as the Federated States of Micronesia. Our choice fell upon Mau Piailug, a master navigator from the atoll of Satawal whom I had come to know when he visited Hawai'i in 1973. Although Mau's navigational methods differed in some details from what is known of Polynesian methods, as Lewis's extensive research had shown, such differences can be considered as variations of a common Pacific island system of navigation. Hence, we felt that Piailug could adapt his skills to the task at hand and guide our canoe to Tahiti and return in a manner closely similar to the way Polynesian navigators had once done.

In his comprehensive study of Pacific island navigational practices, *We the Navigators*, Lewis has described in detail the methods used by Pacific Islanders.[15] A brief sketch of these methods drawn primarily from his book provides some background for understanding how Mau Piailug and then Nainoa Thompson have been able to guide *Hōkūle'a* over many thousands of miles of blue water.

All navigators must be able to: (1) orient themselves and set an accurate course toward their destination; (2) keep track of

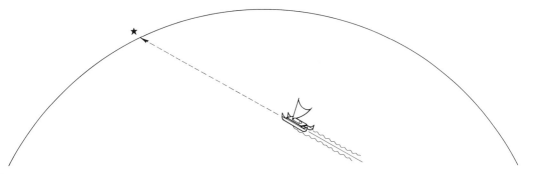

Figure 8. Sailing toward a star low on the horizon.

position en route and make any necessary course corrections;
(3) make landfall on the island or place along a coastline to
which they are heading. To accomplish these the modern navigator uses a variety of instruments, charts, mathematical calculations, and a spherical coordinate system of latitude and longitude. The traditional Pacific island navigator had none of these
tools, but instead employed a number of noninstrument methods which can be sketched in terms of these three main navigational tasks.

Orientation and Course Setting

Because of the rotation of the earth, stars appear to rise in the
east and set in the west, intersecting the horizon at points, and
following paths across the sky that do not change perceptibly
during a navigator's lifetime. Pacific Islanders have long used
these regularities to orient themselves and to guide their canoes
toward destinations far beyond sight range.

At night the navigator points the prow of his canoe toward
the rising or setting point of the star that has the same bearing
as his destination (fig. 8). When sailing across wind and current,
the navigator picks a star course sufficiently to one side or the
other of the direct course to compensate for the estimated leeway and current drift (fig. 9). When the key star marking the desired course is too high in the sky to give a good directional
reading, or when it is below the horizon, the navigator must follow other stars that rise and set at the same or nearly the same
points on the horizon. When clouds block the segment of the

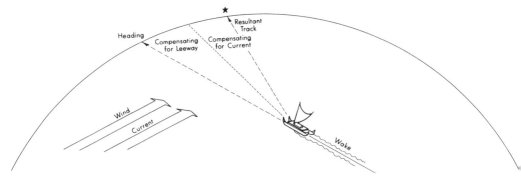

Figure 9. Compensating heading to take into account current and leeway.

sky where the key or secondary stars appear, the navigator must know the pattern of all the stars and constellations to be able to orient himself by reference to any part of the night sky that might be visible.

During the day the navigator orients himself on the sun and the pattern of the ocean swells. The sun can best be used in the early morning and late afternoon when it is low on the horizon. The navigator must, however, be aware that the rising and setting points of the sun shift daily, and constantly recalibrate the bearing of the sun by watching each morning where it rises with respect to the fading star field of the dawn sky. When the sun rises too high in the sky to serve as a precise directional guide, the navigator can use the pattern of ocean swells to keep the canoe on course—as he must do anytime it is so solidly overcast that he cannot discern the position of the sun. Similarly, when it is too overcast at night to see any stars, planets, or the moon, the navigator falls back on the ocean swells to keep himself oriented.

The ocean swells most useful to the navigator are not those raised by local winds, but rather long, regular swells generated by steady winds blowing over long stretches of ocean, or by distant storm centers. Amidst the often confusing pattern of swells coming from several directions at once, the navigator picks out the most prominent and regular of the swells and keeps track of their alignment in reference to horizon stars (or the rising or setting sun) so that he can use them for orientation anytime the sky becomes overcast or the sun is too high in the sky to yield an accurate bearing.

The best-known traditional stellar navigation system in the Pacific is the one employed by a few dozen traditional naviga- tors who still practice this ancient art on remote atolls in the central Caroline Islands of Micronesia—including Satawal, Mau Piailug's island. Carolinian navigators are particularly noted for what has been called their "star compass," which they visualize as a series of bearings along the horizon known by the rising and setting points of the key stars and constellations. That writ- ers commonly call this conception a "star compass" is perhaps unfortunate for it is not a physical instrument like a magnetic compass. It is a purely mental construct, a conceptual direction system by which the navigator mentally divides the horizon sur- rounding him. Although he may demonstrate this mental con- struct to his pupils ashore by placing a circle of pebbles on a mat to indicate the rising and setting points of the key stars and constellations, the navigator sets sail only with a conceptual vi- sion engraved in his mind through years of study and practice.[16]

Like their Western counterparts, Carolinian navigators divide the horizon around them into thirty-two points or bearings, as did, according to evidence from the Cook Islands to be discussed below, at least some Polynesian navigators. Although one might argue for a historical connection between the Western directional system and these oceanic counterparts, a case can also be made for their independent evolution in European seas and the Pacific Ocean, for they can all be derived by a simple process of division and subdivision: first divide the circular horizon into the four cardinal points, then bisect the angle between these to mark the intercardinal points, and then repeat this process twice more until thirty-two evenly spaced points result. Unlike, however, the Western practice of naming the points by such directional terms as north, northwest, north-northwest, and north by west, the points of the Carolinian directional system are known by the actual rising and setting points of the most prominent stars and constellations closest to them. Since these do not rise and set exactly at the points derived from the successive bisections, charting the Carolinian conception on paper (or by coral rocks placed on a mat) yields irregularly spaced bearings (fig. 10).

Although we do not know as much about the now largely for- gotten Polynesian methods as we do about the still-practiced Carolinian ones, there can be no question that the Polynesians set their courses by the stars and other celestial bodies, and did

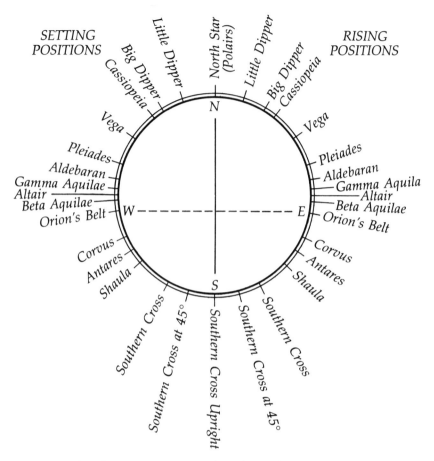

SETTING
POSITIONS

RISING
POSITIONS

Figure 10. Carolinian star compass (Goodenough 1953, 6).

so skillfully. For example, both Cook and Banks wrote about Tahitian stellar navigation methods, as did the Spanish navigator Andia y Varela who visited Tahiti in 1774, four years after Cook first touched there, and penned the following succinct entry in his journal about how the Tahitians navigated:[17]

> When the night is a clear one they steer by the stars; and this is the easiest navigation for them because these being many, not only do they note by them the bearings on which several islands with which they are in touch lie, but also the harbours in them, so that they make straight for the entrance by following the rhumb of the particular star that rises or sets over it; and they hit

it off with as much precision as the most expert navigator of civilized nations could achieve.

Although these and other accounts make it clear that Polynesians used star bearings for navigation, we do not have any descriptions from Polynesia of a stellar directional system as detailed as those we have from the Caroline Islands of Micronesia. This may be because Polynesians did not conceptualize any such system, or simply because no one bothered to record their ideas before they were lost. There is, however, an intriguing Hawaiian text that seems to refer to a stellar direction system similar to the Carolinian one, though not unambiguously so. Two contemporary Hawaiian scholars, Rubellite Kawena Johnson and John Mahelona, consider that part of the astronomy text dictated in the mid-nineteenth century to the Hawaiian historian Samuel Kamakau by Kaneakaho'owaha, an astronomer who served King Kamehameha I, refers to a stellar direction system that was engraved around the perimeter of a gourd and used for instructing students to navigate by the stars.[18]

Although evidence for Polynesian stellar directional systems may be unclear, information recorded in the nineteenth century from several archipelagos indicates that the navigators there conceptualized a wind-rose in which the horizon was divided into up to thirty-two points named according to the winds that characteristically blow from each point. Figure 11 shows the thirty-two-point wind-rose from the Cook Islands as drawn and described by the nineteenth-century missionary, William Wyatt Gill, who wrote that the islanders used a large gourd to symbolize the distribution of winds. Small holes were drilled in the lower part of the gourd to correspond to the *rua matangi*, the "wind pits" from which the various winds blow, and then plugged with pieces of tapa cloth which supposedly could be manipulated to control the wind:[19]

> Should the wind be unfavourable for a grand expedition, the chief priest began his incantation by withdrawing the plug from the aperture through which the unpropitious wind was supposed to blow. Rebuking this wind, he stopped up the hole, and advanced through all the intermediate apertures, moving from plug to plug, until the desired hole was reached. This was left open, as a gentle hint to the children of Raka [the god of winds] that the priest wished the wind to blow steadily from that quarter.

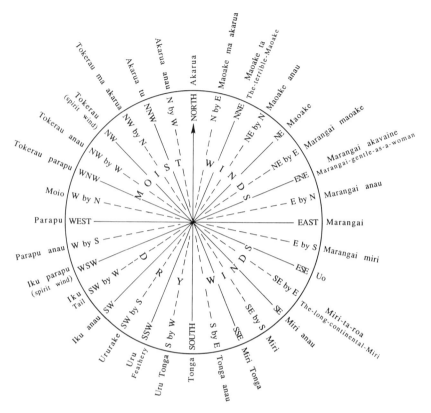

Figure 11. Cook Island wind compass (Gill 1876, 320).

Gill wryly added, however, that because the priest would have had "a good knowledge of the ordinary course of the winds, and the various indications of change, the peril of the experiment was not great."

Polynesian wind directional systems are reminiscent of the wind-rose of eight points formerly used by Mediterranean sea-farers, in which each point (or "petal" of the "rose") is named for the prevailing winds that blew from that direction. Given the shifting nature of the winds in the Mediterranean, it has been said that early mariners there must have been "able to rec-ognize these winds either by their characteristics of temper-ature, moisture content, etc., or else by association with the sun, moon, or stars, otherwise it would be hardly possible to use a wind-rose for purposes of navigation with any degree of certainty."[20] Similarly, it seems likely that Polynesian navigators used their wind-roses primarily for conceptualizing directions but ultimately relied on celestial referents to set their course and for steering.

Keeping on Course

Once at sea, a navigator must keep track of his vessel's progress in order to be able to make any course corrections needed to keep heading for his destination and to judge when he is nearing land. Before the days of modern navigational instruments, Western navigators relied upon a procedure called "dead reckoning" whereby the navigator calculates his position from his estimates of the course his vessel has sailed and how far it has sailed from the last known position. Similarly, the island navigator effectively kept track of his vessel by integrating his estimates of course and distance covered to arrive at a mental picture of where he was at any one time—although he employed a conceptual system utterly alien to the Western one based upon compass bearings, miles covered, and latitude and longitude lines.

Again, because the ongoing navigational tradition of the Caroline Islanders is so well documented, we know much more about Carolinian methods of dead reckoning than we do about specifically Polynesian ones. The Carolinian navigator conceptualizes his canoe's progress through the water by picturing how a "reference island" lying off to one side of the course moves under successive star points along the horizon. This is an abstract construct for picturing a canoe's progress, not a precise measure, as the reference island is too far off the course line to be seen from the canoe. The navigator, nonetheless, knows where the island is in relation to the island from which he sails and the island toward which he is heading. Essentially what he does is envisage his progress in terms of how the bearing from the canoe toward the reference island shifts from one star point to another along the horizon. As the bearing to the reference island moves from one star point to the next, the canoe is said to have completed one *etak*, or segment, of the voyage. Thus, when the requisite number of *etak* has been crossed, the canoe should be off the target island.

On the 117-mile voyage from Woleai atoll to Olimarao atoll,

the island of Faraulep, lying 70 miles off the course line (far beyond sight range) and almost equidistant between the two, provides the reference island that enables the navigator to break
the voyage up into six *etak* of about 20 miles each (fig. 12). At
the beginning of the voyage Faraulep lies under the Great Bear
rising. When, as the canoe sails toward Olimarao, the navigator judges that Faraulep lies beneath Kochab rising, the first
etak has been completed. As the voyage continues, the navigator visualizes Faraulep moving progressively beneath Polaris,
Kochab setting, Great Bear setting, Cassiopeia setting, and finally, when Olimarao is reached, the *etak* island lies beneath
Vega setting.[21]

Because figure 12 portrays the islands from above, it gives the
impression that, like his Western counterparts, the Carolinian
navigator takes a "God's eye" view of his vessel's progress. In
fact, the Carolinian navigator looks outward from his canoe,
which he considers to be stationary, to the islands and stars
which he considers to be moving past his canoe. This seemingly
incomprehensible conceptualization actually parallels the common practice of Western seamen of saying that a channel marker
is "drawing abeam," or that an island is "falling astern," when
it is obvious that it is the vessel, not the channel marker or
island, that is moving. The Western sailor applies this vessel-
centered perspective only to objects he is looking at, however.
When he considers objects over the horizon, or when he thinks
about a voyage in the abstract, he normally switches to the
God's eye view of looking down on his chart as though looking
down at the ocean from a great height, visualizing the fixed islands and his vessel's progress over the surface of the sea.

The Carolinian navigator, not familiar with the concept of
representing the earth's surface on a chart, retains the vessel-
oriented perspective even for objects he cannot see. Looking outward from the canoe with his mind's eye, he visualizes the reference island off to one side of the course and how it changes
bearing from one star point to another as the canoe sails toward
the destination. The modern navigator reads his knotmeter and
compass to gauge the progress of his vessel in terms of miles
run at a heading of so many degrees and then plots this upon a
chart on which the sea is overlaid with a grid of latitude and
longitude lines. When the proper number of miles has been run
off in the right direction, the destination should appear. His tra-

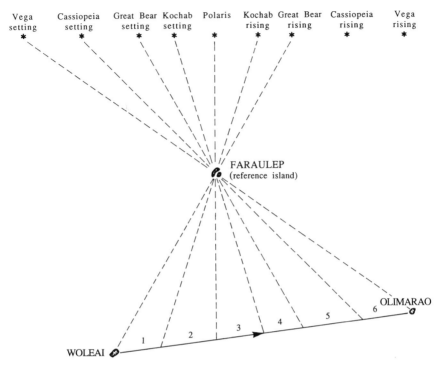

Figure 12. Voyage from Woleai to Olimarao using changing star bearings over the reference island Faraulep to segment voyage into etak *(Alkire 1970, 53; Lewis 1972, 136).*

ditional Carolinian counterpart keeps everything in his head, mentally converting his observations of the canoe's progress through the water into visualized changes in the bearing of the reference island and how these segment his course line. When the bearing marking the completion of the final segment of the voyage is attained, his canoe should be off the target island. Both systems use mental constructs—miles and degrees, latitude and longitude lines, reference islands over the horizon, and bearings from reference islands to star compass points—that cannot actually be seen in the sea or sky. Both systems work.

In addition, for voyages made in a north or south direction, an island navigator can also judge his progress by the changing angular elevation of stars above the horizon. This can be illustrated by reference to a special case, that of Polaris, the Pole Star so named because it lies almost directly above the North Pole and thus hardly appears to move as the earth rotates beneath it.

Hawaiian astronomers named Polaris *Hōkū-pa'a*, literally the "immovable star," and further recognized that its angular elevation above the horizon decreased as one sailed south, and would disappear below the horizon if one sailed far enough south. For example, Kaneakaho'owaha's astronomy text states that "you will lose sight of the *Hōkū-pa'a*" when you sail far to the south, and, referring to the portions of the southern sky not visible from Hawai'i, that then "you will discover new constellations and strange stars."[22]

Unlike Polaris, all other stars appear to move across the sky. To judge accurately their changing height above the horizon as one sails north or south, it is necessary to observe them as they cross the meridian, that is, as they reach their highest elevation above the northern or southern horizon in their passage across the sky. To continue the example from Kaneakaho'owaha of what a navigator would see sailing south from Hawai'i to Tahiti: as Polaris declines in the northern sky and then disappears below the horizon, the Southern Cross (which, contrary to common belief, is visible from Hawai'i, though low on the horizon) would rotate higher and higher in the southern sky the farther southward he sailed. Reversing that course, and sailing north from Tahiti to Hawai'i, the navigator would see the Southern Cross culminating progressively lower in the southern sky as he sailed north. Then, after crossing the equator, Polaris would come into view and move progressively higher and higher above the northern horizon as the voyage northward progressed.

Based on fragmentary accounts, including one by the nineteenth-century Hawaiian writer Kepelino Keauokalani, Lewis has proposed that Polynesian navigators once used this principle of changing stellar elevations on voyages headed north or south in a particularly precise manner by carefully observing stars that passed directly above specific islands.[23] A star's declination is its celestial latitude, that is, its angular distance north or south of the celestial equator. As it progresses from east to west across the sky, a star passes directly above all places on the globe whose latitude equals its declination. If, therefore, a navigator knew what star passed directly above his target island, he would be able to judge when he was approaching the latitude of that island by observing when the star whose declination marked the island (i.e., had the same declination as the island's latitude) was passing almost directly above him as it crossed the sky.

The star *Hōkūle'a* (Arcturus) provides a case in point, for it now passes virtually right over the magnificent stone works that make up the famous *pu'uhonua*, or sanctuary, of Hōnaunau on the southwestern coast of the island of Hawai'i. In other words, its declination and the latitude of Hōnaunau are the same: 19° 27′ North. A navigator sailing north from Tahiti for Hawai'i would therefore see *Hōkūle'a* climb higher and higher in the sky until, when his canoe had reached the latitude of Hōnaunau, Hawai'i, the star would appear to pass directly overhead (i.e., pass through his zenith). Observation of the changing elevation of *Hōkūle'a* could therefore have been used to help a navigator know when he was approaching the island of Hawai'i—although not far back in the past as star declinations slowly shift over the centuries because of the slow wobbling of the earth on its axis.[24]

Lewis had actually tried this method on his voyage from Tahiti to Aotearoa aboard *Rehu Moana*. By adjusting the stays of his mast to make it vertical to the surface of the sea, and then by sighting up the mast, Lewis was able to ascertain what stars were passing directly overhead and thereby keep track of his latitude as he sailed southwest to Aotearoa.

Such zenith observations cannot, however, be used to set and maintain a course because a star at its zenith does not yield a fixed bearing with reference to the globe. *Hōkūle'a*, for example, passes directly above all places on earth located along 19° 27′ North latitude and therefore looks the same at its zenith no matter what the longitude of the observer. The Hawai'i-bound navigator sailing north from Tahiti who wished to use *Hōkūle'a* to judge when he had reached the latitude of Hawai'i would still have to gain his bearings by reference to the rising and setting points of the stars, and then use his observational and dead reckoning skills to keep the canoe heading on the proper course to Hawai'i.

Making Landfall

Small islands, particularly low atolls, are easily missed at sea if all one relies on is the visual sighting of the island itself. The tops of the tallest coconut palms provide a navigator with the first visual sign of an atoll but cannot be seen until a canoe is within 10 to 12 miles of the island. Pacific navigators look for signs of islands in the clouds, the pattern of ocean swells, and the flight of birds. High islands may interrupt the flow of trade wind clouds, causing a noticeable piling-up effect long before the peaks themselves can be seen. The shallow lagoons of some atolls may cast a greenish reflection upon the undersides of passing clouds, and ocean swells bouncing back from an island ahead, or curving around it, provide subtle clues for another remote sensing technique. In many areas the favorite landfinding aids are those birds—primarily the terns, noddies, and boobies—that sleep on land but fly out to sea each day to fish. Navigators searching for land welcome the sight of these birds, particularly if seen in the early morning flying out to their fishing grounds, or at dusk winging their way back to their island roosts, for they then give an indication of the direction of land as well as its proximity.

The traditional navigator's task of finding land is considerably lightened by the fact that most islands in the Pacific do not stand alone in the ocean, but form multi-island archipelagos, most of which stretch for hundreds of miles. The southeast to northwest trend of most of the long chains in tropical Polynesia stems from the interaction of the Pacific lithospheric plate that forms the ocean floor and the "hot spot" sources of magma beneath it. As this plate has slowly moved to the northwest, lava from these hot spots has periodically punched through the ocean floor to form the island chains.

The Society archipelago provides the classic example of this process. The islands show a progression from the youngest islands in the southeast to the oldest in the northwest—from Mehetia, a small, rocky outcropping southeast of Tahiti that emerged from the sea less than a half-million years ago and which has yet to be surrounded by a coral reef, to the atolls of Bellingshausen and Scilly over three hundred miles to the northwest where the only evidence of the volcanic outpouring from the hot spot that formed the chain are the coral rings that outline where now eroded and submerged volcanic islands once stood. In between are the progressively older high islands of Tahiti, Moʻorea, Huahine, Raʻiatea, and Tahaʻa, all of which are surrounded by barrier reefs, and the "almost-atolls" of Borabora and Maupiti where fully developed barrier reefs enclose broad lagoons and eroded remnants of the mountainous cores of these islands which first broke the surface of the sea about four million years ago.

In their southeast to northwest orientation and relative age, the Hawaiian Islands similarly betray their origin in the interaction of the moving Pacific plate and a fixed hot spot source of magma that is now forming the newest island of the chain under the surface of the sea off the southeast coast of Hawai'i Island. Conveniently for the navigator attempting to make long ocean crossings, the Societies, the Hawaiian chain, and other such chains of volcanic islands and atolls furnish much larger and easier to find targets than a lone island. When heading for one island in an archipelago, the navigator can intercept the chain at any point along its length, reorient himself, and then proceed to the target island.

Preparing for the Voyage

Hōkūle'a was launched early in 1975, following which we embarked on a series of sea trials around the Hawaiian Islands designed both to test the canoe and to develop our ability to sail it. *Hōkūle'a* proved to be a seakindly vessel, remarkably smooth and stable even in high winds and seas, and also a good learning vehicle for developing our skills in sail handling and the initially daunting task of steering such a large canoe. Nonetheless, the canoe had its tender points, and we did not always pay enough attention to these. How vulnerable *Hōkūle'a* was to swamping was brought home early one morning while the canoe was being sailed hard into the wind from Kaua'i to O'ahu, to complete a circumnavigation of the Hawaiian chain. The leeward hull, which was depressed low in the water as the canoe heeled under the pressure of the wind on the sails, was carelessly allowed to fill with water. With the gunwales of the hull awash, it proved impossible to bail the water out, so the canoe had to be towed back to port.

This accident brought the vessel under close scrutiny by the Coast Guard, which has the duty to prevent any vessel from leaving port that it considers to be unseaworthy. Although earlier voyagers may have sailed with open hulls which were prone to swamping, we were required to install a series of watertight compartments in the hulls as a safety measure without which we would not be authorized to leave port again.

The First Voyage to Tahiti

On 1 May 1976 *Hōkūle'a* sailed from the island of Maui under the command of Elie "Kawika" Kapahulehua, an experienced catamaran sailor who, since he grew up on the remote island of Niʻihau where everyone still speaks Hawaiian, is one of those rare Hawaiians who is perfectly fluent in his native language. By holding the canoe close to the wind (but not so close as to lose too much speed) we were able to make up the 500-mile difference between the longitude of our departure point on the western end of Maui and that of Tahiti, so that we arrived at our destination after thirty-two days at sea and two days spent on an atoll in the Tuamotus.

As expected, during the first part of the voyage the northeast trades of the Northern Hemisphere enabled *Hōkūleʻa* to slant toward the southeast. At about 9° north of the equator we entered into the doldrums zone between trade wind belts where for the next week we experienced a series of calms interspersed with brief spells of light, shifting winds. During this trying time, the canoe made a little more easting, apparently pushed by the Equatorial Countercurrent that flows strongly if irregularly to the east in this zone between the trade wind belts. Once the canoe left the doldrums and entered into the southeast trade wind belt, the southerly component of those winds combined with the westward flowing current to push the canoe onto a southwesterly course. For several days it even looked like the canoe might lose all the hard-won easting gained in the previous weeks and miss Tahiti by a wide margin. Fortunately, however, as we approached Tahitian waters the winds became more easterly, allowing the canoe to head slightly to the east of south, and make landfall on Mataiva, the westernmost atoll of the Tuamotu chain, from which we were able to sail easily to Tahiti (fig. 13).[25]

The navigational component of the experiment was equally successful. To prepare Mau Piailug for the voyage, David Lewis briefed him on the geography of the islands in this part of the Pacific and the winds and currents that could be expected along the way, all information that an early Polynesian navigator acquainted with this route would have carried in his head. In addition, to alert Mau of how the elevation of stars above the northern and southern horizons would change as the canoe sailed farther and farther south, we held training sessions in Honolulu's Bishop Museum planetarium to graphically show how, for example, as one sailed toward Tahiti Polaris sank lower and lower on the northern horizon until it disappeared at the equator while the Southern Cross curved higher and higher in the

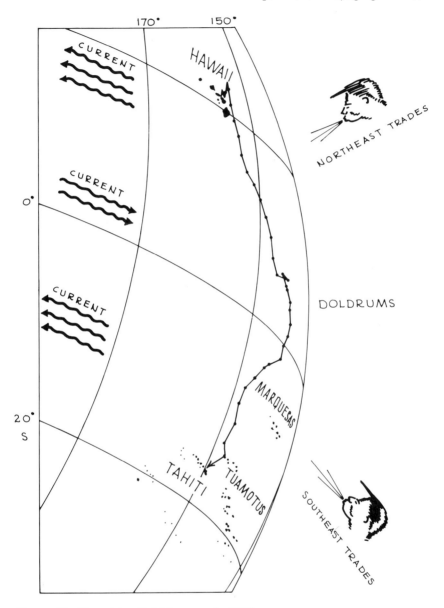

Figure 13. Hawai'i to Tahiti course in 1976.

sky. During the first few days of the voyage, Mau received further coaching on the pattern of winds and currents from Rodo
Williams, a veteran Tahitian seaman on the crew who the year
before had sailed a yacht from Tahiti to Hawai'i and could there-

fore provide Mau with a firsthand account of what he could expect to encounter.

After tacking northwest from Maui around the island of Hawai'i, sails were set for the long slant to the southeast against
the trades. During that time of the year, the constellation Scor-
pius (known to the Hawaiians as *Ka Makau Nui o Maui*, "The
Great Fishhook of Maui") rises in the southeastern sky early in
the evening.[26] Mau wanted to point the canoe east-southeast toward the rising position of Antares, a reddish star in the constellation, a heading which after the effects of current and leeway would result in a course toward the southeast. However,
most of the time the wind was too easterly and forced the canoe
onto a course more toward the south-southeast.

Mau showed those handling the long steering sweeps what
star to point toward and how at other times to use the sun,
swells, or trade wind to hold a steady course. During the brief
spells of wind in the doldrums, Mau had to be especially alert to
keep the steersmen from going off course. Denied any celestial
indications of direction by the leaden skies, those steering could
not easily detect the wind shifts and hence tended to inadver-
tently follow the veering wind—until Mau, who was the only
one on board who could consistently orient himself on the confused welter of swells characteristic of the doldrums region,
would calmly direct them back on course.

As the wind that sprang up after leaving the doldrums blew
from the south-southeast and began forcing the canoe westward,

Mau monitored the canoe's heading closely with reference to the Southern Cross. In his stellar direction system, this constellation provides five directional points: first, as it rises above the horizon; second, as it rises to a 45° angle; third, as it is upright (at this time the axis of the cross indicates due south); fourth, as it slants over to 45°; and fifth, as it sets on the horizon. Toward which of these five positions the canoe's prows pointed gave a clear indication of heading, though leeway and current drift had to be added in to estimate the resultant course. When, for example, the prows framed the Cross setting at 45°—as it did when the wind was most southerly, the resultant course was actually toward the setting position of the Cross, or roughly southwest.

The declining elevation of Polaris above the northern horizon, its final disappearance at the equator, and the concomitant rise of the arc transcribed by the Southern Cross across the southern sky gave a rough indication of the southward progress of *Hōkūle'a*. Mau, however, conceived of our progress in terms of his *etak* system, in which he employed the Marquesas archipelago as his "reference island." For example, when the voyage began, the Marquesas—located 600 miles south of the equator and some 500 miles to the east of the projected course—was at approximately the same bearing as the rising point of Antares and then "moved" north through Mau's directional system as the canoe sailed southward until, as the Tuamotus neared, the bearing to the Marquesas was located between the rising points of the Pleiades and Vega.[27] It might seem incredible that Mau was able to adapt his *etak* system of reckoning from the relatively short voyages made between the Caroline Island atolls he knew so well to such a lengthy crossing in utterly foreign seas, but that proved to be the case. As the canoe neared the Tuamotus on the thirtieth day at sea, Mau told us that we would soon see these coral islands, and then Tahiti the day after. A few hours after he made this statement, we spotted white fairy terns indicating land was near, and soon thereafter the trade wind swell stopped, a sign that there was an island or islands ahead of us that was blocking the swell. Late that night the dim outline of the atoll of Mataiva was spied off to starboard, and had the canoe not stopped there to enjoy the welcome of the islanders, the next day we would have seen Tahiti just as Mau had said.

The return voyage to Hawai'i took only twenty-two days because of the favorable angle of the strong steady trade winds along the route. Unfortunately, because Mau had returned to Satawal soon after his arrival in Tahiti, the canoe was navigated home by modern methods. Although it had not been possible to have both legs of the voyage navigated by traditional means, by guiding *Hōkūle'a* to Tahiti, Mau Piailug had dramatically demonstrated how wrong Sharp had been in limiting navigated voyages to only 300 miles. This navigational feat, plus the performance of the canoe in gaining enough easting to reach Tahiti and then in speeding back to Hawai'i to complete the roundtrip, effectively demolished Sharp's artificial limits on Polynesian voyaging capabilities.

Sharp, who died in 1974, would probably not have agreed with that conclusion. Predictably, given his utter dismissal of Lewis's *Rehu Moana* experiment, he had reacted strongly when, in 1967, I published the rationale and outline for an experimental voyage between Hawai'i and Tahiti. Modern geographical knowledge, he proclaimed, would render it and any other contemporary experiment invalid. Then, in 1971 when I was editing a series of papers on voyaging and navigation research for the Polynesian Society, Sharp took the occasion to bombard me with a series of letters telling me how wrong I was. For example, he wrote me that "you're in grave jeopardy if you go on sticking to your views on Polynesian navigation and experimental voyages" and went on to explain how he was only "trying to be helpful because you shouldn't with a long career before you as a professional become identified with discredited or dubious views."[28]

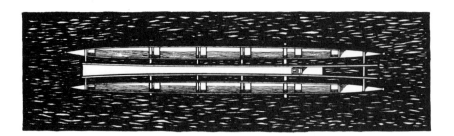

3

CULTURAL REVIVAL

A Cultural Goal

Our purpose in building *Hōkūleʻa* and then sailing her to
Tahiti was actually twofold. In addition to resolving issues about
Polynesian seafaring, we wanted the canoe and the voyage to
serve as vehicles for the cultural revitalization of Hawaiians and
other Polynesians. In the centuries that have followed their disastrous encounter with the outside world and its epidemic dis-
eases, weapons, and institutions, Hawaiians, and to a greater or
lesser extent other Polynesian groups, have become more and
more alienated from their heritage of oceanic exploration and
voyaging. For example, when we started the project the great
majority of Hawaiians knew little or nothing about sailing canoes, traditional navigation methods, or the rich oral literature
about voyaging back and forth between Hawaiʻi and Tahiti that
inspired our voyaging plan. It was this estrangement from seafaring skills and traditions that we wanted to reverse. We therefore started the project with the premise that Hawaiians should
take principal roles in planning the project and running the
Polynesian Voyaging Society and, above all, in the construction
and sailing of *Hōkūleʻa*. Our hope was that from this participa-
tion knowledge of and pride in Polynesia's rich oceanic heritage
would grow and spread, giving Hawaiians and other Polynesians

an added degree of cultural strength with which to face the challenges of today.

For me, this dual role of the project had its beginning back in 1966 when I had brought *Nālehia* to Hawai'i for paddling and sailing trials. I had asked some of my Hawaiian friends dating back to my surfing days in Hawai'i—Tommy Schroeder, "Rabbit" Kekai, and "Nappy" Napoleon—to help me with those trials. They, and friends they brought along, all paddled for the Waikiki Surf Club, then the leading outrigger canoe racing team in the islands. At first they were a bit skeptical about the research agenda of testing how well *Nālehia* sailed and could be paddled. Once, however, they started taking *Nālehia* out to sea and began thinking about how the first people to reach Hawai'i, their own ancestors, had sailed here in such a double canoe, they warmed to the project. To some of them in particular, their growing skill at handling the canoe seemed to give them a new sense of identity as heirs to a great seafaring tradition that went back thousands of years. In at least one case, there was even an immediate practical result of this cultural awakening, which was then being featured in the Honolulu newspapers and on the local television stations. A young paddler just out of high school who had been having trouble getting a regular job was able to land a career position with Hawaiian Telephone largely on the strength of his identification with the project and the dedication to it that he so enthusiastically communicated to the interviewer from the telephone company.

Although upon returning to Hawai'i in 1970 to teach at the University of Hawai'i I was anxious to organize an experimental voyage to Tahiti, I wanted to broaden the project beyond the original research focus before beginning. Sailing a voyaging canoe to Tahiti and return and navigating her by traditional means would, I thought, nurture and spread this cultural awakening more widely, as well as demonstrate the worth of ancient canoe and navigational technology. Upon meeting with Tommy Holmes and Herb Kane in early 1973 and hearing that they shared my dream of sailing a canoe to Tahiti, and of making the voyage culturally meaningful as well as scientifically useful, I felt the time was right to start the project. Tommy and Herb brought to the project unique strengths that went far beyond my skills and experience. In addition to being a dedicated racing canoe paddler who loved to defy the odds by surfing his canoe down 30-foot waves, Tommy was also well known in local business and philanthropic circles and had an enthusiasm for public entrepreneurship that he put to further use after the voyage by founding the Hawai'i Maritime Center. Although Herb was of Hawaiian descent and had been born in Hawai'i, he had spent most of his life in the midwest where he had become a highly successful commercial illustrator (as well as a catamaran sailor on Lake Superior). Herb therefore brought to the project an unusual combination of artistic skill and a passion for getting back to his native culture that seemed ideal for designing the canoe and working out a strategy to make the project significant to his fellow Hawaiians.

In addition to serving as vice-president of the Polynesian Voyaging Society and developing the overall design of *Hōkūle'a*, Herb took the lead in implementing the project's cultural goals. He and the other Hawaiian directors of the Polynesian Voyaging Society made a special effort to spread word of the project among Hawaiians, to develop support throughout the islands, and, above all, to recruit Hawaiian crew members for the voyage. In addition, while we trained for the voyage, Herb skippered the canoe around the Hawaiian archipelago, making contact with Hawaiian groups at each island and using the canoe as a floating classroom of traditional maritime arts. The Society also presented a series of lectures to the general public and to schoolchildren to acquaint them with Polynesian seafaring and our project and held special canoe workshops where participants were taught how to sail *Nālehia*. In addition, we published a series of children's books based on the legendary voyages between Hawai'i and Tahiti and our plan to duplicate one of those crossings.

Although we had hoped that our research agenda and our efforts at cultural revival would reinforce one another, in practice it proved most difficult to join the two—particularly as anxiety rose with the approach of the departure for Tahiti. The mid-1970s was a time of growing exasperation among Hawaiians with their status as a dispossessed minority in their own land, and a number of them came to see the experimental side of the project as just one more arbitrary imposition on Hawaiians by the dominating culture. Some even advocated that we cancel the voyage to Tahiti and back and instead just use the canoe in Hawaiian waters as a vehicle of political protest. In this highly charged atmosphere, made even more volatile by filmmakers who were encouraging revolt to gain dramatic footage, insistence that we keep to the original plan led to conflict that delayed our departure for Tahiti and continued to plague us on the way there.

Despite this conflict, however, the overall impact of the voyage was overwhelmingly positive, culturally as well as scientifically. For example, although the Tahitians were aware of our problems, they focused on the accomplishments of the voyage. During the planning period I had flown to Tahiti (where I had conducted research for several years during the early 1960s) to tell Tahitian leaders about the project and to urge that they join in the effort. They had responded by forming the Tainui Society as a sister organization of the Polynesian Voyaging Society in order to spread word among the Tahitians and other French Polynesians of the nature and goals of our effort, and to act as our host when we arrived. So successful were they that the day of our arrival was declared a holiday, and over fifteen thousand people crowded around the shores of Pape'ete harbor to welcome us to Tahiti. Later we sailed to the nearby island of Ra'iatea to make a pilgrimage to the ancient stone *marae*, or temple, of Taputapuātea, where we were welcomed by elaborate rituals, chants, and speeches that breathed new life into this long-deserted center of the ancient religion.

The remarks made to the Hawaiian crew members by a particularly eloquent orator bear repeating for they express how well our voyage was appreciated:[1]

> This is a magnificent day for us because of the research you have undertaken at sea, research into the way of life of our Polynesian ancestors from distant antiquity. We celebrate your voyage to our island in your canoe, a voyage that has made today a great occasion for recalling the past of our homeland. This is our homeland—Ra'iatea, which long ago was called Havai'i. It is from here that your ancestors left to sail over the great ocean. They settled on the islands they discovered, and now you have returned. The people of Polynesia have been overjoyed to hear of your voyage. You are our brothers.

Although we may not have agreed that the first Hawaiians necessarily came from Ra'iatea or any other Tahitian island (because of the linguistic evidence indicating Hawai'i may have been settled from the Marquesas long before any Tahitians arrived), we felt that this statement summed up what we had been trying to accomplish on a cultural level. The voyaging canoe, and the navigational feats of their ancestors, had been brought back into the Tahitian consciousness—so much so, in fact, that a few years later the design of a double canoe was placed in the center of the flag of French Polynesia to serve as a symbol of the seafaring origins of the nation.

The flawless performance of the return crew, composed primarily of young Hawaiian men and women who had flown to Tahiti to sail the canoe home, did much to focus everyone in Hawai'i on the achievements of the voyage. In particular, the Hawaiians were proud of *Hōkūle'a* as the beautiful sailing vessel that had demonstrated the maritime skills and accomplishments of their ancestors. Social historian George Kanahele even credits the canoe with helping to ignite a Hawaiian cultural renaissance that burst forth at that time.[2]

Relearning Navigation

Despite the great cultural impact of *Hōkūle'a* and the pride felt by Hawaiians that the canoe had been designed, captained, and largely crewed by Hawaiians, there was one missing element: no Hawaiian was able to navigate as their ancestors had once done. By guiding *Hōkūle'a* to Tahiti solely by naked-eye observations of the stars, swells, and other natural signs processed without even the aid of pencil and paper, Mau Piailug had given the Hawaiians a glimpse of an intellectual skill that had once been basic to their culture but had seemingly vanished.

Quietly, a young Hawaiian crew member named Nainoa Thompson set out on his own to learn the old ways of navigating, initiating a personal quest that eventually was to lead the project to new levels of cultural and scientific accomplishment. When first recruited as a crew member in 1974, Nainoa, then a college student, had virtually no knowledge of the stars or of celestial navigation techniques, traditional or modern. As he worked on the project and learned how to identify Polaris, the Southern Cross, and other stars and constellations, Nainoa became fascinated with the idea that these and other objects and patterns in the sky and sea could be used to navigate to distant islands without charts or instruments. He took an astronomy course at his college and began studying Lewis's *We the Navigators* and other descriptions of Pacific Island navigational methods. Although Nainoa did not sail on the Hawai'i to Tahiti leg of the 1976 voyage and therefore had no opportunity to watch Mau in action, his enthusiasm for noninstrument navigation was reinforced by the experience of sailing on *Hōkūle'a* back to Hawai'i. During that crossing he had a chance to try out some of the techniques he had read about, such as steering on the stars and using Polaris to judge latitude, and also began developing some of his own ways for reading the sky.

Once back in Hawai'i, Nainoa continued to study the sea and sky, taking every opportunity he could to observe the stars, swells, and wind patterns when sailing on *Hōkūle'a* and when going out to sea in his own fishing launch. His approach to the night sky went far beyond the memorization of where the stars rose and set and the use of these bearings as points on a stellar compass. He searched the stars for patterns and relationships in their nightly passage across the sky that might help him to orient himself and find his way to land. When, for example, Nainoa was puzzled by a problem concerning the motions of the sun and moon, he turned to the staff of Honolulu's Bishop Museum Planetarium. This inquiry led to many sessions under the planetarium dome during which Nainoa and planetarium lecturer Will Kyselka spent hour after hour studying the simulated sky between Hawai'i and Tahiti as seen at various latitudes and at the different seasons and times of the night, as well as trying out new ideas that Nainoa had for using the stars, moon, and even the planets for finding his way across the sea.

In April of 1977, a year after the first voyage, Nainoa had a chance to practice his newly learned skills on a sea trial designed primarily to determine the feasibility of leaving for Tahiti by sailing along the western, leeward coast of the island of Hawai'i instead of tacking around the island before turning south, as we had done in 1976. As they sailed southward, Nainoa set the course and judged the progress of the canoe by his methods, while another crew member employed a sextant, chronometer, and star tables in order to provide a check on the accuracy of Nainoa's navigation. Although the canoe was sailed only a little farther south than the latitude of the southern tip of Hawai'i Island, the results of the trial looked promising. Sailing southward along the leeward side of Hawai'i Island seemed to provide a smoother start than tacking through bumpy seas around the island, and Nainoa's sense of direction and dead reckoning proved to be very close to the target. Accordingly, plans were formulated to sail all the way to Tahiti the following year, 1978.

Unfortunately, *Hōkūle'a* left Honolulu without an escort vessel, casting off at dusk with small craft warnings flying. As the heavily laden canoe entered the Kaiwi channel between O'ahu and Moloka'i islands the winds were picking up to gale or near-gale force. After crossing the main body of the channel, *Hōkūle'a* ran into trouble around midnight in the steep seas generated in the shallow water over the Penguin Bank. As the narrow-stanced canoe heeled over under the pressure of the strong winds, seas washing over the depressed, leeward hull were not bailed out fast enough. The hull quickly filled with water, and before the sails could be taken down the strong wind turned the listing canoe completely over, dumping into the sea the emergency radio beacon, the only means there was for triggering a rescue. Although all the crew survived the capsize, a valiant attempt made the next day to paddle a surfboard to land in order to alert the Coast Guard of the vessel's plight cost the life of Eddie Aikau, a world champion surfer who was making his first trip on *Hōkūle'a*. At dusk a passing aircraft spotted the overturned canoe, after which the Coast Guard rescued all who had remained on board and then towed the battered but still structurally sound vessel back to Honolulu. Eddie Aikau, however, was never seen again.

This tragedy caused many to drop out of the project. Those who, like Nainoa, stayed with the project dedicated themselves to rebuilding the canoe and then to safely completing this aborted second voyage to Tahiti. While the canoe was being repaired and plans for another attempt were being formulated, Nainoa intensified his efforts to study ancestral ways of navigating, as well as to work out his own ways of using the stars to navigate without instruments. He even went so far as to fly to Tahiti in order to engrave upon his mind the way the stars and constellations looked at that more southerly latitude. Still, despite all these efforts, Nainoa was not fully confident that he really knew enough to sail the canoe to Tahiti as Mau Piailug had done. Consequently, he flew to Saipan in the Northern Marianas group to seek out Mau, who had just sailed his outrigger canoe there from his home island of Satawal located 500 miles to the south, and to ask for his help in furthering his education in the art of navigation.

Mau had originally been attracted to the project by more than the navigational challenge presented by the voyage to Tahiti. He had also empathized with the Hawaiians over their loss of once vital maritime skills and wanted to play a role in their relearning of these. Mau, who was then in his late forties, had seen that the old navigators were dying off in his culture and that very few young men knew much about the old methods. Fearing that traditional navigation would one day disappear in his islands just as it had in Hawai'i, he had been trying to prevent that by teaching the young men of Satawal the skills that had earlier been passed on to him. Despite, however, such efforts as taking Satawalese youths on the voyage to Saipan, Mau was not optimistic about getting them to really learn how to navigate. He complained that they were too busy with school and too attracted to Western ways to undertake the rigorous course of study and apprenticeship necessary to become a navigator, and that, furthermore, they did not seem to care or even realize that traditional navigation was dying and could be lost forever.

Mau was therefore delighted to find such a highly motivated pupil as this young Hawaiian. After hearing Nainoa's earnest appeal, Mau flew to Hawai'i in late 1979 in order to prepare him for the voyage. Mau began by going over the basics with Nainoa: the star compass, the rising and setting points of key stars and constellations, and the dominant swell patterns. They worked together first on land, and then at sea, going out in Nainoa's fishing launch for realistic exercises in stellar and ocean swell orientation, as well as in spotting those birds that indicate when land is near. Mau was an exacting master. He expected his pupil to take the information given him, digest it, think about it, and then come back with further questions—but not about the identification of particular stars or details. As a man from a nonliterate culture where memory skills are highly developed, Mau expected Nainoa to grasp immediately any information given him and then to come up with questions that showed he was thinking ahead and anticipating how he might apply what he had learned. The young Hawaiian proved to be an apt pupil for this approach, for it was in his nature to develop his own way of looking at things and his own way of solving problems.

The system Nainoa developed is therefore neither specifically Carolinian nor Polynesian. It is a unique mixture which, though based on traditional Pacific methods, includes concepts and techniques that Nainoa had worked out for himself. None of these were consciously adapted from modern celestial navigation which Nainoa deliberately avoided learning. Rather, they grew out of his own study of the stars. However, even though Nainoa's system may not be a carbon copy of an indigenous system, because he developed it on a traditional Pacific base and employs it at sea without the use of any instruments, charts, or written materials, his efforts to guide *Hōkūle'a* to distant landfalls can tell us much about the possibilities and limitations inherent in Polynesian and other related Pacific Island ways of navigating.

The bare-bones outline of Nainoa's system given below will furnish the reader with some insight into the key principles and procedures he uses to navigate.[3] Such a summary cannot, however, tell exactly how Nainoa navigates. As he himself emphasizes when introducing fledgling navigators to the principles of noninstrument navigation, although the system is based on logical, matter-of-fact principles, applying them at sea is an art. To develop his own skills took Nainoa years of inquiry and practice, and, as he stresses to his pupils, he is still learning how to guide a canoe to distant landfalls by observing the stars and other celestial bodies, studying the ocean swells and wind patterns, watching for the appearance of navigator birds and other clues indicating the approach to land, and then integrating all his observations and experiences to make his navigational decisions.

Orientation and Course Setting

Like traditional navigators, Nainoa employs observations of stars rising on the eastern horizon or setting in the west, plus Polaris, the Southern Cross, and other circumpolar stars, to orient himself and set a course. He has developed his own star compass based on the cardinal points, with north and south being defined by Polaris and the long axis of the Southern Cross, and with east and west being at right angles to the north-south line. He calls these cardinal directions by their traditional Hawaiian names:

Hikina	East, the "coming" in the sense of where the sun rises
Komohana	West, the "entering" in the sense of where the sun sets
ʻĀkau	North, to the "right" of the observer facing *Komohana*
Hema	South, to the "left" of the observer facing *Komohana*

To further refine his compass, Nainoa halves each quadrant formed by the cardinal points and then halves the resultant sectors twice more to come up with a thirty-two-point compass with equal sectors of 11.25° each (fig. 14). Nainoa calls these sectors "houses" in the sense that each one is the home where particular stars rise or set. The houses at the cardinal points are known by those directional referents: *Hikina, Komohana, ʻĀkau,* and *Hema.* The midhouses of each quadrant, that is, northeast, southeast, southwest, and northwest, he calls *Manu,* or "bird." For those houses where the sun rises and sets, Nainoa has chosen three names, which like *Manu,* repeat in each quadrant.

Lā	where the "sun" rises and sets
ʻĀina	the direction toward "land"
Noio	the "brown noddy tern" that leads the navigator to land

For the polar houses, Nainoa has chosen:

Haka	"empty" for the emptiness of the polar regions
Nā leo	the muted "voices" of the stars
Nā lani	"the heavens"

As the house names repeat in each quadrant, to specify directions fully requires a compound name, which Nainoa finds most convenient to express in a combination of English and Hawaiian: for example, Northeast *Manu,* or Southwest *Noio.* Although it might seem clumsy to have these repeating sector names, and hence the necessity of compound referents, Nainoa developed this system for a purpose. A navigator would like to

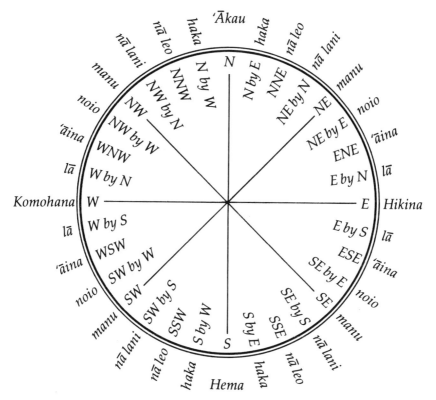

Figure 14. Nainoa Thompson's star compass, showing Hawaiian names and English equivalents.

be able to set a course and steer on stars that are rising or setting at more or less the same heading as the island toward which he is sailing. However, because there are often no distinctive stars that happen to be rising or setting at the desired heading, and because even when there may be stars with the right bearings low on the horizon they are sometimes obscured by clouds, the navigator must develop the ability to set a course on any distinct stars that may be visible along the horizon—on those rising or setting astern, or off to port or starboard, as well as on those rising or setting in the direction of the desired heading.

Following both Mau's teachings and traditional Polynesian precedents, Nainoa visualizes *Hōkūle'a* as a bird, a *manu*, flying with wings outstretched. This visualization, plus the use of repeating names for his compass houses, helps him employ stars located in any direction for course setting and steering. When, for example, Nainoa sets the bow of the canoe (the prow pieces of which are known as *manu* in Hawaiian, and are shaped like the highly stylized heads of birds) toward southeast *Manu* he knows that the stern of the canoe points back to *Manu* in the opposite, northwest quadrant, and that the wings (i.e., 90° to port and starboard) point to the *Manu* houses in the adjacent northeast and southwest quadrants. As he also knows what stars would be rising or setting in these four houses at the time he is sailing, this gives him four choices for course setting and steering, not just one. To envisage the utility of this system, imagine a canoe sailing toward southeast *Manu* when clouds are covering all the stars rising along that sector of the horizon. In this situation, the navigator can backsight over the stern on any appropriate stars setting in the opposite direction of Northwest *Manu*, or he can switch to steering on any good horizon stars that may be visible in one of the *Manu* houses 90° to the port or starboard of the heading. (On headings other than *Manu*, while the bow and stern always point to houses with the same name, the "wing" headings differ, though in a regular pattern that is easily learned.)

In the even spacing of the thirty-two houses, Nainoa's compass is like the thirty-two-point Western mariner's compass and, intriguingly, the Cook Island compass with thirty-two wind points illustrated in the previous chapter—although he did not set out to copy either of these. Nainoa's compass and that used by Carolinian navigators have some significant differences, however. Whereas the directions of the Carolinian compass are marked by the rising and setting points of navigational stars and thus are unevenly spaced along the horizon, in Nainoa's compass his houses are evenly spaced regardless of the rising and setting points of his navigational stars. Furthermore, where his compass is aligned on the cardinal points, the Carolinian compass is aligned on the star Altair, which rises 8.5° North of due east. Nevertheless, despite these differences, Nainoa, like Mau, carries his compass in his mind and can mentally cast it around the horizon whenever he can align himself on directional cues furnished by the stars or other celestial objects or, with less accuracy, on the swells.

On cloudy nights when neither stars nor the moon can be seen Nainoa orients himself on the ocean swells. In the morning and late afternoon he uses the sun for orientation. At midday when the sun is too high in the sky to indicate direction, or when the sky is too cloudy to discern the exact position of the sun, he judges direction from the pattern of ocean swells, which he keeps track of by periodically calibrating them against horizon stars or the sun when low in the sky. For those hazy, partially overcast nights when the stars are difficult to make out, but the moon or planets can be seen, Nainoa uses celestial methods he himself has developed to obtain rough bearings. His "cut of the moon" is an imaginary line through the horns of the crescent moon. It yields a north-south line when the sun is on the celestial equator but progressively deviates from that line as the sun moves north or south during the seasons. By keeping tabs of the changing angle of the cut of the moon in relation to his star compass during periods of clear skies, it is possible to get a rough approximation of direction when clouds obscure the stars but not the moon. Similarly, the changing positions of the bright planets and their relation to the star field can serve as directional guides whenever it gets too hazy to see the stars.

Keeping on Course

Nainoa did not attempt to master the Carolinian *etak* system of dead reckoning and instead developed his own methods of dead reckoning based in part on Mau's teachings and supplemented by various ways he had worked out to judge latitude from the stars.

Before a voyage, Nainoa develops a "reference course line" to represent the track he estimates the canoe will follow given expected wind and current conditions at the particular time of year. On a route, such as that between Hawai'i and Tahiti, where the canoe traverses two or more different wind and current zones, the reference course is actually a series of connected lines, each specific for the conditions of the particular zone. Once the voyage begins Nainoa keeps mental track of the heading of the canoe (based on the bearings of stars, the sun, and the moon, and the direction of the ocean swells) in relation to the reference course line which, though drawn on a map before departure, exists aboard the canoe only in the navigator's head. He pictures the deviation of the canoe off to one side or another of the reference course line in terms of so many "houses" (stellar compass points) and miles run since the last estimate, combining the two with a statement like: "Today we sailed 100 miles three houses west of the course line." This system serves to simplify dead reckoning immensely. Instead of keeping every twist and turn of the canoe in mind over the entire voyage, each day the navigator needs only to take his estimate of the canoe's offset and add or subtract it from the previous day's offset to come up with a new estimate of the canoe's position in relation to the course line.

On a north-south route, such as between Hawai'i and Tahiti, deviation from the reference course will be to the east or west of the line, and is therefore somewhat analogous to an estimate of longitude. This system, however, is neither centered on a fixed meridian such as that of Greenwich, England, nor is it expressed in degrees of longitude. It is focused on the course line specific to the voyage and the zone in which the canoe is sailing and is phrased in terms of how many "houses" and how far the canoe has deviated from the course line.

Nainoa also employs another dead reckoning method derived from Mau's teachings: progressively visualizing how far and in what direction the canoe has sailed from the starting island, and the direction to the target island and how many more miles must be sailed to reach it. He finds this method to be particularly useful when sailing along an east-west route, such as during the 1985 crossing from Rarotonga to Aotearoa which is analyzed in detail in chapter 5. For example, after leaving Rarotonga in the Cook Islands, each day Nainoa summarized the course made good by saying that the canoe was, for example, 170 miles from Rarotonga on a heading of southwest *Nā Lani* (southwest by south). Then, as the canoe progressively came closer to the destination, the Bay of Islands of the North Island of Aotearoa, Nainoa oriented his thinking toward the target by saying, for example, that the Bay of Islands was 450 miles ahead on a bearing of southwest *Noio* (southwest by west).

In addition to visualizing the progress of the canoe in terms of a reference course line, and bearing and distance from the departure point or to the destination, Nainoa also employs the concept of latitude in his navigation system. In fact, he has developed a number of methods for making fairly precise estimates of his latitude.

The angular height of Polaris above the horizon is virtually

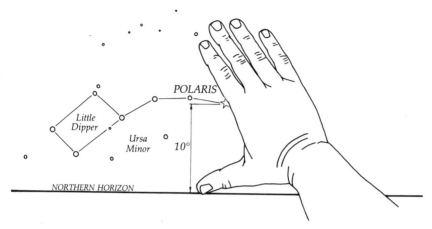

Figure 15. Estimating latitude by using the hand to measure the angular height of Polaris.

equal to the latitude of the observer, a relationship that early navigators from Europe and Asia also used to their advantage. Thus, if Polaris appears to be 10° above the horizon, the observer's latitude is approximately 10° north of the equator. Nainoa worked out a way of measuring the height of Polaris by extending his right arm, placing his outstretched thumb along the horizon, and then gauging where Polaris intersects his upright fingers (fig. 15). For example, O'ahu lies just over 21° north of the equator. Polaris, which from O'ahu appears elevated a little over 21° above the horizon, hits Nainoa's hand just at the top of his index finger. By experimenting in the planetarium and the night sky Nainoa has been able to calibrate his hand so that he can make a fairly accurate estimate of the height of any star that lies fairly close to the horizon.[4]

This method cannot, however, be used when sailing in the Southern Hemisphere where Polaris is below the horizon. For sailing south of the equator (and also for supplementing his use of Polaris in the Northern Hemisphere), Nainoa developed a method for judging latitude from pairs of relatively closely spaced stars that cross the meridian at virtually the same time. He hit upon this method when he realized that when such a pair appears upright in the sky the two stars lie directly on the observer's celestial meridian (the imaginary line connecting the north and south celestial pole and passing directly overhead),

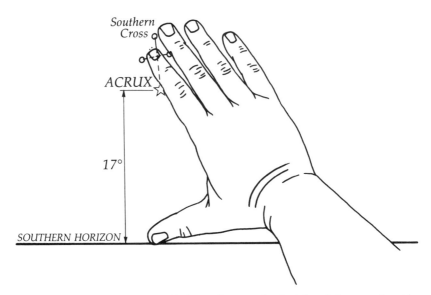

Figure 16. Estimating latitude from the angular height of Acrux when the Southern Cross is upright. (Since at the Equator Acrux is 27° above the horizon, if the star is observed to be 17° above the horizon the observer must be at 10° North latitude.)

and thus indicate true north or south depending upon which hemisphere you are in. He then discovered that he could obtain latitude from such pairs of meridional stars as accurately as he could from Polaris, requiring only that he memorize the angular height above the horizon of the bottom star of each pair when passing through the meridian at the equator. When an upright star-pair is observed, the latitude of the observation is given by the difference between its angular height above the horizon and the angular height it would have if seen from the equator.

The two stars that form the long axis of the Southern Cross are ideal for this method. At the equator, when the constellation is upright in the sky (and therefore is crossing the meridian) the bottom star of the Cross (Acrux, which actually is a double star), is approximately 27° above the horizon. Therefore, if the height of the bottom star of the upright cross were observed to be 17°, the latitude of the observer would be 10° North, a result obtained by subtracting the observed elevation of 17° from 27°, the elevation of the star above the horizon as seen from the equator (fig. 16).

With some star pairs Nainoa can also use what he calls "proportional spacing" to determine latitude almost at a glance. For example, at the latitude of Honolulu the bottom star of the upright Southern Cross is midway between the horizon and the topmost star of the Cross (6° from the horizon to the bottom star; 6° between the bottom and top stars). When sailing north from Tahiti the approach to the latitude of Hawai'i can therefore be judged by looking astern at the Southern Cross, as well as sighting on Polaris in the north. As the Southern Cross descends lower and lower in the sky with the progress of the canoe northward, the spacing between the horizon and bottom star and the bottom and top stars become progressively closer to one another until at the latitude of Hawai'i they are equal.

Still another, though more restricted, method Nainoa developed for measuring latitude involves the simultaneous rising or setting of two stars. In his nocturnal observations he discovered that two stars will rise simultaneously at only one specific latitude. For example, at 21° North latitude Arcturus and Spica rise together. But as one travels southward Spica rises progressively earlier than Arcturus. Hence, sailing north from Tahiti Nainoa could roughly monitor his progress homeward by watching the gap between the rising times of the two stars grow smaller and smaller.

Although Nainoa has tried the method used by Lewis of estimating latitude by sighting which stars are passing directly overhead, like Mau he does not use it, preferring to employ observations of the angular height of Polaris and of meridional star-pairs to estimate latitude.

In practice, Nainoa combines his reckoning of the canoe's deviation from a memorized reference course line (or of the distance and bearing from the departure point or toward the destination) with his estimations of latitude by star observations to keep a running idea in his head of the canoe's position. This is not a mechanical process, however. Sometimes dead reckoning estimates based on course and distance made good and those derived from observing Polaris or meridional star-pairs are greatly at odds, requiring some judgment to reconcile the two.

Because Nainoa uses the concepts of miles as well as degrees of latitude in his dead reckoning, his system cannot be considered purely traditional. Yet although his estimates may be reckoned and phrased in ways that sometimes may depart from traditional navigational thinking, they are nonetheless derived from virtually the same naked-eye observations of heading, speed of the canoe, and elevation of stars above the horizon that are employed in traditional navigation. Furthermore, when Nainoa estimates miles sailed, or the distance from a departure point or to a destination, or calculates how many degrees *Hōkūleʻa* is above or below the equator, he does so mentally without benefit of pencil and paper or charts of any kind.

That Nainoa employs some Western concepts to express his dead reckoning is not surprising. Although not trained in modern celestial navigation when he developed his system, Nainoa had been schooled in mathematics, including geometry and trigonometry. It was therefore natural for him to conceptualize the changing position of the canoe in terms of Western units of distance and angle, just as it is natural for Piailug to conceptualize the changing position of a canoe in terms of bearings over reference islands, *etak* segments sailed, and other concepts alien to the Western mind. Although the ways in which the two navigators phrase the product of their dead reckoning calculations may seem radically different, they both represent workable non-instrument solutions to the problem of keeping track of where they are at sea and thus may be considered to be functionally analogous.

Making Landfall

Of the three main methods for expanding the sighting range of a single target island—observing cloud effects over islands, detecting interruptions in the swell pattern caused by islands, and watching for land-finding birds—Nainoa has focused primarily on the latter. He has learned how to identify the species of terns, boobies, and other birds that serve best as indicators of land and also how to judge when, because of the number of birds sighted and their behavior, land is truly nearby.

The 1980 Voyage

The 1980 voyage to Tahiti and return proceeded much like the first one, except that both legs were navigated without instruments and by a Hawaiian rather than a Micronesian. The voyage was also distinctive in that a system was developed for remotely tracking the canoe by satellite, for the systematic recording on board the canoe of Nainoa's dead reckoning estimates, and then for the post-voyage comparison of the two data sets so that we could assess the accuracy of noninstrument navigation on a day-by-day basis, and not just by the final proof of landfall.

Oceanographers Dixon Stroup of the University of Hawai'i and William Patzert (then of the Scripps Institute of Oceanography, University of California) arranged to construct an accurate track of *Hōkūle'a* through the ARGOS system of position determination. The ARGOS system, a cooperative project operated by the French national space agency with the U.S. National Aeronautics and Space Administration (NASA) and the National Oceanic and Atmospheric Administration, is widely used by oceanographers to track drifting buoys, by meteorologists to track balloons, and by biologists to track such animals as bears and sea turtles. Because the object being tracked carries only a small automatic radio beacon, the ARGOS system was ideal for the navigation experiment. Before the departure for Tahiti, the radio beacon was turned on and sealed, together with its battery pack, in a waterproof housing, and then installed on the canoe; except for a battery change in Tahiti, the unit required no attention by the crew.

The radio beacon continuously transmitted a series of precise signals that were received and recorded by whichever of a pair of satellites in polar orbit was within range of the canoe. The recorded information was then transmitted from the satellites to an ARGOS ground-station, from where it was relayed to the ARGOS system center in Toulouse, France. The position of the radio beacon at the time of each satellite pass was then computed and relayed from France to the Hawai'i Institute for Geophysics of the University of Hawai'i, where the data was stored in a computer file. An average of six position fixes a day, each with a position accuracy of a few hundred meters, were obtained for *Hōkūle'a* throughout the voyage, which, when plotted on a chart, provided us with a fairly accurate picture of where the canoe had sailed.

While these remote sensing data were being collected and transmitted to Honolulu, on board the canoe, at each sunrise and sunset a crew member interviewed Nainoa and recorded his estimates of where the canoe was at the time, phrased in terms of bearing and distance from the reference course line, or from the point of departure or destination, or both. Upon our return to Honolulu we converted the position information from the interviews into a series of latitude-longitude intersections, which were then stored in the computer file along with the satellite fixes. Then, using a special program, the computer plotted the two series of position points on a chart and calculated the bearing and distance between each of Nainoa's position estimates and where the canoe actually was at the time.

This precise plotting and comparison of the actual and estimated tracks of *Hōkūle'a* during this voyage (figs. 17, 18) refuted one of Sharp's main contentions: that errors inherent in setting and holding a course on star, sun, and swell bearings, and in estimating the effects of unseen currents, must inevitably and rapidly accumulate to throw a canoe hopelessly off course, thereby making long navigated voyages impossible. After sailing over 2,000 miles of blue water, on each leg Nainoa was able to bring *Hōkūle'a* to the target island; and whatever misestimates he made along the way did not add up to throw his reckoning completely off course. If anything, this suggested a proposition directly opposite from Sharp's: for skilled navigators, "errors" in course setting, steering, and dead reckoning are likely to occur randomly, and the longer the voyage the more opportunity there is for such random "errors" to cancel out one another.

The crossing from Hawai'i to Tahiti shows how such canceling out can occur (fig. 17). At sunset on 30 March, just after *Hōkūle'a* left the doldrums a few hundred miles north of the equator and entered the southeast trades, Nainoa's estimate of the canoe's position was very close to where she actually was. Then, as Nainoa put the canoe on a southward heading, *Hōkūle'a* apparently encountered a narrow current jet moving westward at 2–3 knots, a not uncommon occurrence near the equator where the Coriolis Force is minimal and such current jets may flow rapidly east or west for short periods. Without a land referent, Nainoa did not notice that the canoe was being shoved toward the southwest while sailing across the current jet.[5] So, although for the next ten days Nainoa's dead reckoning track closely paralleled the actual track, because of the unperceived westward jog while crossing the current jet, Nainoa assumed that the canoe was sailing 90 miles to the east of the actual track.

Then, on 11 April, Nainoa decided that his dead reckoning was significantly off because he had not allowed for enough current set westward during the slow passage southward over the previous ten days. Accordingly, he revised the estimate of the

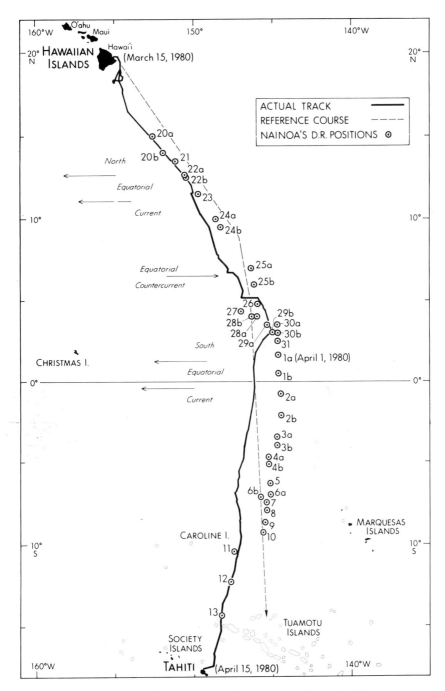

Figure 17. Hawai'i to Tahiti in 1980, showing actual track of Hōkūle'a, *reference course, and Nainoa Thompson's dead reckoning (D.R.) positions estimated at sunrise (marked by "a" following the date) and sunset (marked by "b").*

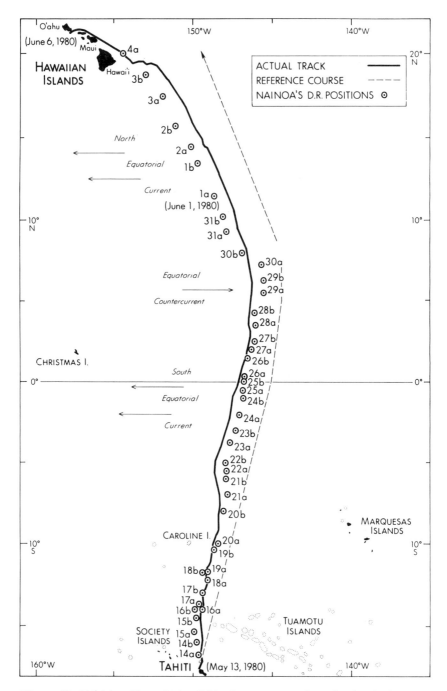

Figure 18. Tahiti to Hawai'i in 1980, showing actual track of Hōkūle'a, reference course, and Nainoa Thompson's dead reckoning (D.R.) positions estimated at sunrise (marked by "a" following the date) and sunset (marked by "b").

canoe's position considerably to the west, placing it almost exactly on *Hōkūle'a*'s actual track. But this revision, however accurate it appeared to be, was apparently based on another misestimate. Oceanographer Dixon Stroup and his colleagues had been monitoring the current between Tahiti and Hawai'i through instrumented buoys dropped from a U.S. Navy patrol aircraft at the same time *Hōkūle'a* was sailing. The data transmitted from the buoys indicated that the current in this region was, contrary to Nainoa's expectation, moving very slowly westward.[6] In effect, therefore, the overestimate of current strength south of the equator canceled out the oversight of how the canoe had been pushed sharply to the west by a brief current burst north of the equator, bringing the estimated position of *Hōkūle'a* remarkably close to its actual position.

That a Hawaiian had so successfully navigated *Hōkūle'a* both ways between Hawai'i and Tahiti made this voyage all the more significant. Not only had Mau's achievement on the 1976 voyage to Tahiti been replicated and then extended, but for the first time in many centuries a Polynesian navigator had guided a canoe back and forth over the long sea road between Hawai'i and Tahiti. Nainoa's achievement particularly impressed the many Hawaiians who followed the progress of the canoe through daily reports on radio and television and in the newspapers. For them, the outstanding accomplishment was that a native son of Hawai'i had revived long-lost and recently doubted ancestral skills, demonstrating both their worth and that a modern Hawaiian youth was capable of the immense intellectual effort and discipline required to re-learn and apply them. After all the difficulties experienced before and during the first voyage in trying to bring research and cultural revival together, it was immensely gratifying to see how well they reinforced each other on this second voyage.

Extending the Experience

At this point, *Hōkūle'a* could have been honorably retired to a museum, and those who had so successfully sailed her to Tahiti and back could have gone back to work or to school, satisfied with a job well done. But to them, the canoe was a living artifact that should be kept sailing and not just put on display. Hence, they began organizing day sails out of Honolulu

and more extended sails from island to island throughout the Hawaiian archipelago, not only for their own enjoyment but also to use the canoe as a "floating classroom" to teach others, particularly Hawaiian schoolchildren, about the technology and skills that made the initial discovery and settlement of their islands possible.

Though immensely rewarding, these short voyages and the teaching experiences were not enough. The once strong Hawaiian penchant for overseas voyaging—which had last found its expression during the nineteenth century when thousands of Hawaiians had signed on as sailors on passing trading and whaling ships—had been reawakened. Those who had tasted the thrill of sailing *Hōkūle'a* to Tahiti, Ra'iatea, and other islands they had hardly heard of before the project were anxious to go to sea again, and many others who had not been on either voyage wanted a chance to make landfall on a distant Polynesian island. Going back to Tahiti once more was discussed, but a consensus soon developed that *Hōkūle'a* should sail beyond Tahiti to other Polynesian centers, both to extend the Hawaiian experience of rediscovering lost voyaging skills and far-off islands, and to share that experience with kindred Polynesian peoples on a more extended voyage. Thus was born a plan to sail *Hōkūle'a* on a "Voyage of Rediscovery" through seven archipelagos.

4

MORE THAN HALFWAY
AROUND THE WORLD

Hōkūleʻa sailed from Hawaiʻi on 10 July 1985 and returned
home on 23 May 1987, completing the long voyage through Polynesian waters in just six weeks short of two years. In order to be
able to construct an accurate track of the canoe over the entire
route of the voyage, *Hōkūleʻa* was tracked by the ARGOS satellite system described in the previous chapter, and by frequent
position fixes made with the satellite navigation receiver aboard
the yacht *Dorcas*, which followed the canoe as an escort vessel
throughout the entire voyage.[1] Totaling the distances between
satellite position fixes yields a minimum measure of the distance sailed by the canoe: 11,511 nautical miles from the fishing village of Miloliʻi on the southwestern coast of the island of
Hawaiʻi through Polynesia and back to the port of Hilo on the
northeastern coast of that island. If one allows for extra miles
sailed during twists and turns of the canoe's track between position fixes, those side trips taken at some island stops which
were not tracked, and the crossing from the canoe's home island, Oʻahu, to the island of Hawaiʻi to position the canoe for
the departure for Tahiti, it can be said that *Hōkūleʻa* sailed well
over 12,000 nautical miles during the Voyage of Rediscovery, a
distance equivalent to traveling more than half-way around the
world at the equator.

Hōkūleʻa sails comfortably at 6 or 7 knots in brisk, steady trade winds and can accelerate up to 10 to 12 knots or more when broad reaching across strong winds coming from just slightly abaft the beam. But on long crossings, the inevitable calms and spells of light winds plus the squally, stormy conditions when sails have to be lowered brings the average down to around 4 knots. In fact, the satellite fixes indicate that the canoe averaged slightly over 4 knots, or about 100 nautical miles a day during the 118 days at sea on the way from the island of Hawaiʻi to Aotearoa and return.

If *Hōkūleʻa* can sail an average of almost 100 miles a day, why did it take almost two years to complete the voyage? Actually, for most of that period the canoe was tied up alongside a wharf, or beached on dry land, at the numerous island stops along the way. Some of the days spent in port can be accounted for by the need for those crew members making all or most of the entire voyage to return to Hawaiʻi between legs in order to take care of work or family obligations. In addition, there were inevitable delays involved in flying in new crew members from Hawaiʻi to replace those who had only enough time off from their jobs to sail on one leg of the voyage. Still more days at each island stop were devoted to welcoming ceremonies and other cultural events, as well as to the repair and maintenance of the canoe. Even, however, if we had tried to restrict the time spent in welcoming ceremonies, crew rest and changes, and repairs and maintenance to just a week or so at each island stop, the voyage would still have taken much more time than the nearly four months actually spent at sea.

This is because at key points along the route it was necessary to wait for seasonal wind shifts in order to continue on to the next island landfall. No sailor, whether in a Polynesian canoe or a modern yacht, wants to force his vessel against wind and sea when it is possible to wait for more favorable winds to make the same passage. Because the route crossed so many different wind zones, it was inevitable that the canoe would be faced by contrary winds along some segments of the voyage. Rather than attempting to tack against these winds, the strategy was to wait, at times for many months, for the season when we could expect favorable wind shifts that would allow the canoe to set sail for the next island destination. For example, it would have been foolish to push directly on to Aotearoa after arriving at

Tahiti in August, for that would mean sailing into temperate latitudes during the Southern Hemisphere winter when cold and often stormy westerlies frequently blow along the approaches to Aotearoa. Since easterlies usually begin blowing in these temperate latitudes late in the spring, we took our time sailing from Tahiti to Rarotonga and then delayed our departure from there to Aotearoa to catch these favorable winds.

The Winds of Polynesia

To understand the nature of the wind field through which the canoe sailed during the voyage and why we waited for favorable wind shifts to complete those legs of the voyage made against the direction of the prevailing winds, consider an idealized model of the winds that sweep across the Pacific (fig. 19). The Polynesian triangle straddles the easterly trade wind zone and in the Southern Hemisphere extends into the midlatitude zone of westerlies. Except for the doldrums region just north of the equator, easterly trade winds prevail in the tropics (i.e., between the Tropic of Cancer at 23° 27′ North latitude and the Tropic of Capricorn at 23° 27′ South latitude) and typically extend to around 28° north and south of the equator. Except for Aotearoa, all the Polynesian islands and archipelagos are within the trade wind zone, although Rapa, the southernmost of the Austral Islands, and Rapa Nui at the very southeastern corner of the triangle lie on the edge of that zone. North and south of the trade wind zone are belts known for strong westerly winds. Extending from 34° to 47° South latitude, the islands of Aotearoa comprise the only part of Polynesia that lies wholly in latitudes where such westerly winds blow for much of the year.

The easterly wind flow of tropical and subtropical Polynesia, and the westerlies that sweep over Aotearoa, are part of the global circulation of wind generated by the differential solar heating of the planet.[2] Maximum solar heating occurs at the equatorial bulge where surface winds are typically light and variable, or absent altogether. There the heated surface air rises high above the ocean's surface and splits into two upper air streams, one flowing northward, the other southward. As these air streams travel toward the poles they cool, and some of the cooled and thereby heavier air descends to the surface in a band generally centered at around 30° North latitude and 30° South latitude

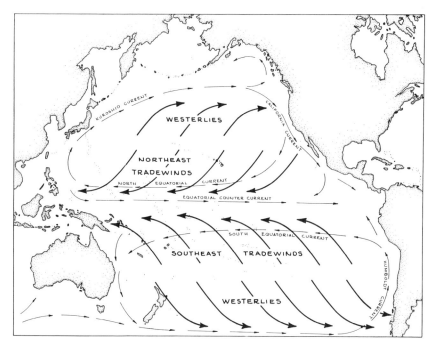

Figure 19. Idealized model of the prevailing winds and ocean currents in the Pacific.

(fig. 20). This region of high pressure, called the "horse latitudes" by British sailors, is known for its prolonged calms.

After having been cooled by its journey northward, and dried by its descent to the surface, some of the air in the horse latitudes then returns to the tropics. It does not flow directly south or north, however, because of the Coriolis Force. The earth's rotation to the east and the increasing circumference of the globe toward the equator makes the southward-flowing winds appear to twist to the west in relation to the earth's surface, so that in the Northern Hemisphere they blow from the northeast quadrant, and in the Southern Hemisphere from the southeast quadrant. These northeasterlies and southeasterlies are the famous "trade winds," so named, some say, from the crucial role they played in enabling sailing ships to carry trade around the world before the days of steam propulsion.[3]

Some of the air descending at around 30° flows poleward rather than back to the equatorial region. As it does so the earth's rotation and the decreasing circumference of the globe gives the

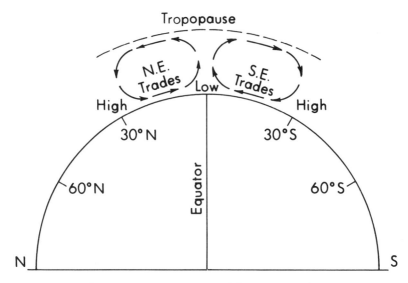

Figure 20. Schematic representation of the equatorial convection cells, the surface segments of which give rise to the northeast and southeast trade winds (Harvey 1976, 102). In the eastern Pacific the southeast trade winds regularly extend over the equator into the Northern Hemisphere.

wind an apparent twist to the east, giving rise to the midlatitude westerlies. During the days of sailing ships, vessels bound from Asia to North America or bound from the east coast of North America to Europe would sail westward before these midlatitude westerlies.

Intense cooling at the poles produces a dense surface air flow toward the equator which, skewed toward the right by the earth's rotation, generates the polar easterlies. At about 60° these polar easterlies and the midlatitude westerlies meet, causing the surface air to rise and then split at high altitudes where some flows back toward the equator and some flows back to the poles. Figure 21 shows an idealized model of these global surface winds and the air circulation cells of which they are part.

A glance at figure 19 indicates that some segments of our voyage had to be made against the direction of the prevailing winds. In particular, the southwestward passage from Rarotonga to Aotearoa and then the subsequent eastward passage from Samoa to Tahiti look most difficult, for in both cases the course is contrary to the direction of the dominant winds: against mid-

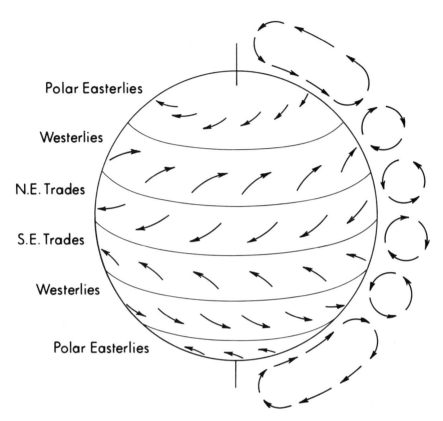

Figure 21. Schematic representation of global convection cells and surface wind belts (Brierly 1985, 17).

latitude westerlies to reach Aotearoa, and against easterly trade winds of the tropics to reach Tahiti.

Those who oppose the idea that Polynesians migrated eastward into the Pacific have focused upon the problem of sailing against the prevailing trade wind direction to buttress their theories. Heyerdahl, for example, makes his contention that the easterly trade winds would have prevented canoes from migrating eastward across the Pacific the linchpin of his theory that only voyagers from the Americas, sailing before the easterly trade winds and drifting with the accompanying currents, could have settled Polynesia. Similarly, those who think Māori legends of numerous voyages made from a homeland in tropical East Polynesia to Aotearoa must be fictions often stress the difficulty canoes would have had in sailing southwest against the cold and stormy westerly winds guarding the approaches to Aotearoa.

Although real, this problem of sailing against the direction of the prevailing winds is not at all insurmountable. Figure 19 is an idealized model that can only show the most common, or prevailing, wind flow, not seasonal variation or the more episodic disturbances in the wind field due to the passage of high and low pressure systems. The phrase "prevailing wind" refers to relative, not absolute, dominance. Even those global winds considered to be the steadiest, the trade winds, do not always blow. Periodically they falter to be replaced by calms and by spells of westerly winds that provide opportunities to sail eastward. Nor do westerlies blow unceasingly in the midlatitudes, forever preventing voyagers from sailing to the west. A drawing such as figure 19 cannot, therefore, be invoked to deny the possibility that ancient mariners could have sailed in a direction contrary to the portrayed wind flow, for the arrows are meant to illustrate average wind directions, not seasonal variation, much less wind shifts linked to passing high and low pressure systems.

Polynesian mariners, I contend, were acutely aware of these seasonal and shorter-period variations in wind direction and exploited them to sail in the direction they wished to go. As Tupaia told Cook, the Tahitians knew that westerly winds interrupted the trades during the Austral (Southern Hemisphere) summer, and they waited for their arrival before trying to sail to the east. Similarly, Māori traditions indicate that pioneering voyagers knew that the best time to head southwest from central East Polynesia to Aotearoa was in the late Austral spring when easterly winds, rather than westerlies, began to blow along the midlatitude approaches to Aotearoa. Later chapters will explain how we were able to replicate this strategy of waiting for seasonal wind shifts to sail *Hōkūle'a* from Samoa to Tahiti, and from Rarotonga to Aotearoa.

Prehistorically Significant
Legs of the Voyage

We do not claim that ancient voyagers ever sailed between Hawai'i and Aotearoa just as we did. Yet the Voyage of Rediscovery did take the canoe over a number of the seaways of Polynesia that, according to our current understanding of Polynesian prehistory, were pioneered by early migrants or traveled by later

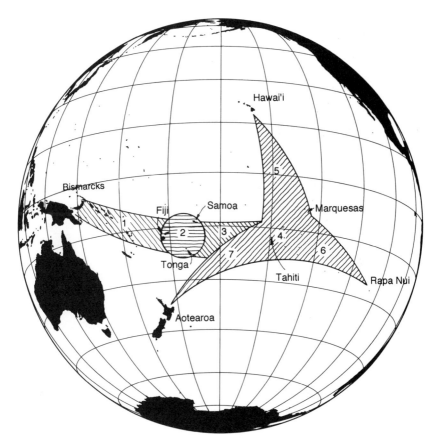

Figure 22. Main Migration Sequence: (1) from the Bismarck Archipelago to Fiji, Tonga, and Samoa (Lapita); (2) West Polynesia formative region; (3) from West to East Polynesia; (4) Central East Polynesia; (5–7) dispersion to Hawai'i, Rapa Nui, and Aotearoa.

voyagers. As such, the record of our voyage applies directly to questions concerning Polynesian migration and postsettlement voyaging over these routes, and more generally to major issues concerning the dispersion of the Polynesians and the ability of the consequently scattered populations to communicate with one another over the seaways separating them.

Figure 22 attempts to provide a visual impression of current thinking derived from linguistic, archaeological, and legendary evidence about the general trend of migration from islands offshore New Guinea to the western edge of Polynesia and then within that region. It indicates only broad directions of movement, not specific migration routes from one island to another. The reasons for this deliberate vagueness will become clear in chapter 8, where issues in reconstructing Polynesian migration and postsettlement communication between archipelagos are discussed in detail. Here only an outline of current thinking about the trend and sequence of Polynesian settlement, plus a few words about postsettlement voyaging, are given in order to provide a spatial and temporal framework for analyzing particular legs of the Voyage of Rediscovery.

Lapita voyagers appear to have moved rapidly from the Bismarcks through the archipelagos of eastern Melanesia, reaching the western edge of Polynesia at around 1500 B.C. according to the earliest radiocarbon dates, and by more conservative estimates at least by 1000 B.C. There they settled the islands in and around the archipelagos of Fiji, Tonga, and Samoa, a region that, with the exception of the main islands of Fiji and their immediate outliers, now makes up the cultural province called West Polynesia. Ancestral Polynesian culture appears to have begun evolving from its Lapita roots in these islands, and to have become archaeologically identifiable there by approximately 500 B.C. Exactly when the movement eastward to the rest of Polynesia (called East Polynesia even though one group, Aotearoa, lies to the west of West Polynesia) began is very much open to question. Some prehistorians think that the migration eastward to central East Polynesia, which is composed of the Cooks, Societies, Marquesas, Tuamotus, and Australs, did not get started until West Polynesia was thoroughly settled and ancestral Polynesian culture had emerged. Others, however, propose that the movement from the Bismarck Archipelago to central East Polynesia was a continuous process without any pause in West Polynesia. Unfortunately, the earliest radiocarbon dates available so far from East Polynesia (around 500 B.C. for agricultural disturbance in the Southern Cooks, and around 200 B.C. for occupation sites in the Northern Cooks and the Marquesas) do not settle the issue. Although these dates might seem to indicate a pause, it can also be argued that archaeologists have not yet found the evidence for the earliest movement into East Polynesia.

Although the exact sequence and dating of the initial colonization thrust to the east may be in dispute, there is a fair degree of consensus that canoes sailing from the central region of

East Polynesia undertook the long voyages to Hawai'i, Rapa Nui, and Aotearoa to settle the far corners of the Polynesian triangle. Radiocarbon dates from archaeological excavations indicate that emigrants from below the equator were established in the Hawaiian archipelago by at least 400–600 A.D., although some archaeologists point to signs of increased erosion from around 0 A.D. as evidence of agricultural activity and hence settlement at that time. On the basis of less secure archaeological work, it is thought that Rapa Nui may have been reached by around the same period of 400–600 A.D., and at least one archaeologist has cited early environmental disturbance in Aotearoa as evidence that the first colonizers of Aotearoa may have also arrived around this time. Most archaeologists, however, believe that these islands were settled centuries after Hawai'i and Rapa Nui, perhaps even as late as between 900–1200 A.D.[4]

As can be seen in figure 22, three segments of our voyage more or less coincided with main directional trends of Polynesian migration: (1) from Samoa to Tahiti; (2) from Tahiti to Rarotonga to Aotearoa; and (3) from Tahiti to Hawai'i. The legs from Samoa to Tahiti and from Rarotonga to Aotearoa have been chosen for separate and detailed treatments in chapters 5 and 6. These chapters are not arranged according to the order in which the legs were sailed, but according to the logic of the questions concerning Polynesian migrations that they address. Chapter 5 analyzes how we sailed from Samoa to Tahiti in order to provide some insight into how a double canoe can be sailed against the trade wind direction from West Polynesia to central East Polynesia, the crucial first step in the spread of the Polynesians throughout the triangle. Chapter 6 analyzes how we sailed from Rarotonga to Aotearoa in order to demonstrate how earlier voyagers might have moved out of the tropical heart of East Polynesia and into the temperate zone to reach this southwesternmost Polynesian outpost.

The third chapter devoted to a particular leg of the voyage, chapter 7, departs from this pattern of focusing on pioneering migration routes to look at the question of intentional voyaging back and forth between already settled archipelagos. On the basis of language comparisons, studies of characteristic artifacts, and analyses of Hawaiian oral traditions to be discussed in chapters 8 and 9, the Marquesas Islands have come to be considered by many as the most likely jumping-off point for the first settlers to reach Hawai'i, whereas Hawai'i and Tahiti are thought to have been connected during a period of two-way voyaging that occurred well after Hawai'i had originally been colonized. Accordingly, chapter 7 examines the round-trip voyage from Hawai'i to Tahiti and return composed of the first and last legs of the Voyage of Rediscovery in order to shed light on the problems of maintaining two-way communication between widely separated archipelagos, rather than on the issue of from exactly where and how Hawai'i was settled.[5]

Voyage Summary

Before plunging into the chapter-length analyses of these crucial segments of our voyage, an outline of the entire journey is presented below. In this outline, the two segments of the voyage not covered in chapters 5 through 7, the legs from Tahiti to Rarotonga and Aotearoa to Samoa, are described in more detail. The crew members who sailed on each leg are listed in appendix A.

Hawai'i to Tahiti:
10 July–12 August 1985 (fig. 23)

During the late spring and the first few weeks of summer, storm-free, trade wind conditions can generally be expected along the Hawai'i to Tahiti route. The crossings in 1976 and 1980 had been undertaken during the spring in order to be able to have enough time, after resting in Tahiti, to return to Hawai'i before midsummer when the tropical storms generated well to the east of Hawai'i spin westward and often pass just to the south of the islands. In 1985, because the canoe did not have to be immediately sailed back to Hawai'i, there was no pressing need to leave for Tahiti so early. Accordingly, the crossing was scheduled for June in order to take advantage of the steady winds that can generally be expected then. But problems in getting the canoe and the escort vessel ready delayed departure until July, putting the canoe at sea months later than the previous two crossings. In retrospect at least, it should not therefore be surprising that conditions encountered on this third crossing turned out to be significantly different from those met on the previous two.

Instead of reasonably steady trades, interrupted only by the predictable appearance of doldrum calms between the northeast

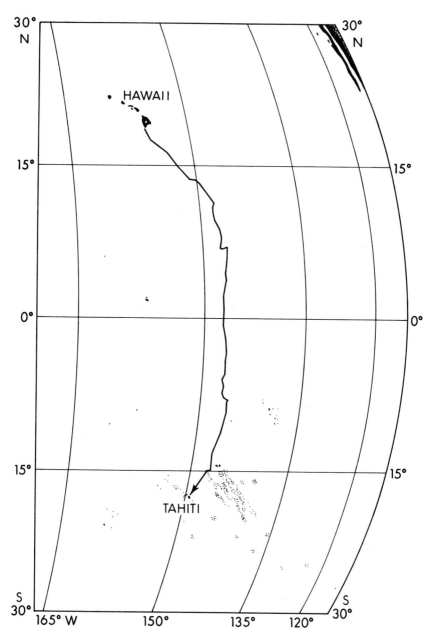

Figure 23. Hawai'i to Tahiti, 10 July–12 August 1985.

and southeast trade wind belts, the canoe experienced a series of calms, squalls, and adverse winds where steady trades were expected, and the doldrums were displaced several degrees north of where they had been encountered on the previous two voyages. These conditions, plus the repeated sightings—in seas south of the equator which are empty of islands—of birds that ordinarily indicate the close proximity of land, turned what had been expected to be a routine crossing into a major challenge. Nonetheless, after working the canoe through the calms and spells of adverse winds and having the navigation thrown off by the anomalous bird sightings and overestimates of the westward trend of the course, Nainoa and the crew brought the canoe to a landfall on Rangiroa atoll in the northwest Tuamotus and then sailed directly from there to Tahiti to complete the voyage in thirty-two days.

Tahiti to Rarotonga:
30 August–14 September 1985 (fig. 24)

There was no rush to sail directly from Tahiti to Rarotonga, for expected wind patterns dictated that the departure from the Cooks to Aotearoa should be delayed until November. Accordingly, a more leisurely route was planned, one that would take the canoe from island to island through the Societies, and then through the Southern Cooks and on to Rarotonga, the southwesternmost island of that group. In part this was a cultural cruise and in part it was a navigational exercise in island-finding. Nainoa planned to make landfalls on a number of small islands along the way to meet with fellow Polynesians and to give himself and other crew members practice in the difficult task of locating coral atolls and small volcanic islands.

From the port of Pape'ete, at the northwestern tip of Tahiti, *Hōkūle'a* sailed across the narrow channel to Mo'orea. The canoe had been invited to Mo'orea by the *Pupu Arioi*, a group interested in reviving and sharing Tahitian spiritual traditions that drew its name from the Arioi Society, an unusual organization that was flourishing in Tahiti at the time of first contact with Europeans and was at once a religious cult dedicated to the god 'Oro and a community of performing artists devoted to spreading his worship. During the feast that followed the canoe's arrival, Abraham Pi'ianai'a, a fluent speaker of Hawaiian and a

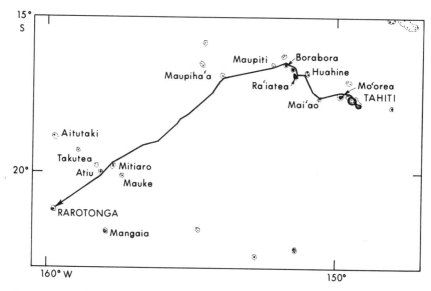

Figure 24. Tahiti to Rarotonga, 30 August–14 September 1985.

professional sea captain and geographer who was then directing the University of Hawai'i's Hawaiian Studies Program, translated the welcoming speeches into English for the rest of the crew and then replied in Hawaiian—the basics of which the Tahitians understood because of the closeness of the two languages. Abe, then seventy, was serving aboard *Hōkūle'a* with his son Gordon, director of the Hawaiian Studies Program at Honolulu's Kamehameha Schools and the captain for this leg, and with his grandson, Chad, who at sixteen was the youngest member of the crew.

The *Pupu Arioi* leaders explained that one of the reasons that *Hōkūle'a* had been invited to Mo'orea was to have the crew take part in a fire walk to prepare them spiritually for sailing through Te Ava Mo'a, literally "The Sacred Pass" through the reef surrounding the island of Ra'iatea, our next stop after Mo'orea, that leads directly to the great stone *marae*, or temple, of Taputapuātea. When we made a pilgrimage aboard *Hōkūle'a* to Taputapuātea in 1976, because of a mix-up we had not sailed through Te Ava Mo'a, as traditionally required of canoes heading for the *marae*. This had greatly upset one of the orators at the *marae*. Centuries before, he said, a *tapu* (taboo, i.e., sacred

restriction) had been placed on the surrounding lands that could only be lifted by a canoe returning from distant islands carrying descendants of those who had migrated from there—but only if the canoe sailed into the lagoon through the sacred pass. Particularly since the ancient name for Ra'iatea was Havai'i, the Tahitian way of pronouncing Hawai'i, the orator had thought that *Hōkūle'a* must have been destined to lift this *tapu.* Hence, he had been terribly disappointed when we sailed into the lagoon through the wrong pass. The orator had died just before *Hōkūle'a* had reached Tahiti on this voyage, and the *Pupu Arioi* had taken it upon themselves to make sure that this time the crew understood the importance of sailing in through the correct pass.

Once the crew was made aware of the symbolic and spiritual significance of the forthcoming passage, they readily agreed to undergo ritual purification by walking over blistering hot rocks heated in a giant earth oven, the *umu tī*, so-called because such large ovens were once used for cooking the starchy roots of the *tī* plant (*kī* in Hawaiian; *Cordyline terminalis*). After fasting that night, the crew was awakened at dawn and handed crisp white *pāreu* wraparounds and *tī*-leaf leis to wear. They were then led through the moonlight to the 20-foot long pit where flames still flickered beneath the large, smooth rocks over which they were to walk. Four large torches were lit, and once everyone was gathered around the pit Tevi, the spiritual leader for the walk, struck the stones and flames with a bundle of shiny green *tī* leaves while delivering his prayers. Once the flames subsided, Tevi started across the pit with precise and measured steps as he tested the steadiness of the hot stones. Upon reaching the other side, he turned and unhurriedly retraced his steps.

Then it was the crew's turn. Tevi motioned to Abe Pi'ianai'a, the elder of the group, to start. Abe carefully stepped from one stone to the other across the pit. Despite the heat radiating up from the rocks and the red-hot coals beneath them, Abe and then one after another of the crew made it across the pit, and then back again, without incident. Although initially the idea of walking across the fire pit had caused some anxiety, once Tevi had performed the ritual and conducted the first walk, a calmness had set in. As crew member Jo-anne Kahanamoku Sterling expressed it in her diary:[6]

> When it was my turn to make the walk, I seemed to be having trouble with my balance as I tried to step on exactly the same rocks as the person in front of me. But I felt no fear. In fact, I felt a sense of calm and a realization that this ritual was a one-in-a-lifetime experience for me.

After resting all day, the crew reassembled aboard *Hōkūle'a* and, setting sail at night, pointed the canoe southwest to get a view the next day of Mai'ao, a small island 45 miles away which combines a low ridge of volcanic origin with an encircling, atoll-like ring of coral and sand. After passing Mai'ao early in the afternoon, the canoe was turned north to Huahine, a large high island some 55 miles to the north-northwest. Using backsights on Mai'ao, and guided by Puaniho Tauotaha, a Tahitian crewman originally from the leeward Societies, the crew steered to the northwest in order to pass to leeward of Huahine well clear

of its reef. That night, the sight of surf breaking off to the starboard announced the canoe's arrival, safely to leeward, off the barrier reef surrounding Huahine.

After Huahine, the canoe made the short sail to Ra'iatea, where *Hōkūle'a* and her crew had a duty to perform. Upon approaching the barrier reef fringing the island, and making sure they had the right pass, the crew sailed *Hōkūle'a* through Te Ava Mo'a, thereby lifting the ancient *tapu* and clearing the path, they were told, for all canoes, material and spiritual, to return to this island that had long ago been called Havai'i. After anchoring in the lagoon, the crew waded ashore to the magnificently restored *marae* of Taputapuātea. After a brief ceremony before the *marae's* imposing central altar composed of great slabs of coraline stone, they returned to the canoe and proceeded through the lagoon to Uturoa, the main town and port of Ra'iatea.

From Uturoa, the canoe was sailed in a few hours across the channel to Borabora, the last major island in the Society chain. Gusty, rainy trade winds from the south kept the canoe three days in Borabora. Finally, at midmorning on 7 September, the weather cleared and *Hōkūle'a* set sail for the small high island of Maupiti, the twin peaks of which appeared as a faint smudge on the western horizon.

The plan was not to stop at Maupiti, but to sail close to it, then veer slightly to the south to head for the atoll of Maupiha'a, using the bearing from Maupiti to set the course. This strategy assumed an average speed of 4 knots, which would put the canoe, after sailing the rest of the day and through the night, within sight range of Maupiha'a sometime the next morning. Unfortunately, light winds so slowed the canoe that, according to Nainoa's reckoning, *Hōkūle'a* would not come within range of the atoll until the following night—a moonless night at that. Nevertheless, despite the poor visibility that night, Mau Piailug finally spotted the thin dark outline of the atoll ahead. This landfall greatly encouraged Nainoa. He had made two other landfalls on atolls, on Tikehau in 1980 and on Rangiroa earlier in this voyage. But in both cases he had not been aiming for those particular islands, but rather was only trying to intersect the Tuamotu chain somewhere along its western end in order to be able to orient himself for the final run to Tahiti. Particularly after the difficulties he had just experienced in navigating from Hawai'i to Tahiti, finding Maupiha'a on such a dark night greatly boosted his confidence of being able to locate small and isolated islands.

The next task was to reach Rarotonga, over 400 miles south-west of Maupihaʻa. The strategy for sailing to this southwest-ernmost island in the Cook group was similar to that used for reaching Tahiti from Hawaiʻi: first make a landfall on one of the chain of islands screening the target island; and then, once oriented, make the final run directly to the target island. From Maupihaʻa four small islands screen Rarotonga: Maʻuke, Mitiaro, Atiu, and Takutea. Upon passing Maupihaʻa, the canoe headed directly for Maʻuke, the southernmost of these islands which lies some 270 miles from Maupihaʻa. Then, after calculating that the canoe had covered two-thirds of that distance, Nainoa altered the course slightly to the north in order to maximize the chance of making a landfall on one of the four islands. The plan was to arrive in the vicinity of these islands during the daylight hours of the third day out of Maupihaʻa in order to have maximum visibility. Unfortunately, the third day dawned gray and cloudy, raising the possibility that the canoe might slip through the screen of relatively tiny volcanic islands and atolls without a sighting of even one of them. But at about 11:00 A.M. white fairy terns flew by, and almost immediately afterward sharp-eyed Peter Sepelalur, Mau Piailug's nephew, spotted underneath the low clouds an island off the port beam. It was a small high island, probably either Maʻuke or Mitiaro, thought Andy Tutai, the Cook Islander aboard the canoe. When the canoe pulled up to the island, the crew learned from an islander who paddled out in his canoe that they had made landfall on Mitiaro.

The rainy weather and lack of a safe anchorage prevented a stay at Mitiaro, so just before dusk the canoe set sail for Raro-tonga, some 140 miles to the southwest. Overcast skies that night provoked some anxiety about running onto Atiu, an is-land 50 miles west-southwest of Mitiaro located just to leeward of the direct course to Rarotonga. Orienting the canoe by the swells, Nainoa was able, however, to guide the canoe safely past Atiu that night, steering around its leeward, northern shore. After sailing steadily southwest the next day and into the evening, at around midnight the shadowy outline of the mountain peaks of Rarotonga appeared on the horizon. After two weeks of island-hopping through the Societies and Cooks, *Hōkūleʻa* was right on target.

Rarotonga to Aotearoa:
21 November–8 December 1985 (fig. 25)

Soon after arriving on 14 September, the canoe was pulled out of the water, and the crew flew back to Hawai'i. This recess was dictated by nature. Māori traditions as well as modern wind records indicate that the best time to sail to Aotearoa is late in the Austral spring when large high pressure systems typically pass slowly from west to east across the seas between tropical East Polynesia and Aotearoa, bringing the easterly wind flow needed for sailing from Rarotonga to Aotearoa.

The crew returned to Rarotonga in early November and, after putting the canoe back into the water, made ready for a mid-November departure to catch the expected easterlies. Because, however, of a lingering subtropical disturbance, *Hōkūle'a* was not able to sail until 21 November, at which time a large high pressure system spread over the ocean southwest of Rarotonga, bringing the easterly winds necessary for the passage. The wind continued to blow primarily from the east throughout virtually the entire voyage, as first one, then another, and then a third high pressure system moved slowly across the seas between Aotearoa and Rarotonga. Only during the transitions between these systems, when troughs from low pressure systems to the south extended northward across the canoe's path, was *Hōkūle'a*'s southwestward progress slowed by light, variable winds.

Making a landfall on so huge an island target as presented by Aotearoa presented no great navigational challenge, even considering that over 1,600 miles of open ocean lay between Rarotonga and there. Nevertheless, Nainoa wanted to reach the coast of the North Island as close to the Bay of Islands as possible, both as a point of pride and because our Māori friends had prepared a formal welcome and safe anchorage there. To orient himself as precisely as possible for the final run to the Bay of Islands, Nainoa was trying to intercept the Kermadecs, a chain of small volcanic islands, two-thirds of the way to Aotearoa. In particular, he wanted to sight Raoul, the northernmost and largest island of the chain. But light, northerly winds encountered just as the canoe was approaching the Kermadecs forced *Hōkūle'a* onto a course that took her slightly to the south of Raoul. Fortunately, just before dawn the outline of a small island was spotted ahead, and as the sun rose the canoe sailed between

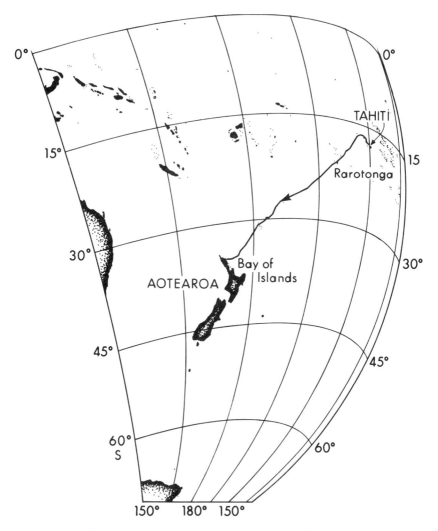

Figure 25. Tahiti to Rarotonga, 30 August–14 September 1985; Rarotonga to Aotearoa, 21 November–8 December 1985.

Macauley and Curtis Islands, the southernmost of the Kermadecs, giving a perfect reference point for sailing directly to the Bay of Islands.

Strong easterly winds revolving around the third high pressure system encountered on the voyage sped *Hōkūleʻa* to within striking distance of Aotearoa in just four days, and, although the wind died down just as land was in sight, the canoe was able to enter the Bay of Islands late in the afternoon of 8 December, to complete the crossing of 1,650 miles in just sixteen days.

Aotearoa to Samoa: 1 May–25 May 1986 (fig. 26)

The canoe was scheduled to sail from Aotearoa to Samoa in order to position her for the crucial crossing from Samoa to Tahiti. Because there is no generally accepted evidence indicating direct voyaging between Aotearoa and Samoa or other points in West Polynesia, this was regarded solely as a positioning leg, not an attempt to retrace any traditional route. Accordingly, the strict rules concerning the passing of navigational information from the escort vessel to the canoe's navigator were relaxed once during the first part of the crossing to give a position check to Chad Baybayan, who was then practicing the navigational skills he had picked up sailing with Nainoa.

The canoe was made ready for an early April departure at the beginning of autumn when the westerlies begin to reassert themselves, yet the weather has not yet turned very cold. Unfortunately, the weather did not immediately cooperate. High pressure systems bringing northeasterly winds to the Bay of Islands kept the canoe in port for three weeks, and it was not until the late afternoon of 1 May that steady westerlies allowed *Hōkūleʻa* to set sail to the north-northeast.

Chad Baybayan navigated the first segment of this leg to the Kermadecs, with Nainoa standing by for advice and back-up. As it turned out, Chad needed no help, for he kept the canoe right on course for the Kermadecs as she sailed north-northeastward before southwest winds. Four days out, a position check from the *Dorcas* confirmed the accuracy of Chad's course, and the next day—after holding the canoe on the same heading—the rocky peak of Raoul Island, the largest of the Kermadecs, appeared on the horizon ahead.

Having made landfall on the Kermadecs, the next task was to cross the almost 500-mile gap to Tongatapu, an uplifted coral island at the southern end of the Tongan Archipelago, where Nukuʻalofa, the chief port and the capital of this island kingdom is located. Nainoa took over the navigation on this segment. Soon after clearing Raoul Island, the wind lightened and then started blowing out of the southeast and east. Early the next

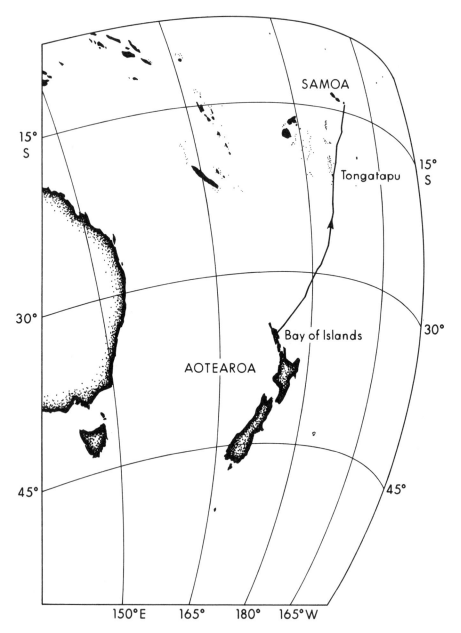

Figure 26. Aotearoa to Tongatapu, 1–11 May; Tongatapu to Tutuila, Samoa, 14–25 May 1986.

morning, just before dawn, a long-dreaded event occurred. As the canoe was sailing in the freshening easterlies, a crewman fell overboard when his safety line snapped as he was leaning outboard of the leeward hull to relieve himself.

He gave no cry. But Nainoa had seen him step over the gunwale to squat on the rail lashed low down to the water and was therefore alerted to the possibility he had fallen overboard when he saw the crewman's yellow rain hat go floating by. After quickly checking the rail and seeing it vacant, Nainoa yelled, "Man overboard! All hands on deck!" Then the repeatedly practiced man-overboard drill began. The navigator turned on a bright, flashing light attached to the base of a long man-overboard pole that was weighted to float upright in the ocean, and threw the pole over the stern rail, while the captain, Leon Sterling, stood by the line attached to the fast disappearing pole to keep it smoothly paying out of the baskets in which it had been carefully coiled for just such an emergency. Then the crew members on watch, and those who came scrambling out of their sleeping bags and onto the deck, brought the canoe into the wind and quickly lowered the sails to stop all forward motion. By this time, however, some 2,000-plus feet of line had payed out.

All the while Nainoa had been keeping his eye on the flashing light at the base of the pole, hoping to see a second light go on, for each crewman had been instructed that if he fell overboard he should swim for the pole and then turn on the second light mounted at the top of the pole to alert those on the canoe that he had reached the pole. But all Nainoa could see was the intermittent flashing of what seemed to be a single light. He did not dare pull the line in, for he had no idea whether the crewman might be at the end of it or not. Instead, Nainoa grabbed a surfboard and paddled toward the light. To his great relief, he found the crewman clinging to the bobbing pole. In fact, the cold but alert crewman had turned on the second light, but because the two lights never flashed at the same instant, it had been impossible to tell from the canoe that both lights were on.

Once the two were safely back on board, the sails were raised and *Hōkūleʻa* got underway again. Soon thereafter the easterlies began to strengthen. When these reached gale force the next night, the crew had to take down the regular sails to lessen the danger of being rolled over by the winds, then gusting to between 40 and 50 knots, and the mounting seas. In their place small storm sails were raised, enabling the canoe to keep safely on course and make about 3 knots. After three days of these gale force winds and high seas, the weather started to moderate, and soon thereafter Tongatapu and neighboring Eua island were spotted ahead.

After the stop to Tongatapu, the plan was to sail, from island to island, up the Tongan chain, and then to continue on to the island of Tutuila in American Samoa. Because of the many closely spaced islands and reefs in the Tongan chain, particularly in the Ha'apai group immediately north of Tongatapu, the government of Tonga was asked to provide an experienced Tongan navigator. Sione Taupeamuhu, a professional sea captain, was chosen to pilot the canoe and joined the crew aboard *Hōkūle'a* when they set sail on the night of 14 May. The plan was to cross the 50 or so miles to the Ha'apai group at night so that the Tongan navigator would have the advantage of daylight to pilot the canoe through the maze of low-lying islands and reefs that make up the group.

During the night crossing Nainoa navigated as usual, using the stars to direct the steersmen to keep the canoe heading straight for Nomuka, an island about 140 feet high at the southern end of Ha'apai. As Nainoa kept his eyes on the stars through the night and from time to time directed the steersmen to adjust their course, the Tongan navigator carefully but silently watched the Hawaiians. It seemed to the latter that Sione was skeptical that they could really bring the canoe to Nomuka without instruments. At dawn, however, when Nomuka appeared right on the horizon as planned, the Tongan's demeanor changed. Impressed by what he had experienced, the deeply moved Sione stepped up to Nainoa and said to him, "Now I can believe the stories of my ancestors."

Upon clearing Nomuka, it was Sione's turn to impress the Hawaiians. For twelve hours he stood on the step of the forward mast and directed the steersmen safely past reef after reef and through narrow channels between islands, bringing the canoe to Lifuka, the principal island of Ha'apai, located at the northern end of the group. He further showed his mettle as a pilot a few days later on the crossing to Vava'u, the northernmost group in the Tongan archipelago some 70 miles north of Lifuka, when the canoe arrived off the main island of 'Uta Vava'u in the dark of night. Instead of waiting offshore until dawn, Sione calmly proceeded to direct the nervous crewmen to keep heading for the island, and then—while it was still dark—to enter and steer down the long narrow channel between two fingers of land leading to the anchorage.

After waiting five days in Vava‘u because of northeast winds blowing from virtually the exact direction of the next destination, the island of Tutuila in American Samoa, the wind finally became more easterly allowing the canoe to set sail. After an uneventful three days of sailing in strong trade winds and building seas, Sione was the first to sight Tutuila off in the distance, a further testament to his abilities, for the others on board could not make it out until another twenty minutes or so had passed.

Samoa to Tahiti: 7 July–21 August 1986 (fig. 27)

Although information gathered by Cook and other early European visitors indicated that Polynesian voyagers wishing to sail to the east would wait for westerly wind reversals common during the Austral summer, because of the frequency of tropical cyclones at that time of the year Nainoa decided not to attempt a summer crossing from Samoa to Tahiti. Instead, he scheduled the voyage for midwinter when these cyclones are extremely rare. Although the trade winds have a reputation for blowing most steadily during the Austral winter, meteorological records consulted by Nainoa indicated that these winter trades can be briefly interrupted by passing low pressure troughs that bring short spells of westerly winds. He therefore reasoned that, by a combination of sailing before these passing westerly winds and then tacking when the trades returned, it might be possible to reach first the Cook Islands and then Tahiti.

Hōkūle‘a set sail from Ofu Island of the Manu‘a group of American Samoa on 7 July bound for the Southern Cooks. At first the canoe was sailed southward, close-hauled against the east-southeast trades. Three days later, the passage of a low pressure trough brought the desired wind shift. As the wind rotated counterclockwise around the compass over the next two and a half days, Nainoa exploited the successive northerly, westerly, and southerly winds to head directly east toward the Southern Cooks. Then, when the trades returned on the 13th, the canoe was forced onto a northeast course. Enough easting had been

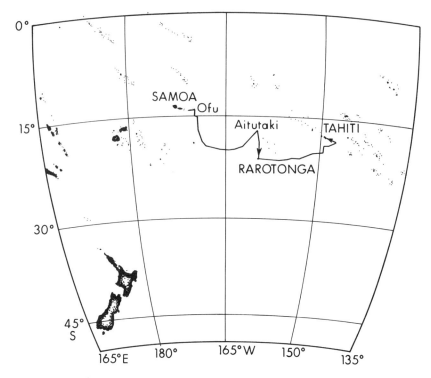

Figure 27. Ofu, Samoa to Aitutaki, Southern Cook Islands, 7–16 July 1986; Aitutaki to Tahiti, 11–21 August 1986.

gained, however, to allow the canoe to be tacked to Aitutaki, located just one day's sail north of Rarotonga.

After almost a month's stay at Aitutaki, *Hōkūle'a*, navigated by Chad Baybayan, continued on to Rarotonga. The next day, 12 August, the canoe set sail for Tahiti, with Nainoa navigating. A trough was then approaching Rarotonga, bringing northwesterly winds ideal for reaching to the east. Nainoa reasoned that the trough would enable the canoe to head east for two or three days before the trades returned and that by then tacking against the trades (and if lucky getting a further boost to the east with the passage of another trough) the canoe could be worked to Tahiti. Instead of this anticipated sequence, the trough and accompanying northwesterly winds stayed with the canoe virtually without interruption for the next week. These unexpectedly persistent westerlies actually pushed *Hōkūle'a* to the east of Tahiti until, on 20 August, the trades finally returned and allowed the canoe to tack back, westward, to Tahiti.

Tahiti to Hawai'i: 2 April–23 May (fig. 28)

The original plan had been to sail back to Hawai'i via the Marquesas in order to retrace the route from that archipelago that may have been followed by the first voyagers to reach Hawai'i. Toward that end, *Hōkūle'a* was sailed from Tahiti to Rangiroa atoll in the Tuamotus to get into position for the difficult crossing to the Marquesas. Nainoa hoped for trade winds from the southeast, or better yet from the south-southeast, in order to be able to head northwest to that archipelago. Instead, the canoe was pinned down at Rangiroa by northerly winds which were part of the widespread disturbances of an El Niño event then developing. Finally, on 24 April, after waiting almost three weeks, *Hōkūle'a* was able to set sail from Rangiroa when a tropical cyclone forming just north of Samoa brought an easterly wind flow to the northern Tuamotus.

By then, however, there was not enough time left to work the canoe to the Marquesas before going on to Hawai'i, for *Hōkūle'a* had to reach Kualoa on the north shore of O'ahu by 23 May for a special ceremony to take place there as part of the "Year of the Hawaiian" celebrations then being held in Hawai'i. So, Nainoa directed the canoe onto a more northerly course designed to bring her directly to the eastern, windward side of the island of Hawai'i, from where it could be sailed along the northeastern flank of the chain to Kualoa.

Even without the side trip to the Marquesas, the voyage home turned out to be much more difficult than the previous return trips to Hawai'i. From Rangiroa, it took twenty-eight days to reach the windward coast of the island of Hawai'i, a week longer than it had taken to sail the longer distance from Tahiti to the same latitude in 1976 and in 1980. Unlike those two previous trips, when strong, steady trades made for fast sailing, this time the trades blew only sporadically, forcing the crew to wait out the calms and squalls and to tack whenever the wind came out of the north. Despite the slow progress northward, however, the canoe was able to reach Kualoa on the morning of 23 May, just in time for the ceremony celebrating the successful completion of the voyage, which was the contribution of *Hōkūle'a* and her crew to the "Year of the Hawaiian."

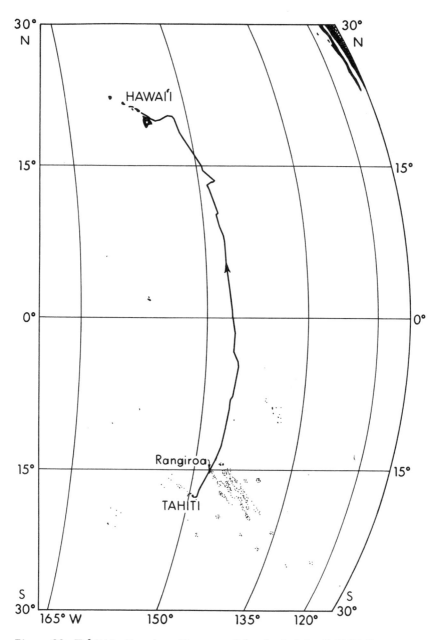

Figure 28. Tahiti to Rangiroa, Tuamotu Islands, 2–4 April 1987; Rangiroa to Hawai'i, 24 April–23 May 1987.

5

WAIT FOR THE WEST WIND

Why were the islands of Polynesia settled by a lineage of sea-farers that stemmed ultimately from the faraway Asian side of the Pacific and not by people from the much closer shores of the Americas? The answer to this question may lie in the way islands are distributed across the Pacific. Starting with Taiwan, the Philippines, and Indonesia, a virtually continuous series of archipelagos extends far out into the Pacific to the eastern edge of Polynesia. In contrast, except for a few island clusters and lone islands relatively close offshore, thousands of miles of open ocean lie between the Pacific coast of the Americas and the easternmost islands of Polynesia: Hawai'i, the Marquesas, and Rapa Nui. Whereas the spread of islands from Southeast Asian shores eastward seems to have encouraged successive genera-tions to sail farther and farther out into the ocean by rewarding them with island after island on which they could settle, the great stretches of open ocean between the western shores of the Americas and Polynesia apparently provided little opportunity or incentive for Native Americans to expand across the Pacific.[1]

Yet, however inviting to oceanic expansion the spread of is-lands from Southeast Asia to Polynesia may have been, the im-mense distances of the open Pacific and the westward flow of the dominant winds and currents must have greatly tested the ability of these seafarers to keep pushing eastward across the

*With Paul Frost, Richard Rhodes, and Nainoa Thompson

ocean. Indeed, the challenges posed to would-be migrants from the west become progressively greater the farther east one sails. Whereas at the western edge of the Pacific most islands can be seen from one another, interisland distances increase to hundreds of miles in the central Pacific, then to thousands of miles in the eastern Pacific. Furthermore, as the island gaps grow larger, so does the problem of sailing eastward against the increasingly dominant trade winds and accompanying currents.

These challenges brought forth a vigorous maritime response. Fundamental was the development of the double canoe as a stable and seaworthy vessel adapted to carrying all the people, their provisions, and their breeding stock of plants and animals needed to establish colonies on the increasingly distant and species-poor islands. Similarly crucial was the evolution of ways of systematically searching unknown seas and of locating islands there. Yet, however basic large, stable watercraft and blue water navigational skills were to this oceanic expansion, in order to penetrate so far and so fast across the Pacific these seafarers also needed to learn how to use variations in the flow of oceanic winds to sail eastward against the direction of the dominant trade winds and ocean currents. This chapter addresses this third basic adaptation for oceanic expansion by analyzing how in 1986 we sailed *Hōkūle‘a* eastward across Polynesia from Samoa to Tahiti by utilizing westerly wind shifts.

The Impermanent Trade Winds

In making his case for the American origin of the Polynesians, Heyerdahl claimed that the islands of Polynesia could not have been colonized directly from the west because "the permanent trade winds and forceful companion currents of the enormous Southern Hemisphere" would have prevented canoe sailors from the Asian side of the ocean from sailing through tropical latitudes to the east. As late as 1981, in a review of *Hōkūle‘a, the Way to Tahiti*, my book on the first voyage to Tahiti, Heyerdahl was still flatly asserting that "until the days of Captain Cook and modern sailing ships, no vessel, not even the Spanish caravels, were able to enter the Pacific triangle except from the American side."[2]

If the trade winds of the Pacific were, in fact, permanent, it would indeed have been most difficult for the ancestral Polynesians to have sailed a canoe directly eastward over long distances. To be sure, Polynesian double canoes are excellent sailing vessels. When sailing on a beam reach (with the wind blowing at right angles to the hulls) or a broad reach (with the wind blowing abaft the beam, or greater than 90° to the hulls) they move easily and swiftly through the water (fig. 29). However, although double canoes can sail to windward, they cannot do so as well as a racing yacht equipped with a deep keel or centerboard. To attempt to sail a double canoe as close into the wind as a racing yacht would be self-defeating. As she points closer and closer into the wind, a double canoe slows noticeably and begins to make so much leeway that little progress can be made directly into the wind, particularly when sailing against a strong current.

Instrumented sailing trials with the Hawaiian double canoe *Nālehia*, and the long slant across and slightly into the trade winds made by *Hōkūle'a* when sailing from Hawai'i to Tahiti in 1976, indicate that a double canoe progresses most efficiently to windward when she is sailed "full and by," that is, sailing as close to the wind as possible without making too much leeway or losing the full drive of the sails. Sailing full and by against a 15- to 20-knot wind a double canoe can do around 5 or 6 knots and "make good" a course of around 75° off the wind (calculated by measuring heading against the true direction of the wind, then subtracting leeway). Because a double canoe cannot point much closer to the wind without greatly losing efficiency, when sailing to windward it is necessary to make long, shallow tacks first to one side and then to the other of a straight line course to an upwind goal, which means the canoe must be sailed over almost 4 miles of ocean for every mile made directly to windward (fig. 30).[3] A 500-mile voyage made tacking directly to windward would therefore be almost 2,000 miles long in actual sailing distance, and a 1,000-mile voyage would be almost 4,000 miles long. Struggling against a current accompanying the wind would, in effect, increase these sailing distances even more.

Certainly Polynesians were able to tack their canoes over moderate distances to windward without great difficulty and could sail them on long slants across and angling across and moderately into the wind as we have done between Hawai'i and Tahiti. But the slow forward progress to windward of their vessels when tacking back and forth makes it seem unlikely that Poly-

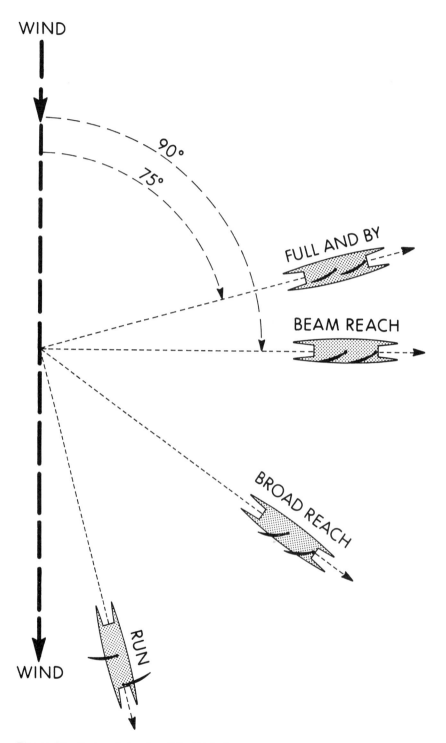

WIND

90°

75°

FULL AND BY

BEAM REACH

BROAD REACH

RUN

WIND

Figure 29. Best points of sail for Hōkūle‘a.

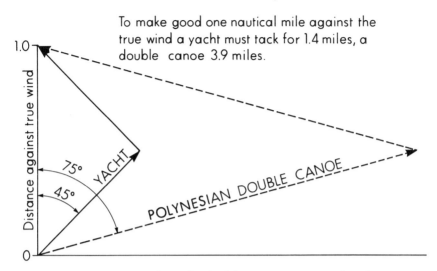

Figure 30. Distance a yacht and a double canoe must travel tacking against the wind.

nesian sailors would ever have sailed directly upwind to distant islands. Particularly for migrating canoes heavily loaded with men, women, and children, as well as their supplies, plants, and animals, such voyages would have become impossibly long as well as highly dangerous because of the stress of pushing against pounding head seas. In 1975 Jim Siers, a New Zealand photographer, had canoe builders from Tarawa atoll in the Micronesian nation of Kiribati (formerly the Gilbert Islands) build a big outrigger sailing canoe for an attempt to sail south-southeast from there to Fiji, and then due east to Tahiti. Despite the V-shaped hull of his canoe, called *Taratai*, she sailed no better to windward than *Hōkūleʻa* and, leaking badly from working to windward, just barely made it to Fiji. Siers then consigned the canoe to a museum and constructed a second Micronesian-style outrigger canoe with a very deep, V-shaped hull made from plywood which he christened *Taratai II*. While working to windward east of Tonga, however, the *Taratai II* broke up when the booms holding the outrigger float snapped in the heavy seas, dumping Siers and his crew in the ocean.[4]

Actually, the main issue is not the exact degree to which Polynesian craft could sail to windward, or their ability to stand up against pounding head seas. Even sailors with modern yachts of superlative windward characteristics do not relish tacking long distances directly into the wind and bucking the accompanying seas. Instead, they prefer to seek out zones of favorable winds for crossing the oceans. For example, after sailing their Manila Galleons before the trade winds from Mexico to the Philippines, the Spanish did not try to return east by sailing directly into the trades. Instead, they headed north from the Philippines in order to get out of the trade wind zone and into the belt of westerlies found in higher latitudes. Then they turned east to sail before these westerlies until sighting land somewhere along the North American coast, after which they turned south to reach Acapulco or one of the other Mexican ports. Polynesians and their immediate ancestors searching for islands to the east could also have tried to sail north (or south) out of the tropics to catch the midlatitude westerlies. But, given their open canoes and lack of warm clothing, they would probably have found it difficult to survive for long in the cold seas of these latitudes. Besides, those pioneering voyagers who discovered and settled the islands strung across the South Pacific from Southeast Asia eastward into the Polynesian triangle had a shorter, warm-weather alternative to lengthy, roundabout voyages made via the higher and colder latitudes: they could stay in the tropics and wait for the west wind.

Not only did Heyerdahl have the direction of settlement wrong, but he also attributed a permanence to the Pacific trade winds that does not exist. This error is not uncommon. Indeed, it is encouraged by the way these winds are usually described and graphically illustrated. Saying that trade winds prevail in the tropical Pacific does not mean they blow for 365 days of the year. The word "prevailing" really only refers to a statistical dominance over the year, but not during every season, month, or week. Similarly, whereas a chart showing trade wind patterns, such as figure 19 in chapter 4, may usefully picture the dominant direction of the wind flow over the entire year, it tells us nothing about the many times during the year in which the wind does not blow steadily out of the east. In reality, although the Pacific trades are among the steadiest and most regular of global winds, they nonetheless wax and wane and are periodically replaced by westerlies for days, weeks, or sometimes even months at a time.

The wind flow on the western side of the tropical South Pacific exhibits a marked monsoonal pattern with two distinct wind seasons: the Austral (Southern Hemisphere) winter when easterly trade winds generally prevail, and the Austral summer when westerly winds regularly intrude. According to meteorologists, this monsoon pattern arises from the intense heating of the Australian continent during the summer. During the winter, the trade winds blow more or less regularly out of the southeast and across Melanesian waters, northern Australia, and the Indonesian archipelago (fig. 31). With the coming of summer, however, the increased solar radiation causes a low pressure trough to be formed over northern Australia and to extend eastward over the Coral Sea (fig. 32). As the surface winds tend to flow toward regions of low pressure, this means that the wind flow on the northern flank of the trough is from the west and northwest.[5]

These summer westerlies periodically extend far out into the Pacific beyond the Australian monsoon trough. So marked is the seasonal alternation of winds in the South Pacific that in many of the island cultures two main seasons are distinguished: a trade winds season and a westerlies season. For example, the people of Tikopia, a Polynesian outlier located in Melanesian waters just off the eastern end of the Solomon Islands chain, divide the year between *tonga*, the period from April until September when southeasterly trade winds prevail, and *raki*, the period from October until March when the trades are largely replaced by westerlies.[6] Summer westerlies become more and more episodic, however, the farther one moves east across the Pacific. Consider, for example, figure 33, a depiction of wind patterns across the Pacific during January at the height of the westerlies season. The arrows, which depict mean wind flow based on reports from ships and shore stations accumulated over the last century, clearly show a corridor of westerly winds leading from the Bismarck Archipelago almost to Fiji. Although these summer westerlies periodically extend into the Polynesian triangle, they do so less frequently than is the case in the western Pacific. At Tahiti, for example, spells of westerlies may come only every few weeks and last no more than a week or so. Therefore, even during January, the month when these westerlies are most common in Polynesian waters, the only effect they have on the arrows indicating mean wind direction is to skew them from east to northeast.

To appreciate visually how spells of westerlies can periodi-

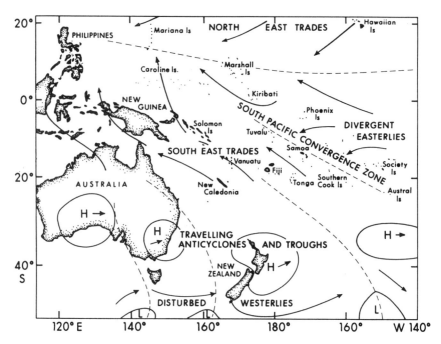

Figure 31. Stylized Austral winter wind circulation in the southwest Pacific (Steiner 1980, 9; Hessell 1981, 43).

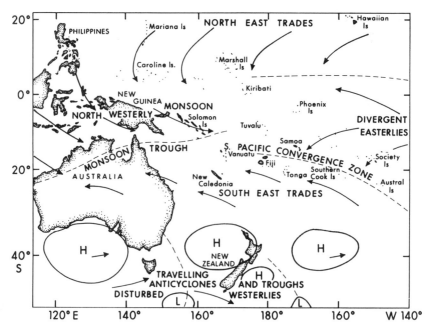

Figure 32. Stylized Austral summer wind circulation in the southwest Pacific (Steiner 1980, 9; Hessell 1981, 42).

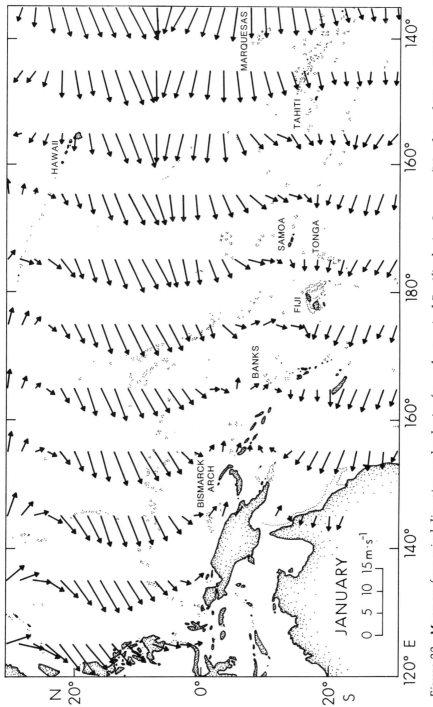

Figure 33. Mean surface wind direction and velocity from the tropical Pacific during January (Wyrtki and Myers 1975, fig. 1a).

cally sweep across Polynesian waters, we need to consult a chart that shows how the winds are flowing at a particular time, such as figure 34 which portrays by means of streamlines the surface wind circulation on 16 January 1979 at the height of a weather system that for over a week brought strong westerly winds across Polynesia as far east as Tahiti.

The main thrust of migration into the Pacific appears to have generally followed the flow of these summer westerlies, suggesting that early canoe voyagers must have used these winds to move across the tropical South Pacific. Their descendants were certainly well acquainted with the alternating rhythm of easterlies and westerlies and knew how to exploit them to sail where they wanted to go. In Melanesian waters, there are memories, and in some cases surviving vestiges, of various trading networks along the coast of New Guinea and among islands to the east where canoe sailors were similarly dependent upon seasonal alternations of wind patterns to facilitate their voyaging. That Polynesian sailors at the time of European contact were familiar with the spells of summer westerlies common in their waters and knew how to use them to sail to the east is documented, as we have seen, in the testimony of Tupaia recorded in Cook's journal, as well as in the writings of other early European navigators, scientists, and missionaries.[7] Furthermore, in Indonesia, one of the few places in the world where large amounts of freight are still regularly carried by sailing craft, traders still use this monsoonal wind pattern to sail east along the Indonesian chain before the westerlies, and then, with the return of the trades, to sail back to the west.

On the basis of the periodic occurrence of summer westerlies in Polynesian waters and their documented use for sailing eastward by Polynesian mariners of the early contact period, it has long been hypothesized that the pioneering voyagers who first sailed from west to east across Polynesia did so primarily by exploiting westerly wind episodes to sail east, tacking to windward only when and if the westerlies dropped and were replaced by easterly trade winds.[8] This chapter reports on our efforts to test the feasibility of this way of moving eastward by sailing *Hōkūle'a* from Samoa to Rarotonga and from there on to Tahiti and explores the implications of this experimental crossing for understanding the colonization of Polynesia.

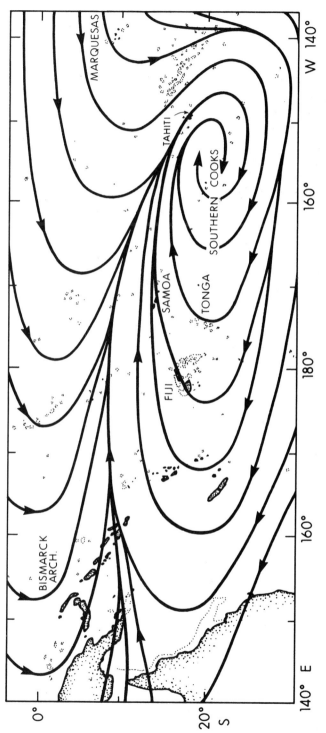

Figure 34. Surface wind analysis for 16 January 1979.

Sailing Strategy

After sailing north from Aotearoa to Tonga and then on to Samoa, *Hōkūle'a* was in position to attempt the eastward crossing. By electing to sail from Samoa to Rarotonga and Tahiti we did not intend to imply that the initial migration eastward from the Polynesian homeland necessarily followed that exact route. Although the Samoan group is a leading candidate as a dispersal point from the West Polynesia homeland region, voyages to the east may also have been made from the Tonga group, or possibly from Futuna, Uvea, or other smaller islands outside these two groups. Besides, because we obviously already knew the location of Rarotonga and Tahiti, as well as that of all the other East Polynesian islands, we were hardly in a position to re-create an early discovery voyage. That would have required that we strike out randomly to the east, without any foreknowledge whatsoever of any archipelagos and islands that might be found there. Actually, our choice of East Polynesian landfalls was in large part dictated by other reasons. We had sailed to Aotearoa via Tahiti and Rarotonga and were obligated to call upon these islands on the way back in order to fulfill pledges made to Tahitians and Rarotongans on the way to Aotearoa. Nonetheless, despite our geographical knowledge, and port-of-call obligations, we believed that by attempting to cross the ocean gap between Samoa and Tahiti we could learn much about the sailing problems faced by early voyagers who had headed east from the West Polynesian homeland, and how these may have affected the settlement of East Polynesia.

Upon Nainoa Thompson, the navigator of *Hōkūle'a*, fell the responsibility of determining the sailing strategy to be followed. The task was formidable because a course straight from Samoa to Rarotonga and then on to Tahiti would take the canoe almost directly against the direction from whence the trades generally blow. After reviewing the wind patterns and considering what had been learned from sailing *Hōkūle'a* over the previous ten years, Nainoa concurred that it would be extremely difficult to try to tack against the trades to Rarotonga and then to Tahiti and that the best hope of reaching these islands would be to exploit westerly wind shifts to make the required easting. However, although he also agreed that the Austral summer, with its episodes of summer westerlies, would be the time of year when we would most likely be able to find winds good for sailing east, Nainoa rejected the idea of sailing during the summer. The bursts of westerlies that occur then, he argued, are often blustery and accompanied by heavy cloud cover and rain. Furthermore, the summer period when westerlies are most prevalent is also the hurricane season when tropical disturbances are most likely to cross the route between Samoa and Tahiti, particularly during major El Niño events such as that of 1982–1983 when four tropical storms did so. Accordingly, for the safety of crew and canoe, Nainoa ruled out trying to exploit the summer westerlies to sail east.

Instead, he proposed a variant of that strategy. Upon studying the daily meteorological charts for the preceding several years, Nainoa and University of Hawai'i meteorologist Thomas Schroeder found that even during the Austral winter, when the trade winds are normally most dominant, brief spells of westerly winds occasionally interrupt the trades when low pressure troughs emanating from subtropical depressions to the south reach into the tropics. This suggested to them that it might be possible to exploit the westerlies generated by these passing troughs to work the canoe to the east.[9] Accordingly, Nainoa proposed to make *Hōkūle'a* ready for a midwinter departure, then wait for the coming of a low pressure trough at which time he and the crew would try to sail the canoe as far east as possible with the westerly winds that would accompany the passage of the trough. Once the trough had passed, Nainoa was prepared to slant obliquely across the trades while waiting for another trough in order to gain an additional boost to the east. Through a combination of exploiting the westerlies of passing troughs, and slanting against the trades while waiting for the next trough, Nainoa hoped that *Hōkūle'a* could be worked first to Rarotonga, and from there farther eastward to Tahiti. If, however, the troughs did not extend into the tropics that year, Nainoa knew that it would be a long and hard struggle to try to make easting by tacking back and forth against the trades, and that it might not be possible to reach Tahiti, or even Rarotonga.

An Embarrassment of Westerlies

The Austral winter of 1986 turned out to be highly favorable for sailing to the east, although we did not fully realize that un-

til *Hōkūleʻa* was well out to sea and did not completely understand what had occurred until after the voyage when we could
analyze the meteorological data for the South Pacific gathered
by satellites and surface stations. Nainoa's study of the meteorological charts of the South Pacific for previous years had revealed an uneven pattern. During the winter of 1984, for example, the trades had broken down seven times with the passage of
low pressure troughs. During the winter of 1985, however, the
trade winds appeared to have stayed solidly in place all winter
long, for he could find no evidence of any troughs significantly
interrupting them. The first indications that the 1986 winter
might be more like 1984 than 1985 came from daily meteorological charts of the southwest Pacific consulted before departure. These showed that a major disruption of surface wind
circulation patterns over a large part of the South Pacific was developing: low pressure troughs were beginning to extend into
the tropics, sweeping across the route the canoe would follow
to Tahiti, bringing with them wind shifts that looked ideal for
sailing eastward.

In the typical winter pattern shown in figure 31, trade winds
dominate the route between Samoa and Tahiti. These blow primarily from the southeast between Samoa and Rarotonga, and
more out of the east from Rarotonga to Tahiti. These southeast
trades and "divergent easterlies" usually meet in a cloudy region called the South Pacific Convergence Zone, which is typically located along a line that runs southeast to northwest from
the Austral Islands between the Southern and Northern Cook
Islands toward Kiribati (formally known as the Gilbert Islands).
Well south of the trades, along the latitude of Aotearoa's North
Island, high pressure systems move from west to east. Slightly
to the south of these highs and alternating with them, low pressure systems also move from west to east.

Sometimes troughs extend far enough north from these low
pressure systems to reach into tropical latitudes where they interrupt the trades and bring westerly winds. The winter of 1986
proved to be unusual in that respect. The traveling highs were
centered about 10° farther south than normal and were persistent and slow moving. Pressures at their centers were also higher
than normal. These displaced highs and anomalous upper air
conditions at the same latitude blocked the normal passage of
the low pressure systems, shunting some of them to the north

between 25° and 35° South latitude before they could continue their eastward movement. The troughs from these displaced lows therefore extended farther north than usual, repeatedly reaching into trade wind latitudes where vertical coupling between them and an unusually persistent and quasi-stationary upper air trough located between Tonga and Tahiti acted to intensify surface disturbances. In addition, the South Pacific Convergence Zone was largely absent. The subtropical ridges of high pressure extending from the migrating highs were also displaced farther north than usual and tended to connect to the semipermanent high pressure system centered to the southeast between the Austral Islands and South America. This combination of displaced troughs and ridges frequently interrupted the trades and gave rise to long periods during which the winds were ideal for sailing eastward to Tahiti (fig. 35).

Actually, "westerlies" seldom blow directly out of the west. Sailors use the term to refer to any winds with a westerly component, that is, to winds from the northwest and southwest as well as straight out of the west. In fact, winds blowing from the northwest or southwest are best for sailing due east, as a canoe generally sails best on a broad reach, with the wind coming over the stern at an angle, rather than directly from astern (fig. 29). Moreover, a canoe can still make good progress to the east reaching across a north wind, or a south wind, or even sailing into a wind blowing from slightly to the east of either north or south. Typically, the passage of a low pressure trough through the trade wind zone causes a counterclockwise rotation of the wind that usually brings at least two or three days of such "westerlies" favorable for sailing to the east. The first sign of the approach of a trough is usually a shift in wind direction from southeast or east to northeast. As the trough comes closer the wind becomes more and more northerly, until, as the trough passes, the wind starts coming from west of north, then more out of the west, then out of the southwest, then out of the south, and so on until, once the trough has completely passed, the easterly trade winds return.

Some critics, of course, may wish to object to our use of modern weather data and meteorological theory to plan a re-creation of an ancient voyage. To be sure, by consulting satellite photographs, daily weather maps, and detailed weather records we could plot the occurrence of these westerlies before departure

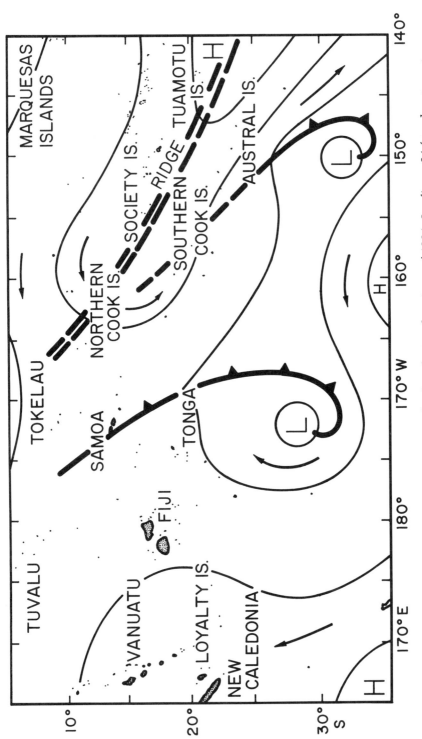

Figure 35. Stylized wind circulation between Samoa and Tahiti during the winter of 1986. See figure 36 for a key to meteorological symbols used. Arrows indicate surface wind direction.

and explain their origin. Nevertheless, although early Polynesian mariners lacked such modern aids, they must have had a deep practical knowledge of weather matters that comes to people whose lives depend upon the sea. Certainly the European explorers who took the time to become acquainted with Polynesian sailors praised their meteorological skills. For example, concerning the two Tahitians he took with him from Tahiti to Ra'iatea, the Spanish navigator Andia y Varela reported that:[10]

> What took me most in the two indians [Tahitians] whom I carried from Otahiti [Tahiti] to Oriayatea [Ra'iatea] was that every evening or night they told me, or prognosticated, the weather we should experience the following day, as to winds, calms, rainfall, sunshine, sea and other points, about which they never turned out to be wrong: a foreknowledge worthy to be envied, for, in spite of all that our navigators and cosmographers have observed and written anent [about] the subject, they have not mastered this accomplishment.

While their sea-level perspective and lack of knowledge of global weather dynamics might seem limited to us today, had such weather-wise Tahitians wanted to sail to the east during a winter such as that of 1986, they surely would have seized upon the unseasonable westerlies just like we did. Furthermore, although before the voyage Nainoa enjoyed a "God's-eye" view of the weather furnished by satellite photographs and detailed meteorological charts, once at sea he was in the same situation as the Tahitians who sailed with Andia y Varela and other early Polynesian sailors who had only their observations of the wind, clouds, and swells made from sea level to guide their sailing decisions—and he probably acted more or less as they would have.

From Samoa to Aitutaki

In early July of 1986, Nainoa and part of the crew flew from Honolulu to American Samoa in order to join the canoe and the rest of the crew at tiny Ofu Island in the Manu'a group at the easternmost end of the Samoan chain. Although they arrived just as a low pressure trough was approaching, they were not able to ready the canoe for departure quickly enough to take advantage of the accompanying wind shift. By the time the canoe was ready, the westerly winds had passed and the trades were reestablished.

Nonetheless, Nainoa chose to leave then, setting sail on the afternoon of 7 July, by which time a small high spreading eastward along 25° South had become embedded in the subtropical ridge extending to the west from southeast of Tahiti, bringing a flow of easterly winds north of the ridge axis and into the region where *Hōkūleʻa* was sailing (fig. 36). With the east-southeast trades then blowing, the canoe could have been sailed either to the north-northeast or to the south. To sail north-northeast would have taken the canoe away from Rarotonga and eventually out of range of any troughs extending up from the south. Nainoa therefore chose to make a long slant to the south—both to approach the latitude of Rarotonga (which, at 21° 15′ South, is almost 350 miles south of the latitude of Ofu) and to get farther to the south in order to be in a better position to catch any passing troughs. For the next two days, 8 and 9 July, the trades continued blowing from between east by south and east-southeast. As long as the wind had a major easterly component, *Hōkūleʻa* was able to hold a course to the south by sailing on the port tack. Briefly, however, when the wind shifted more toward the south, to avoid being forced to the west the canoe was put onto the starboard tack and headed east-northeast until the wind shifted back around to the east.

As navigator, Nainoa's role was to set the course for the steersmen to follow and to make sure the canoe stayed on course by constantly monitoring the ocean swells, the sun by day, and the stars at night, and by mentally tracking the canoe's heading and speed. Mau Piailug was sailing with his colleague, but as a guest and an advisor, rather than as a back-up navigator, for the Micronesian master was by then fully confident of Nainoa's abilities. Serving as captain on this leg was Milton "Shorty" Bertelmann, a quiet, intense *Hōkūleʻa* veteran who was in charge of the crew as well as the setting of the sails, maintenance of the canoe, and the like. Shorty, a contractor from the island of Hawaiʻi, had sailed on *Hōkūleʻa*'s first crossing from Hawaiʻi to Tahiti in 1976 and had already skippered the canoe on the Hawaiʻi to Tahiti and Rarotonga to Aotearoa legs this voyage.

Others on board from the island of Hawaiʻi were: Clay Bertelmann, a rancher and Shorty's younger brother; Ben Lindsey, a fireman and farmer; and Teʻikiheʻepo "Tava" Taupu, a Marquesan long resident on the Kona coast of Hawaiʻi where he maintains the quasi-traditional Polynesian houses of a luxury resort. Representing the island of Molokaʻi was paramedic Mel Paoa.

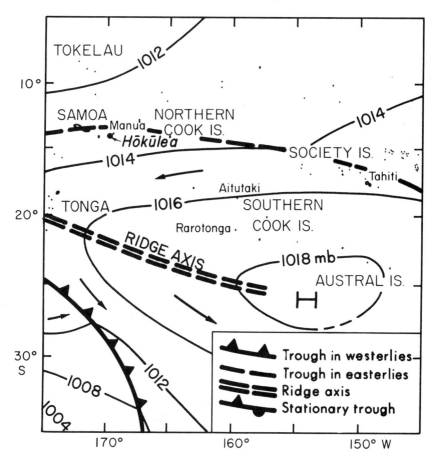

Figure 36. Surface weather map for 7 July 1986. This map, and subsequent weather maps, depict conditions at 1400 Rarotonga Time. Sea-level pressure is indicated in millibars in this and subsequent weather maps. Arrows indicate surface wind direction.

From the island of O'ahu were: Harry Ho, a Honolulu architect who was also in charge of the provisioning of the canoe for the entire voyage and other logistical chores; Bernard Kilonsky, a meteorologist from the University of Hawai'i; and Pauahi Ioane, a young student who was the only woman on board as well as the only crew member fluent in Hawaiian. Completing the crew was Tua Pittman, a tall, young Cook Islander who worked for Air New Zealand in Rarotonga.

On 10 July the wind began to shift to slightly north of east as *Hōkūle'a* approached the axis of the high pressure ridge. This can be seen in figure 37, which also shows westerlies strength-

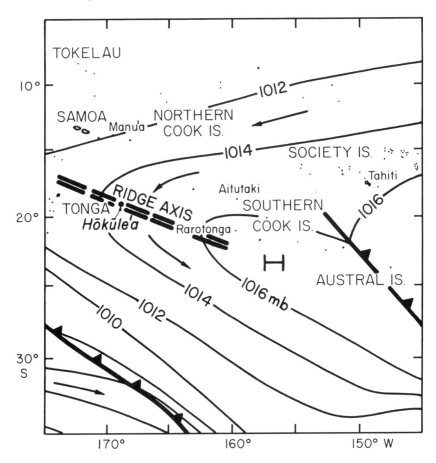

Figure 37. Surface weather map for 10 July 1986.

ening farther to the southwest as a major trough was approaching the ridge axis. With the wind blowing from slightly north of
east, Nainoa was able to put the canoe onto a southeast course.
He anticipated that soon they would be able to sail more directly to the east, for Nainoa interpreted the wind shift as a sign
that a trough was approaching and that the wind would therefore continue to shift in a counterclockwise direction. The next
day, 11 July, the wind continued shifting to the north as expected,
and then became light and at times variable, a sure sign that the
trades had broken down. Once the wind was coming from the
north, *Hōkūle'a* was able to sail due east in fairly clear skies
and calm seas. On the 12th a line of dark clouds to the south-

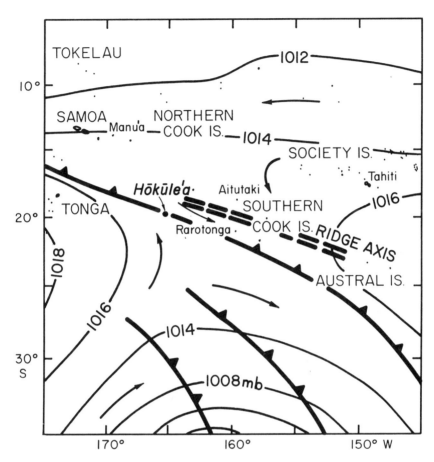

Figure 38. Surface weather map for 12 July 1986.

west announced the approach of the trough. The crew tried to
keep the canoe sailing in front of the trough, but it was moving much faster than the canoe could sail and soon engulfed
Hōkūleʻa with clouds and rough seas. As the trough passed, the
wind shifted quickly to the northwest, then to the west, and then
finally to the southwest (fig. 38), all directions that allowed the
canoe to continue to be sailed due east. By the morning of the
13th, however, the trades started coming back as the wind shifted
from south to south-southeast, and then in the late afternoon
started blowing directly out of the southeast, forcing the canoe
to sail to the east-northeast.

On the 14th and 15th the boisterous trades developed more of an easterly component, forcing the canoe onto a northeasterly course. Nainoa figured that if they continued sailing northeast for a day or so more, they could then tack south to Rarotonga. At this point, the *Dorcas*, the yacht serving as the canoe's escort vessel, began experiencing trouble in the strong winds and heavy seas. *Hōkūle'a*, which was rigged with extra large sails in anticipation of having to tack in light airs, was moving too fast for the heavy cruising yacht, and at one point in squally weather the crew was forced to lower all the sails to wait for the *Dorcas*. Then, on the evening of the 15th, Dan Wright, captain of the *Dorcas*, signaled that he was having trouble with his mainmast and would have to head for a port in order to make repairs. Accordingly, by mutual agreement, Dan disclosed the canoe's position to Nainoa so that an accurate course could be laid to the nearest island, Aitutaki, which lies 140 miles due north of Rarotonga. Nainoa then had *Hōkūle'a* tacked south to Aitutaki, where she arrived on the morning of 16 July.

As on previous voyages, Nainoa had been keeping track of the canoe's progress by his method of dead reckoning which is based on visual estimates of speed and course made good, as well as the effect of the current. At the time Dan Wright notified him of the canoe's position, Nainoa found that he had underestimated the eastward progress of the canoe by about 125 miles. Such a wide margin of error may have stemmed primarily from the roundabout course sailed, and the consequent difficulty of estimating the canoe's progress, as well as the direction and strength of the current. In addition, because *Hōkūle'a* was sailing with a set of sails larger than the ones usually employed, Nainoa may have slightly, but consistently, underestimated the canoe's speed.

Aitutaki lies almost 650 miles to the east-southeast of Ofu. *Hōkūle'a* had made it there in a little over eight and a half days, sailing a roundabout course dictated by the direction of the winds and Nainoa's strategy for making maximum easting. Although the passage of the low pressure trough brought winds favorable for sailing to the east for only a little over three days, the easting thus gained, plus the smaller amount won when forced to sail to the northeast with the return of the trades after the passage of the trough, was enough to enable the canoe to make it to Aitutaki, a day's sail north of Rarotonga (fig. 39).

Had *Hōkūle'a* not stopped at Aitutaki, and instead had been

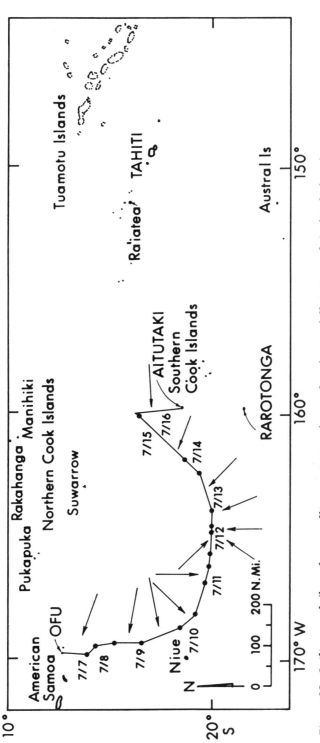

Figure 39. Sailing track (based on satellite navigation fixes taken from a following yacht) of Hōkūle'a from Samoa to Aitutaki during July 1986, and winds (indicated by long, straight arrows) encountered along the way.

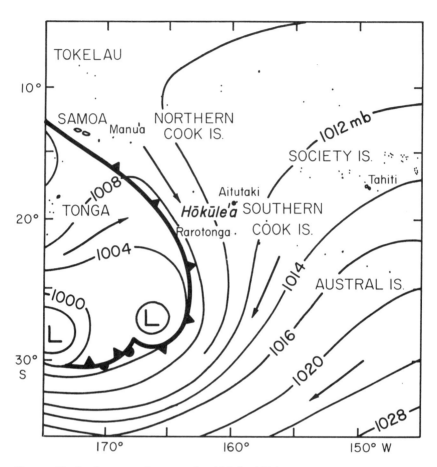

Figure 40. Surface weather map for 16 July 1986.

kept sailing with the trades on the same northeast course, the canoe would have moved into a position from which Tahiti could have been reached. On the afternoon of the 16th, by which time the canoe was anchored at Aitutaki, a depression moving east at 25° South began spreading westerlies northward, and the wind in the Cook Islands began shifting to the north as the trough approached (fig. 40). Had the canoe stayed at sea, it would probably have been possible to exploit the winds of this passing trough to reach Tahiti directly, or at least to attain enough easting so that the canoe could eventually make it to Tahiti by slanting into the trades and then catching the westerlies brought on by the passage of the next trough.

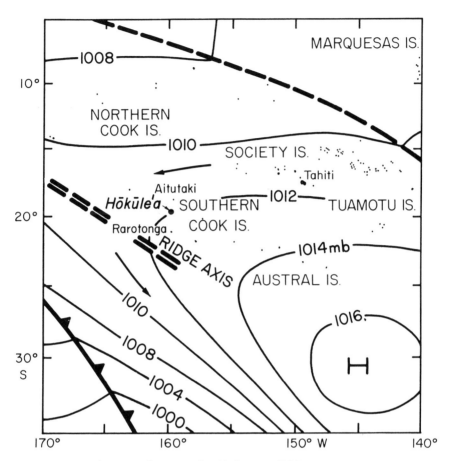

Figure 41. Surface weather map for 10 August 1986.

From Aitutaki to Rarotonga

The crew reassembled at Aitutaki in early August in order to make the canoe ready to sail first to Rarotonga and from there on to Tahiti. As they were working on the canoe yet another low pressure system transited the seas to the south, with its associated trough reaching far north into the tropics. By the time the canoe was ready on 10 August, the trough had passed and clear weather with easterly trade winds had been reestablished (fig. 41). These were ideal for sailing directly south to Rarotonga, and the canoe left just before noon. Nainoa delegated the task of navigating to Rarotonga to his understudy, Chad Baybayan, who when he was not sailing on *Hōkūle'a* worked as a supervisor in a major tourist hotel on Maui. While Aitutaki was still in sight, Chad backsighted on a small *motu* (islet) on the fringing reef, keeping it aligned with one of the peaks of the central mountain core of the island in order to maintain a course due south. As the *motu* was lost from view, the young Hawaiian switched to steering by the descending sun. That night he used the stars, particularly those in the Southern Cross, to keep the canoe on course and was rewarded with a predawn sighting of Rarotonga dead ahead.

From Rarotonga to Tahiti

As Shorty Bertelmann had to return to his work and family in Hawai'i after skippering the canoe to Aitutaki, Nainoa was serving as both captain and navigator for the crossing to Tahiti. Assisting him were Chad Baybayan and Mau Piailug. Other *Hōkūle'a* veterans on the crew included: Harry Ho, who had just made the crossing from Samoa; Michael Tongg, a Honolulu lawyer who had sailed with me on *Nālehia* in the 1960s and who served as president of the Polynesian Voyaging Society at the time of the 1980 voyage; Bruce Blankenfeld, a Honolulu fireman and professional fisherman (and Nainoa's brother-in-law); Abraham "Snake" Ah Hee, a slim, sinuous construction foreman from Maui; and Wallace "Wally" Froiseth, a retired fireman and renowned surfer and sailor from Honolulu who had been working diligently with the project since its inception in the early 1970s. Making their first South Pacific crossings on *Hōkūle'a* were: Glenn Oshiro, representing the island of Lāna'i (located just to the south of Maui) where he manages a service station; Aaron Kalei Young, a Honolulu fireman who like Mike Tongg had participated in the *Nālehia* experiments during the 1960s; and Richard Rhodes, a graphic artist who had just retired from the University of Hawai'i where he specialized in scientific illustration.

To reach Tahiti, Nainoa intended to employ the same strategy of exploiting favorable winds brought on by the passage of low pressure troughs as had been used on the Samoa to Aitutaki leg. Since Rarotonga, at 21° 15' South latitude, lies almost four degrees south of Tahiti (17° 30' South), the canoe was in a good position to reach Tahiti through a combination of sailing east with the westerlies, and then north-northeast against the trades whenever they reasserted their dominance. Accordingly, Nainoa planned to wait for the passage of a trough in order to sail eastward, keeping south of Tahiti until forced to the north by the return of the trades.

Hōkūleʻa entered Avarua harbor on Rarotonga in the early afternoon of 11 August. As the wind had already begun to swing to the north, indicating the approach of another trough, it was tempting to leave that evening to take full advantage of the favorable angle, but waiting ashore was an exchange of speeches and gifts between the *ariki*, the traditional chiefs, of Rarotonga and the leaders of the Polynesian Voyaging Society, to be followed by a lavish feast.

The canoe left the following morning, sailing east on the port tack with 12 knot northerly winds (fig. 42). By the morning of the next day, 13 August, the wind had shifted to the west. Around 9 A.M. the canoe was engulfed by heavy rain, and the wind appeared to switch from northwest to southwest, apparently indicating that the trough was passing (fig. 43). The rainy, overcast skies that completely hid the sun, and seas confused by shifting winds, made it practically impossible to know whether the canoe was on course. At times Nainoa was tempted to take the sails down and drift until he was able to gain a firm indication of direction. Since, however, navigational accuracy was less important than making easting, Nainoa kept the sails up and tried to keep track of all the wind shifts in order to maintain the canoe on an easterly heading.

To Nainoa, the wind appeared to switch to the south at midday, and then, at sunset, to the southeast, as would be expected with the passage of a trough. That night, however, the wind started shifting back, clockwise, toward the southwest, and then went calm. Nainoa had the sails triced by drawing the booms and sails up against the mast while waiting for the wind to pick up again. It was a most confusing night. Judging from the few directional cues he could get from occasional glimpses of the moon through the overcast and from studying the turbulent seas, Nainoa reckoned that when the wind did start to pick up again it had shifted further around in a clockwise direction to the north. This did not immediately make sense. Had the trough actually passed the canoe, the wind should have continued to shift counterclockwise until it came from the east-southeast

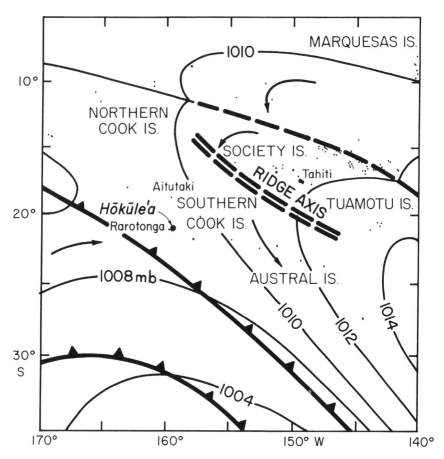

Figure 42. Surface weather map for 12 August 1986.

trade wind direction, as had occurred on the way to Aitutaki. So, Nainoa kept the sails triced for a few hours more until he finally got a glimpse of Jupiter and the moon setting which confirmed that the wind had indeed shifted back to the north and indicated that somehow they were forward of the trough again. He then ordered the sails let out and the canoe be put on the port tack to resume sailing eastward. Judging from the meteorological charts consulted after the voyage, what had happened was that a small depression traveling in the rear of the trough along about 27° South had generated a strong north to northwest wind field which then merged with and reactivated the main trough (fig. 44).

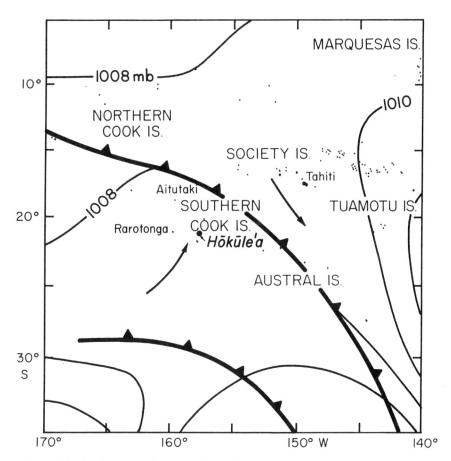

Figure 43. Surface weather map for 13 August 1986.

While sailing so close to the trough brought favorable winds, the overcast skies associated with the reactivated trough (fig. 45) continued to make navigation extremely difficult. On the night of the 15th Nainoa made an observation of a star in the constellation Cassiopeia, the only good star sight he had been able to make for several nights. According to his method of estimating latitude from the elevation of a star at the time of its meridional passage, this sight indicated that the canoe was sailing along latitude 23° South, not along 20° 25′ as Nainoa had mentally calculated by his dead reckoning method of keeping a cumulative estimate of course and distance made good. If true,

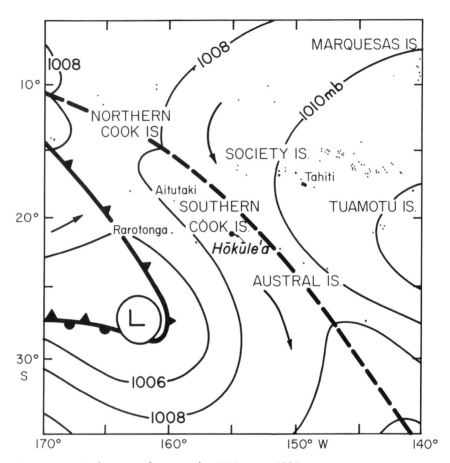

Figure 44. Surface weather map for 14 August 1986.

that would have meant that they were getting uncomfortably close to the Austral Islands and therefore should turn more toward the north. On the next day, 16 August, the sight of patches of seaweed drifting from north to south further confused the situation. If, on the one hand, they had been sailing as far south as 23°, then they would have been in the midst of the Austral Islands, and the seaweed might therefore have been coming from Rurutu, the northernmost island of that group. If, on the other hand, they were at 20° 25', the seaweed would most likely have been coming from the westernmost islands of the Society chain far to the north of them.

This confusion over the canoe's position was cleared up that

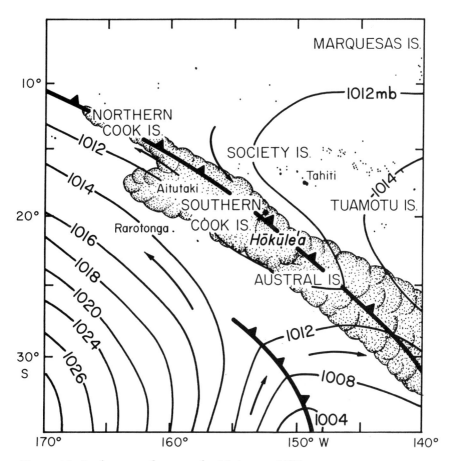

Figure 45. Surface weather map for 16 August 1986.

night when Nainoa made several star sights that seemed to indicate that his observation of the previous night was in error and that they were really sailing at about latitude 21°, safely north of the Australs but still well below the Societies. (Satellite navigation fixes from the escort yacht *Dorcas* indicate the *Hōkūleʻa* was actually sailing at about 20° 15′, some 45 miles north of where Nainoa estimated.) So sure, in fact, was Nainoa that they were not within close range of land that he ignored the sighting made that day of a few boobies and white terns, land-based birds that can mean that land is nearby.

At this point Nainoa would have liked to have been closer to Raʻiatea, as plans called for a stop there to pay a ceremonial visit at the ancient stone temple of Taputapuātea before making landfall on Tahiti. But the northerly winds would not allow the canoe to be sailed due north to Ra'iatea. With northerly winds the canoe could continue to sail on the port tack to the east-northeast or go over onto the starboard tack and sail to the west-northwest. As Nainoa did not want to sail back toward the west, he gave up the idea of visiting Ra'iatea and concentrated on trying to make directly for Tahiti.

By dawn of the next day, 17 August, even making Tahiti began to look problematic, as it was realized that the persistent northerly winds could force *Hōkūle'a* to sail past Tahiti well south of the island. For a while that day the canoe did seem to get out in front of the trough and move into a region of clearing skies and east-northeast winds that dried off the deck for the first time on the voyage (fig. 46). The wind shift and dry air seemed to indicate that the canoe was entering into a ridge of high pressure and that the trade winds might soon come back in force. The east-northeast winds did allow the canoe to be sailed almost directly to the north on the starboard tack, but that night the wind shifted back to the north as the trough gathered speed and began to catch up with *Hōkūle'a*, forcing the canoe back onto the port tack and an easterly heading. As the squally winds continued to blow from the north, Nainoa realized that not only were they going to be pushed past Tahiti, but they might even be blown into the hazardous labyrinth of atolls of the Tuamotu Archipelago. After worrying for months how they were going to make enough easting to reach Tahiti, Nainoa saw that the problem might soon be how to make enough westing to sail back to the island!

As the northwest winds kept forcing the canoe to the east, the crew could look back to the southwest where a band of towering cumulus clouds appeared to mark the front of the trough. If only, they thought, the canoe could somehow get to the rear of the trough they would find trade winds that would allow them to sail northwest back to Tahiti. Finally, at sunset on the 19th the wind started to shift to the northeast, indicating perhaps that the trough was about to pass them. Then the wind died altogether, and after a brief calm a succession of squalls moved in from the west. The squalls, accompanied by winds blowing up to 40 knots, persisted throughout the night, periodically forcing the sails to be triced and lowered to the deck, totally exhausting the crew. At dawn, a strong wind and a big swell started

coming from the south-southwest, indicating that the trough must be passing, and that *Hōkūle'a* was almost back in the trades. Accordingly, Nainoa ordered the canoe to be sailed to the north-northwest, the direction he thought might bring them to Tahiti.

Although the navigator reckoned that Tahiti was somewhere in that general direction, because of the cloud cover that had plagued them throughout the voyage and had been especially heavy during the last few nights, he was not sure of the exact bearing to Tahiti or how far away the island was. Accordingly, Nainoa planned to keep sailing to the north-northwest until sunset, when, if they had not spotted Tahiti, he intended to start tacking back and forth to the southwest to search out the island.

The latter part of that strategy never had to be put into action. After a few hours of sailing, the mist parted to reveal, just a few miles ahead of the canoe, the steep peak of Mehetia (Me'e-tia), a minuscule volcanic island lying 60 miles east-southeast of Tahiti. From then on the sail to Tahiti was straightforward. The canoe passed Mehetia, and as its lone peak began to disappear astern, the high mountains of Tahiti could be seen rising out of the sea ahead. By then the trough lay to the east of the canoe's position, the skies had cleared, and the winds had continued their counterclockwise rotation so that *Hōkūle'a* was at last sailing in strong southeast trades (fig. 47). For the first time since leaving Rarotonga, Nainoa and the crew could relax.

By the late afternoon the canoe was sailing along the rugged

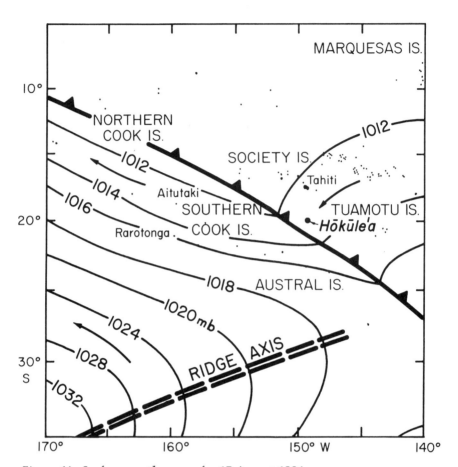

Figure 46. Surface weather map for 17 August 1986.

shore of Tahiti-iti, the uninhabited eastern end of the island
that is visited only rarely by fishermen and sightseers. The sight
of densely vegetated mountain slopes unscarred by roads or cul-
tivation, and of secluded little bays without a house or other sign
of human presence, gave everyone on board a feeling of what it
must have been like many centuries ago for those first canoe
voyagers to sight this stunningly beautiful island. After waiting
offshore that night, the next morning the canoe was sailed into
the pass at Tautira, a village located midway along the northern shore of the Tahiti-iti peninsula (fig. 48). There a warm welcome from the mayor, Tutaha Salmon, and the many friends of
Hōkūle‘a and her crew from the Maire-Nui canoe racing club,
awaited the weary voyagers.

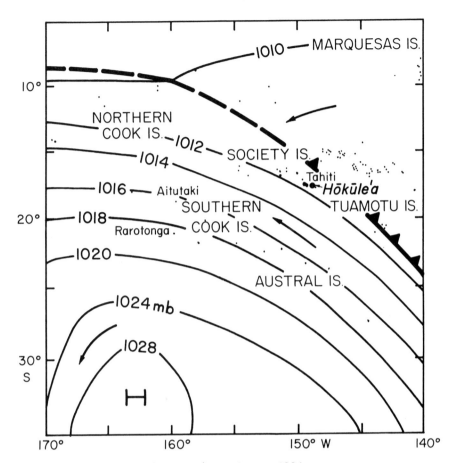

Figure 47. Surface weather map for 21 August 1986.

Winter Westerlies

If any experience could lay to rest the notion, promulgated by
theorists from Martínez de Zúñiga to Heyerdahl, of a permanent trade wind barrier keeping canoe voyagers from sailing
eastward across the tropical South Pacific it would be this one.
Nainoa and the crew were able to sail *Hōkūle'a* from Samoa to
Tahiti during the Austral winter when the trades are supposed
to be at their steadiest. The second part of that crossing, that
from Rarotonga to Tahiti, was especially noteworthy. Instead of
the anticipated hard struggle to reach Tahiti, an embarrassment

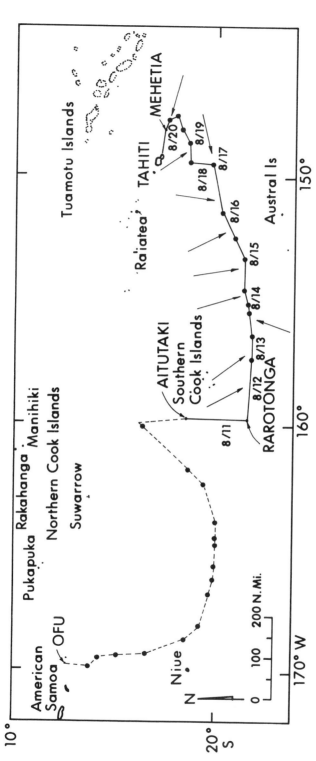

Figure 48. Sailing track of Hōkūle'a from Aitutaki to Tahiti during August 1986.

of favorable northwesterly winds sped *Hōkūle'a* eastward and even forced it past Tahiti before the trades finally returned and allowed the canoe to be sailed back to the northwest to reach the island. Ironically, the low pressure trough that generated these winds needed for sailing east also brought the cloudy, squally weather that Nainoa had wanted to avoid by sailing during the winter instead of the summer. The overcast skies, and the frequent squalls that forced the crew to trice the sails and lower them to the deck so many times that they lost count, made the job of navigating without instruments most difficult. Even so, once the trades returned, Nainoa had an accurate enough idea of the general location of Tahiti to set a course that led to landfall first on Mehetia, and then Tahiti itself.

The favorable winds that enabled *Hōkūle'a* to sail from Samoa to the Southern Cooks and then on to Tahiti may be labeled "winter westerlies" to distinguish them from the more regular summer westerlies. Although these winter westerlies may be much less frequent and enduring than the summer variety, they do seem to occur periodically. In studies of Southern Hemisphere weather patterns, meteorologists have found that the region southeast of the Samoa to Tahiti route is prone to episodes when high pressure systems block the normal passage of lows, shunting some of them onto a more northerly course.[11] On the basis of weather records from Rarotonga, the testimony of experienced sailors and fishermen there, and more general meteorological data, we can roughly estimate that the extraordinary outbreaks of winter westerlies such as those encountered by *Hōkūle'a* in 1985 may occur in Rarotonga waters in about one year out of ten, and that less extensive episodes may occur at least every few years. In addition, therefore, to the westerlies of the summer, it would appear that early seafarers seeking to sail eastward during the winter could also have exploited the periodic if less frequent spells of westerlies that sometimes occur then.

Discussions on how seafarers ultimately originating in Southeast Asia acquired the voyaging ability to expand eastward into the Pacific have centered mostly on the evolution of canoes capable of crossing the progressively wider gaps between islands, and on the development of ways for navigating far out of sight of land. As this crossing from Samoa to Tahiti underlines, it is clear that in addition to voyaging canoes and ways of navigating adapted for long distance exploration and colonization a third maritime adaptation was required. Seafarers had to learn how to exploit periodic spells of westerly winds to keep pressing eastward against the direction from which the trade winds often but not always blow.

6

VOYAGE TO AOTEAROA

Retracing Māori Migration

In early December of 1985, sixteen days after leaving Rarotonga, *Hōkūle‘a* sailed into the Bay of Islands on the northeastern coast of the North Island of Aotearoa. In keeping with the
dual experimental and cultural nature of the Voyage of Rediscovery, this crossing was undertaken both to learn more about
how seafarers from the tropical heartland of East Polynesia were
able to sail to this huge land lying so far to the southwest and to
extend the cultural reach of *Hōkūle‘a* by sailing to a Polynesian
nation whose constituent tribes still express their identity and
claims to land by recalling how their ancestors voyaged to Aotearoa from the legendary homeland of Hawaiki, and where they
landed and made their first settlements.

In sailing to Aotearoa we wished to retrace the general direction of migration to that land, though not necessarily the exact
route. The available evidence indicates that, despite their loca-

*With Chad Baybayan, Bernard Kilonsky, and Nainoa Thompson

tion far to the southwest, the Māori are culturally East Polynesian and their ancestors therefore must have sailed to Aotearoa
from one or more of the islands of the tropical center of East
Polynesia rather than directly from the closer islands of West
Polynesia. But the evidence is not at all clear as to exactly from
which island or islands of central East Polynesia—that region
composed of the Society and Cook groups, and, more peripher-
ally, the Australs, Marquesas, and Tuamotus—the migratory canoes sailed.

Had our voyage been made at the turn of the century, there
would probably have been no hesitation in claiming that in sailing from Tahiti, via the leeward Societies and Rarotonga, to Aotearoa we had actually retraced the Māori migration route. That
was the era when S. Percy Smith, the founder of the Polynesian
Society and the longtime editor of *The Journal of the Polynesian Society*, was searching for the location of Hawaiki, the legendary homeland of the Māori. In various linguistic forms, Hawaiki is found throughout Polynesia: for example, as Savaiʻi and
Hawaiʻi, the largest islands in, respectively, the Samoan and Hawaiian archipelagos; and as Havaiʻi, the ancient name for Raʻiatea.
Smith eventually chose as the immediate homeland of the Māori the region Rarotongans called ʻAvaiki-runga, or "Windward-
Hawaiki," by which they meant Tahiti, Raʻiatea, and the other
islands of the Society group that lie to windward of them. He
proposed that migrating canoes had sailed southwest from the
Societies, stopped off at Rarotonga, and then made the long ocean
crossing to Aotearoa. This scenario was largely accepted by the
next generation of scholars, including the renowned Māori anthropologist known to the outside world as Peter Buck, but called
Te Rangi Hiroa by his fellow Māori.[1]

Recent scholarship, however, has eroded this scenario. The
way Smith cavalierly edited and combined legends to come up
with an impossibly precise historical chronicle of discovery and
then later colonization by the canoes of "the Great Fleet" has
left contemporary scholars dubious of Smith's conclusions and
of any other attempts to use traditions to reconstruct the source,
mode, and sequence of the discovery and colonization of Aotearoa. In fact, the current interpretive fashion has been to deny
that the migration stories have any historical content and instead proclaim them to be myths composed and employed for

pressing claims to land and social status, or simply to be symbolic texts that recorded voyages made not at sea but "inside people's heads." In these interpretations, Hawaiki is not an overseas homeland. Some contemporary scholars grant that the concept of Hawaiki could have been inspired by a place in the far north of the North Island from whence people later moved south to colonize the rest of Aotearoa and speculate that its legendary placement overseas and the tales of harrowing ocean voyages from there to Aotearoa are metaphorical embroideries designed to dramatize the claims to land and status of those who migrated southward. To others, Hawaiki never had a geographical basis; it was a purely mythical concept of an ancestral paradise that was essentially religious in nature.[2]

Furthermore, archaeologists are no longer as willing as they once were to draw arrows on a map indicating that Aotearoa was settled from Tahiti, Rarotonga, or any other specific island or islands of this region, arguing that until comparable excavations of early occupation sites on all the archipelagos in question are conducted it will not be possible to hypothesize from which island or islands the ancestral Māori sailed.[3]

Nevertheless, in sailing from Tahiti to Rarotonga, and from there on to Aotearoa, we found it easy to think that we might indeed be retracing the route followed by at least some of those who reached this distant land. From a seaman's point of view it seems natural that adventuresome Tahitian voyagers headed southwest might have paused at Rarotonga before pushing on. For Tahitians, Rarotonga lies *raro* ("below," i.e., to leeward, with reference to the trade winds), and *tonga* ("south") of Tahiti, and is the central East Polynesian island closest to Aotearoa. The close linguistic ties between Rarotonga and Aotearoa also made us wonder if Rarotonga might have played a more important role in Māori colonization than just as a jumping-off point.[4] We were most impressed, for example, with how easily Sir James Henare and Tupi Puriri, Māori elders who came to Rarotonga to see us off, were able to converse in Māori with our Rarotongan hosts who, incidentally, enjoyed proclaiming that since their canoes settled Aotearoa they are the *tuakana*, elder brothers, in the relationship. Similarly striking was the degree to which Cook Islanders and the Māori seemed to share common voyaging traditions. Although it can be argued that this sharing may

date only from the nineteenth century when indigenous scholars from both areas could have compared and swapped traditions, the Māori leader Sir Apirana Ngata and other authorities
have proposed that it indicates that people from Rarotonga were
the most "decisive ancestors" of the East Coast Māori.[5]

Be that as it may, we do not offer this account of our voyage
as evidence for the precise derivation of the Māori population.
This is a sailing chronicle designed to illuminate the main problem that canoe voyagers leaving any of the islands of central
East Polynesia would have faced in voyaging to Aotearoa: that
of sailing a canoe southwest out of the easterly trade wind zone
and into a region where strong westerlies often blow. We therefore concentrate on the most difficult portion of the route, that
from Rarotonga to Aotearoa along which a canoe must forsake
the warm seas and favorable trade winds of the tropics for the
increasingly chill waters and problematic winds of the higher
latitudes.

Steer Toward the Setting Sun

In preparing for the voyage, Nainoa consulted accounts of
how voyagers had supposedly navigated to Aotearoa following
directions brought back to the traditional homeland of Hawaiki
by Kupe, the legendary discoverer of Aotearoa. For example, in
Elsdon Best's *The Maori Canoe* he read that in the various
accounts the navigators pointed the prows of their canoes toward the setting sun, or just to one side or another of it, during the months of October or November.[6] Although he knew
that heading more or less toward the setting sun at that time of
year would probably assure a landfall somewhere along the immensely long coastline of Aotearoa, as a navigator skilled at using
the stars to set a precise course Nainoa did not see anything
very useful in such seemingly vague directions. Furthermore, he
did not then fully realize that the period specified in the directions for sailing—late in the Austral spring—was so critical to
the problem of finding the right winds to sail so far to the southwest. Accordingly, Nainoa set the Māori sailing directions aside
and concentrated on studying stacks of meteorological charts
and other weather records and on interviewing yachtsmen for
sailing information, in order to answer the question that was

really bothering him: when would be the time of year when the winds would be most favorable for sailing to Aotearoa.

To appreciate the difficulty of reaching Aotearoa from central East Polynesia, consider a highly schematized picture of wind patterns published in a handbook for New Zealand sailors (fig. 49).[7] It portrays Tahiti, Rarotonga, and the other central islands of East Polynesia as lying within the trade wind zone, while Aotearoa is shown as being in the westerlies zone. If such a situation prevailed throughout the year, year after year, it would have been most difficult for voyagers from Tahiti, Rarotonga, or any of the other islands of central East Polynesia to have reached Aotearoa. Initially, they would have found it easy to head southwest toward Aotearoa, for the southeast trades would be blowing abeam of their heading, an ideal situation for fast sailing. But, once they had left the tropics with its favorable trades and warm waters, they would have faced considerable challenges. First, they would have had to traverse the horse latitudes, a belt of calms and light variable winds. Then, once they had sailed below 30° or so South latitude they would have had to force their way against the westerlies and to endure cold seas sweeping across their low-slung canoes as they laboriously tacked into the wind. With the sailing problem so stated, it is difficult to imagine how even one canoe could have reached Aotearoa from tropical East Polynesian waters.

When, however, we consider changing seasonal wind patterns and shorter-term, synoptic variation, it looks much more possible to sail to Aotearoa. Nainoa's study of meteorological reports, pilot charts, and sailing guides, and his interviews with yachtsmen familiar with that part of the Pacific, had convinced him that a canoe had a good chance of reaching Aotearoa if she were sailed there during the right time of the year. In the Southern Hemisphere, the westerlies found to the south of the trade wind belt are most constant during the cold weather months of April through October. Then, as the sun moves south of the equator, the belt of westerlies shifts southward and large, slow-moving high pressure systems bringing easterly winds often dominate in the critical stretch of ocean south of the trade wind zone. Nainoa reasoned that the easterly winds flowing along the northern flank of these passing high pressure systems would give us a good chance to keep sailing toward the North Island

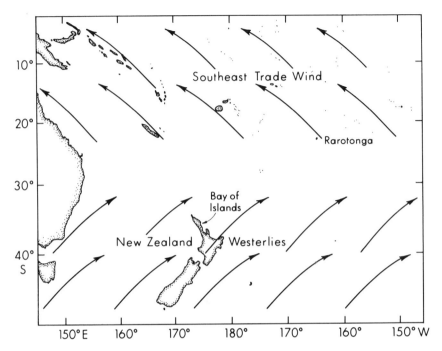

Figure 49. Highly schematized portrayal of general wind patterns in the southwest Pacific (Brierly 1985, 18).

with favorable winds long after the regular southeast trade winds had been left behind. In addition, he reckoned that the warming seas and the extra warmth afforded by the longer days would make for more comfortable sailing at this time of the year.

Yet this is also the season when tropical cyclones are most likely to develop. In this part of the Pacific, these typically form between 5° and 20° South and then move generally in a southeasterly direction before dying out in higher latitudes.[8] Figure 50 shows how the tracks of tropical cyclones of the 1978–1979 season followed this general tendency, with several crossing at right angles the direct course line between Rarotonga and the North Island. Nainoa realized that an encounter with a cyclone, particularly one that had intensified into a storm (winds of 48–63 knots) or a hurricane (winds of more than 63 knots), would put both the canoe and her crew at grave risk. Since he also knew from his research that these tropical cyclones are much more prevalent from late December onward than earlier in the season, Nainoa set the departure from Rarotonga for mid-November,

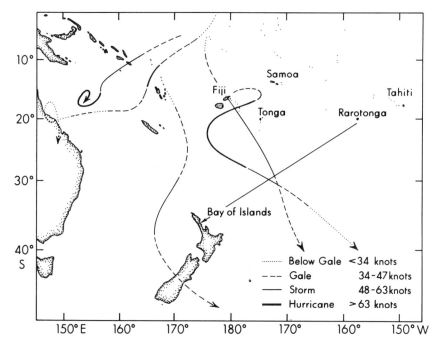

Figure 50. Tropical cyclones in the southwest Pacific during the 1978–1979 season (Revell 1981b, 48).

which also happened to be right in the time window specified in the traditional sailing directions.

Departure from Rarotonga

We flew to Rarotonga in early November to ready the canoe, which had been there since her arrival from Tahiti in June. Instead of the expected clear skies and trade winds, however, we were greeted by cloudy, humid conditions that usually do not develop until mid-December. Then, on the 15th of November, the day we had planned to sail, frigate birds came in from the sea to fly over the ridges of the island, a sure sign, knowledgeable Rarotongans said, that bad weather was out at sea. That evening, strong winds and torrential rain struck the island, making us worry that we may have waited too long before coming back to Rarotonga to start the voyage to Aotearoa—that the summer rainy season, when tropical cyclones are most likely to develop, may have already begun.

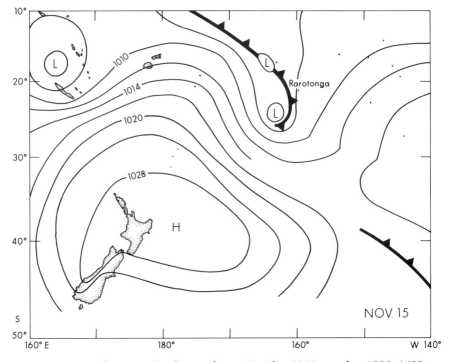

Figure 51. Weather map for the southwest Pacific, 15 November 1985, 1400 Rarotonga time.

Paul Frost of the New Zealand Meteorological Service in Rarotonga showed us on satellite weather maps how the South Pacific Convergence Zone, where trades blowing from north of east and those blowing from south of east converge, was located just to the west of Rarotonga. It was just our luck that this convergence zone, which normally does not move into this region until the mid or late summer,[9] had shifted our way early, bringing the humid, cloudy, and rainy conditions. The satellite weather map for the 15th showed two depressions associated with this convergence, one to the northwest, the other to the southwest (fig. 51). We feared that should the convergence zone stay near the Southern Cooks, we might be in the path of a series of tropical disturbances that could form along the low pressure trough associated with the convergence. We even imagined a worst-case scenario, whereby a disturbance forming to the northwest might develop into a full-fledged cyclone of hurricane force winds and move toward the Southern Cooks, following a path typical for many of the tropical cyclones that have struck these islands.

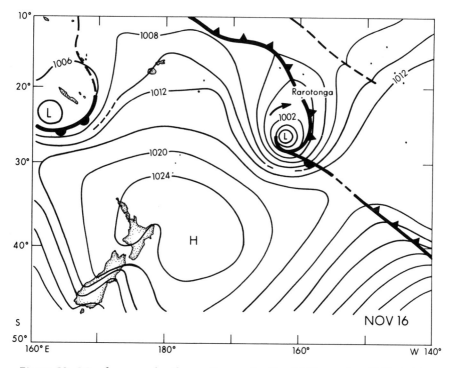

Figure 52. Weather map for the southwest Pacific, 16 November 1985, 1400 Rarotonga time.

(A year later, in January of 1987, Cyclone Sally hit Rarotonga with winds of over 100 knots and violent seas.)

On the 16th, however, the skies cleared, although the weather satellite map showed that the depression to the southwest (fig. 52) had deepened rapidly, with winds of at least 50 knots according to the report of a nearby ship. Fortunately, this was not a tropical cyclone that would be likely to develop into a hurricane and head for the Cooks, but a subtropical cyclone that Paul Frost predicted would soon pass to the southeast of the Cooks, leaving trade wind weather suitable for our departure. Unfortunately, however, it moved so slowly to the east that its cyclonic winds (which revolve clockwise in the Southern Hemisphere) brought day after day of strong southwesterlies to Rarotonga. As these winds were blowing from the direction toward which we wanted to sail, we were forced to remain tied up in Avatiu harbor. The Prime Minister, Sir Thomas Davis, and other experienced Rarotongan sailors assured us, as did Frost, that the wind would eventually shift back to regular southeast

trades. Nevertheless, as the days wore on and the wind continued to blow from the southwest, we became more and more worried that the delay would further expose us to the hurricane dangers of an apparently already early summer season.

Finally, on Thursday, 21 November, the winds shifted to south-southeast, and weather reports indicated clear sailing from Rarotonga for a good part of the distance to our destination. Accordingly, Nainoa decided that we should leave. Early that afternoon, veteran Captain Shorty Bertelmann gave orders to cast off the lines, and we set sail for Aotearoa.

Steering Off the Wind

In addition to Shorty and Nainoa who had overall responsibility for the canoe and for navigation, there were twelve of us on board who were serving as crew members charged with sailing the canoe to Aotearoa. For that purpose, we were divided into three watches. Leon Paoa Sterling, a professional seaman from the island of Hawai'i, captained the first watch. Serving with him were: Dr. Pat Aiu, a Kaua'i physician who also functioned as the canoe's doctor; Honolulu attorney Mike Tongg; and the only man on board who had not sailed on *Hōkūle'a* before— Stanley Conrad, a young Māori seaman chosen to represent his people on the voyage and to serve as pilot in coastal waters off the northeast coast of the North Island, his home region. Billy Richards, a marine researcher from the island of O'ahu and a veteran of the original 1976 voyage to Tahiti, was the second watch captain. Serving with him were: Honolulu fireman Bruce Blankenfeld; Jim Shizuru, a Honolulu businessman and skilled craftsman who had supervised the refitting of the canoe before she left Honolulu; and Honolulu architect Harry Ho. The Marquesan sailor Tava Taupu captained the third watch, on which I served along with Maui islander Chad Baybayan, and Buddy McGuire, a labor relations consultant from Honolulu who volunteered to do much of the cooking on the crossing.

Each watch was on duty for four hours, then had eight off. While on watch we were charged with checking the rigging and sails for chaffing and other problems, keeping the sails trimmed properly, checking the hulls and bailing them out when necessary, taking care of routine maintenance chores, and, above all, steering.

Sometimes keeping *Hōkūleʻa* on course can be fairly easy. In fact, when sailing close into the wind, it is possible to balance the center of effort of the wind's force on the sails with the center of lateral resistance of the hulls to the sideways push of the wind to make the canoe sail automatically to windward without having to use even a single steering paddle. We do this by trimming the sails (that is, adjusting their angle and fullness) and by shifting water jugs and other heavy stores fore or aft to move the center of gravity of the hulls in order to reach just the right balance of forces on the sails and hulls so that the canoe will automatically head into the wind, but then fall off whenever it points too high into the wind. However, in order to sail this way, the desired course has to be aligned to the wind so that the canoe can sail full and by to windward. This has often been the case when sailing from Hawaiʻi and Tahiti and was so the afternoon we left Rarotonga. With the wind coming from slightly east of south, we were able to trim the sails and shift stores in the hulls so that *Hōkūleʻa* naturally sailed close to the wind at just the heading to the southwest that we wanted to maintain.

But, as the wind continued to shift eastward on the second day at sea, 22 November, we were forced to unlash one of the two 18-foot-long steering paddles we keep on deck and run the blade deep into the sea in order to hold the canoe off the wind on the proper heading to the southwest. For virtually all the rest of the voyage the easterly beam winds we encountered forced us to use the long steering paddle to keep the canoe heading for Aotearoa.

Holding a big canoe like *Hōkūle'a* off the wind can some-times be challenging. When steering with strong winds and large, rolling seas coming from abeam, it takes a lot of effort to keep the canoe from yawing wildly. Except when trimmed for automatic sailing to windward, *Hōkūle'a* has a natural "weather helm," a tendency to head up into the wind that is a necessary safety feature for any sailing vessel. Whereas in the advent of a steering failure a craft with the opposite helm, a "lee helm," will head uncontrollably downwind, if the steering mechanism of a craft with a weather helm is disabled the vessel will auto-matically head into the wind until the sails lose their drive and the vessel stops moving forward. The steersman's task, there-fore, is to oppose the natural weather helm and keep the canoe headed off the wind on the desired heading. He does this by shoving the long steering paddle mounted inboard of the wind-ward hull deep into the water in order to move the center of lat-eral resistance of the hull aft and thereby stop the natural swing of the bow into the wind. He has to find just the right position and then constantly adjust it as passing seas shove the bow one way or another. If he doesn't push the paddle deep enough into the water, the canoe will round up into the wind. If he puts it in too deep, the canoe will fall off and run downwind (fig. 53).

Those of us from Hawai'i serving on this leg were all experi-enced in steering *Hōkūle'a* and were looking forward to the challenge of keeping the big canoe on course to Aotearoa. From the time I started experimenting with *Nālehia*, I had always enjoyed steering over sail handling or any other chores. There is something about being able to keep the long hulls of a voy-aging canoe cutting through the seas at just the right angle that is vastly more satisfying to me than any of the other jobs on the canoe. That's why I was delighted to serve with the skilled steersmen on this leg and above all to see what progress had been made in steering techniques since we first began our experiments.

Since they had been introduced to canoe sailing in the mid-1970s, my watch mates Tava Taupu and Chad Baybayan had be-come particularly adept steersmen. They often worked together, particularly during the day when steering often requires a team approach, with one man spotting the sun to set the heading and one man handling the steering paddle. For example, while sail-

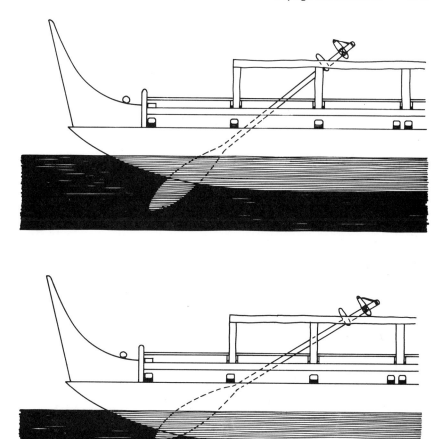

Figure 53. Steering paddle positions.

ing with beam winds and seas on the afternoon of the 23rd, the second day at sea, I watched the two of them making a difficult job look easy. Tava was steering, standing at the aft windward side of the platform between the hulls and gripping the long steering paddle, which extended down at an angle toward the stern where, just below the waterline, the force of the water flowing past clamped the blade to the hull. Although the mechanics of steering required that Tava stand there to exert the proper leverage on the steering paddle, Tava could not see the sun from that position, for it was hidden behind the big forward sail. Accordingly, Chad stood at the opposite, lee side of the platform from where he could spot the sun and relay directions to Tava, as described in this excerpt from my log:

> "Up Tava," Chad, a stocky, round-faced Hawaiian, would call out to the steersman, telling him to pull the steering paddle forward, thereby lifting the blade out of the water to let the canoe swing "up" into the wind and get back on course. Once Chad judged that the canoe was almost back on the right heading, he would shout out a confirming "Right on!" Tava, a quiet, tremendously strong Marquesan, would then shove the blade part-way back into the water to stop the canoe from swinging too far into the wind. But, if Chad was too late in his command, or if Tava didn't push the blade far enough into the water, *Hōkūleʻa* would swing too far to windward past the desired heading, forcing Chad to call out, "Too far, go down a little." Tava would then push the blade deeper into the water to arrest and then reverse the swing of the canoe and make it head "down," that is, to leeward.

As long as the wind kept coming from abeam, which it did for much of the voyage, only one man steered at a time while the others waited their turn at the steering paddle. When, however, the wind moved well abaft abeam, steering became more complicated. For example, after leaving Rarotonga the wind continued moving counterclockwise until by the 26th it was blowing from the east-northeast. With the wind coming nearly straight over the stern the possibility of an accidental jibe grew. A jibe presents a particular danger to the long curved booms of the canoe's two sails, for if the wind is allowed to cross the stern it forces the sails and their booms over onto the other tack, sometimes so violently that the long booms crack under the sudden strain. To guard against such an occurrence, another crewman stood by the other steering paddle (mounted inboard of the other hull), ready to plunge it into the water to stop the canoe from veering too far to starboard whenever a wind shift or passing swells threatened to push it that way. Then, several times when light tailwinds reduced the effectiveness of the side steering paddles, the other two men on watch would unlash the centrally mounted steering sweep, standing by to literally row the stern around one way or the other whenever a jibe threatened.

We tried to avoid running directly downwind, however, unless the winds were very light, as was the case on the 27th. Then, we let one sail all the way out on the port side and the

other all the way out on the starboard side to run "wing-on-wing" before the wind.

High Pressure Easterlies

Before leaving Rarotonga, Paul Frost had told us that a few hundred miles south of the latitude of Rarotonga we had a good chance of being able to make a smooth transition from the southeast trades to light easterly winds associated with migrating high pressure systems that he said could, if we were lucky, take us all the way to the North Island. Typically at this time of year a succession of high pressure areas slowly move east out of the Tasman Sea, across Aotearoa, and then into the open waters beyond. Since in the Southern Hemisphere surface wind circulates counterclockwise around a high pressure system, we could count on easterly winds as long as we were sailing along the northern flank of one of these migrating highs. Our hope, therefore, was that when we moved out of the trade wind zone a high pressure system would be centered to the south of us so that we could sail along the northern flank of the high, taking advantage of the easterly wind flow.

Once at sea, however, we no longer had the counsel of Paul Frost or access to the satellite weather maps. Although for security purposes Jim Shizuru periodically tuned in on weather reports with an on-board single sideband transceiver, this information was not disclosed to Nainoa or the rest of us. According to our experimental protocol, only in the case of a threatening tropical cyclone or other weather emergency was Nainoa to be

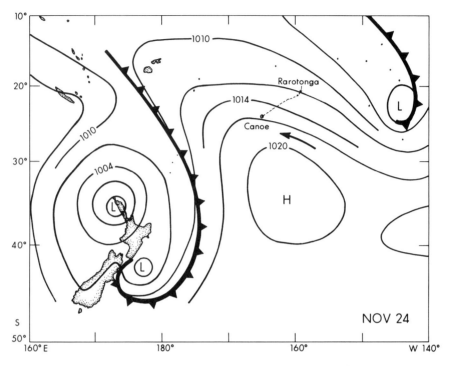

Figure 54. Weather map for the southwest Pacific, 24 November 1985, 1400 Rarotonga time.

told about outside weather reports. Accordingly, we could only look to the wind, to cloud patterns, and to other cues visible from the deck of the canoe in order to estimate when we passed out of the trades and came into the winds circulating around a passing high, if indeed one was there at the time.

During the first few days after leaving Rarotonga, with the wind coming from the southeast and the skies clear except for trade wind cumulus clouds, it looked and felt like we were sailing in the trades. By the 24th, however, when the wind backed around to the east and a high layer of cirrus clouds gave the sky a different look, we began to wonder if we might have left the trades and were sailing in the easterlies along the northern flank of the high we hoped was there. A postvoyage examination of Fiji Meteorological Service weather charts sent to us by Paul Frost shows that this, in fact, had happened (fig. 54). The winds circulating counterclockwise around a high established well east of the North Island bathed us in a strong easterly air flow.

We enjoyed brisk easterly winds throughout the 24th, but on

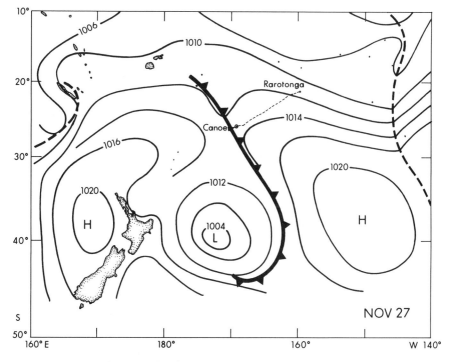

Figure 55. Weather map for the southwest Pacific, 27 November 1985, 1400 Rarotonga time.

the 25th the winds began to lighten and shift farther around toward the northeast, and by the 27th we were virtually becalmed with only very light northeast winds. At the time we were worried that we might be stuck in a calm at the center of the high. Only after the voyage did we learn what had actually happened. The high with its favorable winds had migrated eastward, and a low had developed immediately east of the North Island. In between the two, and just to the west of the canoe, a stationary front had become established and was giving us the calm weather (fig. 55).

The next day, the 28th, dawned cloudy, with light, shifting winds. This made it difficult to stay on course, and for a brief time we actually got turned around and started to head back toward the east. This happened when the sun, which had already risen too high in the sky to yield a clear bearing, disappeared behind the clouds leaving us with only a confused swell pattern to steer by. Then an undetected wind shift apparently turned the canoe around. Leon Sterling felt that something was wrong and asked Nainoa to check our heading against the swells. Because Nainoa could not make clear sense out of the then confused swell pattern, he told us to wait until the sun came out before trying to change course. When it did finally shine through the overcast, Leon's suspicions were confirmed, and we brought the canoe back around to the southwest after our fortunately short detour.

By the evening of the 28th the easterly winds returned, and for the next three days we enjoyed favorable winds, though variable in velocity. Sometimes they exceeded 20 knots and the canoe would speed along at 6 or 7 knots. More frequently, however, they varied between 5 and 10 knots, giving us a speed range of between $2^{1}/_{2}$ and 4 knots. Nonetheless, as the wind always blew from the southeast to east sector of the compass, we had no trouble keeping the canoe headed toward Aotearoa.

Except for the one brief period of calm, during the first ten days after leaving Rarotonga we had been fortunate in having easterly winds to speed us toward our destination. On 2 December, however, our luck began to run out. At about ten o'clock we sailed into a bank of clouds, a light rain began, and the wind began to come out of the north. Showery weather with light, shifting winds continued throughout the day and into the night. The next day, 3 December, was most frustrating. Nainoa was sure that Raoul Island, the largest and northernmost island in the Kermadec Chain, was just over the horizon to the northwest of us, but we found it impossible to sail very far in that direction. Calms, then in the evening light winds from the northwest, kept us from making any significant progress. Later that night flashes of lightning to the north, indicating bad weather in that direction, led Nainoa to give up the effort to reach Raoul and to order the canoe back on a southwest heading toward Aotearoa. Within a few hours an easterly breeze sprang up and we were back on course, sailing with a favorable wind on our beam.

Again, *Hōkūleʻa* had been lucky. As Paul Frost, back in Rarotonga, had been monitoring our progress toward Raoul in relation to a depression then moving across Aotearoa and toward the Kermadecs, he had expected that the strong westerly winds of the depression would push past the Kermadecs and engulf us. At the last minute, however, we were spared as the depression weakened, and the rapid movement of a high eastward gave us

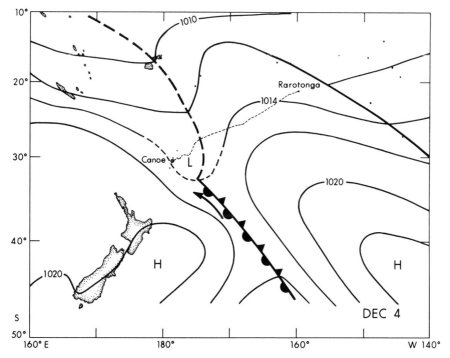

Figure 56. Weather map for the southwest Pacific, 4 December 1985, 1400 Rarotonga time.

good easterly winds again. Instead, then, of fighting headwinds, we were soon back sailing toward the North Island along the northern flank of this new high, though an encounter with the Kermadecs awaited us (fig. 56).

Looking for Raoul

In comparison to finding the little island Rarotonga, hitting the huge target presented by the length of the North Island was not a great navigational challenge. Nonetheless, for reasons of safety as well as professional pride Nainoa wanted to guide *Hō-kūle'a* as precisely as possible toward our target, the Bay of Islands. Particularly as we neared the North Island, Nainoa wanted to have a good idea of where the canoe was at any time so that, should a storm or spell of adverse winds hit us, he would be able to make informed navigational decisions in order to avoid making landfall somewhere well to the north or south of the Bay of Islands, or worse, running aground on some hidden reef.

The Kermadec Islands, a chain of tiny volcanic islands lying across the direct course from Rarotonga to the Bay of Islands a little over two-thirds of the way, provided a natural intermediate target, both from a navigational and historical sense. Sighting any one of the four islands of the chain would tell us precisely where we were and thereby would enable Nainoa to aim exactly toward the Bay of Islands for the last third of the voyage. Of the four islands, the northernmost and largest one, Raoul Island, was the most likely target. With a peak rising over 1,700 feet above sea level, Raoul would be much easier to spot than any of the other three tiny islets. There also seemed to be an historical precedent for stopping at Raoul. According to tradition, the Aotea canoe sailing from Hawaiki to Aotearoa stopped at a small, rocky island, which the voyagers called Rangitahua and which S. Percy Smith identified as Raoul. Furthermore, it has long been thought that the characteristically East Polynesian adzes that have been found on the island could have been left on such a migratory voyage, although recent finds of artifacts made of obsidian originating in Aotearoa would seem to indicate that the island must have been visited from the south as well as perhaps from the northeast.[10]

Keeping the canoe on course at the time of the year we were sailing presented some novel challenges. On most of our previous voyages there had usually been one or more prominent stars setting during the night in the direction the canoe was traveling, making for easy nighttime steering. In late November and early December, however, there are no such prominent stars conveniently setting during the night in the southwestern quadrant of the sky. Hence, those of us steering could not simply pick out a star setting in the direction of the desired course and keep it lined up on one of the twin prow pieces. Instead, we usually had to look astern, or abeam, for stellar guidance.

A number of prominent stars and constellations rising that time of year provided us with handy beacons for backsighting. All we had to do was face aft, line up a star or constellation with one of the high, curving stern pieces or some part of the rigging, and then keep the canoe on course with the steering paddle. The Pleiades, that tight cluster of faint stars Hawaiians call *Makali'i*, was a convenient constellation for backsighting, as were the brighter stars that form the Belt of Orion, particularly when they were low on the horizon. Great care had to be taken, however, in using these stars as they rose higher and higher in the sky and then started curving downward toward the western horizon, for their bearings relative to the course would shift greatly. Nonetheless, under Nainoa's tutelage it was possible to steer on these stars throughout the night as they arched across the sky.

Other favorite steering stars were those in the Southern Cross and the two bright stars that point toward this cruciform constellation. This meant that instead of facing forward or astern when steering, we looked abeam—off to port, roughly at right angles to the length of the canoe. Facing sideways, we would line up the Cross, or the Pointers, with a section of the rail or part of the rigging and then by manipulating the steering paddle keep that alignment as well as wind shifts, passing swells, and our own abilities allowed. Again, Nainoa had to keep us on our toes when steering on these stars because the wide rotation they make around the south celestial pole would greatly throw our steering off if we didn't compensate for it. (When Nainoa took his brief catnaps, Shorty or the watch captain on duty would stand by to make sure that we used these stars correctly for our steering.)

Greatly complicating nighttime steering was the often heavy cloud cover we were experiencing during this part of the crossing. Time and time again our guiding star or constellation, be it astern or abeam, would disappear in the clouds, and we were forced to search out an appropriate star in a clearer sector of the sky. In fact, we soon learned to anticipate this by continually glancing around the sky for alternate steering guides so that when the star we were using was clouded over we could quickly switch to another to stay oriented.

One particularly cloudy night when I was steering I had great trouble keeping any star or constellation in view for long. As the sky was clearest off to port, I was trying to use the Southern Cross as my guide, but when clouds obscured that constellation I had to switch to the two bright stars that point toward the Southern Cross to keep oriented. Then, when I could see that the clouds were soon going to cover up these stars as well, I searched the almost totally overcast sky for familiar stars with which I could orient myself. Finally, off to one side I spotted two fuzzy balls of light I knew: the Magellanic Clouds, which actually are separate galaxies outside of our own. When, as ex-

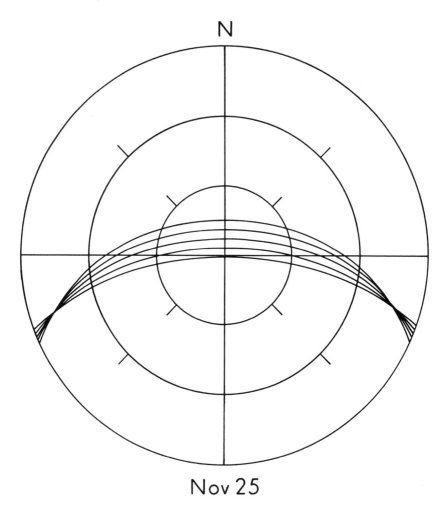

Nov 25

Figure 57. Computer simulation of sun transits for 25 November 1985, latitudes 20°, 24°, 28°, and 36° South.

pected, the pointer stars slipped from view, I switched to the Magellanic Clouds. I remember thinking at the time how strange this all was. Here we were sailing in a canoe across the dark ocean of the third planet out from the sun, steering by a variety of stars light-years away: at one moment by the pointer stars, one of which, Alpha Centauri, is at 4.3 light-years away the closest star to our own, and an instant later by the Magellanic Clouds, whole galaxies of stars that are 160,000 light-years distant![11]

Actually, because the Austral summer solstice was near, we

were steering more hours by the sun than by the nighttime stars. The sun can easily be used for steering at dawn and sunset, for then it is in effect a big horizon star, although one that because of its constantly shifting bearing must be periodically "recalibrated" by comparing its bearing before dawn with the virtually unchanging rising points of the stars. Steering by the sun throughout the day can, however, be difficult, particularly when sailing in the winter with the sun passing far off to the north (or to the south if sailing in the Northern Hemisphere). In our case, however, the timing of the voyage was almost ideal. When we left Rarotonga the sun not only rose and set near our latitude, but came close to passing directly overhead in its daily passage, curving only slightly to the north during the midday hours. (Figure 57, a computer simulation prepared before the voyage, shows the daily transit of the sun during this time of the year.) This situation allowed us to get an easterly bearing from the sun at dawn and hold it until late in the morning when the sun was too high in the sky to judge direction, and then to pick up a westerly bearing as the sun started to descend in the afternoon. Then, as the sun sank toward the horizon we often framed it between *Hōkūle'a*'s twin prowpieces, heading right for the setting sun just as dictated in some versions of the traditional sailing directions for Aotearoa.

On this crossing, Nainoa's method of dead reckoning was essentially the same as that he used in 1980 to navigate *Hōkūle'a* from Hawai'i to Tahiti and return, except that he primarily pictured the canoe's progress in terms of bearing and distance—at first, from Rarotonga, then, as the Kermadecs became closer, to that archipelago, and finally, after clearing the Kermadecs, to Aotearoa—rather than in terms of the deviation of *Hōkūle'a* from a reference course line mentally drawn between Rarotonga and Aotearoa.

Nainoa made these estimates by keeping a purely mental calculation of the cumulative distance sailed by the canoe and the resultant course followed. To do this he had to continually estimate the canoe's speed and its heading in relation to his stellar direction system and then adjust these estimates for how much he judged the canoe was being offset by current and leeway. In addition to the ability to make fairly precise judgments of the canoe's speed (by watching how fast the water flows past the hulls) and heading and how the direction and strength of the current and the angle of leeway may be affecting the actual course, this method calls for a tremendous degree of concentration. Had Nainoa allowed himself the luxury of a chart on which to mark the developing course of the canoe, or even just pencil and paper, the task of integrating all his estimates of heading, speed, current, and leeway and of continually updating the resultant estimate of the canoe's position would have been much easier. However, in order to make this effort more analogous to that of a traditional navigator, Nainoa plotted everything in his head, drawing in his mind a mental map of our progress between islands whose positions, relative bearings, and distances he had committed to memory before leaving. This meant, among other things, that he allowed himself to sleep only in short snatches that totaled only a few hours out of twenty-four, for to close his eyes for any length of time would have been to risk missing crucial changes in speed or deviations in heading that could have thrown his reckoning significantly off course.

In addition, whenever the skies were clear enough and the right stars were in the proper position, Nainoa attempted to make star sights that would enable him to determine his latitude and refine his dead reckoning estimates accordingly. Employing his outstretched hand as a gauge, he would measure the height above the horizon of one or more preselected stars just as they were on the meridian and from that mentally calculate the canoe's latitude in the manner described in chapter 3.

At dawn and dusk Nainoa would dictate his position estimates and latitude sightings, if any, to Chad Baybayan who re-corded them along with observations on the wind, the sea state, the cloud cover, and other relevant factors. Once back in Hono-lulu we translated Nainoa's sunrise and sunset estimates of po-sition into points on the map, which were then plotted in rela-tion to the actual track of the canoe established by the ARGOS satellite system of position determination and the positions re-corded by satellite receiver onboard the escort yacht, *Dorcas*.

As can be seen in figure 58 on which the actual track and the estimated positions are plotted together, the dead reckoning es-timates were fairly accurate for the first third of the voyage. During the first week at sea the difference between the esti-mated and actual positions of the canoe averaged less than 25 miles. During the second week, however, the gap between the two widened to over 50 miles, meaning that Nainoa was either underestimating the speed of the canoe or the strength of the westward flowing current, or both. For example, when at sun-rise on 2 December Nainoa estimated that we were about 140 miles east of Raoul, the canoe was actually about 90 miles from the island.

At the end of the second week, Nainoa began to suspect that the canoe was farther west than he was estimating and told the crew that although his mental calculations indicated that the Kermadecs were still a ways off he wanted them to keep a sharp lookout in case he had underestimated the distance covered since leaving Rarotonga. Accordingly, he told everyone to be on the watch for land-nesting birds, particularly terns, which would indicate close proximity to an island. Soon thereafter four terns appeared off the bow and flew around the canoe for almost a half hour, raising hopes of seeing land soon. But Nainoa cau-tioned us that these might just be a few stray birds fishing far from their island and said that, according to fisheries experts he had consulted in Honolulu, the Kermadecs have an abundance of bird life, and that therefore we should see many terns and other birds when we neared those islands.

Instead of the anticipated swarms of birds, early that after-noon we spotted another kind of wildlife: a pod of whales swim-ming across our bow about a quarter mile off. They soon became aware of our presence (by the vibrations set up by *Hōkūle'a's* twin hulls cutting through the water?), and swam at high speed directly for the canoe. As they came closer, and their huge, box-

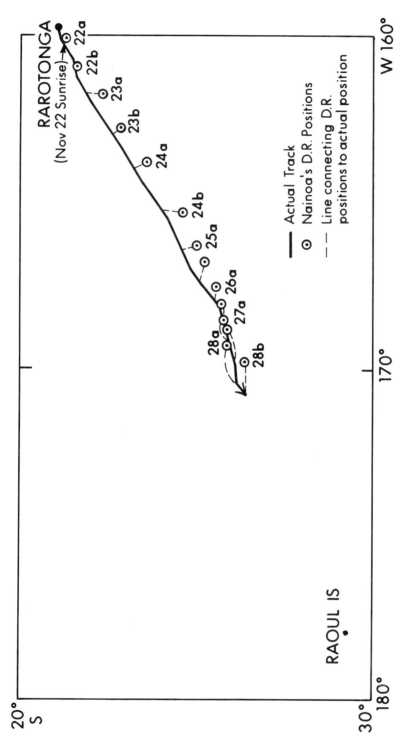

Figure 58. The track of Hōkūle'a and Nainoa Thompson's dead reckoning positions for the first third of the voyage from Rarotonga to Aotearoa.

like heads surged out of the water, we realized that they were sperm whales, the largest of the toothed cetaceans. Although we were initially apprehensive, we could see by the way the whales were eyeing us as they swam around and under the canoe that they were apparently just curious. After investigating us, they swam over to the yacht *Dorcas*, several miles astern, and, after similarly inspecting her, resumed swimming on a heading that appeared to be just slightly east of north.

A couple of hours later we saw off in the distance another pod of whales swimming on roughly the same heading. These creatures, which appeared to be small pilot whales, either did not notice us or were totally disinterested, for they just kept swimming on their course. These two sightings of whales swimming on a heading of approximately north by east were made even more intriguing by the fact that a deep ocean trench lies just to the east of the Kermadec chain and runs in more or less the same direction as the path followed by the whales. This made me wonder if these whales might be swimming along the trench, perhaps for navigational reasons or because the fishing was better, and thus were indicators that the Kermadecs were near.

Later that afternoon a crewman cried out, "Land!" He pointed off to the east-southeast, where he and a few others thought they saw the dark outline of an island. But no one could be sure, for the horizon was then especially hazy and cloudy. Nonetheless, on the chance that Raoul might be off in that direction, we sailed east-southeast for an hour or so—until it became obvious that all we were chasing were phantom islands seen in the outlines of dark clouds.

When we went back to the starboard tack and tried to sail west-northwest to take up our search for Raoul, the wind was coming out of the northwest, making it virtually impossible to make any progress in that direction. This was most frustrating, especially since at dusk we had seen a number of terns winging their way home toward the west-northwest. All through the first half of the night we struggled against light headwinds to sail in the direction the birds had flown, but with little success. Then, when we saw lightning off to the north indicating bad weather ahead, Nainoa gave the order to fall off to the southwest and get back on a direct course to Aotearoa.

Nainoa reckoned that on this heading we would sail through the Kermadec chain somewhere south of Raoul. But he had no

illusions about being able to direct the canoe toward any particular one of the three tiny southern islands or to specify exactly
when we might pass through the chain.

An hour or two after midnight, sharp-eyed Stanley Conrad
spied a dark shape off in the distance a couple of points off the
bow. He thought it was an island—shaped like a huge whale—
but after the previous day's false alarm, he was wary of calling
our attention to it. So he waited, watching to see if it changed
shape, as had the clouds we had been chasing earlier. After
watching it for about an hour, and seeing that it retained its
whalelike form while looming larger on the horizon, Stanley
called over to Tava Taupu who, after peering at the dark outline,
agreed that it indeed was an island. Then, just as everybody
started coming out on deck to see the landfall, another island
began to be barely visible in the dark a few miles almost directly
ahead. As the predawn sky began to lighten, we saw that the
canoe was heading just slightly south of Macauley Island, the
one Stanley had spied first, and directly toward Curtis Island,
the southernmost island of the Kermadecs (fig. 59). We had not
made it to Raoul, but now Nainoa knew exactly where we were.
Accordingly, after passing close by Curtis Island to watch the
steam rising from the fumaroles located on this minuscule volcanic rock, Nainoa was able to set an exact course directly for
the Bay of Islands without the doubts that would have beset him
had we passed through or to one side or other of the Kermadecs
without sighting any of the chain's little islands.

Racing for Aotearoa

As we cleared Curtis Island thoughts turned to what the Māori
leaders Hector Busby (Heke Nukumaingaiwi Puhipa) and Tupi
Puriri had said just before we left Rarotonga. "Be sure to get to
Waitangi on a weekend," they had urged.

Under Hector Busby's leadership, the Māori people of the far
north of the North Island had formed the Tai Tokerau Cultural
Association in 1973, the same year we had founded the Polynesian Voyaging Society in Hawaii. These two organizations had
much more in common than the same foundation year. While
the Polynesian Voyaging Society was being formed to build and
sail *Hōkūle'a*, Tai Tokerau was being organized to relaunch *Nga
Toki Matawhaorua*, a giant Māori paddling canoe 136 feet long

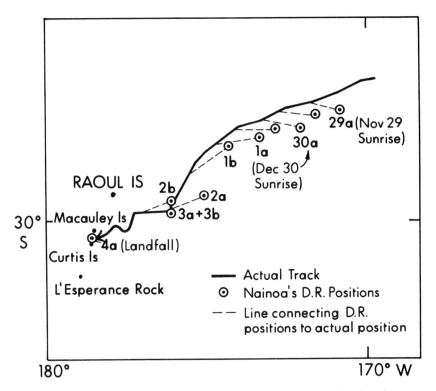

Figure 59. The track of Hōkūle'a *and Nainoa Thompson's dead reckoning positions for the second third of the voyage from Rarotonga to Aotearoa.*

named, we were told, after a legendary canoe that had made a second voyage from Hawaiki to Aotearoa after having been re-carved or, as its name translates, having been "by the adze hollowed out twice." The modern *Nga Toki Matawhaorua* had been constructed for the 1940 centennial of the Treaty of Waitangi between the British and Māori tribal chiefs. But after having been paddled around the Bay of Islands as part of that celebration, the canoe had been high and dry on land until its relaunching. The idea behind this relaunching was to employ *Nga Toki Matawhaorua* as a focus for cultural revival among the Northland tribes, much as *Hōkūle'a* had been conceived as a vehicle for rekindling Hawaiian pride in their voyaging heritage.

Given the similarity in cultural mission of the two groups, it was most appropriate that Tai Tokerau would host *Hōkūle'a* upon her arrival in Aotearoa. This is why we were headed for the Bay of Islands, the home waters of *Nga Toki Matawhaorua*, and specifically for the Waitangi *Marae* located on the shore deep inside the bay, a complex of buildings set upon consecrated ground that forms the cultural center for the region and the home base for the Tai Tokerau group. The members of Tai Tokerau wanted to welcome us by launching their massive canoe to meet *Hōkūle'a* as she entered the Bay of Islands and by ceremonially greeting us on the Waitangi *Marae*. However, as most of the Tai Tokerau people live a considerable distance from Waitangi and are normally busy working during the week, they could mount a proper welcome only on Saturday or Sunday. Hence, the admonition to arrive on a weekend—and the warning that should we enter the Bay of Islands after Sunday evening we would be put under a *tapu* and be required to remain at anchor behind one of the small islands within the bay until the following Saturday morning.

We were in a race against time, for none of us relished the idea of waiting around for days before being able to go ashore. According to the calendar we had been keeping since leaving Rarotonga, we did not clear the Kermadecs until dawn on Wednesday, 4 December. Since, however, Aotearoa lies on the other side of the International Dateline, we actually had passed between Curtis and Macauley islands on the morning of Thursday, 5 December New Zealand time. This only gave us from Thursday through Sunday evening—three and a half days—to make the 450 or so miles from the Kermadecs, which meant that *Hōkūle'a* would have to average almost 130 miles a day, or sail at the average rate of a little over 5 knots.

Hōkūle'a can easily sail 5 or 6 knots, but only with brisk winds. Experience on previous voyages had shown us that given the inevitable periods of calms and light winds a more realistic average to expect would be on the order of 4 knots or 100 miles a day. Once again on this voyage, however, we were lucky, for as we cleared the Kermadecs a dry cold wind began to blow. By midmorning we had 20-knot-plus winds coming from the southeast, approximately 90 degrees to our southwesterly course. Sailing in these brisk beam winds *Hōkūle'a* easily made $5^1/_2$ to 6 knots. The wind remained strong throughout the day but began to weaken after sunset. After a night of slow sailing as we tried to work our way around a series of huge black clouds that seemed to stifle the wind, by dawn we were back in steady winds coming from east-southeast. By late afternoon the wind had

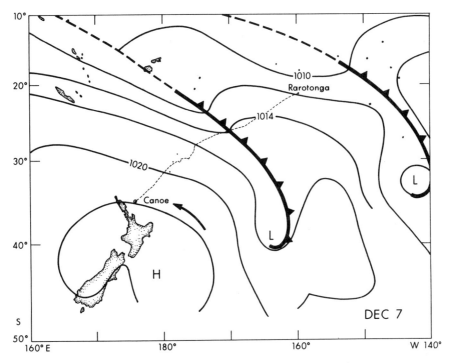

Figure 60. Weather map for the southwest Pacific, 7 December 1985, 1600 New Zealand time.

picked up to 25–30 knots and was driving the canoe toward Aotearoa at 6½ to 7 knots or better. The wind lightened a bit that night and the next day, Saturday, 7 December, but we still made at least 6 knots during that period, speed enough, we thought, to just make it into the Bay of Islands sometime on Sunday.

The weather map for 6 December (fig. 60) shows how a new high had become established in just the right place to give us these strong southeast winds for the final run to the Bay of Islands.

As we approached the North Island Nainoa mentally pictured the expansion of our target in terms of the widening angle between the island's North Cape and East Cape. Upon clearing the Kermadecs that angle had been about 40 degrees. By Saturday, 7 December, Nainoa pictured the angle as having widened to over 150 degrees. Landfall somewhere along the northeastern coast of the island was therefore assured. The question was whether we were headed more or less directly for the Bay of Islands, or to one side or the other of our target. If Nainoa's dead reckoning

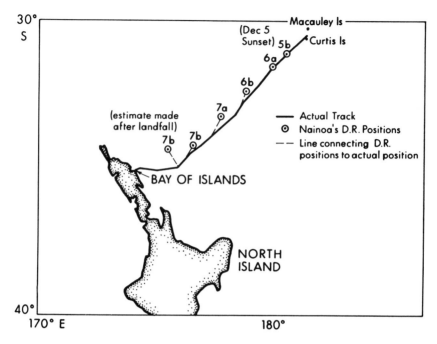

Figure 61. The track of Hōkūle'a *and Nainoa Thompson's dead reckoning positions for the last third of the voyage from Rarotonga to Aotearoa.*

calculations were correct, and we were indeed heading more or less directly toward the mouth of the bay, we had a good chance of reaching Waitangi before sunset Sunday and of enjoying the welcome then being planned for us there. If, however, we might be heading significantly south or north of our target, after making landfall it could have taken as much as a day to work our way up or down the coast in order to reach the Bay of Islands. That would have made it impossible to reach Waitangi before sunset on Sunday, leaving us with the dismal prospect of having to wait offshore until the following weekend.

The sight on Saturday morning, 7 December, of drifting seaweed and a floating log were sure signs that we were approaching shore, although we did not know exactly where we were. Late that afternoon Nainoa estimated that we were about 125 miles east-northeast of the Bay of Islands. That gave us a chance, he thought, of just barely making it to Waitangi before sunset of the following day—if the wind held. (In actuality we were closer than Nainoa had expected—about 100 miles almost due east of the Bay of Islands; fig. 61.) As the sky looked like it was going to be fairly clear that evening, Nainoa hoped to be able to take a sight on the Southern Cross or any other stars that crossed the meridian close enough to the horizon to allow a fairly accurate estimate of their angular elevation above the horizon and from that calculate our latitude so that we could make any required course adjustment. An unusual sighting at sunset made taking the star sight unnecessary, however.

As the sun sank toward the horizon that evening all eyes were drawn toward the reddening disk. Hope was widespread that land might be closer than thought and that we might even be able to see the dark outline of a mountain peak outlined against the setting sun. In actuality, we were treated to a sight which, though initially perplexing, was in a way even more dramatic. Just before the sun should have touched the horizon, the bottom part of the disk began to progressively disappear. At first we were mystified. Then it became apparent that the sun must be setting over a solid bank of dark gray clouds hovering over a coastline, or the land mass itself. Nainoa speculated that even though we were probably too far from shore to have a direct, line-of-sight view of land, we were probably seeing a projected image of the sun setting over the coast, or a cloud bank above it, which was being refracted from below the horizon.

One translation of the name Aotearoa is "long white cloud," stemming, according to some authorities, from when voyagers from Hawaiki spied a white cloud bank over what turned out to be the North Island. Although we had not been privileged to repeat that experience, we had seen the optical effects of either a long gray cloud bank, or the land mass below it, that told us that our destination was just over the horizon.

Because of the need to reach Waitangi before Sunday evening, at this point Nainoa declared the navigation experiment to be at an end and called over to Dan Wright, captain of the escort vessel the *Dorcas*, to alert him that we thought we were nearing land and to ask for a position check. Nainoa told him that on the basis of this sighting he reckoned that we were approximately 75 miles east-northeast of the Bay of Islands. Dan then reported that we were 95 miles from land, almost due east of the Bay of Islands.

The next morning a few scattered peaks standing out above the horizon provided our first actual view of land. Stanley Conrad recognized these as the tops of islands lying off the coast just to the south of the Bay of Islands, and we altered our course to head up the coast directly for the entrance to the bay. To our dismay, after sailing slowly for several hours, the wind began to fail us entirely. In order to assure our arrival before dark we unlashed the outboard motor carried to help us get in and out of harbors and put it into service to keep up speed. Then, late that afternoon, just as we were off Cape Brett about to enter the Bay of Islands, both the wind and our outboard motor died, forcing us to take a tow from a fishing boat in order to make it into the bay in time for the welcoming ceremonies.

Once we had cleared the last of the islands within the bay, a light wind sprang up, allowing us to drop the tow and sail slowly toward *Nga Toki Matawhaorua*, the welcoming canoe manned by some eighty paddlers. The two canoes came together at Tapeka Point. As we lowered our sails, the chanting crew of the Māori canoe paddled over to us to deliver Tai Tokerau's leader, Hector Busby, who, once on board, formally welcomed us in Māori. Following the completion of customs formalities carried out in person by New Zealand's Minister of Customs who had also come on board, we raised sail again and headed toward the Waitangi *Marae* located deep inside the bay.

We arrived offshore the *marae* just as the last of the sun's rays outlined the black-garbed Māori women gathered on the shore, rhythmically calling out *"Haere mai! Haere mai!"* ("Come hither! Come hither!") to welcome us to Waitangi. After anchoring the canoe offshore, we transferred to *Nga Toki Matawhaorua* and were paddled to the beach. We were not, however, allowed to walk ashore ourselves. Instead, pairs of crewmen from the Māori canoe carried each of us in turn through the shallow water onto the beach. We were then escorted to the *marae* for the welcoming ceremonies that, to everyone's delight, had not had to be put off until the following weekend.

You Have Shown That It Can Be Done

Unlike the Tahitian *marae*, the Māori *marae* is not an ancient stone temple of an abandoned religion, but is a busy ceremonial center—complete with meeting rooms that double at night as dormitories, and above all a kitchen and a dining hall that can serve hundreds of people—where community meetings that can last for days are held periodically throughout the year. Before, however, we could enter the *marae* grounds, we faced a ritual challenge by the young men of Tai Tokerau. Painted with designs simulating the tattoos of old and carrying war clubs, they advanced in formation upon us, enacting a vigorous chanting dance in which they tested our friendly intentions with taunting words, upraised war clubs, and by fiercely sticking their tongues out and rolling their eyes at us. After making, at the prompting of our hosts, the appropriately conciliatory response, we were ushered onto the grounds and taken to the broad lawn to the front of the main meeting hall where the elders of Tai Tokerau awaited us. In the welcoming speeches interspersed with songs and dances which continued into the early hours of the next morning speaker after speaker lauded our efforts to re-create the voyages by which their ancestors had sailed to Aotearoa over the legendary *Moana Nui a Kiwa* ("Great Ocean of Kiwa"). For example, Sir James Henare generously declared that:

> You have shown that it can be done and it was done by our ancestors. To me, this is the most important occasion, and I smile, and I laugh, and I shall smile again tomorrow at all the critics who have said it was never done.

The tall, white-haired Māori leader then paid us the ultimate compliment by proclaiming that all those who sailed *Hōkūleʻa* and traveled to Aotearoa to greet her arrival now made up the "Sixth Tribe" of the Tai Tokerau region.

Similar sentiments were expressed by elders at Waimirirangi *Marae* when, several days later, we traveled to the far north of the island to be welcomed by the people of Aupouri, Stanley Conrad's tribal group. To our Māori hosts we had dramatically demonstrated how their ancestors had sailed from far off Hawaiki to settle this land and how those who said that it could not have been done intentionally did not know what they were talking about.

We deeply appreciate the sentiments our voyage to Aotearoa have evoked and are proud of the role *Hōkūleʻa* is playing in renewing pride in the sometimes maligned Polynesian voyaging heritage. We cannot, of course, claim that our crossing exactly replicated an early canoe voyage to Aotearoa or use our experiences to prove conclusively any particular theory of discovery and settlement. Nonetheless, we believe that our voyage has demonstrated how it is possible to intentionally sail a double canoe from Rarotonga to Aotearoa during the late spring and lends support to the hypothesis that the original Māori settlers exploited the easterlies common in that season to make their way to Aotearoa.

It took just over sixteen days for *Hōkūle'a* to cover the 1,650 miles between Rarotonga and the Bay of Islands. Accurate course setting and steering as straight a course to the Bay of Islands as the wind would allow certainly helped us make such a relatively speedy passage (fig. 62). Dan Wright, the skipper of the yacht following us, was amazed at how little the canoe had deviated from a direct rhumb line, declaring that a yacht equipped with modern navigational equipment and easy-to-handle wheel and rudder system, and subjected to the same wind patterns, could hardly have done better. But however much skillful navigation and steering may have cut down our time at sea, the fact remains that we would not have been able to reach Aotearoa so directly had we not enjoyed the relatively steady easterly winds generated along the route by the high pressure systems that dominated the seas between Rarotonga and Aotearoa during our passage.

Undoubtedly, timing the voyage for late spring greatly raised our chances of getting easterly winds along the route. But we were also very lucky to have enjoyed virtually uninterrupted easterly winds all the way to the Bay of Islands. Although many yachtsmen sailing along this route at this same time of year have experienced similarly favorable wind conditions and consequently fast passages to Aotearoa, some have had to contend with calms, variables, and some spells of westerlies along the way. This happened to the *Hawaiki Nui*, another double canoe, built in Tahiti under the leadership of the Māori carver Matahi Whakataka (Greg Brightwell), which sailed from Tahiti to Rarotonga a month after we did and left Rarotonga for Aotearoa just six days after us. Where we enjoyed almost continuous easterlies from a succession of high pressure systems, the *Hawaiki Nui*, which took a more southerly course than we did, ran into much more variable conditions and took a month to reach Aotearoa. Similarly, when in November and December of 1965 David Lewis conducted his pioneering noninstrument navigation experiment from Rarotonga to the North Island aboard the catamaran *Rehu Moana*, spells of light variable winds kept him at sea for almost a month.[12]

Nonetheless, although the more mixed wind conditions and

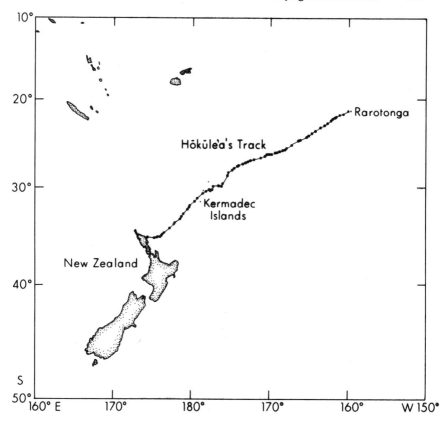

Figure 62. The track of Hōkūleʻa *from Rarotonga to Bay of Islands, showing daily positions.*

consequently slower sailing times of *Rehu Moana* and *Hawaiki Nui* should be kept in mind when estimating how long it would have taken canoes to sail to Aotearoa, the fact remains that despite being slowed by spells of unfavorable winds both craft made it to their destination. Clearly, the experimental voyage of *Hōkūleʻa*, and those of *Hawaiki Nui* and *Rehu Moana*, as well as the many successful crossings between Rarotonga and Aotearoa made by yachts at this time of the year, indicate that the late spring is a good time to sail along this route.[13]

The dangers of trying to sail to Aotearoa earlier in the year had been on our minds as we were working our way to the Bay of Islands because of a bit of intelligence we had picked up just before we left Rarotonga: a brand new yacht being delivered to Auckland had left Rarotonga a month or so before us and then had subsequently disappeared without a trace. Although we had no way of knowing for sure that the vessel had gone down in a storm, it seemed a likely hypothesis judging from the many tales told about yachts running into strong and stormy winter westerlies in these seas. While, for example, we were sailing to Tahiti in 1976, the photographer on board had told about how his father had been lost at sea when the yacht on which he was sailing from Auckland to Tahiti vanished in tempestuous winter seas.

The Chiefly Red of the Pohutukawa

In addition to specifying sailing times in terms of the Māori lunar calendar, Māori traditions contain a more indirect, botanically phrased reference to the time of year when voyages to Aotearoa were supposedly made. In tales about the arrival of the famous *Aotea, Arawa,* and *Tainui* canoes, it is said that the bright red blossoms of the *pohutukawa* tree caught the eye of voyagers as they approached the shore. Thinking that they were seeing immense numbers of red-feathered birds perched in the trees, the weary travelers threw their battered and salt-encrusted *kura,* or red-feather headdresses, into the sea in the expectation of being able to make new ones ashore. "The chiefly color of Hawaiki is cast aside for the chiefly red of the new land that welcomes us," one of the voyagers is said to have exclaimed in anticipation. To his chagrin, and that of his fellow voyagers, upon landing and approaching the trees they realized that what they had really seen were not red-feathered birds but crimson flowers.[14]

We, too, were attracted by the scarlet blossoms we saw on the *pohutukawa* trees around the shore of the Bay of Islands, but for a different reason. The blossoms looked to us just like the *lehua* flower of the *'ōhi'a* tree found in the uplands of Hawai'i, which is not surprising since the *'ōhi'a* and *pohutukawa* are closely related species of the genus *Metrosideros* of the myrtle family.[15] We even discovered later that there is a linguistic tie between these distantly separated species, for the people of Te Aupouri, where Stanley Conrad comes from, call theirs *kahika* which, given the equivalency of the Māori *k* and the Hawaiian glottal stop ('), is a cognate of the Hawaiian *'ōhi'a.*

The close similarity of the two species made us all the more curious as to why the seemingly trivial incident involving the *pohutukawa* blossoms should be so prominent in Māori voyaging tales. Our host, Tai Tokerau leader Hector Busby, had a ready answer for us. He related how when he was a boy the elders of his tribe used to tell him that he should watch for the *pohutukawa* trees to bloom, for that was the time of year when, they told him, "our ancestors arrived from Hawaiki." Along the northeast shore of the North Island these trees bloom in late November and in December, the period which, as our crossing had demonstrated, the slow passage of large high pressure systems make it possible to catch easterly winds all the way to Aotearoa. This story element would therefore seem to encode botanically the best time to sail for Aotearoa, supporting those sailing directions phrased in terms of the lunar calendar that dictate a late spring departure.[16]

7

SAILING BACK AND FORTH
BETWEEN HAWAI‘I AND TAHITI

The voyage *Hōkūle‘a* made in 1976 from Hawai‘i to Tahiti and return set a new standard in experimental voyaging, for it was the first time a reconstructed craft had sailed both ways over a long oceanic course. *Hōkūle‘a*'s passage to Tahiti and back in 1980 replicated the 1976 voyage and extended its significance in that both legs were navigated without instruments. Considered together, the first leg of the Voyage of Rediscovery from Hawai‘i to Tahiti in 1985 and the last leg from Tahiti back to Hawai‘i in 1987 comprise the canoe's third roundtrip between these two Polynesian centers. To have made not one but three roundtrip crossings between such distantly separated islands stands as an accomplishment unparalleled in the field of experimental voyaging, particularly since *Hōkūle‘a* was guided by noninstrument navigation techniques on all legs except the return one to Hawai‘i in 1976.

*With Tai Crouch, Thomas Schroeder, E. Dixon Stroup, Nainoa Thompson, and Elisa Yadao

The Route and the First Two Roundtrips

Although the alignment of the Hawai'i-Tahiti route across the trade winds lends itself to two-way voyaging, it is not totally ideal, for the islands do not fall exactly on a north-south line, and the trade winds do not blow constantly from due east. If Hawai'i and Tahiti were on the same meridian of longitude, and if the trade winds and accompanying currents came directly out of the east, sailing both north and south between the two would present no problem at all. It would simply be a matter of sailing a canoe on a reach across the easterly trade winds, pointing only slightly into the wind in order to make up for leeway and the westward set of the ocean currents that accompany the trades. But the meridian of Tahiti lies hundreds of miles to the east of that of Hawai'i, and the trade wind and current flow varies significantly along the route. In fact, the route crosses three separate wind zones, each with a distinctive ocean current flow: the northeast trade winds, the doldrums, and the southeast trade winds.

Northeast Trade Wind Zone

During the Northern Hemisphere summer, the northeast trade winds are usually dominant roughly from around 28°–30° North (some 400–500 miles north of Hawai'i) to around 9° North (about 600 miles south of Hawai'i). Although these winds are named for the quadrant from which they blow, their actual direction in the zone between Hawai'i and their southern limit is more typically east-northeast than straight northeast. In this zone the North Equatorial Current flows westward with an average speed of about a half a knot, or around 12 nautical miles a day.

Doldrums

Although it is sometimes possible to sail from one trade wind zone to the other without interruption, sailing vessels frequently have to work their way slowly through the doldrums, a band of calms and light, variable winds punctuated by squalls, heavy overcast and rain, and sometimes interrupted by still, cloudless, torrid days. This band is typically 200–300 miles wide and is located during much of the year between approximately 4° and 9°

North. Here the Equatorial Countercurrent flows eastward, typically at around 12–24 miles a day.

Southeast Trade Wind Zone

Although the Southeast trade winds are centered in the Southern Hemisphere, in this part of the Pacific they typically cross over the equator and extend as far north as the southern limit of the doldrums, generally located around 4° North (240 miles from the equator). Although below the equator these winds typically blow from between east and southeast, as they cross the equator and flow toward the low pressure trough of the doldrums they become more southerly, particularly during the summer. Like its Northern Hemisphere counterpart, the South Equatorial Current of this zone flows westward at about 12 miles a day.

The south-southeast slant of the route from Hawai'i to Tahiti means that a canoe has to be worked hard to windward against the trade winds in order to make up the deficit in longitude. The strategy we adopted in 1976 and 1980 was to try and gain as much easting as possible in the northeast trades and the doldrums in order to get to the east of Tahiti, and then, when sailing in the southeast trades, to hold onto as much of that easting as possible in order to keep from being driven to the west of Tahiti. As detailed in chapters 2 and 3, those first two voyages to Tahiti were accomplished more or less as expected. Upon clearing the island of Hawai'i, the east-northeast angle of the trades enabled the canoe to sail to the south-southeast and, before entering the doldrums, to attain a position about 160 miles to the east of the meridian of Tahiti in 1976 and 125 miles to the east in 1980. On both voyages, as the canoe slowly crossed this shifting zone of calms and light variables, the eastward flowing Equatorial Countercurrent gave *Hōkūle'a* a welcome boost eastward, pushing the canoe still farther to the east of Tahiti (to a point about 285 miles to the east of Tahiti in 1976 and 225 miles in 1980). Then, again on both voyages the canoe was able—despite the unfavorable, south-southeast angle of the trade winds encountered immediately upon exiting the doldrums—to hold onto enough of these hard-won miles of easting to make landfall in the western Tuamotus and from there easily sail to Tahiti. Both crossings took slightly over a month—32 days in

1976 (plus 2 days spent at the atoll of Mataiva) and 31 days in 1980—and it was equally remarkable that the landfalls in the Tuamotus were within about 15 miles of each other.[1]

On both crossings, however, some problems were experienced. In 1976 the south-southeast trades encountered upon exiting the doldrums extended much farther south than had been anticipated and pushed the canoe onto a course that would have taken it to the west of Tahiti had not the wind finally become more easterly some 650 miles south of the equator. That shift enabled *Hōkūle'a* to turn back to the south-southeast to make a landfall on Mataiva, the westernmost atoll of the Tuamotus, and from there to sail to Tahiti. In 1980 gale-force trade winds encountered soon after clearing the island of Hawai'i forced the canoe to lower sails and drift for a while and then to tack to the northeast to regain lost easting before continuing on its course to the southeast. Thereafter sailing conditions were fairly mild and the canoe reached first the Tuamotus and then Tahiti without incident.

Both times, the navigation also proceeded more or less as planned. The generally good visibility over the route (except in the doldrums where overcast skies frequently obscured the sun, moon, and stars) enabled Mau Piailug in 1976, and Nainoa Thompson in 1980, to utilize star sights to keep the canoe on the right heading or monitor its heading whenever adverse winds forced the canoe off the intended course. Although in 1976 the novelty of the long route into unfamiliar seas and Southern Hemisphere skies may have made it difficult for Mau Piailug to keep in mind the exact track of the canoe as it curved toward Tahiti, the canoe made landfall in the Tuamotus just about as he had anticipated. In 1980, the postvoyage comparison of the satellite-derived track of the canoe with navigator Nainoa Thompson's estimates of where the canoe was sailing revealed that (except for one period when an unexpectedly strong current affected the canoe) he was fairly accurate in mentally tracking the canoe's progress and in visualizing where the canoe would make landfall in the Tuamotus.

The windward position of Tahiti made the legs home to Hawai'i much easier and faster than the outbound ones. Both times *Hōkūle'a* was able to sail swiftly back, reaching across strong and relatively steady trade winds (with, fortunately, minimal doldrum conditions at the convergence of the southeast and north-

east trade wind systems) to draw abeam Hawai'i in slightly under twenty days in 1976, and in twenty-two days in 1980. From
there, the canoe was able to sail downwind to O'ahu in a few
days to complete the voyages in twenty-two and twenty-six days,
respectively. Although without the services of Mau Piailug the
1976 return to Hawai'i had to be navigated by modern means,
in 1980 Nainoa Thompson employed his noninstrument systems to guide *Hōkūle'a* back to Hawai'i accurately and without
incident.

Because these first two roundtrips had been so successful, we
did not focus on the Hawai'i-Tahiti route when planning the
Voyage of Rediscovery. Instead, we concentrated on those legs
of the voyage where *Hōkūle'a* had not yet sailed, particularly on
those routes where it seemed likely that the canoe might encounter adverse winds or rough weather, such as the route from
Samoa to Tahiti and that from Rarotonga to Aotearoa. This confidence about being able to sail routinely between Hawai'i and
Tahiti was to be shaken by doldrum calms alternating with sharp
squalls where steady trades were expected, winds that blew from
the "wrong" quarter, and scores of land-finding birds that flew
around the canoe when she was still far from land. This recounting of *Hōkūle'a*'s third roundtrip between Hawai'i and Tahiti
highlights these and other seeming anomalies and the problems
they engendered, particularly for navigation, to show how even
under such adverse conditions it is possible to sail a double canoe between these two widely spaced Polynesian centers and to
do so without instruments or other navigational aids.

Hawai'i to Tahiti: 1985

Both in 1976 and in 1980 the canoe had sailed for Tahiti during the early spring in order to have enough time to reach Tahiti
and then sail back to Hawai'i before the late summer when
tropical disturbances, some of which develop into hurricanes,
periodically form far to the southeast of Hawai'i and then spin
northwestward on trajectories that often cross the sailing route
between Hawai'i and Tahiti and occasionally intersect the Hawaiian chain. Because in 1985 the canoe was continuing on to
the Cook Islands and New Zealand after reaching Tahiti, there
was no need for so early a departure in order to be able to get

back to Hawai'i before the summer hurricane season. Nonetheless, a late spring or early summer sailing was scheduled so that the canoe would be at sea when there would be a high probability of steady trades and a low probability of storms. Unfortunately, however, because of delays in arranging for an escort vessel and then getting her ready for the voyage, the canoe was not able to leave until the second week of July, putting her on the seaway to Tahiti several months later than on the previous voyages and at a time when tropical storms begin developing north of the equator.

The Northeast Trade Wind Zone

Early on the afternoon of 10 July, *Hōkūle'a* left her anchorage off the little fishing village of Miloli'i, located on the rugged, lava-strewn South Kona coast of the island of Hawai'i. As the waters off this coast are sheltered from the trades by the massive slopes of Mauna Loa, the canoe did not pick up the trade winds until late that night after she had cleared Ka Lae, the island's southernmost point, and was sailing in seas clear of any obstructions to windward for thousands of miles. With the trades blowing steadily and the canoe riding over the accompanying trade wind swell, the crew settled down to the routine of holding the canoe as close to the wind as possible without losing speed in order to gain maximum easting in the northeast trade wind belt.

Captain Shorty Bertelmann and navigator Nainoa Thompson were joined by ten other crewmen for this first leg of the voyage. These included a number of veteran *Hōkūle'a* sailors: Tava Taupu and Clay Bertelmann from the island of Hawai'i; Harry Ho, Buddy McGuire, and Jim Shizuru from O'ahu; and Mau Piailug from Satawal atoll. Completing the crew were Dr. Larry Magnuson, a physician from Kaua'i who served as the canoe's doctor; Richard "Tai" Crouch, a former student of mine who, after earning a B.A. degree in anthropology and an M.A. in Pacific Islands Studies at the University of Hawai'i, was teaching at Honolulu's Punahou School; Dennis Chun, the coordinator of the Hawaiian Studies program at Kaua'i Community College; and Thomas Reity, Mau's nephew and apprentice from the island of Satawal.

The satellite-derived track (fig. 63) shows that *Hōkūle'a* made

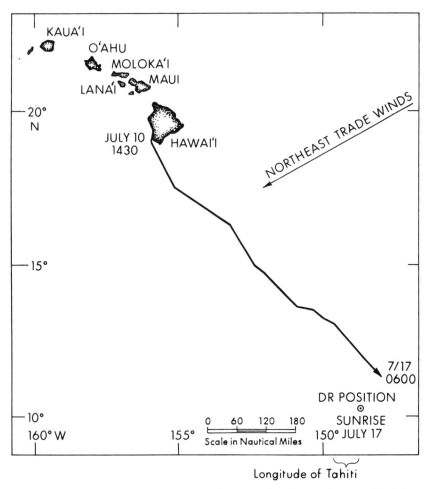

Figure 63. Making easting in the northeast trades during first week of the 1985 voyage of Hōkūle'a from Hawai'i to Tahiti.

good progress to the east as she slanted across the trades during this first segment of the voyage, for the canoe reached 148° West longitude, a degree east of the meridian of Tahiti, on the morning of 17 July after just six and a half days at sea. Compared to the eastward position reached by the canoe in 1976 and in 1980 at the same latitude (11° North; 660 miles north of the equator), at this stage of the voyage the canoe was making much better progress to windward than on the previous two crossings.

Although the overall direction of the wind, averaging between east-northeast and northeast, was favorable for gaining easting, the weather conditions were unexpectedly uneven. The clear skies and fairly steady winds enjoyed upon clearing Ka Lae had soon given way to heavy cloud cover, shifting winds, and the occasional squall. Then, on the 14th, at about 13° 30′ North, the canoe ran into a weak tropical disturbance that brought sharp squalls with strong, variable winds and heavy downpours, alternating with periods of absolute, oily calm. At first, Nainoa had interpreted these conditions to mean that the canoe had entered the doldrums, raising the unwanted prospect that this zone might then be especially wide and consequently would delay the canoe for longer than the week it took to transit the doldrums in 1976. To everyone's relief, however, after a couple of days of this disturbed weather trade wind conditions returned, indicating that the canoe had not yet reached the doldrums.

During this period Nainoa and the crew were able to keep the canoe headed southeast, despite the shifting winds that required constant adjustments in steering and periods of total cloud cover when the canoe had to be guided by the swells, which was not at all easy to do in the confused seas engendered by the frequent wind shifts. At this time Nainoa's dead reckoning calculations were fairly close to the actual track of the canoe, although toward the end of that first week he was beginning to place the canoe to the southwest of its true position. For example, at sunrise on 17 July, when the canoe was actually at about 11° 20′ North and 148° 05′ West, Nainoa placed her about 70 miles to the southwest (fig. 63).[2]

The Doldrums

On the afternoon of the 17th, the trade winds died again. There followed over the next six days classical doldrum conditions: calms, punctuated with squalls and spells of wind that shifted all around the compass, as well as periods of heavy cloud cover and soaking rains. An infrared weather satellite image (fig. 64) shows a markedly cloudy convergence zone that blanketed the region until the 22nd, when it began weakening as tropical storm Ignacio approached several hundred miles to the east-northeast of the canoe. At that point, however, the canoe was not yet out of the doldrums; throughout the daylight hours of the 22nd and far into the night squall after squall struck the canoe.

Hōkūleʻa

Figure 64. Infrared satellite image of heavy cloud cover on the afternoon of 17 July 1985 as Hōkūleʻa *enters the doldrums.*

Not until the morning of the 23rd did the skies really clear and steady winds come back for the first time in almost a week, indicating, it seemed, that the canoe had exited the doldrums and entered the zone of southeast trade winds. At this point the canoe was at about 7° 30′ North, which meant that the doldrums, entered at 11° North, had been several degrees north of where they had been encountered in 1976 and 1980. Only after the voyage when we examined weather records did we realize that at this time of year the doldrums are often displaced to the north, for the convergence zone between the two trade wind belts shifts progressively northward as the summer wears on and does not migrate southward until the Northern Hemisphere begins to cool with the coming of winter. Similarly, our retrospective study of weather records reminded us that the encounter with the small tropical disturbance just before reaching the doldrums, and then the approach of tropical storm Ignacio, were also not that unusual for this time of year, as the frequency of tropical disturbances in this region goes up with the increased warming as the summer wears on.

The Southeast Trade Wind Zone

As expected, the trade winds encountered upon exiting the doldrums had a marked southerly component that forced the canoe onto a course slightly to the west of south. This led Nainoa to consider tacking to the east, for he was worried that the canoe may not have gained enough easting in the northeast trades and the doldrums and that the long spell coming up of sailing in the southeast trade wind belt might see them driven to the west of Tahiti. He nonetheless decided to remain on the port tack, for to go over on the starboard tack would mean that the canoe would be heading slightly north of east. The miles of easting to be gained on that tack would have been welcome, but the northerly component of the course would have eventually taken the canoe back into the doldrums region, something definitely to be avoided. So, there was nothing to be done but to keep the canoe sailing on the port tack as close to the wind as possible and hope that after they crossed the equator the winds would start coming more out of the east than the south.

Throughout this first day in the southeast trades, the 23rd, and well into the following night, Nainoa kept the canoe on the port tack. According to Nainoa's reckoning, after factoring in leeway and current drift to the west, this resulted in the track curving toward the southwest. Then, at about one in the morning of the 24th a squall hit with winds gusting up to 50 knots, forcing the crew to lower the sails to the deck. After the squall had passed and the sails were raised, another squall hit, and the sails were lowered again. After drifting with sails down until dawn, a wind sprang up from the south. This time Nainoa decided to take the opportunity to tack in order to gain easting and so gave the order to raise the sails and go onto the starboard tack. The canoe stayed on that tack—first heading due east, then, as the wind shifted a little toward the south-southeast, slightly north of east—until early in the afternoon when the wind became more easterly and Nainoa had the canoe put back onto the port tack to resume sailing southward.

During this period between sunrise on 23 July and the early afternoon of the 24th Nainoa's dead reckoning estimates began to diverge significantly from the satellite track of the canoe. Where the satellite fixes indicated that the track started to curve slightly southeastward, then made an abrupt turn to the east followed by a slight swing to the north, Nainoa estimated that *Hōkūle'a* continued to sail toward the southwest. So, by the morning of the 25th when the canoe was actually at about 6° 15′ South and 146° 45′ West, Nainoa's dead reckoning placed *Hōkūle'a* over 200 miles to the west-southwest of there (fig. 65).

It is not clear from the notes and tape recordings made during the voyage, or from Nainoa's recollections after the voyage, exactly why he reckoned that the canoe was being pushed by wind and current toward the southwest when her track seems in fact to have curved toward the east. A simple mental slip of not including in his dead reckoning the tack eastward on the morning of the 24th would account for only part of the difference, as before then Nainoa's position estimates and the satellite fixes had already begun to diverge, perhaps because he did not anticipate the effect of the eastward-flowing Equatorial Countercurrent.

The speed of the Equatorial Countercurrent, which is typically encountered in the doldrum belt between about 4° and 9° North, varies seasonally, generally being weakest in May–June and strongest (approaching 1 knot, on the average) in September–November. Nor is its speed uniform across the width of the flow; faster and slower bands can occur in an unpredictable pattern.

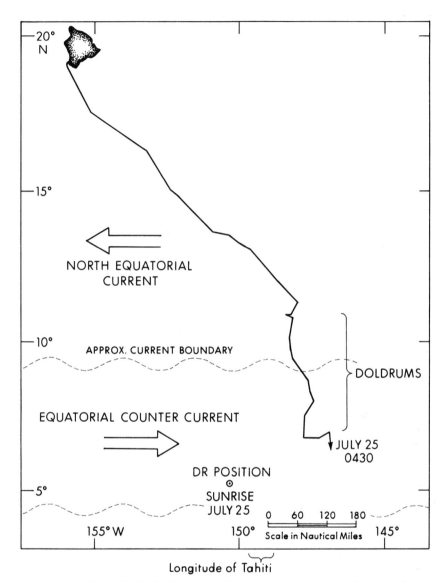

Figure 65. Through the doldrums and into the southeast trades, 25 July 1985.

In 1976 and again in 1980 *Hōkūleʻa*'s track bulged markedly to the east when crossing the doldrums, indicating the effect of the Countercurrent. In contrast, the 1985 track shows no such marked deviation eastward while transiting the doldrums, which is not surprising since the doldrums were encountered above the usual northern limit of the Countercurrent. Only during the last day and a half of doldrum conditions, after *Hōkūle'a* had crossed 9° North, did the canoe's course turn slightly to the southeast, which may indicate that she was then in an outlying band of the Countercurrent, though probably not the main stream, for toward the end of the doldrums the canoe's course turned back toward the southwest. When, on the first day out of the dol-drums (23 July), the canoe's course began curving back toward the southeast, *Hōkūle'a* may have actually entered the main body of the eastward-flowing current, particularly since at the time Nainoa was sure that the canoe was heading southwest. Then, the sharp turn of the course eastward when the canoe was drifting with sails down in the early hours of the 24th would seem to indicate that *Hōkūle'a* was then in the grip of a strongly flowing Countercurrent band. If so, when the canoe was tacked east just after sunset, this current would have accelerated her progress eastward.

Whatever the exact cause of the sudden widening of the gap between the estimated and actual course of the canoe—a mem-ory lapse about tacking east, the unperceived effects of the Equa-torial Countercurrent, or more probably a combination of these—the toll on Nainoa's mental concentration of the unexpectedly adverse weather conditions experienced so far must have been a contributing factor. Particularly after the wildly shifting con-ditions of the first few days and the unwelcome encounter with a tropical disturbance right before entering the doldrums, these northerly displaced doldrums and their debilitating calms, squalls, and overcast skies were particularly hard on the navigator. To be constantly working to catch whatever wind there was while making sure sudden squalls did not overwhelm the canoe was tiring enough. But the added tasks of keeping the canoe on course by reading vague clues from the confused swell pattern when leaden skies denied any view of stars or sun, and of keeping in mind all the twists and turns of the track in order to have a men-tal picture of where the canoe was at all times, had utterly ex-hausted Nainoa.

On the 23rd, once the canoe finally cleared the doldrums and was back in trade winds, Nainoa voiced his concerns about the problems he was having keeping his mind on the situation:

> The thing that has been so hard about these days is that I can't go to
> sleep because if I go to sleep we'll have no idea of where we're go-

ing. That's what is so tough about this kind of adverse weather . . . you can't rest. It is showing that when I am fatigued my thinking is not clear. I know I'm making mental errors. I'm in the position where I need rest to keep my head clear, but I can't because of the situation.

The westward deviation of Nainoa's dead reckoning estimates from the canoe's actual course greatly increased when Nainoa apparently overestimated the westward set of the South Equatorial Current as the canoe was sailing southward toward and then across the equator. At that time, Nainoa reckoned that the canoe's track was being displaced just slightly to the west of south by the westward-flowing current that typically accompanies the southeast trade winds. The satellite track shows, however, that the canoe was sailing virtually due south, with only some minor deviations first to one side and then to the other. As a result, at dawn on 1 August when the satellite fix showed the canoe to be at 3° 22′ South and 146° 59′ West, Nainoa's reckoning placed her almost 300 miles to the west-southwest of where she actually was (fig. 66).

The tape-recorded interviews made during this period indicate that Nainoa was extremely worried about the possibility that ever since they had entered the doldrums the current had been setting strongly toward the west, each day skewing the canoe's course farther in that direction. For example, after exiting the doldrums Nainoa speculated that there may have been no countercurrent at all in the doldrums and that instead "all the days we sat there we were getting shoved to the west." Then, while sailing southward after the doldrums, he frequently referred in his interviews to the danger that a continued current flow westward might push them farther and farther to the west. At one point, Nainoa and interviewer Tai Crouch even joked that the canoe might end up being driven so far to the west as to make landfall on Maupiti, a small high island that is the westernmost permanently inhabited island in the Society chain.

Part of Nainoa's concern about a strong current set to the west may have stemmed from the unsettling experience on the 1980 voyage, recounted in chapter 3, when a swift but unperceived current jet pushed the canoe 90 miles to the west. Although after the 1985 voyage Nainoa did not recall having been especially worried about being again driven westward by another such unperceived current jet, in his interview on 27 July with Tai Crouch he mentions that the canoe was then nearing

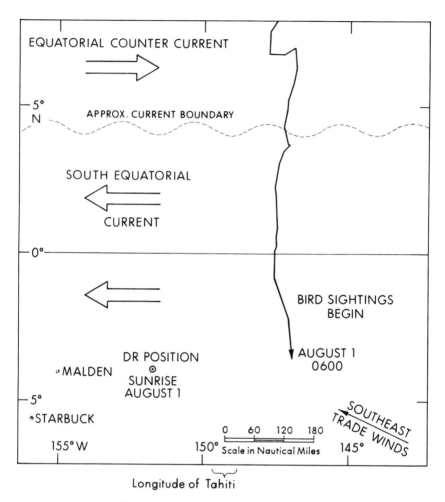

Figure 66. Across the equator and into the Southern Hemisphere, 1 August 1985.

the latitude of 3° North where *Hōkūle'a* encountered the current jet in 1980 and speculates that they might again be set west by such a current.

Whatever contributed to this overestimate of westward current set, it is important to note that Nainoa had no way to check his estimates of how far the canoe was being pushed to the west by reference to the stars. Unlike estimates of movement north or south which can continually be checked and revised with ob-

servations of Polaris or other stars that yield a measure of latitude from their elevation above the horizon, there is no way for
Nainoa to determine movement east or west through sighting
on the stars, for to do so would require a chronometer in order
to calculate longitude. Because Nainoa has no means to check
and revise his estimates of movement along the east-west axis,
there is always the danger that misestimates can accumulate in
one direction, skewing his dead reckoning farther and farther to
the east or west. Although in 1980 the failure to perceive the
strong current set to the west when the canoe was just north of
the equator was later offset by an overestimation of the westward set of the current south of the equator, on this voyage Nainoa's misestimates of current set were mostly additive, leading
to a progressively greater divergence westward of his dead reckoning relative to the actual track.

Further complicating the situation after the canoe crossed the
equator were numerous sightings of land-finding birds: primarily what appeared to be white fairy terns, called *manu-o-Kū*
in Hawaiian (literally "bird-of-*Kū*," one of the major Hawaiian
gods), plus some grayish terns that looked like the Hawaiian
noddy tern (*noio*) and a few booby birds and frigate birds. Seeing
a few stray booby birds was no cause for alarm, for as had been
shown by a similar sighting far from land in 1976, juvenile boobies without nesting responsibilities often wander widely over
the ocean. But starting at about 2° South, the almost daily sightings of snow-white fairy terns flying singly and in small flocks
could not be so easily discounted, for these birds have a reputation of seldom straying in any number more than 50 miles or so
from land.

When the birds were first spotted at the end of July, Nainoa
reckoned that they might possibly be coming from Malden and
Starbuck, isolated coral outposts in the Southern Line Islands located far to the west of the intended course to Tahiti. But although the bird sightings tended to reinforce his belief that the
canoe had been set far to the west by the South Equatorial Current, the more Nainoa thought about it, the less sure he was, for
he reckoned that these islands were still 200 miles to the west
of where he thought the canoe was, too far away to be the source
of the birds. (At the time the islands were actually about 500
miles west of the canoe's position; fig. 66.)

This perplexing situation led Nainoa to speculate that either the current had set the canoe much farther to the west than he had assumed, or that he was mistaken in his identification of the birds as fairy terns, or, alternatively, that the fairy terns in this part of the Pacific have a greater range than those he was familiar with in Hawaiian and Tahitian waters. Close-up sightings of these birds in the following days confirmed that indeed they were fairy terns, but the question of whether or not sighting these birds meant that the canoe had been pushed as far west as the Southern Line Islands was not to be satisfactorily resolved until the end of the voyage.

On 2 August, the canoe sailed into a zone of convergence with doldrum-like cloudy skies, squalls, calms, and variable winds that lasted for four days, leading the crew to call it the "second doldrums." Passage through this disturbance further exhausted Nainoa, making it even more difficult for him to deal with the issue of whether or not they were sailing as far west as the Southern Line Islands. Although Nainoa tended to assume the worst-case scenario that the bird sightings confirmed that they were passing close by the Southern Line Islands, he continued to suspect that the sightings might be false clues of the close proximity of land. For example, during the evening interview on 5 August, Nainoa speculated that his reckoning might be so far off that instead of sailing in the longitude of the Southern Line Islands, the canoe could actually be sailing directly toward the Tuamotus. The next morning, when his reckoning told him that the canoe should be passing between Caroline and Vostok islands, Nainoa said that if no birds were seen they might indeed be sailing north of the Tuamotus instead of farther to the west.

But many terns were seen throughout the next day, apparently confirming that they actually were near Caroline and Vostok. Yet, because the birds followed a pattern of flying out from the west, and then returning to the west, Nainoa concluded they had not passed between Caroline and Vostok islands as anticipated, but had passed to the east of the islands. The birds, he reasoned, must have been flying out to fish in seas to the east of Caroline Island (the easternmost of the two islands), and then returning westward to that island to feed their chicks and nest there for the night. Accordingly, Nainoa revised his reckoning to bring the estimated position of the canoe to the east of Caroline (fig. 67).

But the next day, 8 August, Nainoa started shifting his as-

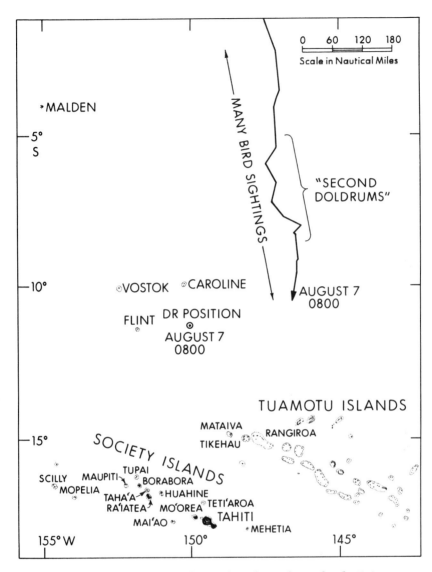

Figure 67. Passing to the east of Vostok and Caroline islands, 7 August 1985.

sumed position back toward the west, for according to his latitude estimates based on star sights the previous nights the canoe
should have then been approaching the latitude of the northernmost of the Tuamotu Islands. Since he saw no signs of land—
either from birds flying out to sea from islands to the south-

east, floating debris, or the blockage of the southeast trade wind
swells—that indicated they were nearing this extensive archipelago, Nainoa reverted to his earlier assumption of the extreme westward set of the canoe, and once again began worrying about being driven so far west as to be lucky to make land
at Maupiti at the far western end of the Societies.

That evening of 8 August the wind shifted to almost due
east, allowing the canoe's track to trend to the east of south, giving Nainoa hope that they might make a landfall on Borabora or
Taha'a, the two high islands immediately to the east of Mau-

piti. The following day, the 9th, flocks of birds and a change in the swell pattern, plus a glimpse of a passing aircraft, led to the expectation that land was very near. As night fell and fairy terns repeatedly flew directly over the canoe, Nainoa and the crew anxiously searched for land but could see nothing. Rather than keep sailing southward and risk running aground on the barrier reef of whatever island was out there, the sails were lowered to the deck and the canoe drifted while everyone continued looking for land in the darkness.

Finally, a few hours before dawn, in the dim moonlight, sharp-eyed Thomas Reity, Mau's nephew, spotted the tops of coconut palms poking above the horizon. *Hōkūle'a* had made landfall on an atoll. But which atoll was it: one of those scattered along the northern edge of the Societies, or one in western Tuamotus? Here Nainoa's estimate of the canoe's latitude was crucial. Mataiva, Tikehau, and Rangiroa at the western end of the Tuamotus all lie at about 15° South, whereas the atoll outliers of the Societies are just a little north of 16° South. So, when his star observations indicated that the canoe was at about 16° South, Nainoa ruled out the Tuamotu atolls in favor of those along the northern edge of the Societies. Since Nainoa did not think the canoe had been driven as far west as the atolls of Bellingshausen or Scilly at the far western end of the Societies, his choice fell on Tupai, a small atoll just to the north of Borabora.

As the canoe started sailing westward along the coast of the atoll, it became apparent, however, that they could not have made landfall on tiny Tupai, which is only about 4 miles long, for the morning light revealed the vista of coconut palms stretching in both directions as far as the eye could see. They had reached the Tuamotus after all, Nainoa concluded, because neither Tupai nor any of the other Society Island atolls is large enough to present such a scene. He even correctly surmised that it was Rangiroa, because of the great length, 44 miles, of this largest of Tuamotus atolls (fig. 68).

It took much of the day to sail westward along the coast of Rangiroa, round its western cape, and then pass through the channel between it and the atoll of Tikehau just to the west. At a little after noon on the next day, Sunday 12 August, after an uneventful passage to Tahiti made reaching across the trades, *Hōkūle'a* sailed into the lagoon and landed at Ta'aone beach a few miles to the northeast of Pape'ete harbor to complete the voyage thirty-two days after leaving Miloli'i.

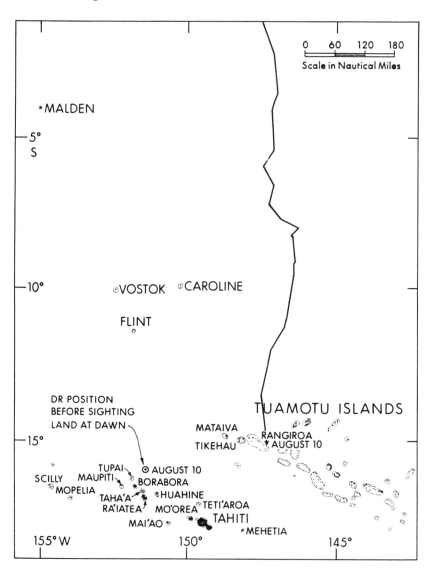

Figure 68. Landfall on Rangiroa atoll, 10 August 1985.

A Voyage of Surprises

Compared to the first two trips to Tahiti, this third crossing had been full of surprises: the displacement of the doldrums several degrees north of where they had been located the previous two voyages, the equally unexpected encounters with a small depression immediately north of the doldrums, and then, south of the equator, the spell of doldrum-like conditions and the repeated sightings of fairy terns and other land-nesting birds when the canoe was really hundreds of miles from land. These unanticipated conditions made the voyage more difficult, especially for Nainoa who overestimated both how far the canoe had been set west by the current and its progress southward. The latter was not simply a matter of overestimating the speed of the canoe: all but the first three of Nainoa's latitude estimates based on star observations were too far to the south by an average of slightly over 50 miles. Whatever the exact cause of these overestimates—fatigue from the weather conditions, lack of practice (it had been five years since the last time Nainoa had undertaken to navigate over such a long route) or a combination of these and perhaps other factors—during the last two-thirds of the voyage they combined to skew Nainoa's dead reckoning positions to the west-southwest of the canoe's actual course (fig. 69).

Nonetheless, despite these difficult conditions and navigational problems they caused or at least made worse, *Hōkūle'a* made its landfall on Rangiroa in the northwest Tuamotus close to the 1976 and 1980 landfalls (about 70 miles east of the 1976 landfall on Mataiva, and some 55 miles east of the 1980 landfall on Tikehau), and from there sailed without difficulty to Tahiti just as had been done in 1976 and 1980. Although the eastward curve of the track of the 1985 voyage is more irregular than those of the two previous voyages, figure 70 shows how on all three voyages the canoe followed more or less the same curving route to Tahiti through the three wind and current zones. Clearly, even given the far from ideal conditions encountered in 1985, the voyage between Hawai'i and Tahiti is well within the capabilities of a double canoe such as *Hōkūle'a*.

In terms of noninstrument navigation, landfall on Tahiti would also appear to be repeatedly attainable—primarily because Tahiti is not a lone island lost in the vastness of the open ocean, but is one of many islands that form an arc extending eastward from Bellingshausen atoll at the western end of the Societies for over a thousand miles to the atolls on the eastern fringe of the Tuamotus. It would be difficult, though not at all impossible, for a competently crewed canoe approaching from Hawai'i to slip through this long arc without anyone aboard spotting an island. Once any island along the arc was sighted, then identi-

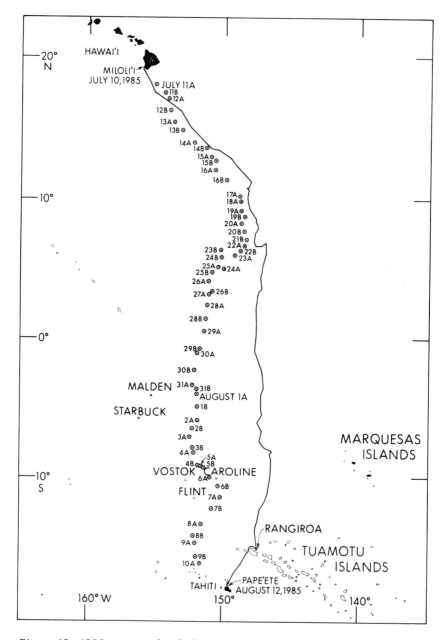

Figure 69. 1985 voyage of Hōkūle'a *from Hawai'i to Tahiti showing actual track of the canoe and Nainoa Thompson's dead reckoning (D.R.) positions estimated at sunrise (marked by "A" following the date) and sunset (marked by "B" following the date).*

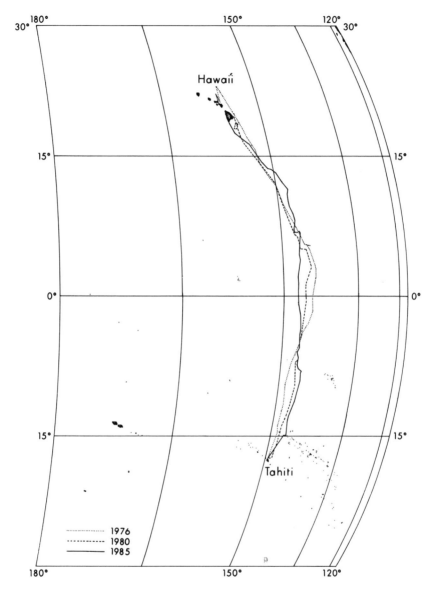

Figure 70. 1976, 1980, and 1985 voyages of Hōkūle'a *from Hawai'i to Tahiti.*

fied, a navigator acquainted with the Societies and Tuamotus would then know the direction and bearing to Tahiti and, given the right wind conditions, could sail there. Thus a landfall anywhere along the Society or Tuamotu chains should enable a canoe to reach Tahiti.

Had Nainoa's worst-case scenario come true with landfall at the western end of the Societies, *Hōkūle'a* could still have made it from there to Tahiti, either by laboriously tacking to windward or waiting for more favorable northerly or westerly winds. But there turned out to be no need to resort to either of these tactics. Nainoa may have reckoned that the canoe had missed the Tuamotus and been driven to the west of Tahiti, but just as occurred on the last two voyages *Hōkūle'a* had arrived off the western Tuamotus, the ideal location along the Society-Tuamotu island arc to make landfall on the way to Tahiti. Although the dead reckoning may have been somewhat off on this first leg of the voyage, steadfast application of the strategy of sailing hard against the trades succeeded once again in bringing the canoe safely to Tahiti.

Tahiti to Hawai'i: 1987

After sailing from Samoa to Tahiti in mid-1986, *Hōkūle'a* was hauled onto dry land at the village of Tautira at the eastern end of the island. There, under the able direction of Mayor Tutaha Salmon, our Tahitian friends erected a shelter over the canoe, while the crew returned to Hawai'i.

Early in the Northern Hemisphere spring of 1987 an advance party flew down from Hawai'i to put the canoe back into the water and ready her for the voyage north. Instead of returning directly to Hawai'i, as was done in 1976 and 1980, the plan was to sail home via the Marquesas. That rugged archipelago, not the Society Islands, is the leading candidate for the homeland of the original settlers of Hawai'i—primarily because the Hawaiian language appears to be more closely related to Marquesan (specifically Southern Marquesan) than Tahitian or any other Polynesian language. The plan was to sail first to the Marquesas and from there head for Hawai'i following the sea trail over which, if the language relationship is telling, the first voyagers to discover Hawai'i may have set sail some 1,500 to 2,000 years ago.

Because the Marquesas lie far to the east, to windward, of the meridian of Hawai'i, we were anticipating a swift passage home from there sailing on a broad reach. Sailing the 700 miles from Tahiti northeast to the Marquesas posed a problem, however (fig. 71). To sail there on one tack would require winds almost directly out of the southeast, yet in this region the trades most commonly come from somewhere between east and east-

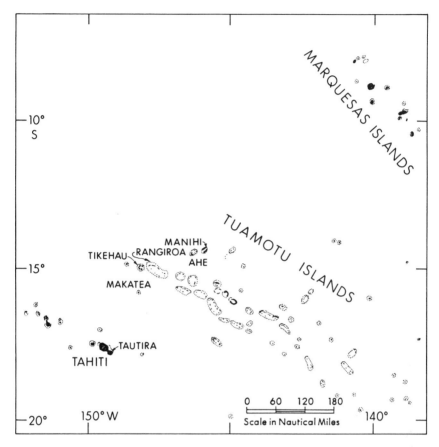

Figure 71. Tahiti, the Tuamotus, and the Marquesas.

southeast. Furthermore, a direct route would take a canoe into an area of the Tuamotus where the islands are especially closely spaced, leaving little room to maneuver, particularly if sailing hard on the wind. To wait at Tahiti for a spell of westerly winds in order to get a boost directly to the east was a possibility but one fraught with danger, for that would mean heading straight into the Tuamotus with boisterous winds pushing the canoe, and a high probability of overcast skies and poor visibility along the horizon. That would be a sure recipe for disaster when approaching any atoll chain, but particularly so for the Tuamotus, which the eighteenth-century navigator Bougainville had so aptly named the "Dangerous Archipelago" because of its many reefs and the swiftly flowing currents between them.

Rather than tempt fate, Nainoa decided on a more prudent strategy. First, he would wait on Tahiti for fair, trade wind conditions and then sail directly to the Rangiroa located 170 miles to the north-northeast at the western end of the Tuamotu chain. Once there, he would wait for a spell of steady trades with a strong southerly component in order to be able to sail to the northeast and try to make it to the Marquesas on one long tack.

Normally, it would have been advisable to wait at least until late May or early June to attempt this sail, for by then the unsettled weather of the Austral summer usually gives way to a pattern of trade wind dominance. But *Hōkūle'a* was scheduled to be back in Hawai'i by 23 May for a welcoming ceremony planned as major part of the statewide "Year of the Hawaiian" celebration. This made it necessary to leave by late March at the latest in order to have enough time to make it to Rangiroa, wait there for the right winds to reach the Marquesas, and then sail from there to Hawai'i. Such an early departure meant that *Hōkūle'a* would be sailing before the trade wind pattern of the Austral winter months might be fully established.

Tautira to Rangiroa

On previous legs of the Voyage of Rediscovery Nainoa and the crew had been experimenting with larger sails than had been used on earlier voyages. Although the regular sails were well adapted for sailing in strong winds, the new, larger sails were designed to make the canoe sail faster in light winds, a particular advantage for going to windward when forward speed is all important. On this final leg home, these experiments were taken a step further by putting an extra-large sail on the after mast, increasing sail area and changing the balance of the rig in that the after sail was then larger than the forward sail. To accommodate this rigging change, Wally Froiseth, an expert craftsman and long-time *Hōkūle'a* sailor, scarfed onto the after mast and boom the extensions needed in order to carry the big sail. In addition, the step for the after mast was moved forward almost six feet to the next *'iako*, as Hawaiians call the cross beams linking the hulls, to balance the forces acting on the sails and the hull so that the canoe could be more easily steered, as well as to make it easier to sheet in the larger sail.[3]

The canoe was ready to sail in late March, but first a ceremonial visit to Pape'ete was in order to inaugurate a striking stone structure, loosely modeled on an ancient *marae* and dedicated to *Hōkūle'a*, that the City had erected at the beach where the canoe had first landed in 1976. On 29 March, after the ceremonies, *Hōkūle'a* returned to Tautira to wait for a spell of steady trade winds to make the 170-mile trip to Rangiroa. But light, variable winds and overcast skies kept the canoe from leaving until the morning of 2 April, when a breeze from east-southeast started blowing. Unfortunately, after sailing three hours northward, the wind started coming out of the north-northeast, forcing the canoe onto a course west of north. Then it became light and variable, and rain squalls swept over the canoe. By evening the canoe had been forced back to a point about 10 miles northeast of Tautira, where she was hove to for the night.

An easterly wind started blowing before dawn, and at mid-morning the canoe got underway again. Three-quarters of the way to Rangiroa was the upraised coral island of Makatea, which, if it could be spotted during the night, would give an exact fix for a landfall on Rangiroa for the following morning. Although there was some concern that the canoe might be set to the west of the island by the current, several hours before dawn the dark outline of Makatea appeared to port, giving the needed navigational fix. Late that morning land-nesting birds were sighted. Then, a half hour later a line of surf, then the sight of coconut palms, announced the presence of land ahead. Nainoa correctly assumed that they had made landfall on Rangiroa and so turned the canoe westward to sail along its southern shore and then north through the channel between Rangiroa and the neighboring atoll of Tikehau. The canoe then entered Avatoru, the main pass at the northwest end of Rangiroa, and anchored in the atoll's huge lagoon.[4]

Waiting for the Trades

Once anchored at Rangiroa, those who had joined the crew just for the Tautira-Rangiroa leg flew back to Tahiti, and from there on to Hawai'i, while new crew members flew in to replace them. For the return to Hawai'i, Shorty Bertelmann and Nainoa Thompson were serving as captain and navigator, respectively. Six other experienced *Hōkūle'a* sailors anchored the crew: Tava Taupu, originally from the Marquesas but long resident on the island of Hawai'i; Chad Baybayan and Snake Ah Hee from Maui; Bruce Blankenfeld and Mike Tongg from O'ahu; and from Kaua'i, Dr. Pat Aiu, who was again serving as the canoe's doctor. Five additional crewmen represented the main island groups where the canoe had stopped along the way: Puaniho Tauotaha, a champion racing canoe paddler from Tautira, Tahiti; Tua Pittman, the Cook Islander who had made the crossing from Samoa to Aitutaki; Stanley Conrad, the Māori youth who had sailed from Rarotonga to his native Aotearoa; Sione Taupeamuhu, the skilled Tongan sailor who had piloted the canoe through the reef-strewn Ha'apai Archipelago; and Eni Hunkin, a Samoan high chief, who was also the Lieutenant-Governor of American Samoa. Rounding out this diverse crew were: University of Hawai'i oceanographer Dixon Stroup, a longtime board member of the Polynesian Voyaging Society, and reporter Elisa Yadao and cameraman Cliff Watson of Honolulu's television station KGMB, who were making a documentary of the voyage.

To sail to the Marquesas, a steady wind from the southeast, or south-southeast, would have been ideal. That would have enabled the canoe to sail northeast, safely clear Ahe and Manihi atolls that lie just to the east-northeast of Rangiroa, and then head directly for the Marquesas some 500 miles farther to the northeast. Unfortunately, however, the wind started coming out of the northeast, and over the next two and a half weeks varied between northeast and northwest. These unwelcome northerly winds, often accompanied by overcast skies and spells of rain,

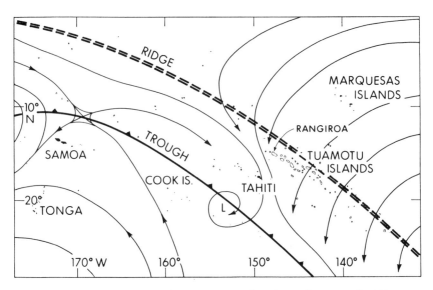

Figure 72. Surface wind analysis 7:00 P.M. (local time), 16 April 1987, showing El Niño trough bringing westerly winds to Tahiti and northerly wind to the Tuamotus.

blocked *Hōkūle'a* from leaving Rangiroa, for they were from the worst possible quarter for sailing to the Marquesas. To be sure, they might have allowed the canoe to sail eastward to reach the longitude of the Marquesas (from where, if the wind then shifted back to the trade wind direction, the canoe could head north for that archipelago). But the sea directly to the east of Rangiroa is filled with atolls. Although Nainoa could have tried to thread the canoe past these, he judged the risk to be too great, and so *Hōkūle'a* remained tied up in the Rangiroa lagoon.

This long delay forced abandonment of the plan to sail home via the Marquesas, for there was simply not enough time left to try to reach that archipelago and still make it back to Hawai'i for the 23 May celebration. To make matters worse, these northerly winds were far from ideal for sailing directly back to Hawai'i. To be sure, at times the canoe could have headed northwest or west-northwest on the starboard tack, but it would not have taken too many days of sailing on such a course to have put the canoe to the west of the meridian of Hawai'i—when the navigational strategy called for an approach from the eastern, windward side of the islands.

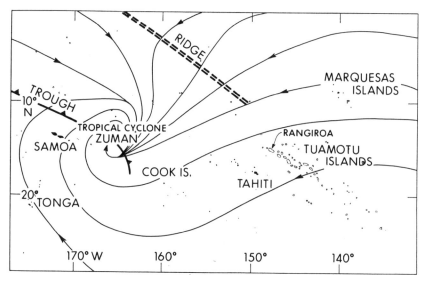

Figure 73. Surface wind analysis 7:00 P.M. (local time), 23 April 1987, showing tropical cyclone Zuman disrupting El Niño trough, bringing easterly winds to the Tuamotus.

These anomalous northerlies were apparently part of a widespread El Niño disruption of atmospheric and ocean circulation that had been developing over the South Pacific during the Austral summer of that year and was extending into the early fall.[5] The monsoon trough of the southwestern Pacific had shifted eastward, bringing the northerlies that were keeping *Hōkūle'a* from sailing (fig. 72). A break in these winds did not come until after almost three weeks of frustrating waiting in the lagoon of Rangiroa. Such a monsoon trough is a spawning ground for tropical cyclones,[6] and at this time a tropical cyclone formed to the north of Samoa in the El Niño–extended trough and began to affect wind flow to the east. As the surface wind analysis in figure 73 indicates, by the evening of 23 April, this cyclone, christened Zuman and by then located at 16° South and 168° West, was bringing an easterly wind flow over Rangiroa.

The Southeast Trade Wind Zone

The next afternoon, on 24 April, twenty days after arriving at Rangiroa, *Hōkūle'a* finally cleared the pass and headed for the equator 900 miles away. The desired heading was not due north,

but somewhat east of north so that by the time the canoe entered the northeast trade wind zone she would be well east of
the meridian of Hawai'i. Fair skies marked by only a few cumulus clouds and a 15-knot breeze blowing out of the east-
southeast which enabled the canoe to make good a course
toward the north-northeast led everyone to hope that the unwelcome conditions that had kept the canoe at Rangiroa were
over at last and that they would have a swift crossing to Hawai'i.

Hopes for uninterrupted trade wind sailing held up only until
around midnight, when a series of intense squalls forced the
sails to be triced, leaving the canoe to drift aimlessly until the
trades returned a few hours after dawn. But the gusty winds that
soon developed proved to be too strong for the big sail then
being carried on the after mast, and a smaller, heavy weather
sail had to be substituted. Even with this smaller sail, the canoe
was able to make a good 6 knots in the trades, which sometimes
reached 30 knots or more. Strong winds continued throughout
the 25th and into the 26th when they shifted to the north of
east and forced the canoe onto a heading almost due north.

At midmorning on the 26th, when the canoe was at about
10° 50' South and 146° 35' West, Nainoa spread into the sparkling blue sea the ashes of Dan Wright, the owner and skipper of the escort vessel *Dorcas*, who had tragically died from a
sudden illness that struck him while the yacht was anchored
off Mo'orea after the leg from Rarotonga to Tahiti. Having the
Dorcas, crewed so competently by Dan and his family, shadow
the canoe throughout the Voyage of Rediscovery had proved
to be invaluable from the point of view of documentation and
safety. At this point, however, the broad-beamed cruising yacht—
now being sailed by a hired captain and crew—was having trouble keeping up with the fast-moving *Hōkūle'a*. Several times
during this period of strong trades, the crew was forced to trice
the sails as the *Dorcas* faded from sight astern and each time
wait a couple of hours for the yacht to catch up.

At about 10:30 on the night of 27 April, after a day and a half
of boisterous winds, the sails went limp, leaving *Hōkūle'a* to
drift at about 9° South (540 miles from the equator) until dawn
when light easterlies began blowing. These held for several
hours, until the wind veered to the north, then west of north,
forcing the canoe to tack to the east. At this point Nainoa, who
was then correctly estimating that the canoe was less than 300

miles due west of the Marquesas, reckoned that if the wind held and they could keep heading east there might still be a chance to call on these islands. Unfortunately, the northerly winds lightened late that afternoon, then went flat at around 10:00 P.M., eliminating, to everyone's disappointment, the last possibility for making a call upon this remote archipelago that is thought to have played a vital role in the early history of Hawai'i.

At dawn on the 29th a light wind started coming out of the south, then the southeast, allowing the canoe to slowly sail in a direction slightly east of north. Although the canoe was once again on the desired course of north by east, by now Nainoa was thoroughly disillusioned with the idea that after their long wait on Rangiroa they might enjoy smooth trade wind sailing back to Hawai'i. In his tape interview that morning, Nainoa stressed how the "weird weather" of this voyage—the squalls, calms, and northerly winds—erased any notion that the ancient Polynesian voyagers could always count on steady trade winds in this part of the Pacific. The anomalous wind conditions associated with the El Niño event had not been left behind. Once Cyclone Zuman moved farther to the southeast, the easterly wind flow that had enabled the canoe to sail from Rangiroa had faded, and the "weird weather" that followed was apparently part of the widespread anomalies associated with the renewed intrusion of the monsoon trough into the East Polynesian waters.

Despite the presence of the trough, however, Nainoa and the crew were to continue to enjoy brief periods of trade wind–like conditions between squalls and spells of northerly winds. For example, during the night of 29–30 April, right after Nainoa had recorded the remarks quoted above about how strange the weather had been, the canoe was sailing in 10–15 knot winds from the east-southeast, with mild seas and clear skies—all of which led Nainoa to exclaim in his interview the following morning how this had been the first time they had been able to sail through the whole night without having to trice the sails because of squalls or stop for the lagging escort vessel. Unfortunately, this good weather continued only until the late afternoon, when the canoe had to fall off to the north-northwest to avoid a mass of towering black clouds that had suddenly loomed up on the horizon. But this weather system proved too big to avoid, and it soon engulfed the canoe, bringing humid sticky weather, gusty winds, and messy, rough seas. Then, several hours after sunset, squalls forced the crew to trice the sails once more and sit out the bad weather. At this point the canoe was about four degrees, or some 240 miles, south of the equator.

By around two that morning (1 May) the squalls had passed, and the wind started to blow steadily, but out of the east-northeast. This forced the canoe onto a course toward the north-northwest, causing Nainoa to speculate in his interview the following day that if they kept on this course they might end up being driven west of the meridian of the island of Hawai'i, a concern that was to grow as the voyage wore on.

Although the wind briefly shifted back toward the east-southeast during the daylight hours of 2 May, by which time the canoe was just a degree and a half (90 miles) south of the equator (fig. 74), that evening the wind switched back to east-northeast. For the next five days the canoe encountered light winds that came mostly out of the east-northeast and northeast, forcing her onto a course slightly to the west of north as she crossed the equator on 3 May and headed toward the zone between 4° and 9° North where the doldrums are normally found.

Contrary to expectations, the canoe reached and then crossed this zone unimpeded by any doldrums. As they sailed north-ward, the crew could see huge convection clouds, punctuated from time to time with lightning flashes, developing behind them along the southern horizon, but they seemed always to be able to stay ahead of the threatening build-up. Yet the lack of boisterous northeasterlies with well-developed trade wind swells made Nainoa hesitate to believe that they had escaped the doldrums so easily. But, on 6 May, by which time they had reached 7° North and had enjoyed a full day of sailing in strong winds from the northeast by east and what looked like the beginning of organized trade wind swells, Nainoa conceded that maybe they had missed the doldrums and were indeed in the northeast trade wind zone. Perhaps, he speculated in his interview that evening, there had been no doldrums because, in the absence at the time of a well-developed southeast trade wind system, the northeasterlies had simply extended southward across the belt where the doldrums are commonly found and had even penetrated into the Southern Hemisphere.

Analysis of meteorological data after the voyage indicates that it is not unprecedented for the doldrums to be absent or weak during April, but that the extension of the east-northeasterly

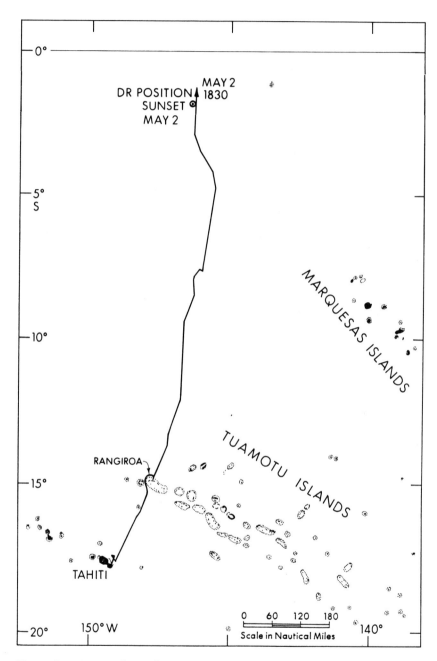

MAY 2
DR POSITION 1830
SUNSET
MAY 2

0°

5°
S

10°

MARQUESAS ISLANDS

TUAMOTU ISLANDS

RANGIROA

15°

TAHITI

0   60   120   180
Scale in Nautical Miles

20°   150° W   140°

Figure 74. Approaching the equator, 2 May 1987.

trade wind belt south of the equator was most unusual—though perhaps understandable in the context of the basin-wide anomalies in wind flow associated with the El Niño condition that had then developed.

A comparison of the actual track of the canoe during this period with Nainoa's dead reckoning positions shows that for the first time since leaving Tahiti the two diverged significantly. Up until 2 May, when the canoe was a hundred or so miles south of the equator, Nainoa's dead reckoning positions had fallen fairly close to the actual track, sometimes even right on it. As the canoe had sailed further toward and then across the equator in the light northeast and east-northeast winds, however, the dead reckoning positions fell progressively farther and farther to the west of the actual track. While the canoe was actually sailing at this time on a bearing about 7° or 8° to the west of north, Nainoa's estimates indicate that he thought the canoe's track was bearing some 20° to the west of north. As a result, by sunrise 7 May, Nainoa's dead reckoning was some 150 miles too far to the west (fig. 75).

Two factors may have combined to throw Nainoa's reckoning off. First, he may have overestimated the westerly set of the current, as he apparently had done in these same latitudes when sailing to Tahiti in 1985. Second, he may have been too conservative in judging the windward performance of *Hōkūle'a* against these light northeast and east-northeast winds and the relatively smooth seas that accompanied them. The larger sails (particularly the extra-large after sail) which the canoe now carried may have been more efficient than expected in going to windward in these light airs.[7]

The Northeast Trade Wind Zone

Hopes for strong, steady trades and fast sailing for the rest of the way to Hawai'i did not last long. The winds lightened during the daylight hours of 7 May and shifted progressively northward, forcing the slowly sailing canoe to veer toward the northwest and making Nainoa worry once more about ending up to the west of the island of Hawai'i. Although the wind direction improved that night, during the next day the winds turned more northerly, forcing the canoe once again to the northwest. Then around sunset, the wind shifted all the way around to north,

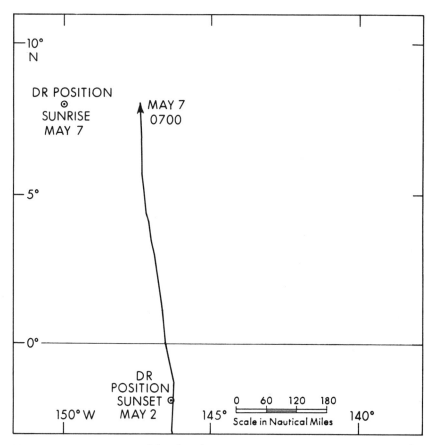

Figure 75. Divergence of dead reckoning and actual positions north of the equator, 2–7 May 1987.

forcing the canoe to be tacked due east until around two the next morning (9 May), when the wind shifted back to the northeast allowing the canoe to change tack again and resume sailing toward Hawai'i. At this time *Hōkūle'a* was at about 10° 15′ North, a little over 600 miles north of the equator.

In addition to constantly watching the swells so that he could use them for steering during cloudy periods or when the sun was too high in the sky for orientation, Nainoa also kept a lookout for the sudden appearance of big swells, as these can provide an advance warning of any storms that might lie in the canoe's path. For example, in his interview on the morning of the 9th, Nainoa pointed out the large, highly developed swells

that were coming from the north and proposed that these indicated that a subtropical depression was moving somewhere
north of Hawai'i, interrupting the normal trade wind flow. The
surface wind analysis for 7:00 A.M. (Hawai'i time) on 7 May
shows that in fact a well-developed subtropical disturbance
(known among Hawai'i meteorologists as a "Kona low") was
then centered northeast of Hawai'i at 28° North, and 149° West
(fig. 76). This disturbance was producing brisk northerly winds
along longitude 150° West and the strong north swell that Nainoa noticed when it reached the canoe.

Although the wind continued to come from the northeast
and east-northeast for the next day and a half, at sunset on 10
May the canoe, then at about 13° North, sailed into a weather
front, and the wind once more shifted counterclockwise until it
was again coming out of the north. To keep from being forced
westward, Nainoa had the canoe tacked to the east; he assumed
that this was just a small front and that they would soon pass
through it and be able to resume sailing toward Hawai'i. The
weather system proved to be larger than expected, however,
and, except for one short spell of tacking northward when the
winds briefly became more easterly the canoe continued sailing
to the east across the northerly wind field for the next thirty-six
hours.

While the canoe was sailing on this eastward tack, the frigate
U.S.S. Brewton, directed by position information radioed from
the escort vessel, rendezvoused with *Hōkūle'a* in order to evac-
uate Dixon Stroup, who had a fast-spreading and potentially
life-threatening leg infection. The efficiency and goodwill with
which the frigate's captain, Commander Paul Mallet, and crew
carried out this operation typified the relations our project has
enjoyed with the U.S. Navy and the Coast Guard as well. As
professional seamen, Navy and Coast Guard personnel have followed the voyages of *Hōkūle'a* with keen interest, particularly
because they fully understand the difficulty of navigating long
distances without modern instruments. We especially appreciate their willingness to make the rendezvous with the canoe without revealing any position information that would have
compromised the navigational effort.[8]

At dawn on 12 May, the wind shifted a bit toward the east,
and Nainoa gave the order to go back on the starboard tack, even
though the north-northeasterly direction of the wind forced the
canoe onto a northwesterly course. *Hōkūle'a* continued sailing

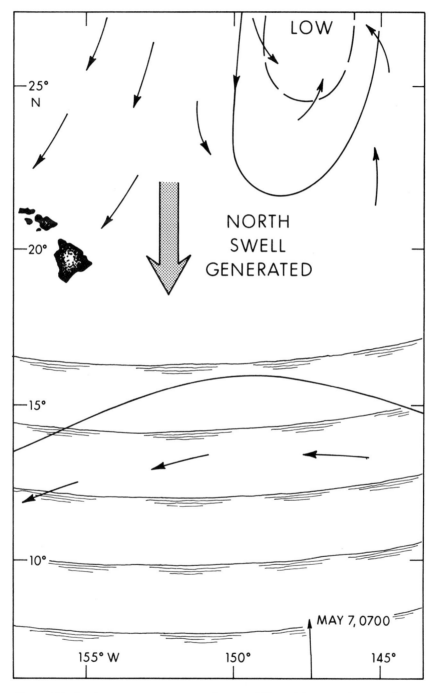

Figure 76. Low pressure system northeast of Hawai'i generating north swells, 7 May 1987.

northwestward in these light north-northeasterly winds until the 13th, when, during a period of shifting winds, Nainoa had the canoe tacked to the east, then back to the northwest, and then eastward once more before turning back to the northwest once the light northeasterlies became reestablished. Despite this tacking back and forth, during the early morning hours of 14 May the canoe did manage to cross the 15th parallel of latitude (900 miles north of the equator and almost to within 400 miles of the southernmost point of Hawai'i). That morning the motor vessel *Ma'alaea* rendezvoused with the *Dorcas*, bringing diesel fuel from Hawai'i to replenish the yacht's tanks that had been emptied in trying to keep up with the canoe on the lengthening voyage. The *Ma'alaea* also brought to *Hōkūle'a* Tua Pittman, the crew member from Rarotonga who had been forced to leave the crew at Rangiroa when he had dislocated his shoulder while the canoe had been detained there by adverse winds. Tua was most grateful for this chance to rejoin the crew to finish the voyage.

By this time Nainoa was beginning to feel unsure of his dead reckoning. In particular, he was wondering whether or not the canoe was really headed toward the island of Hawai'i as his mental calculations indicated, or whether the canoe might be headed to the west of the island on a course that would greatly complicate making a safe landfall. The source of his doubt was the extraordinary character of this voyage. As Nainoa put it in his interview on the 14th:

> By far this is the strangest trip in terms of being so against the average. . . . To me, it is the biggest challenge I have ever faced for a number of reasons. One is the length of the trip; it is the longest voyage so far. Two is the weather; the weather has been so unpredictable that you can't stay on a regular sail plan. Three is that we have had to sail perpendicular to our course line so many times. So, given all that . . . [it] is going to be real interesting to see exactly where we end up.

Elsewhere in the interviews he gave during this period, Nainoa stressed how he was not prepared for so much tacking back and forth across the course to Hawai'i and wondered how it might be throwing off his ability to estimate how far they were deviating east or west from the projected course line. In addition, he expressed concern about how his preoccupation with

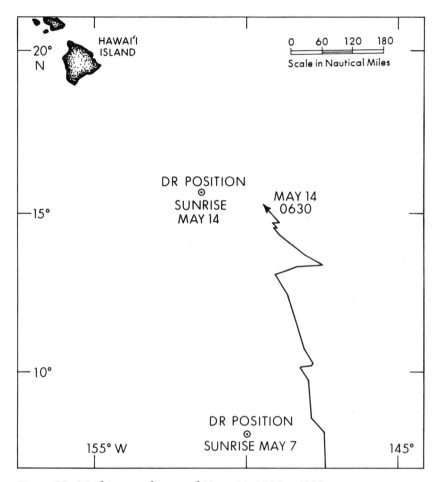

Figure 77. Working north toward Hawai'i, 14 May 1987.

the rendezvous first with the *Brewton* and then with the *Ma'a-laea* may have led him to make mistakes in his dead reckoning. Yet judging from the plot of his position estimates, Nainoa's navigation did not really suffer during these tacking episodes and the two rendezvous (fig. 77). If anything, the gap between his estimates and the actual track of the canoe that had opened up when the canoe first encountered northeasterly winds actually shrank during this period. For example, whereas on 7 May Nainoa's dead reckoning had been some 150 miles west of the actual track, at dawn on 14 May, when the canoe was at about

15° 15' North and 149° 24' West, his estimates placed her about 120 miles to west-northwest of the actual position.

Nainoa was, of course, unaware of the true position of the canoe and could only rely on his own estimates. Although these indicated that the canoe was heading almost directly toward the island of Hawai'i, given his conservative nature Nainoa was prepared for the worst-case scenario: that, in reality, they were being forced onto a course that would push the canoe to the west of the island. Nainoa wanted to reach the latitude of the Hawaiian chain just to the eastern, windward side of the island of Hawai'i, after which the canoe could be turned downwind and to sail westward toward an archipelago target 315 miles wide, measured from Ka Lae at the southern end of the island of Hawai'i to the northern shore of Kaua'i. If, however, the canoe were approaching the archipelago directly from the southeast, heading in the same northwest direction as the trend of the chain, the width of the target would be greatly narrowed. And, to state the worst-case scenario, if the canoe were being forced by the unfavorable winds onto a course that would take her so far west of the island of Hawai'i that even the towering peaks of the island could not be seen as the canoe sailed past it, a landfall along the chain could become problematic, particularly if continued northerly winds kept making it difficult to work further to the north.

Fortunately, from the 14th on, the wind became a bit more easterly, allowing the canoe to be sailed on a more northerly course. The sailing was frustratingly slow, however, for the wind remained very light and irregular. For example, in his interview on 16 May, when the canoe was approaching the latitude of the island of Hawai'i, Nainoa states that although the wind was out of the east-northeast where it should be,

> the weather is still, I think, certainly not back to trade wind conditions because there is no force in the wind; it is really weak. . . .
> We are just lucky to have these big sails that can push us along through this small stuff and still make four and one-half knots.

At this time, Nainoa's estimates of the canoe's position became particularly crucial. The main Hawaiian islands extend from the Ka Lae, Hawai'i at 18° 56' North to the northern shore of Kaua'i at 22° 14' North. Based on star sights during the previous night, at midday on 16 May Nainoa placed the canoe at about 18° 30' North—within sight range of the island of Ha-

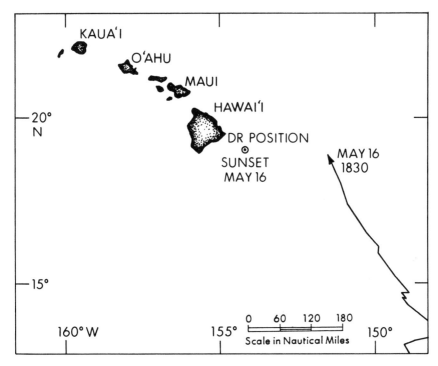

Figure 78. Drawing abeam of the island of Hawai'i, 16 May 1987.

wai'i if the canoe was in fact heading toward that island. Look-outs posted throughout the day saw no sign of land, however, for in fact the canoe was actually well to the east of Hawai'i. Although Nainoa's estimate of latitude was basically correct, he was reckoning that the canoe was over 150 miles west of where she actually was (fig. 78).

The wind died on the 17th, forcing the crew to lower the sails to the deck in order to prevent chafing as well as damage to the booms as the canoe was rocked violently from side to side by the confused seas. Smoother seas that evening allowed the sails to be raised to take advantage of very light northerly breezes to sail toward the west-northwest. These conditions led Nainoa to comment once more in his tape-recorded interview about how weak the wind was in latitudes where he was used to sailing in brisk trades:

> From 10° North we virtually had no trade winds. We had wind sometimes in the trade wind direction—for slight periods from the east-northeast, but with no strength in it. . . . The absence

of the normal trade winds—the most consistent wind belt on earth—in the trade wind season is just really baffling.

The frustration of being held up by light, fluky winds at this last stage of the voyage may have made Nainoa forget how variable the trades can be this time of year. Actually, May is not known for consistent trades in Hawaiian waters. It marks the transition from *ho'oilo*, the winter rainy season, to *kau*, the summer dry season. During this transitional period the trades are often light and frequently may fail altogether before becoming steadier during the summer months. For example, during May 1987 the steadiness of the trades at Honolulu (based on a value of 100 percent for blowing from the same direction during the entire month) was only 67 percent, while in June it was 89 percent and in July was 94 percent.[9] A major factor in this seasonal decline in the steadiness of the trades is the Tropical Upper Tropospheric Trough. This trough, which is most evident at 35,000 feet above sea level, moves over Hawai'i as it shifts north with the coming of summer. As it passes over the islands each May, disturbances formed along the trough often cause the surface pressure to fall and the trades to weaken or fail.[10] (The resultant warm, muggy conditions are often termed "termite weather" in Honolulu, in that the heat and humidity triggers evening flights of termites.) The surface wind analysis for 1:00 A.M. on 18 May, when *Hōkūle'a* was stalled east of the island of Hawai'i by very light northerlies, reveals the disturbed conditions near the islands (fig. 79). The trough lay directly over the islands, and a meteorological buoy anchored southeast of Hawai'i Island showed north-northeast winds of just 5 knots.

During the day on the 18th the canoe sailed to the northwest in order to gain a few more miles against these light north-northeast winds. Nainoa's worst-case dead reckoning indicated that they might possibly be passing just to the west of Hawai'i Island and that if they kept heading northwestward they would make land somewhere along the middle of the chain. Nonetheless, even though sightings of oily waste and bits of paper and plastic floating in the water seemed to indicate land to the north or northeast, Nainoa was beginning to express some doubt about this possibility. Perhaps, he wondered, the canoe was not west of Hawai'i Island, but instead was sailing to the east of it. Despite these doubts, however, Nainoa wanted to keep sailing northward as far as 20° 30' North. At that latitude, he reckoned that

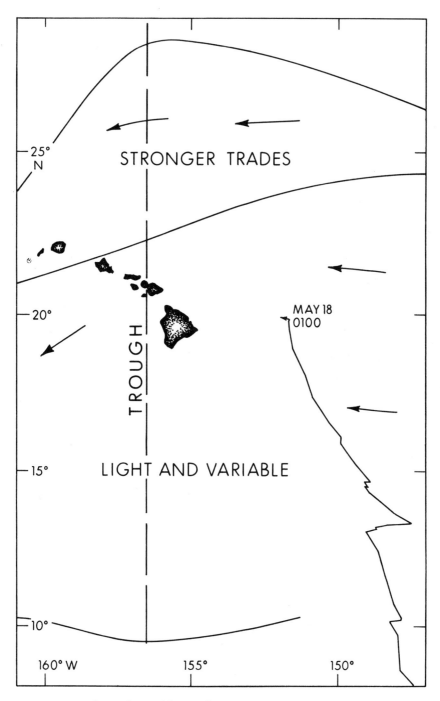

Figure 79. Light and variable winds in Hawaiian waters, 18 May 1987.

if they were in fact west of the island of Hawai'i, they would be able to see the towering volcano of Haleakalā on Maui, or the islands of Kaho'olawe or Lāna'i off the southern shore of Maui. Or, if they had been driven even farther to the west, once it became dark they would be able to see the loom cast in the skies by the bright lights of Honolulu off to the north.

That night Nainoa got what he considered to be an excellent view of Polaris, and estimated from its elevation above the horizon that they were at 21° North, or a little south of there. Since they had seen no indications of land the previous day other than a few stray sooty terns (*'ewa 'ewa* in Hawaiian), and no lights or other signs of land to the north during the night, Nainoa concluded that he had indeed overestimated the westward deviation of the canoe's course, and that in fact they were to the east of the island of Hawai'i. Accordingly, Nainoa had the steersman turn the canoe downwind to head westward toward where he now deduced the island of Hawai'i must lie.

The next day, 19 May, Nainoa guessed that they might be about 120 miles away from the island, and that Mauna Kea, the 13,784-foot volcanic peak in the north of the island where some of the world's largest telescopes are located was then bearing southwest by west. His estimate was not too far off the mark, for the canoe was then located about 140 miles east by north of Cape Kumukahi, the easternmost point of Hawai'i located midway along the island's windward coast. After almost a month of struggling northward against frustratingly inconsistent winds, and after radically revising his dead reckoning calculations when land did not appear where he had estimated it should, Nainoa had been quickly able to reorient his thinking and develop a mental image of where the canoe was in relation to land that was essentially correct, if not precisely accurate.

As the canoe slowly sailed westward in light winds on the 19th, more sooty terns were sighted. Because of previous experiences on the various legs of the entire voyage with seeing a few terns flying around when the canoe was far from land, Nainoa did not set great store in this sighting, but at this point he conceded that these terns might be signs of land nearby. More intriguing was the sight of a lone albatross, for this was the first one he had ever seen flying around Hawai'i. Nainoa recalled in his interview that evening that a colony of these wide-ranging birds had recently become established on Kaua'i and that maybe this bird was from there.

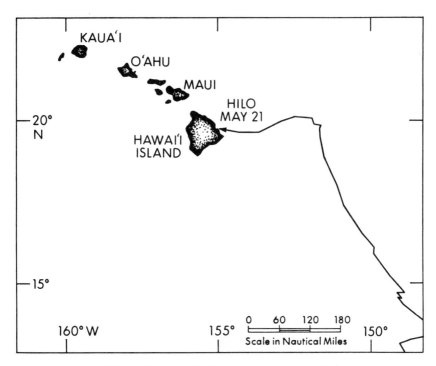

Figure 80. Landfall on the island of Hawai'i, 21 May 1987.

The next day, 20 May, Nainoa began to think that he may have overestimated the latitude and so directed the steersmen to steer a little to the south of west, a heading that in fact made the canoe point almost directly toward Cape Kumukahi. That day, as the canoe slowly sailed along in the light airs, much rubbish floated by, and more sooty terns and big brown albatrosses were seen. More telling as true signs of land, Nainoa thought, was the sight of four *manu-o-Kū*, as everyone on board called the sparkling white fairy terns.

That night, a loom of light was seen ahead, and, despite the extremely poor visibility, the next morning land was sighted ahead under the clouds. *Hōkūle'a* had come home, successfully concluding the navigation experiment (fig. 80). The next priority was to get the canoe to O'ahu in time for the welcoming celebration planned for the 23rd, just two days away. As the winds continued very light, *Hōkūle'a* was taken under tow to Hilo for customs inspection and other formalities before continuing along the island chain toward O'ahu. Late in the afternoon of the

22nd, *Hōkūle'a* anchored off Kalaupapa Peninsula on the north shore of the island of Moloka'i to pick up crew members who had flown in to join the canoe for the final arrival at O'ahu. The crew was given supper ashore by the residents; this quiet re-entry to Hawai'i was a welcome pause before the hectic day to follow.

About midnight the canoe left Kalaupapa, still under tow in the calm, and shortly after dawn arrived off the entrance to Kāne'ohe Bay which leads directly to Kualoa. Just before the canoe was to make its ceremonial entrance, the wind at long last picked up, enabling the canoe to sail majestically into Kāne'ohe Bay, surrounded by a fleet of paddling canoes, yachts, and power craft. Finally, the twin prows of *Hōkūle'a* nosed onto the sands of Kualoa, the same shore where the canoe had been launched twelve years earlier. Just as thousands of people had seen *Hōkūle'a* first take to the sea at Kualoa, so thousands more now welcomed the canoe and her crew home with chants, dances, and orations.

The Longest Leg

The return to Hawai'i took longer than any other leg of the entire Voyage of Rediscovery (fig. 81). Largely because of the enforced stay on Rangiroa, almost two months elapsed between the time the canoe left Tahiti and her arrival at Kualoa. Even the sail from Rangiroa to Hilo took a comparatively long time: twenty-eight days in comparison to the twenty-two days it took in 1976 to sail the greater distance from Tahiti to a point abeam the island of Hawai'i, and the twenty-four days it took to cover that same distance in 1980. The northerly winds, overcast skies, and squally conditions brought on by the El Niño delayed *Hōkūle'a* for weeks in Rangiroa and then made sailing north to the equator tortuously slow, while north of the equator, the lack of strong and consistent northeast trades further lengthened the voyage.

These conditions severely tested Nainoa's navigation as well as the crew's sailing skills and stamina. Although the canoe more or less followed the same course northward as she had on the previous crossings, the 1987 track differed in detail from the other two (fig. 82). On the two previous trips back to Hawai'i, *Hōkūle'a* had sailed fast on the starboard tack for most of the trip, with minimal variations in heading and speed, all of which

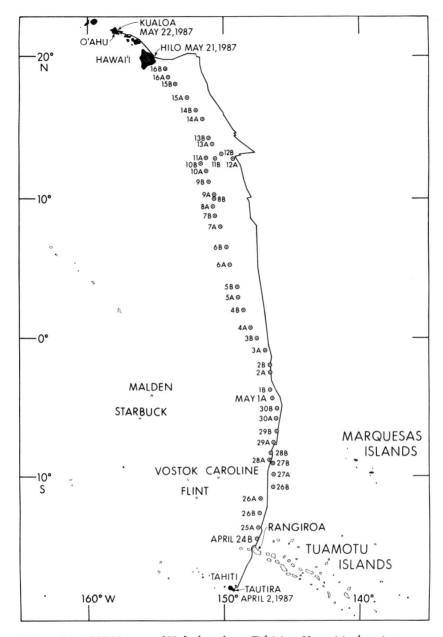

Figure 81. 1987 Voyage of Hōkūleʻa from Tahiti to Hawaiʻi, showing actual track of the canoe and Nainoa Thompson's dead reckoning (D.R.) positions estimated at sunrise (marked by "A" following the date) and sunset (marked by "B" following the date).

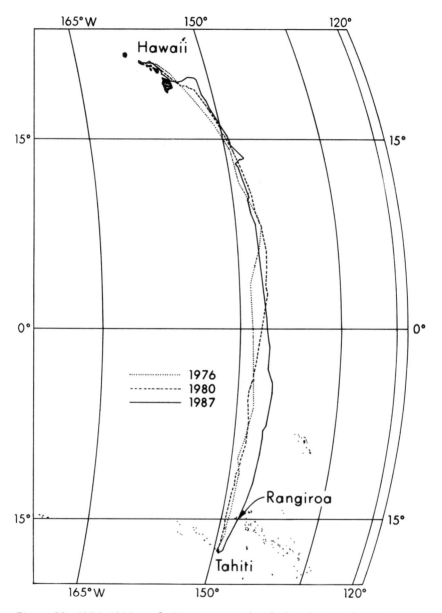

Figure 82. 1976, 1980, and 1987 voyages of Hōkūleʻa *from Tahiti to* Hawaiʻi.

made the navigation relatively straightforward. In 1987, however, the canoe had to be worked north, rather than getting an easy ride, which in turn complicated navigation. Shifting winds forced many tacks, with the heading often departing widely from the reference course, while the light winds extended the time at sea, all of which contributed to skewing Nainoa's dead reckoning positions to leeward of the actual track of the canoe. Yet, even though toward the end of the voyage Nainoa was worried that the canoe was passing to the west of the island of Hawai'i, in fact he had managed to sail the canoe to the eastern side of the island, just as originally planned. When no signs of Maui or O'ahu appeared to the north where his reckoning indicated land might lie, Nainoa was able to quickly readjust his thinking to mentally visualize the canoe's correct position to the east of Hawai'i. In spite of everything, the ultimate test of landfall was passed once more.

Long-range, Two-way Voyaging

This third roundtrip voyage of *Hōkūle'a* between Hawai'i and Tahiti demonstrates how even under adverse conditions it is possible for a voyaging canoe, navigated without instruments, to sail back and forth between these distantly separated outposts of the Polynesian nation. Not only, therefore, can we forget the limit of 300 miles that Sharp so arbitrarily imposed on the Polynesians' ability to make intentional voyages, but we should also open our minds to the possibility that Hawai'i was not always so isolated as was apparently the case when European voyagers first visited the archipelago in the late eighteenth century. To be sure, our three roundtrip voyages between Hawai'i and Tahiti do not prove that the legendary voyages back and forth over this route celebrated in Hawaiian oral traditions actually took place. Nonetheless they do demonstrate how well the double canoe and noninstrument navigation methods are adapted for sailing over the thousands of miles of blue water separating Hawai'i from Tahiti. After our voyages, it is no longer possible to assume that the great stretches of ocean which lie between Hawai'i and the other Polynesian islands necessarily barred two-way communication between Hawaiians and their kinsmen in the South Pacific.

Yet, that we have made three roundtrips between Hawai'i

and Tahiti cannot be taken to mean that Polynesians could have sailed freely back and forth between virtually any set of islands in their oceanic realm. Strictly speaking, our experimental findings gained in sailing around Polynesia are highly specific to particular routes and their characteristic wind conditions, to particular seasons of the year or to weather cycles of shorter or longer periods, and to the size of the destination formed by the target island and any surrounding or screening islands. For example, the alignment of Hawai'i and Tahiti across the trade wind field, and the extensive navigational targets presented by the great length of the Hawaiian chain and the even wider east-to-west spread of the Society and Tuamotu chains, work together to greatly enhance the prospects for voyaging back and forth over this route. Conditions over some other interarchipelago routes in Polynesia are even more conducive to two-way communication, whereas over others they are much less favorable. Voyaging possibilities over each of the sea ways between the many islands and archipelagos of Polynesia must be separately assessed in order to develop realistic models of the degree to which interaction and isolation may have shaped the evolution of the many constituent cultures of the widespread Polynesian nation.

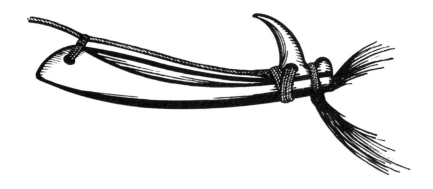

8

PUTTING VOYAGING BACK INTO POLYNESIAN PREHISTORY

When we began experimenting with reconstructed double canoes in the mid-1960s, a new generation of archaeologists then applying modern excavation and interpretative methods in the Pacific were questioning long-held ideas about Polynesian migration and voyaging. Many of these archaeologists rejected assumptions about intentional exploration and settlement, followed by widespread voyaging thereafter, in favor of the view that each island had somehow been fortuitously settled by a canoe-load or two of Polynesians and that the resultant colonies had developed in relative if not total isolation from all but their nearest neighbors.

Such minimalist thinking about Polynesian voyaging and settlement was in part a reaction to the extreme "migration mentality" of earlier students of Polynesian prehistory who pictured canoes sailing freely back and forth across the Pacific and sought to explain the development of each island society in terms of the diffusion of cultural traits brought in by voyagers from various islands, or by the overlayering of one migratory wave over another. But it also reflected a major shift in archaeological thinking brought into the Pacific by researchers trained in the United States and Britain where the longstanding culture history paradigm with its focus on the migration of peoples and the diffusion of culture traits was being replaced by attempts to reconstruct the way of life of a group through archaeology, and to study adaptation to the environment, cultural evolution, population growth, innovation, and other processes as though they were internally generated within a closed system.[1] Although not all archaeologists working in Polynesia adopted the extreme antimigrationism of the self-styled "New Archaeologists" of this period, even those who retained an interest in tracing migrations and searching for connections between island cultures seem to have been constrained by this closed-system, ahistorical approach to parsimoniously limit their models to the least number of voyages possible needed to explain the settlement of the islands and any subsequent contacts between them.

Although at first glance Polynesia might seem an unlikely place for such antimigrationism to have taken hold, to archaeologists imbued with this way of thinking, as well as to social anthropologists who were then experimenting with their own version of closed-system modeling of the evolution of individual Polynesian societies,[2] the region provided a virtual laboratory where they could develop their reconstructions and analyses of internal cultural processes without having to take into account external influences. Basic to their thinking was the assumption that the vast stretches of open ocean separating the island societies surely must have formed a barrier to the flow of people, their artifacts, and their ideas, rather than a highway for migration, exchange, and communication. They therefore found Sharp's theory about random, accidental settlement followed by virtual isolation to be most enticing. By embracing it, not only could they shed assumptions about voyaging feats they found incredible, but they could feel free to develop their own analyses of internal processes and behaviors confined to the island or archipelago in question without having to worry about any complications that intentional exploration and colonization, multiple settlement, and postsettlement voyaging might bring.

For example, archaeologists who came from Britain to Aotearoa in the 1950s to establish archaeology as an academic discipline there regarded tradition-based reconstructions of Māori migrations involving sequential waves of migrants, great fleets of canoes, and two-way voyages between Aotearoa and the legendary homeland of Hawaiki to be unnecessary to their concerns, as well as being products of unsound scholarship. Following from their training in England, where culture-historical reconstructions based on successive migrations were being superseded by analyses focusing on internal cultural processes, they wanted to be free to concentrate on the development of Māori society in terms of the evidence for local adaptation and change revealed in their excavations. They, their students, and their colleagues proceeded to develop a fascinating portrait of how people from tropical islands learned to survive and then flourish on massive islands located far to the south in cool temperate latitudes, but one in which the maritime heritage of the Māori celebrated in their traditions was conspicuously missing.[3]

Such isolationist thinking did not long go unchallenged, however, although at first the strongest criticism came primarily from outside archaeology and was mostly directed at Sharp's then influential downgrading of Polynesian sailing and navigation capabilities rather than archaeological thinking per se. For example, by means of a massive series of computer simulations, a team led by geographer Gerard Ward demonstrated how random drift voyaging alone could not account for either the Polynesian thrust to the east, or the long voyages to Hawai'i, Rapa Nui, and Aotearoa.[4] Then, the early experiments with *Rehu Moana* and *Nālehia* indicated how Polynesian canoes and navigation methods might be employed to make long voyages, while the ethnographic work by David Lewis and anthropologist Tom Gladwin in Micronesia and a few other areas of the Pacific where traditional navigation had survived into the twentieth century clearly demonstrated how it was possible to navigate from island to island without instruments.[5]

The Māori linguist Bruce Biggs was the first to attack head-on what he called the "simplistic view of Polynesian settlement" inherent in the unidirectional, least-moves modeling then being applied. Echoing the admonition of linguistic theorist Leonard Bloomfield to remember that a family tree diagram of related languages is merely a statement of linguistic method, not a portrayal of actual events, Biggs warned archaeologists not to be misled by spare diagrams of the branching of Polynesian languages. They should be taken simply as models of language relations, he said, not as literal statements of historical reality. Although Biggs admitted that these diagrams might seem to imply a unilineal series of migrations and branchings without any backtracking or communication between branches, he argued that neither the logic of linguistic classification nor the empirical record of word borrowing and language replacement among Polynesian islands supported such a view. Accordingly, he called for a theory of "multiple intra-Polynesian migration and settlement" to account for the complex reality of interisland voyaging and communication which lay behind the story of Polynesian settlement and subsequent cultural developments.[6]

As these critiques were appearing, archaeologists started paying more attention to evidence they themselves were finding in their excavations on various Polynesian islands that indicated both intentional colonization and widespread postsettlement voyaging. Shell vegetable scrapers, domesticated animal bones, and other signs in the lower levels of archaeological sites pointed to settlement by planned colonization voyages on which were carried the plants and animals necessary to reproduce an agricultural economy, and intrusions and disruptions found in the higher levels cast doubt on isolationist assumptions about purely internal cultural development and in some cases supported local traditions about the impact of newcomers.[7] These discoveries, plus those being made on islands along the migration trail to Polynesia indicating that the Lapita ancestors of the Polynesians had moved rapidly into the Pacific and exchanged raw materials, pottery, and other goods widely among the islands they colonized,[8] led archaeologists to start giving voyaging a more dynamic role in their thinking about Polynesian prehistory than allowed for in parsimonious models of random settlement followed by isolation.

Starting in the 1970s Auckland University's Roger Green, whose wide-ranging interests had always included cultural historical reconstructions, took the lead by analyzing the culture of the Polynesians and their Lapita ancestors in terms of adaptations to the challenges of moving from New Guinea and adjacent islands of what he calls "Near Oceania" to "Remote Oceania," the open Pacific beyond these closely spaced islands. He has since been joined in this line of thinking by his colleague Geoffrey Irwin and a number of other archaeologists who are now making intentional exploration and colonization central to their models of Pacific settlement. In addition, it is becoming commonplace to uncover evidence of widespread postsettlement voyaging and work it into analyses of the evolution of particular island societies as well as of regional networks of linked islands and archipelagos. Archaeologists are no longer looking at the different island societies of West Polynesia as isolates. Instead they see them as parts of a communication sphere marked by frequent inter-island voyaging and the flow of goods, ideas, and people, a regional perspective that is now being fruitfully extended to central East Polynesia. Even such formerly discredited ideas as those about the settlement of Aotearoa by multiple canoes arriving during the same general time period, and the influence on cultural development of two-way voyaging between the central islands and such peripheral outposts as Hawai'i, are now being given a hearing once more.[9]

The role of the experimental voyages of *Hōkūle'a* in this rethinking about Polynesian voyaging and prehistory has been to provide information and insights on the performance of voyaging canoes and traditional ways of navigating needed to understand how people were able to expand so far and wide over the Pacific and to maintain a degree of inter-island communication after initial settlement. Results from our first long voyages have already been widely cited by archaeologists and have been instrumental in their adoption of more realistic views about the role of voyaging in Polynesian prehistory.[10] To continue this process of introducing nautical insights into the reconstruction of Polynesia's past, this chapter applies findings from the Voyage of Rediscovery and our most recent thinking about sailing and navigation to problems and issues in Polynesian colonization and postsettlement voyaging.

Eastward Expansion

Although it might seem incomprehensibly daring for anyone to have intentionally left the security of the rich and varied islands and archipelagos of West Polynesia to search in unknown seas for islands that may or may not be there, it must have made good sense to the early Polynesians. After all, their ancestors had been rewarded with landfalls on island after island as they sailed farther and farther into the Pacific. Moreover, they must have been greatly encouraged to keep sailing east when they made a startling discovery upon penetrating beyond the Solomons: because only they had the technology to sail so far into the ocean, each new island over the horizon was theirs alone to

settle. Their descendants who continued eastward across Polynesia therefore had every reason to believe that they would find
still more uninhabited islands to colonize. In addition, flotsam
and jetsam brought by the trades and westward-flowing ocean
currents would have provided concrete evidence that still more
islands lay to the east. Furthermore, as Peter Buck and other
nautically informed writers have pointed out, exploring eastward makes good sailing sense.[11] To sail east against the direction of the trade winds (but not, as we have pointed out, necessarily against the trades themselves) is the prudent way to search
for new lands, for the explorer always has the ability to return
home when the trades are blowing.

A traditional tale collected by Bruce and Mary Biggs from the
island of Cikobia in the Fiji archipelago tells of the search for
islands on which to settle undertaken first by the chief, Matai-
welu, and then continued by his sons. Although the islands in
question are few and relatively closely spaced, the tradition provides a rare glimpse into how the islanders themselves phrased
the search to windward for uninhabited lands. The tale begins
with Matai-welu sailing first to Cikobia. Because the island was
already occupied, Matai-welu asked the reigning chief there to
"please allow me to look for a land of my own." In response to
the question of where he would look, Matai-welu replied that "I
will search upwind only" and departed with the blessing of the
resident chief. After sailing upwind, Matai-welu and his sons
reached the island of Qele-levu, and, finding it to be uninhabited,
they settled there. After living there for a while, the maturing
sons begged their father to be allowed "to look for our own
lands upwind from here." With their father's permission, they
set sail and found the uninhabited island of Vutuna on which
one of the sons settled.[12]

That generations of voyagers such as Matai-welu and his sons
succeeded in moving eastward, discovering and settling one uninhabited island after another as far as Rapa Nui, is unarguable.
How they managed to span the great ocean gaps to the east of
Tonga and Samoa, and the rate and sequence of their expansion,
are issues that are far from settled, however.

As noted, during the 1960s and 1970s, archaeological thinking about this expansion across Polynesia was heavily influenced
by a linguistic family tree model of how languages branch off
from one another (fig. 83). Just as linguists drew single lines to

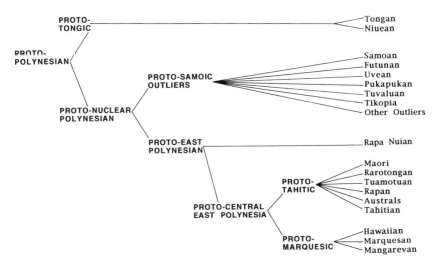

Figure 83. Family tree model of the branching of Polynesian languages.

outline the branching off of Proto-East Polynesian from the parent language, and then separate lines from Proto-East Polynesian to each East Polynesian language, so did archaeologists think about Polynesian expansion in terms of the least number of one-way voyages needed to account for the settlement of all the archipelagos. Such modeling typically started with a single migration from a specific West Polynesian homeland to the archipelago in East Polynesia where proto-East Polynesian language and culture became differentiated in isolation, and then a repetition of this process for the founding of each separate East Polynesian language and culture. Before archaeological excavations were undertaken in central East Polynesia, the leading candidate for the East Polynesian homeland was the Society Group, with Tahiti and Ra'iatea considered to have been most central for cultural development and subsequent dispersion. When, however, excavations undertaken in the Marquesas and Societies during the late 1950s and early 1960s indicated that the Marquesas may have been settled earlier than the Societies, and directly from West Polynesia, the Marquesas came to be considered by many as the primary East Polynesian homeland. The Society Islands were then relegated to the status of a secondary dispersal center after their settlement from the Marquesas, a conception that only slightly complicated this spare model of Polynesian expansion.

Voyaging research has undercut such unidirectional, least-moves modeling. As long as it was considered to be extremely difficult to sail from West to East Polynesia, it made some sense to think about East Polynesian colonization in terms of a single migration to an archipelago which then became the source for subsequent population dispersal throughout the region. Now, after the long voyages of *Hōkūleʻa*, particularly the 1986 crossing from Samoa to Tahiti, the movement eastward looks to be much less difficult than formerly assumed. Our demonstration of how to use periodic disturbances in the winter trade winds to sail from Samoa to Tahiti, along with a renewed appreciation of the ethnohistorical information on how Polynesians sailing at the time of European contact were exploiting the more regular summer westerlies to sail to the east, as well as the recent realization of how massive westerly wind flows characterize El Niño events, virtually forces us to consider the possibility that there could have been many colonization voyages to East Polynesia.

The major El Niño event of 1982–1983 and intensive research on such periodic disturbances in wind and current flow conducted over the last decade and a half have led to an appreciation of how these events may have played a role in the movement east across Polynesia. Roughly once or twice a decade warm, equatorial water floods down the coast of Peru, smothering the upwelling of cold, nutrient-rich water with a devastating effect on marine life. As these periodic disturbances typically occur around Christmas, they are known by the name *El Niño*, or "The Christ Child." These warm currents are not strictly local in nature, but are part of basin-wide changes in oceanic and atmospheric circulation. Linked with their appearance is a reversal of the usual atmospheric pressure gradient across the South Pacific of high in the east and low in the west, which is known as the "Southern Oscillation." This oscillation manifests itself in a weakening of the trade winds and the outbreak of prolonged and intensive periods of westerlies, generally during the summer season. With the weakening of the trades and the outbreak of westerlies, the surface of the sea across the South Pacific, which is normally higher in the west than the east because of the stress of the trades, begins to level off, triggering water pulses and flows that eventually result in warm, equatorial water inundating the cold water upwelling off the Peruvian coast.[13]

Although these El Niño westerlies are generally strongest and most prolonged in the western and central Pacific, they often spread into the eastern Pacific. For example, even the comparatively mild El Niño of 1987 brought westerly winds as far east as the western Societies, as well as the northerlies that kept *Hōkūle'a* anchored in the lagoon of Rangiroa atoll so long. In 1982–1983 a particularly massive El Niño brought a prolonged outbreak of westerlies that spread over much of central East Polynesia and at times extended to Rapa Nui and beyond. Although Polynesian mariners may not have realized the full meteorological and oceanographic ramifications of the wind shifts they experienced during such disturbances, because of their intimate knowledge of the environment they certainly must have recognized that these periodic events brought prolonged spells of westerly winds good for sailing to the east and probably more than once exploited them when they wanted to search for new lands far over the eastern horizon, or to pay a visit to already settled islands lying in that direction.[14]

Over the centuries, ambitious voyagers from Samoa, Tonga, and perhaps also from some of the smaller groups and islands of West Polynesia, seeking to find and settle new lands to the east, could have exploited regular summer westerlies, El Niño westerlies, and winter westerlies. They need not, however, have necessarily sailed only to the nearest islands to the east, the Cooks. Some exploring and colonizing parties may have passed through or by the Cooks to directly reach islands farther to the east. For example, voyagers sailing from Samoa might have slipped between the Northern and Southern Cooks and made landfall in the Societies, as we probably could have done in 1986 had we not chosen to break our voyage into two legs and stop in the Southern Cooks. Because of their more southerly starting point, Tongan sailors would have been in a particularly favorable position to use the winter westerlies stemming from low pressure troughs extending up from the south to head directly east and intercept the southern end of the Tuamotu chain around the Gambier group, or to head slightly south of east and end up in the Australs. Even a direct voyage all the way to the Marquesas— as has been hypothesized on the basis of the discovery that potsherds found in ancient sites in the Marquesas were made with minerals that geologists source to Fiji—seems possible, particularly during a major El Niño event, such as that of 1982–1983

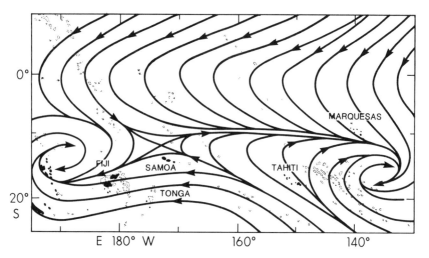

Figure 84. Surface wind analysis for 21 March 1983 showing El Niño westerlies (Sadler and Kilonsky 1983).

when strong westerly winds reached the Marquesas and were dominant there for several months (fig. 84).[15]

Particularly given this multiplicity of westerly wind systems, there is no reason to assume that all islands or archipelagos were settled from one source. For example, the possibility that the Marquesas may have been settled from at least two different island groups in West Polynesia was raised in the last century by Thomas Lawson, a longtime resident of the Marquesas Islands. He collected one legend from the Northern Marquesas about the first settlers there coming from a land called Vevau located far "below" them, a directional referent that in Polynesian sailing parlance means to leeward, and another from the Southern Marquesas about settlement from Hawaiki rather than Vevau. Equating Vevau with the Vava'u group in Tonga, and Hawaiki with the island of Savai'i in Samoa, Lawson proposed that the northern and southern clusters of islands in the Marquesas were settled by separate migrations, one from Tonga and the other from Samoa.[16] The discovery of potsherds at the lower levels of Marquesan archaeological sites that may date back some 2,000 years further muddies this picture. Although some are made from local clays, others have been sourced to Fiji, which raises the question of whether this indicates a migration from there, or simply reflects widespread trading patterns.[17]

The alternation of westerlies from the various systems outlined above with the easterly trade winds implies that sailing back and forth across tropical Polynesia was nowhere near as difficult as assumed in isolationist models. In fact, several writers have recently revived the idea common in the nineteenth century that two-way voyaging was crucial to the discovery and settlement of the islands. For example, archaeologist William Keegan and biologist Jared Diamond from the University of California, Los Angeles stress the importance of the continuous feedback from voyagers returning to the west with news about fertile, uninhabited islands over the eastern horizon in motivating Polynesians to keep moving across the Pacific. Auckland University's Geoffrey Irwin (a rare archaeologist who owns his own yacht) and his colleagues take this reasoning a step further. They hypothesize that the ability of explorers searching to the east for new islands to return home made the exploration and colonization much safer and more efficient than formerly assumed. Those explorers who had found new islands could return home to organize fully equipped colonizing expeditions; those who found nothing could run for home before their food and water gave out. In addition, writing primarily about the ancestral Polynesian movement from the Bismarcks to Tonga and Samoa, archaeologist Patrick Kirch from the University of California, Berkeley has proposed that voyaging back and forth between outposts on the frontier of colonization and those in the rear would also have facilitated oceanic expansion in the sense that small and struggling outposts on the frontier of settlement would thereby have had continuing access to the needed resources of larger, more settled communities in the rear.[18]

Prior knowledge of Pacific geography means, of course, that we could not have realistically re-created an exploratory voyage into unknown seas. Nevertheless, based on practical experience gained in sailing thousands of miles through Polynesian waters, it seems likely that early Polynesians would have been able to search the seas to the east for lands on which to settle and, at least in some cases, to sail back to their home island to spread word of their discoveries so that fully equipped colonizing expeditions could be sent out. To be sure, the episodic westerlies of the eastern Pacific and their only generally predictable alternation with the trades would not have been as ideal for moving eastward as the more regularly monsoonal wind shifts the Polynesians' Lapita ancestors were able to exploit in their rapid thrust into the mid-Pacific. Nonetheless, in time skilled Polynesian sailors must have been able to learn how to exploit the wind regimes of the eastern Pacific well enough to be able to search for virgin lands over the horizon, return home, and then mount colonizing expeditions to the newly discovered lands.

Similarly, the navigational task of exploring and settling the central region of East Polynesia does not seem extraordinarily difficult. This region should be thought of as a conglomeration of contiguous and near-contiguous archipelagos, not as a dispersed collection of lone islands and isolated archipelagos. The broad spread of islands to the east virtually assures that explorers sailing eastward would have intercepted islands.

Many writers have proposed that Polynesian navigators may have employed latitude sailing both to find their way back home after discovering an island and then sail out again to colonize the new discovery.[19] With this technique, commonly practiced by European navigators before the introduction of the chronometer allowed them to determine their longitude exactly, the navigator sails first to the latitude of his destination, and then turns to sail along that latitude until he makes his landfall. Norse navigators, for example, used this method to sail out to their island colonies in the Atlantic. Once having found the Faroes, Iceland, and the southern tip of Greenland, the Norse took the latitude of each place by roughly measuring the height of Polaris above the horizon. Upon their return to Norway, they could then find their way back to any of these outposts by first sailing north along Norway's coast until they reached the latitude of their destination, and then turning due west to sail down that latitude until they reached the island in question. Similarly, fifteenth-century Portuguese navigators who were working their way down the coast of West Africa found their way home by sailing long, dog-leg courses based upon latitude sailing. First they sailed northwest across the trades and into the westerlies zone until they reached the latitude of Lisbon, Lagos, or whatever port along the coast of Portugal they were heading for, and then turned their caravels due east to sail downwind directly to their home port.[20]

Although Pacific island mariners were certainly capable of using latitude sailing to help them find their way to a known destination, as we learned upon raising the question with Mau while preparing for the 1976 voyage, their own methods were probably more refined than those employed in prechronometer European navigation. Mau found the idea of sailing first to the latitude of an island and then turning to sail directly along that latitude until you reached the island to be curiously unprofessional. Essentially, he asked: Why sail way out of your way on long, dog-leg courses, when it was possible to use the stars and dead reckoning to sail directly for an island? He did, however, advocate setting a course so as to arrive at an island destination just on its windward side, so that if you missed your target you could always turn downwind to search for it. As we have seen, where possible Nainoa has tried to follow Mau's counsel, taking care to arrive at or near the latitude of his target island on its windward side, but not so far to windward of the island as to have to sail downwind for days to reach it.

The high level of Polynesian voyaging skills does not mean, however, that the expansion eastward was accomplished solely through linked exploration and colonization voyages. Judging from oral traditions from the late prehistoric era and some eye-witness reports from the Marquesas to be cited later, groups of men, women, and children did set sail on one-way expeditions to find and settle new islands. Although famine or defeat in war may have driven many to flee long-settled islands, dire necessity cannot account for the initial Polynesian expansion before the islands became crowded. The lure of empty lands to be found to windward may have been motivation enough for colonizing parties to set out to sea, even without benefit of prior reconnaissance. Furthermore, the Polynesian emphasis on primogeniture encouraged migration even in the best of times. A younger son of a ruling chief could not normally succeed his father, and therefore had every motivation to organize an expedition to find and settle an empty island where he could become the ruling chief.

Although random drift voyages cannot account for the main thrust to the east, some islands within central East Polynesia may have been reached by accident when canoes traveling in the region were blown off course by unforeseen winds, or simply wandered off course through navigational error. Hapless voyagers who made an accidental landfall might then have settled down on the newly found island and never tried to return to their homeland. Particularly, however, if there were only men in the party (as would probably have been the case if they had set out on a fishing or raiding expedition), they would probably have tried to return home and then either mounted their own colonizing expedition or spread the word so that others might organize an expedition to settle the newly found land. A sequence involving an apparently unforeseen discovery of an island, a return to the homeland, and then the launching of a colonizing expedition by others is featured in the traditional history of the linked atolls of Manihiki and Rakahanga in the Northern Cook group. These islands were said to have been discovered on a fishing expedition by a Rarotongan named Huku and then later colonized by his daughter and her husband after the latter had been defeated in battle.[21]

Exactly when the colonization of central East Polynesia began, and how long it took for people to spread over all the archipelagos of the region, are questions hotly debated today. The pattern of radiocarbon dates that began to emerge in the late 1960s from excavations across Melanesia and throughout Polynesia suggested that the rapid thrust of Lapita voyagers into the Pacific essentially ended in West Polynesia and that only after a settling-in period that lasted for upwards of a millennium, or perhaps even longer, was this eastward migration resumed by the Polynesian descendants of these pioneering voyagers. Since the early 1980s this "long pause" hypothesis has been vigorously challenged by Irwin and other archaeologists who see no good reason why there should have been any mid-Pacific lull in this migrational drive to the east. Instead, they propose that the colonization of the Pacific proceeded in a continuous, archipelago-by-archipelago fashion, without any marked pauses.[22]

This issue cannot now be fully resolved by reference to available radiocarbon dates of objects made from organic materials such as wood and bone that have been recovered from cave shelters, ancient dwellings, and other living sites. Radiocarbon dates themselves are not precise. They are subject to contamination at the site itself, or in the handling of the sample, and, in addition, must be calibrated according to various environmental factors. At best they only indicate a period of several centuries—usually quoted in such terms as 650–950 A.D. or 1200 ± 150 B.P. (plus or minus 150 years before present)—within which it is statistically likely that, for example, the tree from which a wooden artifact was shaped, or the bone from which a fishhook was made, was living and taking up the unstable isotopes of ^{14}C on which this dating system is based. Furthermore, there are disagreements as to whether radiocarbon dates markedly earlier than others should be accepted or simply rejected out of hand, and, more fundamentally, whether or not the earliest available radiocarbon dates from excavated living sites necessarily indicate when colonization began. Some archaeologists, for example, hypothesize that the earliest sites in the Cooks and Societies may have been missed because they have been submerged below sea level following island subsidence, or have been buried deeply under sediments washed down from intensively cultivated hillsides, and that new strategies must be developed to search for these sites. Furthermore, there is a movement to break away from relying only on living sites for evidence of early human occupation and to accept that marked vegetation changes, accelerated erosion, and periodic burning revealed in deep cores indicate slash-and-burn farming and therefore the onset of colonization.[23]

Given the imprecision of radiocarbon dating, disagreements over which radiocarbon dates to accept, and more fundamental disputes over whether or not those sites that have been discovered and excavated so far are indicative of the onset of colonization, it is not surprising that various authorities still disagree over whether there has been a pause in eastward migration after the initial occupation of West Polynesia. For example, by stringently applying various principles of what they call "chronometric hygiene," Matthew Spriggs and Atholl Anderson reject all candidate dates from the Cook Islands earlier than the range of 810 to 1170 A.D. and argue that extending this procedure throughout East Polynesia pushes all dates of first settlement there well forward in time, compelling "the retention of an apparent 1300–1600 year standstill in Pacific colonization after the first settlement of West Polynesia." In contrast, Patrick Kirch and Joanna Ellison argue that abrupt changes in stratigraphy, vegetation, and the geochemical composition of soils indicated in cores from drainage ditches around Mangaia island in the Southern Cooks are evidence that agricultural clearing and hence colonization started there by around 500 B.C., and offer this as evidence that there was no significant delay in movement eastward from West Polynesia.[24]

Accepting the date of 500 B.C. for Mangaian colonization does not, however, rule out the possibility that the rate of migration indicated by the rapid spread of Lapita sites from the Bismarcks to the mid-Pacific may have slowed in the eastern Pacific—as might be expected given the more episodic nature of the westerlies and their less regular alternation with the trade winds in the eastern as opposed to the western Pacific. Most authorities would probably agree that it took no more than 500 years for people to migrate the 2,300 or so miles from the Bismarck Archipelago to the archipelagos of West Polynesia, and some radiocarbon dates suggest that the movement may have required no more than a few hundred years to complete. Yet, even using the most conservative date for West Polynesian occupation of around 1000 B.C., the Mangaia evidence indicates that it took another 500 years to move farther eastward to that island, which is considerably less than half as far from West Polynesia as West Polynesia is from the Bismarcks.

Alternatively, even though it may have become progressively more difficult for voyagers to move across Polynesia as rapidly as their ancestors had migrated across Melanesia, they may well have responded creatively to the greater challenges of sailing eastward by trying harder and further refining their craft and sailing strategies so that the rate of expansion was maintained or even accelerated. Since, however, the islands have not been thoroughly sampled for submerged or deeply buried sites and for evidence of the environmental impact of pioneering agricultural activity, it is probably best to reserve judgment until that research has been conducted. Whatever may turn out to be the case, all parties to this dispute would probably agree that however long it took after pioneering voyagers first reached the western edge of Polynesia for their descendants to colonize all the archipelagos of central East Polynesia, the accomplishment of spreading human life over this truly oceanic domain was considerable. In terms of sailing achievements, however, settling these centrally located eastern archipelagos was but a prelude to the colonization of the far-flung islands that now form the defining points of the Polynesian triangle.

Southeast to Rapa Nui

Once the archipelagos of central East Polynesia had been settled, the Polynesians were faced with a situation neither they nor their Lapita predecessors had experienced during the long expansion eastward across the Pacific. The chain of relatively closely spaced islands and archipelagos extending across the ocean had come to an end. Yet some seafarers did go on to colonize the lone island of Rapa Nui, located some 2,300 miles from the South American coast (as well as to occupy temporarily the intervening island of Pitcairn and its even tinier neighbor, Henderson Island). This discovery and occupation of Rapa Nui represents the last known success in the strategy of expanding eastward that had brought this lineage of seafarers so far across the Pacific.

That Polynesians colonized Rapa Nui was a magnificent feat in itself, for the island is a lone volcanic outcropping of only some 50 square miles of land located 1,900 miles directly upwind with respect to the southeast trades from the Marquesas Islands, and 1,100 miles from the temporarily settled islands of Pitcairn and Henderson. Nonetheless, voyagers who probed eastward toward this small and lonely island may have been able to detect its presence while still far from it. Archaeologist Joanne Van Tilburg hypothesizes that the abundant bird life that flourished on and around the island before human occupation may have provided explorers probing this part of the Pacific with a sure indication that land lay over the eastern horizon, and even a bearing toward the island that they could follow.[25] Voyagers who spied flocks of migrating land birds heading east could have converted the observed flight path into a star compass heading, and then sailed directly toward Rapa Nui. Voyagers who approached within 30–40 miles or so of the island, whether by chance or by following a migratory bird route, would then have been treated by the sight of multitudes of terns and other land-nesting birds fishing the offshore waters, a sure indication that land was near. They might even have been able to convert the homeward path of the birds at dusk to a fairly precise star bearing, and then followed that directly to Rapa Nui.

It seems likely that those voyagers who sailed far enough to the east to get within range of the island probably did so by exploiting westerly wind shifts. A prolonged and far-reaching spell of westerlies during a major El Niño event might have enabled voyagers to reach Rapa Nui from as far away as the Marquesas, the source of the Rapa Nui settlers according to some analysts. The two months of predominantly westerly winds that spread at least as far east as Rapa Nui during the major El Niño event of 1982–1983 probably would have allowed a canoe to be worked across the 1,900-mile gap from the Marquesas to Rapa Nui.[26]

Alternatively, Rapa Nui may have been settled by mariners sailing a more southerly route where they would have been in a better position to exploit winter westerlies stemming from low pressure systems passing to the south. Yachtsmen who wish to sail to Rapa Nui (located at 27° South latitude) often head there via Mangareva in the Gambiers (23° South) and its outlier to the east, Pitcairn (25° South), and a number of recent computer simulation studies of canoe voyages purposefully sailed to the east seem to indicate some probability that canoes sailing along this route could have reached Rapa Nui. Perhaps, therefore, early voyagers chanced upon Rapa Nui by following this southern route, or by sailing a parallel if longer course from one of the Austral islands, which extend from Rurutu (22° South) to Rapa (27° South), or in sailing from as far west as Rarotonga (21° South) or Mangaia (22° South) in the Southern Cooks.[27]

A more radical suggestion for the way in which voyagers might have chanced upon Rapa Nui involves exploiting the westerlies that frequently blow in temperate latitudes below the tropics. Square-riggers bound from tropical Polynesia to Chile first sailed south to the "roaring forties" between 40° and 50° South and then turned east to sail before the strong westerlies found in these latitudes.[28] Although Polynesians sailing in an open canoe would have had great difficulty surviving for long in such high latitudes, the experience of the French adventurer Eric de Bisschop points to a way they might have been able to sail along the fringe of these westerlies far enough to reach Rapa Nui.

In 1956 de Bisschop tried to sail a bamboo raft, the *Tahiti-Nui*, from Tahiti to South America in a valiant, if anthropologically misguided, attempt to reverse Heyerdahl's thesis and demonstrate that Polynesians could have rafted eastward to South America. Instead of sailing from Tahiti all the way down to 40° South where he could have been fairly well assured of getting into the westerlies, de Bisschop tried to work his way eastward at around 30° South, hoping to get enough westerly wind there to move east without being exposed to the cold and stormy seas of higher latitudes. The gamble did not pay off. Although de Bisschop and his crew did manage to find enough westerly wind to work their way to within 800 miles of the Chilean coast, it took them over six months to do so by which time their raft was so battered by gales and easterly headwinds that they had to abandon it and accept a rescue by a Chilean naval vessel. Much earlier in the voyage, however, the *Tahiti-Nui* passed just a few hundred miles south of Rapa Nui, which suggests the possibility that some similarly adventurous canoe sailors might have tried to work their way eastward at around 30° South until cold and exhaustion drove them north on a course that fortuitously took them to Rapa Nui.[29]

Whatever wind conditions enabled people to reach Rapa Nui, the voyage (or voyages, if we follow Thomas Barthel's reading of Rapa Nui traditions to the effect that two separate parties landed there)[30] must have been extraordinary. Once there, a return voyage to the west would have been relatively easy. Even a minimally seaworthy craft pointed imprecisely westward would have stood a fair chance of fetching up on an island somewhere in the heart of East Polynesia, as witness the post-World War II adventures of four groups of Rapa Nui youths who managed to sail to the Tuamotus and the Cooks in tiny, makeshift craft. The problems inherent, however, in sailing back to the island— hitting just the right wind conditions for making easting, and then finding such a small target without the aid of a surrounding or screening archipelago—probably inhibited the development of any significant two-way voyaging between there and central East Polynesia, particularly after human settlement impacted the bird populations on Rapa Nui, extinguishing or greatly reducing in number the bird species that must have helped the first human settlers to find the island.

The pioneering archaeologist William Mulloy has written that "the most important and central fact leading to an understanding of Easter Island culture-history is its unusual degree of isolation by sea."[31] Of all the major islands of Polynesia, Rapa Nui may be the one in which isolationist assumptions about single-voyage settlement and the subsequent lack or low level of communication with other islands work best. Indeed, the reason why Rapa Nui culture looks so different from those of other East Polynesian islands may be because over the centuries the people there had little or no opportunity to share ideas and experiences with their cousins far to the west.

North to Hawai'i

Once the Polynesians had settled the archipelagos along the eastern frontier of central East Polynesia, no more island groups lay directly to the east—only, way off to the southeast, the sprinkling of tiny islands from Pitcairn to Rapa Nui. Exploratory parties that may have kept probing eastward for still more archipelagos would therefore have been sorely disappointed by the empty seas they found. The strategy of eastward expansion which had brought their ancestors so far across the Pacific had run out of islands. Since the eastern frontier of their island universe had been reached, and they knew that the islands "below" them to the west were already settled, might some particularly daring sailors have set out to explore unknown seas to the north?

This is not all conjecture. Polynesians did temporarily occupy some dry and barren atolls of the Northern Line Islands located just north of the equator, and of course colonized the Hawaiian Islands, over 1,800 miles northwest by north of the Marquesas. Although Tahiti was long thought to have been the source for the migrants who first settled Hawai'i, comparative analyses of Hawaiian and other central East Polynesian languages which indicate that Hawaiian is basically a Marquesic language has led to the hypothesis that the first people to settle Hawai'i came from the Marquesas Islands. Although this hypothesis may be challenged on the basis of a more complicated settlement scenario involving initial colonization from the Cooks or Societies followed by the repeated arrival of canoe-loads of Marquesans that gave the resultant language its Marquesan character, let us here assume that the language connection points to the initial settlement of Hawai'i from the Marquesas.[32] What, then, can be said about the voyaging conditions between the two groups?

Despite the vast stretch of open ocean that lies between the two archipelagos, the sail from the Marquesas to Hawai'i looks relatively straightforward because of the favorable alignment of the route in relation to the trade winds as well as the large navigational target presented by the long Hawaiian chain. This is not to say, however, that canoes could easily have drifted to Hawai'i from the Marquesas. Neither computer simulation studies nor our own experience in sailing from Tahiti to Hawai'i supports such a scenario; in ordinary conditions a canoe departing the Marquesas would have to be intentionally sailed to Hawai'i.[33] In good weather the passage would be relatively fast, however. As the Marquesas group lies well to the windward of Hawai'i, a canoe could sail there on a broad reach, the most favorable sailing angle for a double canoe. Assuming fairly steady trades such as those enjoyed during the 1976 and 1980 return voyages of *Hōkūleʻa* from Tahiti to Hawaiʻi, and a relatively direct heading, a canoe should be able to cover the 1,800-plus miles between the two archipelagos in some fifteen to twenty days, although extended doldrum conditions, adverse winds along the way, or a meandering course could easily add a week or two to that time.

Why, however, would Marquesan voyagers have sailed so far from their islands, angling slightly downwind on a course that would be difficult to retrace toward islands they had never seen? We know from the independent testimony of two English beachcombers—Edward Robarts and a man known only as "Wilson"—who jumped ship in the Marquesas and lived there during the first years of the nineteenth century that even at that late date Marquesans were setting out to find and settle new lands and that they seem to have left without intending to return. In his diary, Edward Robarts wrote about Marquesan families setting off in canoes to find fertile and uninhabited lands, while Wilson told the visiting American naval commander David Porter that during his stay in these islands some 800 men, women, and children had left in search of islands on which to settle. Although Robarts did not state in which direction the canoes sailed, Wilson specified that canoes set off downwind in search of land to the northwest.[34]

Some of these early nineteenth-century Marquesan emigrants are described as having been forced to leave their valleys by population pressure, war, and drought-induced famine to search desperately for new islands on which to settle. Yet the first people to reach Hawaiʻi from the Marquesas may not have been driven to flee their islands by such dire circumstances, for they settled Hawaiʻi almost 2,000 years ago, presumably before the Marquesas would have become so crowded and conflict-ridden. Perhaps just the lure of new lands lying over the horizon may have been incentive enough for the more adventurous to set sail. The English beachcombers described how the *tauʻa*, the shamanistic priests of the tribes, would exhort their people to take to their canoes by recounting the visions they had received of fertile, well-watered, and uninhabited islands lying over the horizon. If such exhortations were anywhere near as common in the past as they seem to have been in the early 1800s, it seems likely that over the previous centuries many a canoe-load of the adventurous would have been willing to commit themselves to a one-way, downwind voyage to the northwest—particularly if previous efforts to explore the seas to the east had found them to be empty of archipelagos.

Were any signs available to the Marquesans that land might lie far over the northern horizon, or was the discovery of Hawai'i the result of a lucky landfall by seafarers searching randomly in the unknown northwest quadrant? That the sight of Polaris might have led the first settlers to Hawai'i is an intriguing suggestion made by *Hōkūle'a* designer Herb Kane and Abe Pi'ianai'a, the veteran seaman who sailed on the canoe from Tahiti to Rarotonga. Although in the Southern Hemisphere Polaris lies out of sight below the horizon, it can be seen soon after crossing the equator. Kane and Pi'ianai'a accordingly imagine that voyagers who had headed off to the northwest would, after sailing over the equator, have become transfixed by the sight of a star low on the northern horizon they had never seen before, one that remained almost stationary in the sky, inscribing around the north celestial pole a tiny little circle that was only slightly larger 2,000 years ago. They further speculate that the fascinated voyagers would have taken this star, known in Hawaiian as *Hōkū-pa'a*, or "immovable star," as a sign that land lay in that direction and would therefore have headed directly toward it on a northerly course that led them inevitably to the Hawaiian chain. If the great volcanic peak of Mauna Loa on the island of Hawai'i was in eruption at the time, its fiery glow might even have provided a homing beacon for any such voyagers.[35]

Another possibility is that seafarers set a course for Hawai'i by watching the flight path of migratory shorebirds that each year, after sojourning during the Northern Hemisphere winter in the Marquesas, set off for their breeding grounds in Alaska. Three such migratory species are of particular interest: the Pacific golden plover (*Pluvialis fulda; Kōlea* in Hawaiian); the bristle-thighed curlew (*Numenius tahitiensis; Kioea*); and the ruddy turnstone (*Arenaria interpres; 'Akekeke*).[36] The golden plover is especially well known in Hawai'i where they can be seen to flock together just before the annual migration and then, after wheeling around in the air, to head off en masse toward the north. Although parallel observations have not yet been made in the Marquesas, it seems likely that the plover or one or both of the other species may exhibit the same behavior there. If so, observant Marquesans could have converted the flight direction of departing flocks into a star bearing toward the land they knew must lie somewhere over the northern horizon.

A direct course from the Marquesas to Alaska would, however, pass to the east of Hawai'i, probably too far away for detecting land, unless strong northeast trades and accompanying ocean currents north of the doldrums forced an exploring canoe far enough to the west to bring it within sight of Hawai'i—or within range of the daily flight patterns of terns or other land birds flying out each day from the islands to fish at sea. Alternatively, if migratory birds regularly fly from the Marquesas to Hawai'i before turning due north for Alaska, a possibility that has yet to be investigated, their heading from the Marquesas might have given the islanders a direct bearing to Hawai'i.

A return voyage from Hawai'i to the Marquesas looks much more difficult than one from Hawai'i to Tahiti because the Marquesas group lies so far to the east of Hawai'i. A canoe sailing from Hawai'i would have to make almost 900 miles of easting to reach the Marquesas. Sleek, weatherly yachts have to be pushed hard against the wind to make it to the Marquesas; during the attempts to gain maximum easting while on the way to Tahiti in 1976, 1980, and 1985 the closest *Hōkūle'a* has been able to get to the Marquesas was in 1985 when she passed about 375 miles to the west of the islands. Each time the track of the canoe in the northeast trades was headed almost directly for the Marquesas, but then curved off to the south-southwest when *Hōkūle'a* encountered the southeast trade winds. This situation, plus the apparent lack of any Hawaiian traditions of return voyaging to the Marquesas, has discouraged speculation that there might have been any two-way voyaging between the two archipelagos.

Nonetheless, in Hawai'i we have recently been wracking our brains to come up with a viable strategy for sailing to the Marquesas for a very practical reason. Nainoa is now directing a new project to sail *Hawai'i-Loa*, a reconstructed canoe launched in 1993 that was made as much as possible from native materials, from the Marquesas to Hawai'i in order to re-create a "discovery voyage." Since *Hawai'i-Loa* was built in Hawai'i, some way must be found to get her to the Marquesas in order to be in position for the run to Hawai'i. Discussions for sailing the new canoe to the Marquesas have focused on three main options: using spells of southerly and westerly winds that occur periodically in Hawaiian waters during the winter to try and gain a thousand or so miles of easting before turning south for the Marquesas; leaving Hawai'i during a spell of strong, winter trade winds, in hopes of encountering northeast instead of southeast winds south of the equator, as sometimes occurs that time of year;[37] or sailing directly to the Tuamotus, and then using westerly wind shifts to work north-northeast to the Marquesas. All these strategies have their problems, however: the spells of southerly and westerly winds that occur during the Hawaiian winter are unpredictable, often short-lived, and sometimes dangerously stormy; we know of no way to predict when the winds would be northeast in the vicinity of the Marquesas; and, as we learned in 1987, sailing from the Tuamotus to the Marquesas would be highly dependent on getting just the right wind shifts.

Just recently, a fourth option has emerged from an encounter with southerly winds during *Hōkūle'a*'s fourth crossing to Tahiti while sailing to Rarotonga to take part in the Pacific Festival of Arts that was held there in 1992. As the southeast trade winds flow across the equator toward the doldrums trough, they become more southerly, typically blowing from south-southeast. When *Hōkūle'a* encountered these south-southeasterlies on previous crossings, except for brief tacks to the east the canoe was kept sailing to the west of south to make maximum southing in order to reach as quickly as possible the more easterly winds to be found south of the equator. In 1992, however, the steady, light winds encountered just below the doldrums came almost directly from the south, a direction which, if the canoe had been kept on the port tack, would have quickly driven it far to the west. Accordingly, it was decided to use these southerlies to go over on the starboard tack and sail east in order to gain additional easting. This tactic brought the canoe almost to the longitude of the Marquesas before she was put back onto the port tack to sail west-southwest until more easterly trade winds could be reached. Since *Hōkūle'a* could probably have continued to sail due east across these southerlies until she had made enough easting to make a direct slant across the southeast trades to the Marquesas, this experience suggests that whenever such subdoldrum southerlies occurred in the past it might have been possible for resourceful sailors from Hawai'i to have used them to reach the Marquesas.

Of course, at present we do not know whether homesick Marquesans, or adventurous Hawaiians, were ever able to exploit these subdoldrum southerlies, or any other wind conditions, to sail to the Marquesas. Given, however, the difficulty of the route and the lack of any obvious evidence for two-way communication between the archipelagos, at this point of time it is perhaps advisable to stay on the skeptical side about this issue. A successful, two-way experimental voyage between Hawai'i and the Marquesas, particularly if accompanied by newly discovered linguistic, archaeological, or traditional evidence of back and forth movement, would, of course, force a reconsideration of the possibility that Hawai'i may have once been in two-way communication with the Marquesas as well as Tahiti.

Southwest to Aotearoa

Those seafarers who sailed southwest from the tropical heartland of East Polynesia and into temperate latitudes to discover and settle Aotearoa departed even more radically than the colonizers of Hawai'i from the ancestral pattern of expanding eastward. Not only did they head downwind in relation to the trades, but by keeping on such a course they soon sailed completely out of the trade wind zone and into latitudes often wracked by cold seas and blustery westerlies. Indeed, these conditions could help explain why Aotearoa apparently was the last major part of Polynesia to be settled. Seafarers may not have been willing to explore so far downwind and then out of the trade wind zone entirely until all the tropical islands of the Pacific had been discovered and colonized.

In 1985, as we sailed farther and farther from Rarotonga and into cooler and cooler waters we wondered what drove the very first voyagers along this route to keep the prows of their canoes pointed in a direction that was taking them away from warm seas and familiar winds. Were they convinced, as S. Percy Smith and others have proposed, by the annual migrations of the bartailed godwit (*Limosa lapponica*) or long-tailed cuckoo (*Eudynamis taitensis*) that land must lie in that direction,[38] or were they just pressing on to see where sailing with seasonal southeasterlies on their beam would take them? Or, to follow a scenario suggested by at least one Māori legend, after having wandered south out of the tropics, were they racing before early summer easterlies in a desperate bid to find land before their food and water ran out?

Whatever the reason, our experience in sailing to Aotearoa leads us to believe that the discoverers must have been highly motivated to sail so far into strange latitudes and cold seas. We had a dry and comfortable voyage: there was hardly any rain at all, and with beam winds most of the way the canoe took little water over the deck. Furthermore, we were equipped with foul weather gear designed for North Atlantic conditions, as well as fast-drying sleeping bags. Even so, as we moved farther and farther south the nights especially felt cold, and we wondered about the hardships pioneering voyagers must have experienced—especially if they encountered heavy rains or had to drive through drenching head seas. Those early voyagers, who only had rain capes made from pandanus leaves, woven mat ponchos, and *tapa* (bark cloth) to shield them from the elements, must have had compelling reasons for sailing so far to the south and facing the cold seas and winds found there.

Some Māori legends tell of two-way voyaging; for example, Kupe, the legendary discoverer of Aotearoa, is said to have returned to Hawaiki from whence, years later, colonizing parties set out for Aotearoa following the oral directions that Kupe left. Although these and other tales involving voyaging back and forth between central East Polynesia and Aotearoa have been criticized as untrustworthy if not downright fabrications, from a sailing point of view such two-way voyaging would seem possible, though not at all easy. As we have seen, sailing to Aotearoa is not that difficult. The crossing from Aotearoa back to central East Polynesia looks much more challenging, however. The problem is making enough easting to reach the Cooks or islands beyond. In theory, the westerlies common during the winter could have been used to drive a canoe far enough to the east so that, upon entering the trade wind belt, a canoe could have made land somewhere in central East Polynesia. In practice, however, this strategy may have been too hazardous to attempt in open canoes. If the stormy conditions did not overwhelm a canoe, those on board would have been in danger of dying from exposure to the cold wind, rain, and drenching seas common at that time of year. However, during those summers when slow-moving high

pressure systems pass to the north of the North Island, it seems likely that voyagers anxious to sail east might have been able to take advantage of the warmer and more benign westerlies circulating around the southern flanks of these displaced highs in order to get a safe boost far enough to the east so that they could then angle toward the trade wind zone and work their way to Rarotonga or islands beyond.

In September–October of 1992, Hector Busby, the Māori leader who hosted us when we sailed to Aotearoa in 1985, attempted just such a voyage. Using plans that we supplied him, Hector and a group of young Māori apprentices built a double canoe from two giant *kauri* logs (*Agathis australis*), a tree favored by both canoe builders and shipwrights. Hector's goal was to sail his canoe, called *Te Aurere*, to Rarotonga and then back to Aotearoa, retracing a voyage made, according to his family traditions, by one of his ancestors. Unfortunately, an urgent invitation to sail to Rarotonga in late 1992 in order to participate in the coming together of voyaging canoes at the Pacific Festival of Arts led *Te Aurere* to leave Aotearoa while winter conditions were still prevailing. The Arts Festival was scheduled for mid-October, forcing Hector to set sail in late September at the tail end of what had been an unusually cold winter. A series of westerly gales did boost *Te Aurere* quickly to the east, but they so severely battered the canoe and her crew that a decision was made to get the canoe as quickly as possible out of the danger zone and into calmer trade wind waters by having the escorting yacht tow her to the northwest during calm periods between gales. Thus, although *Te Aurere* did finally make it to Rarotonga, she did not do so solely by sailing. Nonetheless, this experience does point out how a voyage from Aotearoa back to the tropical center of East Polynesia might be made under more benign summer conditions. (Bad luck continued to dog the canoe on the return to Aotearoa; when *Te Aurere* was nearing the North Island her mast broke and the canoe was towed most of the rest of the way.)

Polynesian Outliers in Melanesia and Micronesia

Although Aotearoa lies well to the west of the other East Polynesian islands and even slightly west of Samoa and Tonga, it is not the westernmost outpost of Polynesian culture. That distinction goes to Nukuria, an atoll located in Melanesia just to the northeast of New Guinea between New Britain and Bougainville, with two other atolls located almost due north in Micronesia as close runners-up: Kapingamarangi and Nukuoro. These are among the dozen and a half or so "Polynesian outliers," small islands scattered through Melanesia and along the southern fringe of Micronesia that were settled by Polynesians. It can therefore be said that Polynesian settlements truly stretch more than a quarter way around the globe, 96 degrees from Nukuria at just a little less than 155° West longitude to Rapa Nui at little over 109° East longitude.

Formerly a number of theorists thought that these outliers were relic outposts left over from the original Polynesian migration from Southeast Asia into the Pacific. Since, however, Polynesian culture as such did not really exist until it evolved in the mid-Pacific, and since the outlier languages are recognizably West Polynesian in derivation, it is now widely accepted that the outliers were settled in a much later "backwash" movement from West Polynesia. As these outliers lie downwind (with respect to the trades) from West Polynesia, it is not surprising that computer simulation studies have shown them to be the Polynesian islands most likely to have been settled by accidental drift voyages. A simple drift model does not, however, fit with the complex culture histories of these islands now emerging from archaeological investigations and evident in the islanders' own traditions. These traditions feature tales of multiple settlement by both castaways and people deliberately searching for a new island home, as well as of frequent intrusions by marauding canoes from Tonga and other islands to the east.[39]

To Continental Shores?

Did the Polynesian expansion stop with the discovery and settlement of Rapa Nui, Hawai'i, and Aotearoa and the backwash to small islands in Melanesian and Micronesian waters, or did seafarers keep exploring farther until they made landfall on the Americas or Australia? The issue of continental landfall has been repeatedly raised by writers who, impressed by the seeming similarity to Polynesian examples of fishhooks, adze blades, war clubs, and other artifacts found here and there along the Pacific coasts of North and South America and Australia, have proposed that Polynesians must have reached these far-off shores.[40] Most prehistorians have tended to dismiss such claims on the basis that the similarities are coincidental rather than indicative of a real connection, or that those artifacts that are genuinely Polynesian were in fact recently transported as curios to continental regions by Europeans. Yet there is one connection between Polynesia and the continental rim of the Pacific that is widely accepted as genuine: before European contact Polynesians were cultivating the sweet potato, a plant that originated in South America. This has led to the widely discussed hypothesis that Polynesians sailed all the way to South America, picked up the sweet potato there, and then sailed back to Polynesia with this valuable tuber.[41]

There is one great objection to this hypothesis. Such a round-trip seems both complicated and immensely difficult, especially in comparison to the alternate explanation that the sweet potato was brought to Polynesia by Native American raft voyagers. Introduction by a one-way downwind raft trip, rather than by a problematic roundtrip canoe expedition, would seem to satisfy the philosophical principle of Occam's Razor that we should choose the simpler hypothesis over the more complex one. As has been demonstrated by the *Kon-Tiki* expedition and a number of subsequent raft voyages that have also reached Polynesia, the balsa wood raft formerly used along the west coast of tropical South America is well adapted for the long drift to Polynesia. A likely scenario of sweet potato introduction might therefore start with its transport by Native American raft voyagers from South America to the Marquesas or some other point in East Polynesia, from which it was then spread to other islands by Polynesian canoe voyagers.

At first glance, such a scenario seems far simpler than one in which intrepid voyagers sail 4,000 miles to windward with respect to the trade winds all the way from the Marquesas to South America, refit their canoe and load it with valuable sweet potato tubers, and then sail it all the way back to the Marquesas or some other point in Polynesia. Although the return voyage downwind to Polynesia would probably not have posed a great problem to experienced seamen sailing in a sound canoe, the windward crossing to South America would have been most daunting. Between the Marquesas and South America lies an immense body of open ocean dominated by easterly trade winds and bereft of intervening islands, except for Rapa Nui and a scattering of islands off the South American coast.

Nonetheless, granted that a roundtrip voyage from the Marquesas or other points in Polynesia to South America and return might seem almost unbelievably difficult, a case can still be made for Polynesian voyagers fetching the sweet potato from South America. South American rafts were certainly seaworthy and durable enough to have reached Polynesia by sailing before the trade winds and accompanying currents. Yet we need to remember that the Lapita seafarers and their Polynesian descendants, not Native Americans, colonized the oceanic islands of the Pacific—sailing the hard way against the direction of the dominant winds and currents. A scenario involving a Polynesian roundtrip to South America and return is therefore more in keeping with the reality of Pacific migration, even though its complexity and difficulty might appear to go against the principle of choosing the simplest explanation.

To accept such a possibility, we have to come up with a reasonable hypothesis of how Polynesian voyagers could have accomplished the toughest leg of such a roundtrip, that of moving from the eastern edge of Polynesia all the way to the South American coast. Judging from our experience in sailing from Samoa to Tahiti, it seems most likely that the only way to move so far to the east would have been by means of westerly winds. Perhaps particularly determined voyagers might have been able to work the spells of winter westerlies along the southern edge of the trades to make their way that far east, or they might have headed farther south to 40° or so in order to pick up the more regular westerlies to be found there and then sailed before these all the way to the South American coast. Both strategies would have their problems, though. Working that far eastward with spells of winter westerlies would require a fortuitously long series of such events, and going far to the south to pick up the midlatitude westerlies would have exposed the canoe and crew to the chill, rough seas, and boisterous winds often found there on the edge of the "roaring forties" as nineteenth-century sailors nicknamed these latitudes. Eric de Bisschop's account of his harrowing, six-month voyage made mostly between 30° and 35° South latitudes aboard the bamboo raft *Tahiti-Nui* from Tahiti to within 800 miles of the Chilean coast (before the disintegrating raft had to be abandoned) should be read by any armchair voyagers who would blithely propose that Polynesian voyagers successfully pushed their way to the east along this southerly route to reach South America.[42]

But we need to know more about summer sailing conditions in these latitudes before dismissing outright the possibility of a canoe working its way east through this zone. Although the comparable latitudes of the Northeast Pacific do not have the reputation of being as stormy as those in the Southeast Pacific, yachts are not advised to sail through them during the winter, and periodically even large freighters founder in the strong gales and heavy seas then common in these latitudes. Conditions there are much more benign in the summer, however, and yachtsmen wishing to sail from Hawai'i to California typically wait until then to depart. First they sail north to clear the "Pacific High" until they reach the westerlies circulating clockwise around the northern flank of this quasi-permanent high pressure zone. They then head east before the westerlies to make land somewhere along the California coast or farther to the north.[43]

In 1952 I made such a roundabout crossing from Hawai'i to California. Particularly since our broad-beamed ketch sailed no better to windward than *Hōkūle'a*, it seems to me we could have just as easily sailed a voyaging canoe to California. Although there is no compelling evidence to suggest that in prehistoric times Hawaiians or any other Polynesians ever reached California or other points along the Pacific coast of North America, archaeological remains on Necker, a rocky little island located at 23° 35' North latitude, attest that canoe voyagers reached at least that far north along the Hawaiian chain.[44] To sail another ten to fifteen degrees or so north into the westerlies belt would probably have been within Polynesian capabilities, as would have been the long run east to the coast, providing the weather was fair and the westerlies were not too stormy. If similar summer sailing conditions prevailed in the Southeast Pacific during the past two millennia, a canoe voyage made via the midlatitudes to South America might, therefore, not have been totally out of the question.

Starting from Rapa Nui rather than islands farther to the east would have greatly shortened such a crossing, as Rapa Nui is only 2,300 miles off the coast and within 500 to 1,000 miles of the westerlies belt. But to judge whether Rapa Nui could have been a staging base for such a venture, we would have to know whether the wood of the palm trees, the only sizable trees that apparently grew there when the first settlers arrived, could have been used to build voyaging canoes or repair ones originating in central East Polynesia. Whatever the case, once the island had been denuded of these and other trees, building or perhaps even refitting a voyaging canoe there was out of the question, and the Rapa Nui people would have been effectively cut off from sailing to South America as well as sailing to the islands to the west.

Polynesian seafarers seeking to explore far to the east may not, however, have had to start their journey (or its last leg) from Rapa Nui, or even to chance a crossing in southerly latitudes. Especially daring sailors from central East Polynesia might have been able to ride the westerly winds of a massive El Niño disruption of the trade wind field all the way to the South American coast. Although it is not possible to state definitely that westerly winds during the major El Niño event of 1982–

1983 carried all the way to South America, some meteorological records indicate that they may have extended that far, or almost that far.[45] If so, some time in the past, weather-wise explorers from the Marquesas or other islands along the frontier of central East Polynesia might have jumped at the opportunity presented by such an outbreak of El Niño westerlies to explore far enough to the east to land on the coast of what is now Equador or Peru.

Turning to the southwestern frontier of Polynesia, it is similarly not totally out of the question that Polynesian seafarers might have reached Australia, where stone tools that look Polynesian have reportedly been found. The hypothesis that the undoubtedly Polynesian adze blades found on Norfolk Island were brought there prehistorically by Polynesians (and not by later visitors during the European era) has recently been strengthened by the discovery in excavated sites of the bones dated from around 1200 A.D. of that ubiquitous passenger on voyaging canoes, the Polynesian rat (*Rattus exulans*).[46] If Polynesians reached this island, located less than 800 miles from Australia, it would seem possible that by exploiting easterly winds to search far to the west, or by being driven that way by easterly gales, some voyagers might have fetched up on the Australian coast.

Without, however, a lucky find of indisputably Polynesian artifacts or skeletal remains buried deep in a well-stratified and datable archaeological site somewhere along at least one of the coastlines in question, we probably will never know whether Polynesian voyagers ever set foot on any continental beaches. Yet, the lack of such firm archaeological evidence for a Polynesian presence in Australia or the Americas, or of languages and cultural practices there of unarguably Polynesian derivation, does not necessarily mean that Polynesian seafarers never reached the continental margins of their oceanic world. Hungry, tired voyagers would probably not have been a match for any local group that opposed their landing, and even if they found a friendly reception it is doubtful that their distinctively oceanic culture would have long survived intact amongst any group with whom they might have peacefully settled. Even if Polynesian seafarers did manage to sail to the Americas or Australia, their unique cultural adaptation for island colonization, which in effect had made them Polynesians, would not have been easily transplanted onto these alien, already inhabited continental shores.

Post-Colonization Two-Way Voyaging

The question of whether there was any significant voyaging back and forth between widely separated islands and archipelagos after they had been settled has long exercised Polynesian specialists. Because of the voyages made aboard *Hōkūleʻa* between Hawaiʻi and Tahiti, Andrew Sharp's pronouncements about the impossibility of such voyaging have lost much of their appeal. Nonetheless, the idea promoted especially by nineteenth-century students of Polynesian traditions that canoes once sailed back and forth between distantly separated Polynesian centers continues to be regarded with much skepticism, primarily because there seems to be no eyewitness evidence of such voyaging at the time of European contact.

It is commonly believed that the only significant two-way voyaging taking place at the time of European contact was that among the relatively closely spaced islands and archipelagos of West Polynesia and that between the Society Islands and the Northwest Tuamotus in East Polynesia. Yet there exists abundant ethnohistorical evidence of more widespread two-way voyaging activities during the period just before and after contact. For example, when the Spanish navigator Quiros visited the Marquesas Islands in 1595 the Marquesans told him how they raided islands to the south, probably those of the northern Tuamotus where there are numerous traditions about the coming of the fearsome "Hiva" as the Tuamotuans called the invaders from the north. The Bishop Museum monographs reconstructing the cultures on various Polynesian islands are filled with references to canoes sailing here and there. For example, in their monograph on Pukapuka atoll in the Northern Cooks, Ernest and Pearl Beaglehole give detailed navigational directions that the Pukapukans had formerly employed to sail to the high islands of the Samoan group to obtain stone adze blades needed on their coral atoll. The Beagleholes also point out that the Pukapukans voyaged freely for other purposes: "a desire for adventure; desire to visit the lands and peoples that traditions told them lay below the horizon in all directions; . . . desire to advance the prestige of one's paternal lineage as against the others," as well as to flee the island because of some transgression.[47]

We will probably never know to which of the islands on Tupaia's famous map (fig. 3, chap. 1) Tahitians were regularly voyaging. Tupaia is reported to have said that he had sailed from Ra'iatea to an island Cook wrote down as "Mannua." He also talked about sailing ten to twelve days to an island to the west of Ra'iatea, and then taking thirty days to return, figures that would be consistent with sailing westward 1,200 miles to reach Manu'a at the eastern end of Samoa and then working a canoe back to Ra'iatea from there. Although David Lewis argues convincingly from his seaman's point of view that Tupaia was referring to sailing to and from Manu'a in the Samoan group, some other commentators are skeptical. Cook's apparent confusion about some of Tupaia's directional terms, coupled with his poor phonetic rendering of Tahitian words, as well as inconsistencies in the accounts of what the Tahitian is supposed to have said, has led to the suggestion that the "Mannua" in question may be the atoll of Manuae located in the Southern Cooks, not the more distant Manu'a of the Samoan group. In contrast, Tupaia's statement that he had visited "Ohetiroa" (Hiti-Roa; now known as Rurutu) in the Australs seems unarguable since he actually guided Cook to this island. Furthermore, Tupaia told Cook that there were more islands in that direction, including "Oreevavai" (Ra'ivavae), from whence, he said, "fine adzes come over that sea-way to Ra'iatea."[48]

Even, however, if all these examples (save the disputed one involving Manu'a) are accepted as evidence of additional inter-archipelago communication at the time of European contact, it could be argued that most of the voyaging activity in question fell within the limit of 300 miles that Sharp placed on two-way voyaging (or was no more than a hundred or so miles over that limit), and that there is no firm archaeological evidence of any regular communication between more widely spaced islands such as Samoa and Rarotonga (700 miles), the Societies and Rarotonga (700 miles), the Marquesas and Rarotonga (1,200 miles), and Hawai'i and Tahiti (2,250 miles).

Yet traditions have come down to us that tell of canoes sailing back and forth between these and other widely spaced islands and archipelagos. For example, legends from the Southern Cooks recorded by the early British missionaries John Williams and William Wyatt Gill include tales of voyaging between Samoa, Rarotonga, and Tahiti revolving around the adventures of two chiefly voyagers, Karika from Samoa and Tangi'ia from Tahiti. The descendants of Karika living on Rarotonga told Gill that their ancestor came from Manuʻa at the eastern end of the Samoan chain, a contention that Taʻunga, an early nineteenth-century Rarotongan convert to Christianity, was able to confirm while serving as a missionary in Manuʻa where he discovered that the people there still preserved the memory of Karika and his departure for Rarotonga. For sailing back and forth between the Southern Cooks and the Societies, there are a number of traditions, including one recorded independently in both groups. John Orsmond, a British missionary in the Society Islands, collected a legend about annual pilgrimages made by representatives from Rarotonga and other islands to leeward of the Societies to the great *marae* of Taputapuātea on Raʻiatea. The Rarotongan representatives stopped coming, Orsmond was told, after their chief priest was murdered at the temple. When Orsmond's fellow missionary, John Williams, arrived at Rarotonga the people there told him essentially the same story, blaming the Tahitians for the death of their priest and the subsequent suspension of the annual pilgrimages. According to tales collected in 1897 by the German ethnographer, Karl Von Den Steinen, Marquesans once sailed all the way to Rarotonga to fetch red feathers they valued highly for personal adornment and as symbols of status. As for traditions that canoes once sailed back and forth between central East Polynesia and the distant islands of Hawaiʻi and Aotearoa, those telling about voyages between Tahiti and Hawaiʻi are the most extensive and will be treated in some detail in the next chapter.[49]

Two diametrically opposed ways have been offered to resolve the contradiction between the apparent historical evidence for only limited two-way voyaging at the time of European contact and traditional testimony about longer-range voyaging in previous centuries. Nineteenth-century students of Polynesian traditions argued that there had been a period when Polynesians did voyage widely back and forth between distantly separated islands, but that communication spheres had greatly contracted by the time Europeans arrived in the Pacific. In contrast, their modern critics have contended that there is no reason to believe legends indicating that interarchipelago communication was ever more widespread in the past than at the time of European contact. They argue that these traditions are fictional myths clothed in the metaphor of heroic seafaring that were composed and recited by those claiming descent from voyaging heroes in order to support claims to land and status, or simply that they were symbolic expressions of basic metaphysical and cultural concerns unrelated to anything that had ever occurred at sea.[50]

Although such reasoning may be in line with fashionable trends in interpreting oral traditions, a point explored in the next chapter, the idea that voyaging tales are purely "mythical"—in the negative sense that they had nothing to do with voyages that actually took place—can be questioned on the basis of archaeological evidence that either corroborates local traditions or is consistent with them. For example, within West Polynesia archaeologists have demonstrated a widespread movement of pottery and other items consistent with the traditions of frequent voyaging, invasions, intermarriage, and exchange among the many islands of the region. Samoan-style adze blades have also been found outside West Polynesia as far away as the Northern and Southern Cooks in East Polynesia, the Solomons in Melanesia, and Pohnpei in Micronesia. Some of these have even been sourced, through geochemical analysis, to the famous fortified quarry of Tataga Matau, or nearby quarries, on the island of Tutuila in American Samoa.[51] The cache of Samoan-style adze blades found in the remains of an ancient dwelling site on Rarotonga said to date back to between the twelfth and fourteenth centuries A.D. is particularly interesting in that this is the approximate time period when Rarotongan traditions tell of the coming of the Samoan chief Karika. Further archaeological evidence for communication between West Polynesia and the Southern Cooks comes from the island of Ma'uke where a potsherd recently recovered there in an occupation period dated at around the fourteenth century A.D. has been sourced to Tonga.[52]

Although no direct archaeological indications have so far turned up anywhere in central East Polynesia that Māori voyagers ever sailed back to that region, newly uncovered evidence from Raoul Island in the Kermadecs, over 400 miles northeast of the North Island, indicate that some Māori sailed at least that far away from their home islands. Because European visitors had previously found Polynesian adzes and domesticated plants on Raoul, it has long been thought that this rocky island located on the seaway from Rarotonga to Aotearoa might have been the legendary island of Rangitahua where voyagers from Hawaiki are said to have stopped on their way to Aotearoa. The

recent discovery there of cutting tools made from obsidian trace-
able to a volcanic source on Mayor, a small island off the east
coast of the North Island, indicates, however, that Māori voyagers ranged at least as far as Raoul, and opens the possibility
that the island might have been visited on return voyages from
Aotearoa back to tropical Polynesia, such as those mentioned in
Māori traditions.[53]

Concerning the Tahiti-Hawai'i contacts featured in Hawaiian
traditions, although efforts to confirm Tahitian influence through
the identification of specific changes in Hawaiian temple architecture, fishhook types, and other tools, artifacts, and structures
have so far not been widely accepted, as will be argued in the
following chapter the issue is far from closed.

On the Decline of
Long-distance Voyaging

Basic to the rejection by Sharp and others of the notion that
Polynesians once engaged in widespread two-way voyaging between widely spaced islands were the observations of the first
European navigators to touch on Polynesian islands during the
sixteenth, seventeenth, and eighteenth centuries who saw little
in the way of long-range voyaging then going on. Brushing aside
as just so much wishful thinking all the talk by Fornander, Smith,
and other students of Polynesian traditions about a golden age
of voyaging in centuries past, and downplaying evidence for some
voyaging activity during that era that the European navigators
had missed, Sharp and other critics claimed that since the Polynesians weren't making long voyages at the time of European
contact, their ancestors had never done so in the past.

Such seemingly hard-headed logic rests upon the Western
notion of progress common in twentieth-century industrial societies, at least until recently: that the course of human civilization is ever onward and upward, that technology will always
advance, and so forth.[54] Yet, history is full of examples of the
decline as well as the rise of empires, trading systems, and particular technologies. Within the Pacific, for example, there is
solid archaeological and ethnographic evidence for a long-term
decline in the range of voyaging and trading relations in Melanesian waters. The widespread exchange links established thousands of years ago among the newly settled islands extending

from the Bismarcks to Tonga and Samoa did not last. Over the centuries, voyaging spheres shrank until by the time of European contact regular interisland exchange was largely limited to localized trading networks involving relatively closely spaced islands, such as the famous *kula* exchange of the Massim region off the east coast of New Guinea.[55] Recently, Richard Walter and Barry Rolett, two young archaeologists working in the Cooks and Marquesas, respectively, have argued that this process of the buildup and then decline of voyaging links also occurred within and among the archipelagos of central East Polynesia. Walter, for example, documents his claim with archaeological data from the Cooks where he proposes that voyaging networks among the islands became established soon after settlement of the region and persisted until around 1300–1400 A.D. when the various island societies turned inward because of population growth, political rivalries, and other local developments. Recent excavations conducted by Kirch and his colleagues on Mangaia in the Southern Cooks show an abrupt cessation of the importation of pearl shell (for fishhooks and ornaments) at this time.[56]

Further indications of a decline in overseas voyaging in Polynesia can be seen in the types of watercraft in use on the various islands and archipelagos of the region when the European explorers visited them. As a perusal of the pages of Haddon and Hornell's encyclopedic work, *Canoes of Oceania*, demonstrates, in many archipelagos the sailing canoes in use at the time of European contact were adapted primarily for local coastal and intra-archipelago transport and communication and not for long-range voyaging, and on a few islands sailing canoes had entirely disappeared.[57]

Consider, for example, the canoes in use during the eighteenth century at the most peripheral Polynesian outposts of Hawai'i, Rapa Nui, and Aotearoa. Because of their distance from central East Polynesia, these were the islands most likely to have been reached only by craft well adapted for long-range voyaging. Yet it was apparent to the early European visitors to Hawai'i, Rapa Nui, and Aotearoa that the canoes they saw there were not made for undertaking long voyages to distant archipelagos, but rather were designed primarily for coastal use or inter-island sailing within the archipelago in question. The least oceanworthy vessels seen were those from Rapa Nui. Rongeveen, Cook, and other early visitors reported that the islanders had only tiny outrigger canoes, averaging about 10 feet in length. As we now know, massive deforestation had reduced the Rapa Nui to literally sewing together bits of driftwood and whatever scraps of local wood might be available to make their tiny, leaky craft. A more extreme example of how the lack of suitable canoe timber had impacted the ability to build voyaging canoes comes from the Chathams, cold, windswept islands located in the "roaring forties" to the east of the South Island of Aotearoa. Because no trees large enough to build canoes grew there, the people who migrated to these islands were forced to make rafts out of the dried stalks of a local reed.[58]

Although abundant supplies of large trees enabled Hawaiians and Māori to keep building large canoes, if we look at the design of their craft it is evident that they were not designed for long-range voyaging. For example, the rounded cross-section of Hawaiian canoes may be well adapted for handling in the rough, surf-filled seas characteristic of Hawai'i, but it is not ideal for long voyages where a more V-shaped hull form would resist leeway better, apparently indicating that Hawaiian sailors were willing to forego the more weatherly characteristics of voyaging canoes in order to have craft better suited for local conditions. The adaptation of canoes primarily for local use is even more evident in Māori naval architecture. Although some medium-size double canoes were in use in Aotearoa waters at the time of contact, most Māori canoe builders were then using the huge trees available to them to build long, outrigger-less canoes, vessels propelled primarily by paddling and used mainly for coastal travel and raiding.

Yet there were island groups where at the time of European contact overseas voyaging was flourishing. For example, the Tuamotuans were then regularly building and sailing big overseas sailing canoes well adapted for long voyages. The atoll environment of the Tuamotus must have encouraged the maintenance of deep-sea voyaging there. As inhabitants of dry, coraline islands, the Tuamotuans needed to be able to sail to the Societies in order to maintain access to the stone, timber, and other resources to be found on those high islands. In fact, at the time of European contact the Tuamotuans were known as the best canoe builders in the Society Islands, using local trees there to make canoes for Tahitians as well as for themselves.[59]

The contrast between the apparent decline of seafaring on

many of the high islands of Polynesia and its maintenance in the Tuamotus was mirrored in the Caroline Islands of Micronesia. Although the inhabitants of the high islands of Belau (Palau) and Yap at the western end of that chain, and Chuuk (Truk), Pohnpei (Ponape), and Kosrae (Kusae) at its eastern end, retained only limited voyaging capabilities, those living on the low, coral islands in between maintained a vigorous deep-sea voyaging capacity well into historic times. This included not only well-built oceangoing canoes but also the superb navigational skills that have been so helpful to our efforts at re-creating traditional Polynesian navigational techniques.[60]

The other Polynesian group most active in voyaging at the time of European contact were the Tongans. Since the Tongan archipelago is made up primarily of comparatively small, upraised coral islands, it is tempting to speculate that environmental factors may have played a role in Tonga's maintenance of an overseas voyaging capability. Certainly, at the time of European contact, the Tongans were frequently sailing to Fiji and other high islands to obtain stone, timber, and other needed raw materials. Yet their voyaging activities went far beyond that required for survival, and had a political dynamic of their own. In late prehistoric times and extending into the nineteenth century, Tongan canoes ranged widely throughout West Polynesia on missions of exchange, tribute gathering, and raiding to a point where it is possible to talk about a "Tongan maritime chiefdom." The nearby southeastern islands of Fiji became virtual Tongan colonies, and a number of islands to the north of Tonga as far away as Rotuma, over 600 miles to the northwest, fell under the influence of this expansionary maritime power. On the island of Niuatoputapu located between Tonga and Samoa, Tongan overlordship resulted in a Tongan dialect replacing the former language, known to have been Samoic from a vocabulary gathered in 1616 by the Dutch navigator Le Maire. Furthermore, Tongan canoes ranged far into Melanesian waters, as witness the tales of Tongan raids on Tikopia, Anuta, and other Polynesian outliers there.[61]

During the eighteenth century and into the nineteenth, the Tongans were actively improving the sailing characteristics of their canoes. The first Tongan double canoes seen in 1616 and 1643 by, respectively, the Dutch explorers Jacob Le Maire and Abel Tasman were of the *tongiaki* type. When Cook visited Tonga in 1774 on his second voyage into the Pacific, a new type of double canoe called the *kalia* was gaining popularity as the favored voyaging craft. Whereas the Cook and other early observers were not very impressed with the sailing abilities of the *tongiaki*, which was a variant of the basic Polynesian double canoe with a fixed bow and stern, they lavished great praise on the *kalia*. Apparently, the Tongans had been in contact with sailors from Micronesia, where a breakthrough in canoe design had occurred. These sailors had developed a double-ended craft with a movable sail that allowed them to sail more efficiently to windward and avoid the process of tacking by laboriously bringing the bow across the wind as required with orthodox Polynesian craft (and with Western sailing vessels as well). Instead they "shunted" their vessels first to one side and then the other side of the wind by moving the sail and mast from one end of the canoe to the other, thereby changing ends so that the bow became the stern and vice-versa. The Tongans adapted this movable-sail/double-ended configuration, coming up with the *kalia*, a racehorse of a double canoe that could sail circles around the ships of Cook and the other European navigators. (Tuamotuan sailors must have had some contact with the Tongans, if not directly with the Micronesians, for their double-ended, lateen-rigged craft also have the look of Polynesian-Micronesian hybrids.)[62]

One way to think about why some Polynesian groups would have given up long-range voyaging by the time of European contact whereas others maintained or even expanded their voyaging activities is in terms of the costs and benefits of voyaging. Our own efforts at re-creating Polynesian voyaging have certainly taught us how difficult and costly overseas canoe travel can be. Voyaging canoes were and are major capital investments whether the cost is reckoned in dollars, miles of coconut fiber line, or thousands and thousands of hours of labor, and they require constant attention and still more resources to maintain them. In addition, navigators must be trained, and they and their crews must drop everything for months or years on end to wander the seas, requiring those at home to take up the slack for their missing kinsmen. In the economists' jargon, voyaging has its opportunity costs: to build and maintain large sailing canoes and then to provision and sail them to and from distant islands requires the commitment of numerous people and considerable resources that could be used for other projects at home, be they developing irrigated taro systems to expand food production, building temples for communing with the gods, making war on neighboring chiefdoms, or whatever other initiatives might be considered most pressing at the time. For example, rather than organizing overseas voyages, the Hawaiian and Tahitian chiefs of the late eighteenth century were focusing their energies on vying for power in their mature and well-developed societies. As apparently had also occurred in Aotearoa, war canoes, rather than deep-sea voyaging canoes, became the most impressive craft in these two archipelagos.

The high island of Mangareva, located in the Gambier group at the southeastern end of the Tuamotu chain, provides an example of perhaps the ultimate step in canoe devolution. According to Peter Buck's analysis of traditional Mangarevan history, the people there once built large double canoes for use in and around their island and adjacent islands, as well as for sailing to Rarotonga and other more distant lands, but as chiefly rivalries grew they came to use them more and more for invasions and naval battles between rival chiefdoms. This stage lasted until finally a triumphant chief who gained control over the entire island banned all double canoes in "a disarmament scheme" that was, wrote Buck with some irony during the darkest days of World War II, "enforced by the government in power with more success than has attended similar proposals by civilized powers." (Alternatively, on the basis of recent fieldwork archaeologist Marshall Weisler proposes that the severe deforestation of Mangareva spelled the end of voyaging canoes there, which in turn led to the abandonment of colonies on Pitcairn and Henderson islands dependent in part on Mangareva.)[63]

Voyaging can also be costly in terms of lives lost at sea. Although *Hōkūleʻa*'s record of sailing repeatedly to various islands in the South Pacific and then back to Hawaiʻi might seem to indicate that long-distance canoe travel was a fairly safe, even routine, enterprise, our experiences with accidents at sea and those of other recent experimental voyagers, as well as historical reports of canoe disasters, suggest otherwise. When *Hōkūleʻa* sails on long voyages she is followed by an escort boat and carries safety gear dictated by Coast Guard regulations, as well as by the bitter experience of a swamping in 1975 when the canoe was being sailed back from Kauaʻi to Oʻahu, and the tragedy that occurred in 1978 when *Hōkūleʻa* overturned in high winds and steep seas off Molokaʻi island, and Eddie Aikau was lost while paddling a surfboard to shore to get help. Had these accidents, particularly the second one, happened to lone traditional canoes sailing in heavy weather far out to sea, the craft and everyone on board would probably have been lost. According to early historic accounts from Hawaiʻi it was virtually impossible to right a large double canoe that had been overturned, or to bail out a totally swamped one, unless the canoe was close enough to land for it to be towed ashore.[64]

Structural failure of the cross beams or lashings connecting the hulls of a double canoe was even more disastrous than swamping or capsizing; reassembling the hulls and cross beams in a moving sea was virtually impossible. The missionary William Ellis recorded this harrowing tale of the few survivors of a group of thirty-two Tahitians who were sailing from one island in the Societies to another when the hulls of their double canoe separated in a storm:[65]

> It was in vain for them to endeavour to place them upright, or empty out the water, for they could not keep them in an upright position, nor prevent their incessant overturning. As their only resource, they collected the scattered spars and boards, and constructed a raft, on which they hoped they might drift to land. The weight of the whole number, who were now collected on the raft, was so great as to sink it so far below the surface, that they sometimes stood above their knees in water. They made very little progress, and soon became exhausted by fatigue and hunger. In this condition they were attacked by a number of sharks. Destitute of a knife, or any other weapon of defence, they fell an easy prey to the rapacious monsters. One after another was seized and devoured, or carried away by them; and the survivors, who with dreadful anguish beheld their companions thus destroyed, saw the number of assailants apparently increasing, as each body was carried away, until only two or three remained. The raft, thus lightened of its load, rose to the surface of the water, and placed them beyond the reach of the voracious jaws of their relentless destroyers.

Two reconstructed voyaging canoes have been lost at sea during the last two decades, though fortunately all the sailors were rescued by other vessels. In 1975 the *Spirit of Nukuhiva*, a double canoe modeled on the Tongan *kalia* and built by yachtsman Bob Griffith, broke up while bound from the Marquesas to Hawai'i when the cross beams connecting the hulls failed during squally weather. Then in 1977 the *Taratai II*, an outrigger canoe modeled on Micronesian designs and built by New Zealand photographer Jim Siers, broke up while sailing from Tonga to Tahiti when the beams connecting the outrigger to the hull gave way in heavy seas. Fortunately, the yacht escorting the *Spirit of Nukuhiva*, expertly skippered by Bob's wife Nancy, picked up the crew soon after the canoe broke apart. Some days after their accident the weakened survivors from the *Taratai II* were rescued when their raft was spotted by the crew of a tugboat that just happened to be passing along an otherwise deserted seaway while being delivered from South America to Australia.[66]

One of the few attempts to compile canoe loss records was undertaken at the turn of the last century in the Marshall Islands of Micronesia by a seasoned mariner who signed his report as "Captain Winkler of the German Navy." At that time, the Marshallese were still sailing from island to island in their sleek "flying proa" outrigger canoes and could recall the loss over previous generations of many single vessels, and five instances when all or most of the canoes in large flotillas had set sail from their islands but were never seen again. For example, Winkler's informant told him how, in "about 1830, a flotilla of over 100 canoes set out on a voyage. It was destroyed, and only one boat, with the chief's daughter, Ligibberik, on board, drove on an island in the ocean; the others were never heard from again." Even if the round figure of one hundred may represent some exaggeration, the disappearance (primarily because of typhoons?) of all or most of the canoes from five separate flotillas over the preceding century must have represented a major loss for the islanders.[67]

In addition to the recollections found here and there in Polynesian oral traditions of canoes that never returned, there are a number of written reports of canoe disasters gathered from the survivors during the early contact period when Polynesians were still sailing widely back and forth. One such tale came to be recorded because the survivors fetched up on an uninhabited atoll in the Tuamotus where they happened to be met and interviewed by Captain Beechey of *H.M.S. Blossom*. While traversing the Tuamotu archipelago in 1826, the *Blossom* chanced upon the little atoll of Ahunui where the British found a forlorn

group of people who had been stranded on this otherwise uninhabited island. They told the British that the year before they
had set out in a convoy of three double canoes carrying in all
some 150 people from Anaʻa atoll (located 300 miles to the
northwest of Ahunui) to Tahiti, where they wanted to pay their
respects to the young sovereign Pomare II who had just as-
cended to the throne of the nascent Tahitian kingdom upon the
death of his father. As Anaʻa lies about 200 miles due east of
Tahiti, they were expecting that the crossing would take only a
few days of sailing before the easterly trade winds.

Unfortunately the summer westerlies, or "monsoon" as
Beechey called them, came unexpectedly early that year. The
excited celebrants had set out with a fair wind blowing, but just
when they were expecting to see Mehetia, the small volcanic
rock of an island just to the east of Tahiti on which *Hōkūleʻa*
had made landfall in 1986, violent westerly winds forced them
eastward. When the westerlies finally abated, a period of calm
followed after which easterly winds started blowing again, enabling them to head back toward Tahiti. But soon thereafter another spell of westerlies drove them again to the east and separated their canoe from the other two. This was followed by a
hot, dry calm during which the last of their food and water was
exhausted, and some people resorted to drinking seawater. Finally, with the return of the trades, they were able to head
northwest to try to find Anaʻa or any islands that might lie in
that direction. After passing a couple of islands, they landed on
Ahunui, seriously damaging their canoe on the reef. Out of the
twenty-three men, fifteen women, and ten children who had
started out in their canoe, around forty had survived the stormy
westerlies and torrid calms. But these survivors had no idea of
the whereabouts of the other two canoes, which Beechey pre-
sumed had been lost at sea. By the time Beechey had reached
Ahunui the people had repaired their canoe and were laying
in stores to set sail once more for Anaʻa. With the exception
of the one family that Beechey brought back to Anaʻa it is not
known if any of these hapless voyagers ever made it back to their
island.[68]

Given the dangers of the sea, many a canoe must have been
lost with all hands when it swamped, overturned, or broke up
in a storm, and more than a few voyagers must have perished at

sea when they ran out of food and water, or succumbed to exposure, in fruitless attempts to find new islands or sail to known ones. Although we can never know how many people were lost at sea during the Polynesian expansion and subsequent voyaging activities, some idea of the human costs can be gained by estimating that around ten voyaging canoes each carrying at least twenty-five people were lost every year on exploring and colonization missions and on postsettlement voyages of various kinds. Over, for example, the 2,000-year span from 250 B.C. to 1750 A.D., the toll would add up to half a million.

After emphasizing how the vast majority of his fellow Polynesians did reach land in their voyages, Peter Buck phrased in these, more lyrical terms, the inevitable losses at sea of those who for various reasons failed to reach land.[69]

> Others there must have been, as daring and trusting in their star, whose course led them into empty seas. Such unlucky ones sleep beneath the barren sea roads they so vainly followed. If the sea ever gives up its dead, what a parade of Polynesian mariners will rise from the depths when the call of the shell trumpet summons them to the last muster roll! Their numbers will bear witness to the courage of those who dared but failed to reach the land which was not there. For them no human songs were sung, but the sea croons their requiem in a language that they understand.

Obviously, however, the cost of voyaging did not stop the Lapita pioneers and their Polynesian successors from expanding over the Pacific. Neither did it prevent them from voyaging widely back and forth between already settled islands and archipelagos, as traditions detail and recent archaeological work is now beginning to confirm. Indeed, a good case can be made that the establishment of wide-ranging links between islands was critical to the colonization process. Small, vulnerable outposts on the frontier of colonization would have benefited greatly by keeping in contact with the homeland or other newly settled islands, so that the colonists could have access to supplies of critically needed tools and materials, skilled people needed for special tasks, and mates for their maturing offspring.[70]

The Hawaiian tradition of a voyage made back to Kahiki to fetch the breadfruit, the Māori tale of a voyage made back to their homeland to bring the sweet potato, and similar tales told elsewhere in Polynesia suggest that the quest for valuable plants for food, medicine, and other purposes could have been responsible for some communication back and forth between newly settled islands lacking the full complement of cultivated plants and those long-settled ones that could provide the missing tubers, cuttings, or seedlings. In this connection it is interesting to speculate how the sweet potato's arrival in the Marquesas, or any other East Polynesian archipelago, might have led to a flurry of voyages around Polynesia to spread this new and valuable food plant.

Once, however, all the islands had been settled and the new communities were well established, once local resources had been located to ensure local self-sufficiency, and once the sweet potato and other valuable cultivated plants had been distributed, there would seem to have been little in the way of material needs to keep long-range voyaging alive. To be sure, when Europeans entered the Pacific, resource-poor Pukapukans and Tuamotuans were sailing regularly to nearby high islands, the ambitious Tongans were in an expansive phase, and some drought-prone or overcrowded islands such as the Marquesas and Tikopia were spawning one-way exile voyages. In addition, some valuable resources, such as fine basalt adze blades from Samoa and Rurutu, may have been transported widely at the time of European contact. Nonetheless, by then many of the long-settled and mature Polynesian societies seem to have turned inward, largely forsaking long-range voyaging for local concerns.

Yet such utilitarian reasoning ignores an important motive behind many of the long voyages celebrated in Polynesian traditions. There was more to Polynesian voyaging than finding and developing oceanic real estate and then conducting exchanges with other islands. Just as reaction to overpopulation or hard times cannot explain the speed of the Lapita thrust into the mid-Pacific, or why their Polynesian descendants spread so far and wide over the eastern Pacific, so must we look to other than demographic or economic reasons to comprehend fully postcolonization voyaging. Because societies may have advanced to the point where wide-ranging links were no longer crucial to survival it does not necessarily follow that all long-distance voyaging would have immediately ceased. Voyages made for what we might class as religious, romantic, or adventurous purposes may not have left material traces broad and prominent enough to be noticed by the archaeologists of our era, but this does not mean that they were unimportant to the people involved, or above all, as some have claimed, that they never took place.

Like so many cultures around the world explored in Mary Helms's intriguing monograph, *Ulysses' Sail*, knowledge, power, and long-distance travel were intimately linked in Polynesian thought, even though that might not be obvious in reconstructions of Polynesian prehistory based on techno-ecological processes.[71] Such voyages of Polynesian tradition as the Tahitian politico-religious missions to Hawai'i to be discussed in the next chapter, the Rarotongan pilgrimages to the sacred *marae* of Taputapuātea on Ra'iatea that are said to have stopped after their priest was murdered there, as well as the widespread ranging of adventurous Tongan chiefs do not easily fit into any utilitarian mold. Neither can the many tales about voyagers setting sail because of disappointments in love, to search for lost kinsmen, or simply to seek new adventures be dismissed out of hand as so much unfulfilled fantasy.

There are many known instances of voyaging for adventure during the last half century, primarily involving young men who, desperate to escape their small islands and see the outside world, have set sail for distant destinations in small craft and with little or nothing in the way of navigational aids. For example, during the 1940s and 1950s when Chilean authorities restricted the Rapa Nui people from traveling overseas, on eight separate occasions small groups of youths desperate to reach the outside world set off for Tahiti in rowboats stolen from the Chilean navy, or any other small craft on which they could raise a sail. Despite their makeshift vessels and lack of navigational equipment, four of the groups landed on islands scattered from the Tuamotus to the Cooks; the other four disappeared with all hands. Similarly, youths bored with living on Anuta, a tiny Polynesian outlier with less than a hundred inhabitants located off the eastern end of the Solomons chain, are to this day still setting sail in small canoes to see the outside world.[72]

During the late 1920s, the ethnographer Raymond Firth had the good fortune to live for a year on Tikopia, the well-known Polynesian outlier located near Anuta where traditional attitudes toward voyaging, and memories of expeditions taken over the previous century or so, were then still strong. In discussing how Tikopia youths would blithely take to the sea without a worry, Firth wrote:[73]

> Fired by the lust for adventure and the desire to see new lands canoe after canoe set out and ranged the seas, and those members of the crews who returned contributed a great deal to such knowledge of the outside world as the islanders now possess. Fear of storms and shipwreck leaves them undeterred, and the reference in an ancient song to the loss of a man at sea as a "sweet burial" expresses very well the attitude of the Tikopia.

Homelands

For years scholars, travelers, and adventurers have been obsessed with finding the ultimate homeland from whence the Polynesians began their migration. Most thought they had found it among the islands of Southeast Asia or on adjacent continental shores, and in the late nineteenth century it became popular to trace the Polynesians beyond Southeast Asia to India, Persia, or even the Near East. A vocal minority reversed the direction of migration and claimed to have found the Polynesian homeland on the Pacific coast of South America. Even when it was realized that the Polynesian homeland must really be in the middle of the Pacific, at first researchers sought the specific island or archipelago where the descendants of the seafarers who had pioneered this region became distinctively Polynesian in appearance, language, and culture. Although at times Samoa and Tonga have each been put forward as the crucial homeland, the current consensus is that ancestral Polynesian culture did not evolve solely on a single island or within a single archipelago. Because the many islands of West Polynesia found in and around the main archipelagos of Tonga, Samoa, and the Lau group of Fiji were apparently all linked together by travel and exchange during the crucial period when the ancestral Polynesian cultural pattern was emerging from its Lapita roots, this entire region is currently the leading candidate for the long sought-after homeland.[74]

Only recently have prehistorians begun to apply such a regional perspective to central East Polynesia and the differentiation of the variants of Polynesian culture that developed there, a tardiness that probably reflects a lingering reluctance to consider that people living on such far-flung islands could ever have maintained communication links over the great ocean distances of the region. Judging from our voyaging experiments, however, there would appear to have been no insurmountable barriers to widespread inter-archipelago voyaging within central East Polynesia. Particularly when the settlements on the various islands and archipelagos were small and struggling, people may have been greatly motivated by the need for valuable plants, new tools and materials, spouses, and just plain companionship to establish and keep open lines of communication among far-flung communities.

The sharing of cultural innovations and adaptations over a wide area of the central East Polynesian region suggests new ways to look at old problems that have so far defied solution. The reason, for example, why the search for the single island or archipelago that formed the homeland where East Polynesian culture became differentiated from West Polynesian culture has been so fruitless may simply be that crucial innovations and adaptations were spread so widely and rapidly around central East Polynesia by frequent inter-archipelago voyaging that all or most of the region formed the long-sought fount of East Polynesian culture.[75] Similarly, the seeming contradiction between the time depth of central East Polynesian settlement indicated by archaeological investigations and that suggested by comparative studies of the languages within the region may also be resolvable by considering cultural differentiation from this regional perspective. Whereas radiocarbon dates point to the settlement of central East Polynesia beginning as early as some 2,500 years ago, to many linguists the individual languages of the region seem too similar to have been separated anywhere near that long. This apparent contradiction disappears, however, if we consider that the various colonial outposts in central East Polynesia may have been in frequent enough contact with one another over the centuries to share language changes, thereby slowing linguistic differentiation.[76]

The solution to the puzzle of why Rapa Nui culture looks so different from other local East Polynesian cultures and, linguistically at least, more archaic and closer to West Polynesian forms may also lie in the regional nature of cultural processes in central East Polynesia. Although some have proposed that Rapa Nui was so unique because it was settled by West Polynesians who sailed there directly with little or no contact with any groups already established in central East Polynesia,[77] the island's uniqueness may stem simply from its extreme isolation from the regional cultural homeland in central East Polynesia. If, for example, the colonizers of Rapa Nui left central East Polynesia before the regional culture there took on its characteristic form, their descendants would not have had the same opportunity as the people living in the main archipelagos enjoyed to share in all the innovations and changes that subsequently occurred in the heartland. Instead, in their relative isolation the Rapa Nui were left to develop a culture marked by the cult of the *moai*, the great stone statues, and other distinctive features that made them stand out so much from other East Polynesian groups.

The Rapa Nui case may actually be the exception that proves the general rule. The realization that, where wind patterns are favorable and navigational targets are large, Polynesians could sail back and forth between widely separated islands and during some periods seem to have done so with some frequency may upset cherished notions about particular homelands and migration routes, as well as assumptions about single-source settlement followed by cultural development in isolation. The resultant models of multiple migration voyages and episodes of extensive inter-archipelago communication may, however, more closely approach what really happened than allowed for in previous thinking. If so, our experiments will not only have provided realistic insights into Polynesian nautical achievements, but they will also have contributed to putting voyaging back into the prehistory of this vast oceanic realm.

9

THE FAMILY OF THE CANOE

Homecoming

When *Hōkūle'a*'s twin prows touched the sands of Kualoa to complete the Voyage of Rediscovery, the canoe and her crew were welcomed home with chants and dances—some taken from ancient voyaging traditions, others especially composed for the occasion—and then honored with speeches by Governor John Waihe'e, Congressman (now Senator) Daniel Akaka, and other Hawaiian leaders, as well as by traditional chiefs and elders from islands south of the equator. The homecoming was planned as a high point of Hawai'i's "Year of the Hawaiian" celebration because of the key role played by *Hōkūle'a* in helping Hawaiians regain a sense of pride in their culture. Speaker after speaker stressed how this voyage had made all Hawaiians, indeed all Polynesians, proud of their seafaring heritage, giving them extra strength needed to face the challenges of today's world. Governor Waihe'e, for example, proclaimed:

> I am more than just governor—I am Hawaiian, and as I sat there watching *Hōkūle'a* my bones screamed with pride. It is so won-

derful to be Hawaiian in the Year of the Hawaiian, the Year of *Hōkūleʻa*. You know that today we welcome you back with pride because you have established once and for all that our ancestors, our Polynesian ancestors, were masters of their world—and that despite those who doubted just a few years ago, they were able to navigate the seas and to work with the elements to create the civilization that Captain Cook, two hundred years ago, called the most extensive nation on the face of the earth. . . . If they could do that, it seems to me that, conclusively, their descendants have within their grasp the power to face and be masters of their own world. . . . I want to acknowledge those of you who participated in this great voyage of discovery and those others who supported these efforts—and all of you for making this sense of pride, this sense of destiny, so available to each and every one of us on this blessed soil. *Aloha.*

After the welcoming speeches it fell to Nainoa to respond as the leader of the Voyage of Rediscovery and the one who had navigated the canoe all the way to Aotearoa and return. The young Hawaiian navigator, who usually shies away from speaking in public, characteristically began his response by giving credit to others:

There's a big misconception that the navigator sails the canoe by himself. That's not true. I am just the eyes for the canoe and everybody else does the rest. I only decide which way to go, but it's the crew that makes the canoe go in that direction, it's the crew that keeps the canoe safe and floating, and it's the crew that takes care of me.

There was something special, Nainoa went on to say, about those who sailed *Hōkūleʻa* back to Hawaiʻi on this last, homecoming leg of the voyage. In addition to veteran sailors from Hawaiʻi, the crew included representatives from all over Polynesia: Stanley Conrad from Aotearoa, Eni Hunkin from Samoa, Tua Pittman from Rarotonga, Puaniho Tauataha from Tahiti, Sione Taupeamuhu from Tonga, and Tava Taupu from the Marquesas. Their efforts, along with those of the crew members from Hawaiʻi, to bring *Hōkūleʻa* home showed how, Nainoa said, a joining together of people from all over Polynesia had made this voyage and its mission of rediscovery such a success.

This was the last of many celebrations held at the various ports of call along the route of the voyage. Each time ancient glories had been recalled by chants, dances, and speeches, and the progress of the canoe through the islands was praised as a reminder not only of past achievements but also of how Polynesians can shape their future. This transformation of *Hōkūle'a* into a symbol of resurgent pride, and the way this voyage galvanized Hawaiians and other Polynesians, demonstrates how far the cultural revival aspect of our project has progressed since the idea of combining experimental and cultural goals had first been floated a decade and a half earlier.

As an effort in cultural revival, the project shares much with other initiatives around the world wherein people consciously seek to re-create and elaborate ancestral ways for contemporary purposes.[1] Examples from Europe range from the adoption by Scots in the late eighteenth century of the kilt woven in distinctive clan tartans, the bagpipe, and other cultural emblems as part of an effort to forge a distinctive Scottish identity to the Renaissance wherein Western Europeans sought to revive art, literature, and learning through recalling their links with the ancient civilizations of Greece and Rome, and elaborating on selected classical themes from that era. What particularly distinguishes our effort is that from the beginning of the project cultural revival was an integral part of a plan to re-create an almost forgotten technology and systematically test it to find out more about the past. Furthermore, we began our work with the hope that the experimental and cultural sides of the project would reinforce one another—that the reawakened seafaring skills of Hawaiians and other Polynesian participants would enhance the quest for a better understanding of the seafaring accomplishments of their ancestors and that the process of reviving and applying those skills over the long seaway between Hawai'i and Tahiti would also serve contemporary needs.

In the beginning, it was easy to say that experimental research and cultural revival would reinforce each other. Actually making them work together proved to be much harder than we had imagined but in the end has turned out to be much more rewarding than we had ever dreamed. In particular, the success of the second voyage to Tahiti and return and Nainoa's stunning accomplishment of navigating the canoe both ways without instruments, demonstrated, even to the most skeptical, how scientific and cultural goals could be compatible. By the time of the Voyage of Rediscovery, these two facets of the project had become thoroughly enmeshed, and even the most partisan advocates of experimentation and of cultural revival came to respect one another and to try willingly to accommodate each other's concerns. When, for example, crew members who may have been skeptical of the need for experimental procedures and data recording realized how these could provide concrete information on sailing and navigation that spoke well of the genius of their ancestors, they not only accepted the experimental approach but vied for the chance to join in such tedious research tasks as the twice-daily recording of Nainoa's navigational decisions and dead reckoning estimates. At the same time, those planning the voyage placed great emphasis on making it as much of a cultural as a scientific enterprise by, for example, working with the people of the various islands along the route to mark the canoe's arrival and departure with appropriate protocol and ceremonies and to develop cultural exchanges between *Hōkūle'a* crew members and supporters and their island hosts.

This joining together of experimental voyaging and cultural revival has been more than just additive. Cultural and scientific rediscovery have worked together synergistically for mutual benefit. It is no exaggeration to say that the initiative to solve a scientific puzzle through experimental voyaging has led Hawaiians to develop a new appreciation of their nautical heritage which has tremendously boosted their feelings of individual and cultural worth. Furthermore, this last voyage has spread the project's cultural impact throughout the islands of Polynesia, bringing their people together in a collective celebration of their common seafaring past. While *Hōkūle'a* was sailing from island to island during the Voyage of Rediscovery, Sam Ka'ai, the Hawaiian sculptor and crew member on the 1980 voyage, liked to talk about the canoe's cultural mission in terms of the *lei*, the flower garland of Hawai'i, by saying that "just as we string a *lei* out of flowers, so *Hōkūle'a* strings a *lei* of islands."

As the canoe was stringing her *lei*, unexpected gestures of appreciation received along the way added further to the cultural meaning of the voyage. For example, the Tahitians built a modern *marae* on the waterfront at Pape'ete where we first landed in 1976 and, with the canoe's crew and delegates from the Polynesian Voyaging Society in attendance, formally dedicated it to *Hōkūle'a* and the voyaging revival we had sparked. Earlier, upon our arrival in Aotearoa, the Māori leaders who welcomed us to Waitangi had declared that, following their model of counting tribal descent from those who had arrived together on a canoe, we now constituted the "Sixth Tribe" of the northern tip of their island, Tai Tokerau. They have since followed that up by setting land aside on the shores of Tokerau Bay for a Māori-style *marae* where Hawaiians, Māori, and others of this *lei* of islands touched by *Hōkūle'a* can periodically come together.

So, too, has the passion for reviving lost sailing and navigational arts kindled by *Hōkūle'a*, and in particular the skill and enthusiasm with which Hawaiians, Marquesans, Tahitians, Rarotongans, Māori, Tongans, and Samoans have sailed the canoe over their ancestral seaways, enabled the project to fulfill and then extend its experimental mission. In particular, the insistence of the Hawaiians now leading the project that the canoe should continue to sail around Polynesia and their enthusiasm in working with a variety of researchers—oceanographers, meteorologists, astronomers, as well as anthropologists—to document the voyages and analyze the results, has brought forth a wealth of new data and insights on issues of Polynesian voyaging and settlement. Before taking up this synergy in detail, however, we need to consider the legendary basis behind the choice of the Hawai'i-Tahiti route as the seaway over which *Hōkūle'a* was initially tested.

Behold Hawai'i

The homecoming celebration at Kualoa was titled *Eia Hawai'i*, or "Behold Hawai'i," the opening words of a chant said to have first been called out by the bard Kamahualele one morning many centuries ago as the voyaging canoe bearing the high chief Mo'ikeha entered Hilo Bay on the west coast of the island of Hawai'i after a long voyage from distant Kahiki. The chant starts with these lines recalling Hawai'i's relationship with Kahiki:

> *Eia Hawai'i, he moku, he kanaka,*
> *He kanaka Hawai'i——e,*
> *He kanaka Hawai'i,*
> *He kama na Kahiki,*
> *He pua ali'i mai Kapa'ahu,*
> *Mai Moa'ulu-nui-ākea Kanaloa.*

> Behold Hawai'i, an island, a nation,
> Hawai'i is a nation indeed,
> Hawai'i is a nation,
> A Child of Kahiki,
> A royal offspring from Kapa'ahu,
> From Moa'ulu-nui-ākea Kanaloa.

This chant is featured in *The History of Mo'ikeha* (*Ka Mo'o-lelo o Mo'ikeha*), a long narrative tradition about the voyages made between a land called Kahiki and an already settled Hawai'i by Mo'ikeha and his sons. Except, possibly, for a pair of tales about the initial discovery of Hawai'i (which some scholars consider may be nineteenth-century creations), Hawaiian traditions appear to have little to say about the initial colonization of the archipelago.[2] In contrast, a considerable number of well-documented legends, such as that revolving around Mo'ikeha and his sons, about voyaging between a place called Kahiki and already settled Hawai'i would appear to relate to a period when Hawaiians were in communication with islands far to the south. Arguably, this period can be dated back to between the eleventh to the fourteenth centuries A.D. by means of counting the generations in the genealogies of chiefly Hawaiians who traced their descent back to Mo'ikeha and other personages featured in the narratives.

Mo'ikeha was said to be the grandson of Maweke, a great chief from Kahiki who settled on O'ahu sometime between the eleventh and twelfth centuries A.D. and founded the Nana line of chiefs that came to dominate that island and Kaua'i.[3] Although some versions of the story begin with Kahiki, others start in Hawai'i, where Mo'ikeha and his brother Olopana and Olopana's wife Lu'ukia were living in Waipi'o valley on the northwest coast of the island of Hawai'i until great storms and floods devastated the valley and forced the three to set sail for Kahiki.

Once in Kahiki, Mo'ikeha and Lu'ukia became lovers—with Olopana's consent, as siblings often shared spouses in traditional Hawaiian society. After a time, however, Lu'ukia spurned her lover, believing a false rumor spread by an amorous local chief to the effect that Mo'ikeha had slandered her behind her back. The disappointed Mo'ikeha then ordered Kamahualele to make his voyaging canoe ready to sail to distant Hawai'i, the land where his ancestors had settled and where he had been born. After an apparently uneventful voyage, Moʻikeha's canoe pulled into Hilo Bay on the northeastern shore of Hawaiʻi Island, where Kamahualele marked their arrival with the chant quoted above. From there Moʻikeha sailed along the chain, dropping off crew members along the way, until reaching Kauaʻi where he settled down, married the two daughters of the ruling chief of the island, a position to which Moʻikeha succeeded upon the death of his father-in-law.

As his sons grew to maturity on Kauaʻi, the aging Moʻikeha longed to see Laʻa, the son he had left behind in Kahiki, and so sent his youngest Hawaiian son Kila to fetch him. After many adventures at sea and on land, Kila finally located Laʻa and told him of their father's desire to see him. Then Laʻa—called in full Laʻa-mai-Kahiki ("Laʻa-from-Kahiki")—made the long voyage to Hawaiʻi to see his father.

After their reunion on Kauaʻi, Laʻa sailed for Oʻahu and stopped at Kualoa, where he is said to have tarried long enough to father three children by separate wives, and where centuries later *Hōkūleʻa* was launched. Then Laʻa traveled to Maui, where he stayed on the south coast of the Kahiki-Nui district. After tiring of the fierce winds of Kahiki-Nui, Laʻa crossed to the small offshore island of Kahoʻolawe, and from there he set sail back to Kahiki, heading home through the channel between Kahoʻolawe and the neighboring island of Lānaʻi that thereafter bore the name of *Ke Ala i Kahiki*, or "The Way to Kahiki." Later, when he heard that Moʻikeha had died, Laʻa made another roundtrip to Hawaiʻi to fetch his father's bones and bring them back to Kahiki to bury with those of his ancestors.

In this and other voyaging tales Kahiki is portrayed as a marvelous place from whence come cultural gifts and innovations. Laʻa, for example, is credited with bringing a special ritual drum, the hula dance, and a new type of image worship, and another descendant of Moʻikeha is supposed to have later brought the breadfruit to Hawaiʻi. Another series of legendary voyages involving the introduction of a range of religious, social, and political innovations center around Paʻao, a priest, and Pili, a high chief who is said to have founded the line of ruling chiefs that came to dominate the islands of Hawaiʻi and Maui.[4] This cycle opens with a dispute between Paʻao and his brother Lonopele that led to the death of both of their sons and caused the distraught Paʻao to set sail to the north. After battling winds and heavy seas magically sent by Lonopele, Paʻao arrived in the district of Puna on the west coast of Hawaiʻi Island. There he is credited with building the walled *heiau* (temple) of Wahaʻula that still can be seen today surrounded by an immense field of hardened lava that in 1989 flowed completely around the *heiau* but did not destroy it. From Puna, Paʻao continued around the coast to the district of Kohala at the northwestern end of the island where he built Moʻokini *heiau*, a temple with especially high and massive walls that to this day stand out amidst the abandoned sugar cane fields of this windswept coast.

After finding that the chiefs of Hawaiʻi "had become greatly debased by indiscriminate alliances with the common people," Paʻao sailed to Kahiki to fetch the high chief Lonokaʻeho and bring him to Hawaiʻi to rule the islands and introduce proper political and religious behavior.[5] Preferring to remain at home, however, Lonokaʻeho nominated another chief to take his place, Pili Kaʻaiʻea. Paʻao and Pili then sailed back to Hawaiʻi Island where, according to Abraham Fornander's analysis of the legend, Pili "by the assistance of Paʻao was established as the territorial sovereign of that island, Paʻao remaining his high priest." From Pili, Fornander continues, "the ruling Hawaiian chiefs, down to the Kamehameha family, claimed their descent." Furthermore, according to a number of authorities, "the priesthood established by Paʻao under the Ku ritual descended through an unbroken line of kahunas to Hewahewa, under whom the tapus were broken and the old heiau worship was abolished after the death of Kamehameha in 1819."[6]

Abraham Fornander, Nathaniel B. Emerson, and other nineteenth-century interpreters of these tales thought that the voyaging traditions recorded actual persons and events and chronicled a time when canoes sailed freely back and forth between Hawaiʻi and Tahiti. They identified the "Kahiki" of the traditions with Tahiti because of the equivalence of the Hawaiian *k* sound with that of the Tahitian *t*, noting, furthermore, that Kahiki was often pronounced in the Tahitian manner in the leeward islands of Oʻahu and Kauaʻi until the windward island pronunciation (and missionary-produced alphabet based upon it) spread there in the nineteenth century. In fact, the name is still pronounced as "Tahiti" by the people of Niʻihau, the tiny, isolated island off the coast of Kauaʻi where one can still hear the old leeward island way of speaking marked by the use of the *t* and *r* sounds rather than those of *k* and *l*.

Identifying the legendary Kahiki with the island of Tahiti was not as straightforward, however, as this linguistic correspondence would seem to indicate. As Fornander, Emerson, and scholars of their generation had to admit, at the time of European contact Hawaiians typically employed Kahiki in a generalized sense for lands far away rather than as the name for a specific island. Furthermore, as can be seen in Hawaiian texts written in the mid-nineteenth century by the Hawaiian scholars David Malo and Samuel Manaiakalani Kamakau, Kahiki could also be applied to sectors of the celestial dome. To resolve this apparent confusion over whether Kahiki was a specific island or a broad directional referent, nineteenth-century interpreters of Hawaiian traditions proposed that over the centuries since the last voyages between Tahiti and Hawai'i the meaning of Kahiki had shifted from a single island from whence voyagers had once sailed to Hawai'i to a general concept of "overseas," referring to places far beyond the visible horizon.[7]

Thus, the Kahiki of legend came to be identified with Tahiti; Kahiki-Nui, the district on Maui where La'a tarried, was thought to have been named after Tahiti-Nui ("Great Tahiti"), as the Tahitians call the main part of their island; and the channel Ke Ala i Kahiki was considered to have been literally "The Way to Tahiti" through which La'a began his voyage home to Tahiti. The dilemma posed by some versions of the Pa'ao tradition in which the priest is said to have originally come from 'Upolu and Wawau was also resolved in favor of Tahiti, albeit a larger one meaning all the Society Islands. Although some writers identified Pa'ao's home islands with 'Upolu in Samoa and Va-va'u in Tonga, Bishop Museum ethnologist John F. G. Stokes pointed out that 'Upolu was also the ancient name for Taha'a while Wawau (Vavau in Tahitian) was also the ancient name for Borabora, and that therefore Pa'ao came from the Society Islands, or Kahiki, employing that term to denote all the islands inhabited by Tahitian speakers.[8]

This Hawaiian expansion of the meaning of Tahiti beyond a single island is mirrored today in contemporary usage in French Polynesia, *Polynésie Française*, the overseas territory of France which includes Tahiti and the Societies. When contrasting the

Society Islands with the other archipelagos of French Polynesia (the Marquesas, Tuamotu, Gambier, and Austral groups) one
sometimes hears Tahiti used to stand for the whole Society
Group. When talking to foreigners who have no idea of Pacific
geography, Tahitians may even refer to all of French Polynesia
simply as Tahiti, and in searching for a more indigenous name
for French Polynesia that would give the territory instant recognition in the international tourist market, some local politi-
cians have seriously proposed using Tahiti or Tahiti-Nui.

The idea that the voyaging tales precisely related the adventures of real people who had once sailed between Tahiti and
Hawai'i came to be modified by such leading Polynesianists of
the twentieth century as the Māori anthropologist Peter Buck,
Hawai'i folklore specialist Martha Beckwith, and her intellectual successor, the University of Hawai'i's Katharine Luomala.[9]
They pointed out that these tales were too filled with supernatu-
ral and fantastic events and with stock incidents and embellish-
ments of Polynesian storytelling to accept them as literal history. Nevertheless, they did consider that these tales recalled a
time when canoes sailed back and forth between Tahiti and Hawai'i and had been inspired by the exploits of actual voyagers.
For example, in her assessment of the Mo'ikeha legend, Luomala
declared that:[10]

> I do regard the Mo'ikeha story as representative of the spirit and
> type of voyaging between Hawai'i and the south in a period when
> these islanders had seaworthy double canoes and much practical
> knowledge of navigation as well as many motivations—spiritual,
> political, economic, emotional—to make long voyages. I am also
> inclined to accept the names of the principal human characters
> in the tradition as those of Hawaiians who once lived, were famed
> voyagers and high chiefs, and so successful that their contempo-
> raries and descendants told marvelous and entertaining accounts
> of their adventures.

Luomala wrote this in 1979. By that time, however, the idea
that these traditions had been inspired by a period of interarchipelago voyaging had come to be rejected by many younger students of Polynesian prehistory. Five years earlier, for example,
archaeologist Ross Cordy had gone on record as emphatically
denying that the traditions had anything to do with overseas voyaging. To him, the repeated coming and going of canoes over

such a great distance and the marvelous feats of the voyagers branded these tales as fiction. Echoing the proposals of New Zealand scholars that the Māori homeland of Hawaiki was located within Aotearoa itself, Cordy suggested that Kahiki may refer to somewhere in the Hawaiian archipelago and that the legendary coming of high chiefs and priests from Kahiki may be a mythical charter for aggrandizement by ambitious local chiefs at a time in Hawaiian history when population pressures were intensifying social stratification and chiefly conflict. Similarly functionalist sentiments were also expressed at this time by another archaeologist, David Tuggle, who proposed that the coming of chiefs from overseas to rule in plebeian Hawai'i "sounds suspiciously like external justification for internal consolidation of elite power."[11]

Among contemporary social anthropologists, the historical validity of the Hawaiian voyaging traditions has virtually ceased to be an issue of interest, although the fascination with Kahiki and the cultural meaning of the voyaging legends remain. Both Valerio Valeri and Marshall Sahlins, for example, consider Kahiki in a way similar to the current structural-symbolic approach to the Māori homeland of Hawaiki. To Valeri, Kahiki is a spatial metaphor "designating the divine origins," and "the invisible place . . . out of which come the gods, ancestors, regalia, edible plants, and ritual institutions—the life of the Hawaiians and the means to reproduce it." Sahlins adds that "Kahiki was also the original cultural time," as well as the "invisible and celestial realms beyond the horizon, the legendary source of great gods, ancient kings, and cultural good things."[12]

This shift in the interpretation of Hawaiian voyaging traditions from a quasi-historical point of view to the belief that voyaging traditions were mythical constructs designed to justify the status of one ruling line or another, or to express cultural origins and concerns, mirrors the similar transition that has occurred among students of Māori voyaging epics. Both cases reflect a general change in how scholars interpret oral traditions. Whereas four decades ago, Glyn Daniel, a distinguished British archaeologist, wrote that while "myth is an invented story, . . . legend, on the other hand, has a basis of history, however confused and obscured by later additions," in recent decades it has become fashionable to consider all, or virtually all, traditions to be mythical fictions composed for just about any purpose other than memorializing actual events. Buck's division of Polynesian traditions into a mythical period that told about the creation of the earth and life and the adventures of the gods, and the historical period of exploration and settlement that chronicled the efforts of high chiefs and their followers to find and colonize islands, is therefore no longer widely accepted. Instead, now the dominant scholarly view is that all traditions, Polynesian or otherwise, are mythical constructs.[13]

Contrary to this trend, Jan Vansina, a historian specializing in African oral traditions, argues that the historical content of an oral tradition should not be denied outright any more than it should be accepted automatically. Instead, he says that we should consider an oral tradition to be a hypothesis about the past to be tested.[14] By sailing back and forth between Hawai'i and Tahiti we have been indirectly testing the Hawaiian voyaging legends by investigating whether or not traditional technology was adequate for earlier voyagers to have intentionally sailed over this route. To be sure, our voyages do not prove that Mo'ikeha, Pa'ao, and/or any other particular legendary figure once sailed between these islands. Nonetheless, our three roundtrips between Hawai'i and Tahiti do demonstrate that the double canoe and noninstrument ways of navigating are well adapted to the task of sailing over this route. Accordingly, we offer this demonstration to support the thesis that the tales of those heroes whose voyages between Hawai'i and Tahiti are celebrated in Hawaiian traditions could actually reflect an era when Polynesian mariners did sail back and forth between these two centers.

Among those who might go even further and insist upon the absolute historicity of the legends are those Hawaiians who trace their descent back to Mo'ikeha, Pili, Pa'ao (usually through Hewahewa, Kamehameha's high priest who was directly descended from Pa'ao), Maweke (Mo'ikeha's father), and Paumakua (another voyaging chief from Kahiki). Periodically in Hawai'i the descendants of these and other legendary figures associated with Kahiki hold family reunions to celebrate their lineage. Advertisements for reunions of the descendants of Hewahewa, Maweke, and Paumakua appeared, for example, in the October 1989 issue of *Ka Wai Ola o Oha*, the monthly newspaper of the Office of Hawaiian Affairs, a quasi-governmental body of the State of Hawai'i. Furthermore, as part of the current effort of the Pa'ao-Hewahewa descendants to trace their roots, Hawaiian historian Rudy Leikaimana Mitchell has recently documented this lineage in Hawaiʻi and then traveled to the Society Islands where he found that the Tahitian chiefly line from whence Paʻao was said to have come was still remembered by the elders on Borabora (the ancient Vavau).[15] These and other traditional ties between the Hawaiians and the Tahitians were dramatically recalled and celebrated at the *marae* of Taputapuātea on Raʻiatea, when, in September of 1992, *Hōkūleʻa* and her crew stopped by on the way to Rarotonga for the Pacific Festival of Arts and were joined by a contingent of Hawaiian dancers, chanters, and students of ancient traditions, as well as by navigators and sailors from Tahiti, the Cook Islands, and Aotearoa.

Prehistorians, however, look to hard evidence to demonstrate early connections. They would much prefer to test a hypothesis of overseas contact through ancient structures, tools, and other artifacts recovered in systematic archaeological excavations rather than rely upon canoe performance figures, route charts, and landfall records provided by experiments at sea, or upon the testimony of those who claim descent from the voyaging figures in question.

Actually, it turns out that archaeologists working in Melanesia on Polynesian outliers and other islands subjected to Polynesian influence have done precisely that by uncovering material evidence of foreign influence on these small islands that correlates with local traditions of the coming of canoes from overseas. The first such discovery came about in the late 1960s when French archaeologist José Garanger conducted a series of excavations on the island of Tongoa in the Shepherd group of central Vanuatu. These revealed geological evidence of the volcanic cataclysm that, according to legend, had split off the other islands of the Shepherd group from Tongoa and also demonstrated a complete transformation in material culture that correlated with oral traditions about the coming of foreign canoes from the south bringing new people who subsequently established their dominance on the island. Furthermore, Garanger reported that he was able to find the sepulcher of their legendary chief, complete with skeletons and grave goods that fit the orally transmitted description of the internment of the renowned leader, his wives, and his servants.[16]

In 1961, the distinguished New Zealand social anthropologist Raymond Firth published a compilation of oral traditions from the Polynesian outlier of Tikopia, a small, volcanic island located between Vanuatu and the Solomons group. He consid-

ered that these legends were "quasi-historical" accounts that recorded real events critical to the history of Tikopia, such as the
invasion of Tongan raiders, the founding of local lineages by
voyagers from other islands, and the expulsion in times of war
or famine of whole groups of people who were then forced to
take to sea in their canoes. In keeping, however, with the structural, ahistorical way of interpreting oral traditions then gaining popularity in social anthropology, many of Firth's colleagues
thought his monograph to be a hopelessly old-fashioned attempt
to read history into myths that had nothing to do with real
events. For example, in his influential review, British social anthropologist Edmond Leach roundly scolded Firth for believing
that these traditions were quasi-historical legends instead of
myths that required a structural analysis to ascertain their true
meaning. Later, a like-minded New Zealand colleague developed
such an analysis in which he argued that the structure of Ti-
kopian society and its constituent clans and lineages reflected
an internal cultural logic, not the movements of people and other
events portrayed in the traditions.[17]

In 1984, however, archaeologist Pat Kirch and ethnobotanist
Douglas Yen published a detailed report on the prehistory of Tikopia that provided archaeological support for traditions about
the coming and going of canoes and people from other islands
and their impact on the local population. Furthermore, their
excavations revealed that prior to the arrival of Polynesians at
about 1200 A.D. Tikopia had been occupied for some two thousand years by related but apparently culturally distinct seafaring
peoples who also had exchanged tools and materials widely between neighboring islands and archipelagos. In fact, so salient
was the evidence for the complex movement of artifacts, materials, and people to and from Tikopia over a 2,000-mile ocean
range that Kirch and Yen concluded that "the evolution of Tikopia culture owes as much to external factors or immigration
or exchange relations as it does to internal adaptation in response to environmental and sociodemographic pressures."[18]

Accepting, however, that small island societies, such as those
on the Polynesian outliers, might be particularly vulnerable
to changes brought by the arrival of people from overseas still
leaves the question unanswered as to whether voyagers from
Tahiti (or other Polynesian islands south of the equator) could
have made a significant impact on what must already have been

a sizable Hawaiian population spread over the archipelago. Abraham Fornander and such other early students of Hawaiian prehistory as William T. Brigham, the first director of Honolulu's Bishop Museum, and Honolulu publisher Thomas G. Thrum thought so. They advocated an architectural study of Hawaiian *heiau* to see if they could archaeologically document the introduction of a new form of temple from Tahiti, as is implied in the Pa'ao legend and had been posited as an indication of major social change by Fornander. After, however, Bishop Museum researcher John F. G. Stokes's survey of Hawaiian *heiau* conducted over the first two decades of this century was judged to have failed to clearly confirm the posited change, this approach was largely abandoned except, notably, for the efforts of Kenneth Emory. As a young Bishop Museum researcher in the 1920s, Emory detected what he proposed was a distinctly Tahitian imprint on small shrines that voyagers had built on the rocky islets of Nihoa and Necker to the northwest of Kaua'i.[19]

It was not until the 1960s that archaeological data was once more brought to bear on the issue of Tahitian contact. After conducting pioneering excavations of stratified sites throughout the archipelago, Kenneth Emory, then the senior archaeologist at the Bishop Museum, and his colleague at the Museum, Yoshihiko Sinoto, proposed that changes in the form of fishhooks and other tools they found reflected Tahitian influence on a culture that had otherwise evolved directly from its Marquesan beginnings. In response, however, a number of other archaeologists have argued that the comparative analysis of Hawaiian, Marquesan, and Tahitian artifacts on which Emory and Sinoto based their reasoning was flawed by sampling bias and other problems and that it is not now possible to trace the changes in question to any particular island or archipelago, if indeed they have an external source and did not arise in Hawai'i independent of any external influence.[20]

Nonetheless, not all contemporary scholars have dismissed the tradition-derived notion of a connection between Tahiti and Hawai'i. Besides the disputed archaeological evidence there are other indications of prehistoric connections, as the apparent adoption by Hawaiians of such Tahitian innovations as the feather girdle worn by high chiefs to symbolize their status and of distinctively Tahitian words such as those for nights of the moon. Furthermore, according to the Hawaiian folklorist Rubel-

lite Kawena Johnson, the Moʻikeha tradition betrays an intimate knowledge of Tahitian geography. For example, she locates
on Tahiti the sites of Kapaʻahu, Moaʻula-nui-ākea and other
places featured in the chant, cited earlier in this chapter, with
which Kamahualele announced Moʻikeha's arrival in Hilo Bay.
Accordingly, in his general survey of Hawaiian prehistory, Kirch
considers that the spectrum of evidence indicates that there
may be "some element of historical reality in the Hawaiian traditions of multiple contacts." More recently several young archaeologists working in Hawaiʻi—Kehau Cachola-Abad, Tom
Dye, and Matthew Spriggs—have independently called for a re-
opening of the search for archaeological evidence that might
bear on the issue.[21]

Reliving the Voyaging Past

To argue, however, that the voyaging traditions of Hawaiʻi or
elsewhere in Polynesia must be either historical legends or fictional myths would be to ignore the multifaceted nature of these
and other oral traditions. Surely, a voyaging tradition can be at
once historically based, functionally employed, and culturally
structured in the sense that it may have been inspired by an actual voyage or voyages, told and retold to claim land or status
for those who count descent from the voyaging heroes, and laden with cultural symbols and themes. We saw this when *Hōkūleʻa* sailed into Rarotonga's Avatiu harbor on the way to
Aotearoa. As the canoe entered the harbor, the people of the resident tribe, Ngati Uritaua, welcomed *Hōkūleʻa* and her crew with
traditional songs, dances, and oratory filled with references to
the heroic voyaging ancestors and gods of old that were carefully crafted to reiterate their own claim to the surrounding lands
by recalling how their ancestral canoe, *Te-ru*, had landed there
when that part of the island was unoccupied.

Accepting that oral traditions may have historical, functional, and structural features does not exhaust interpretive possibilities, however. Our own experience suggests still another
way to comprehend the voyaging tales, one that brings us back
to the point about the synergism between scientific experimentation and cultural experience made at the beginning of this
chapter. *Hōkūleʻa* was conceived and built to be tested over
the legendary voyaging route between Hawaiʻi and Tahiti. That

well over 2,000 miles of blue water separates Hawai'i and Tahiti was critical to this experimental plan, for Sharp had declared that intentional voyaging was impossible beyond the range of 300 miles. We therefore planned to make a single roundtrip between Hawai'i and Tahiti as a kind of "crucial test" of the Sharp hypothesis about the limited range of intentional voyaging. This plan for a single voyage ignored, however, a salient attribute of the voyaging traditions upon which the choice of route was based: they portray multiple trips made back and forth between the two centers. For example, Mo'ikeha and his sons account for four roundtrips. Although completion of that first voyage to Tahiti and back essentially fulfilled our experimental objective, it did not directly address this issue of multiple roundtrip voyaging.

Indeed, when we initially conceived the project we thought it daring to propose making even one voyage to Tahiti and return. Provided that this voyage was successful, we envisioned that *Hōkūle'a* would then be retired from overseas voyaging and employed in Hawaiian waters as a "floating classroom" for the children of Hawai'i to learn about the technology and skills by which the islands had first been settled. Fortunately, those young Hawaiians who had learned to sail *Hōkūle'a* were not content with this single overseas voyage or, however satisfying for them and their pupils, with conducting learning cruises around the Hawaiian archipelago each summer thereafter. Once having tasted blue water canoe sailing and the thrill of making landfalls on distant shores, they wanted to continue and extend their experiences. Accordingly, it was primarily they who organized and led the second voyage to Tahiti and return in 1980, and then the Voyage of Rediscovery. In so doing, not only has a fuller picture of Polynesian voyaging and navigation emerged, but by making three roundtrips between Hawai'i and Tahiti they have ended up reproducing the legendary pattern of multiple voyaging without having consciously tried to do so.

Similarly, the 1986 voyage to Aotearoa not only took the canoe far beyond the Hawai'i-Tahiti seaway for which she was built, but followed the timing and manner of sailing there contained in Māori traditions even though that had not been originally planned. When Nainoa Thompson prepared for that voyage, he did so primarily by studying meteorological records and orienting his navigational thinking to the star patterns and elevations of unfamiliar southern skies rather than by pouring over traditional texts. Yet his researches led to a sailing plan that largely conformed to that contained in the legends. *Hōkūleʻa* left Rarotonga just at the time of year specified in Māori tradition as being most favorable for sailing to Aotearoa, followed the indicated course toward the setting sun, and arrived when the fabled blossoms of the *pohutukawa* were in full flower— just as, according to legend, they were when the Aotea, Arawa, and Tainui canoes arrived from Hawaiki centuries earlier. Furthermore, in 1985 *Hōkūleʻa* was not the only reconstructed canoe to reach Aotearoa during the voyaging period indicated by legend. *Hawaiki-Nui*, a voyaging canoe built in Tahiti by the Māori carver Matahi Whakataka, sailed in our wake from Tahiti to Rarotonga, and from there headed for Aotearoa, arriving right after us. Then, in the late spring of 1993, the reconstructed Māori double canoe, *Te Aurere*, returned from Rarotonga to Aotearoa after having sailed to Rarotonga to take part in the Pacific Festival of Arts.

In addition to bringing us closer to the manner of voyaging portrayed in the legends, this unanticipated reproduction of voyaging back and forth between Hawaiʻi and Tahiti and the way in which a number of migrating canoes once sailed to Aotearoa through the late spring voyaging window also evokes a quintessentially Polynesian way of thinking about and employing oral traditions which eludes us if we examine them solely in terms of their historical or mythical content. "The Maori himself," writes the Danish student of Māori religion and philosophy, J. Pritz Johansen, "does not make any nice distinction proper between myth and history." To him, myth is history, a history to be recalled and applied to the present, not just relegated to the past. To make his point, Johansen points to proverbs and rituals by which Māori understood their present actions in terms of mythical events from the past. When, for example, a Māori wanted to emphatically say no without abruptly saying so, he would rhetorically answer a request by saying "Should Kupe return?" This joined the new situation with an archetypal event, for the phrase recalls how Kupe himself first uttered these words in Hawaiki as a way of firmly but diplomatically saying no to a plea that he undertake a second expedition to Aotearoa. Similarly, each year Māori farmers would ritually reenact the tale of how voyagers fetched the *kūmara*, the sweet potato, from

Hawaiki and thereby made life fruitful in this new land where the original tropical crops from their homeland grew poorly or not at all.[22]

It is this insight into the Polynesian way of recalling and reenacting events and situations from their legendary past that Marshall Sahlins extends to Hawai'i, arguing that the cross-cultural confusion arising from the Hawaiians' identification of Captain Cook in terms of their mythical archetype of a divine chief returning from Kahiki formed a critical link in the chain of circumstances that led to Cook's death on the shores of Kealakekua Bay. More recently, the Hawaiian historian Lilikalā Kame'eleihiwa has pointed out how, working from a conception of past and present that is anything but unidirectional, ". . . the Hawaiian stands firmly in the present, with his back to the future, and his eyes fixed upon the past, seeking historical answers for present day dilemmas." The Tahitian educator Wilfrid Lucas employs a similar logic when, in discussing cultural renaissance among the Tahitians, he explains how they are "using the past to confront the future."[23] From this perspective on time and history, our efforts to reconstruct voyaging canoes, to relearn long-forgotten navigational skills, and then to test these at sea begin to look much more Polynesian than had originally been intended or even imagined. What began as a project to settle a scholarly controversy by making a single crucial voyage has evolved into a culturally invigorating celebration of Polynesian voyaging wherein a revived Hawaiian enthusiasm for the sea has led them not only to relive the legendary voyaging exploits of their ancestors and those of kindred Polynesians but also to create still more experimental findings and insights critical for understanding this uniquely oceanic chapter of humankind's spread over our planet.

'Ohana Wa'a

The Hawaiian word *'ohana* expresses the strong Polynesian sense of family. According to the noted Hawaiian cultural authority, Mary Kawena Pukui, the term is derived from the taro plant whose starchy roots, or corms, are pounded to make *poi*, the staple of the Hawaiian diet. Taro is propagated by means of its sprouts, or *'ohā*. Adding the suffix *na* extends the meaning to "that which is composed of off-shoots," thus making the

Hawaiian metaphor for family.[24] The Hawaiian *'ohana* is not, however, the nuclear family of industrial society, but rather the extended family composed of all familial off-shoots. Furthermore, it is now commonly extended beyond biological bounds and those of marriage to stand for those who work together for a common cause, particularly one involving cultural revival.

Wa'a is Hawaiian for canoe. *'Ohana wa'a* is then the "family of the canoe," a term that has come to be used for all who have been involved with *Hōkūle'a*, from those who sailed the canoe to those who have contributed to making the voyages possible, or have just been touched by the coming of *Hōkūle'a* to their island. To end this account, let me cite the words delivered by Myron Thompson, Nainoa's father and the president of the Polynesian Voyaging Society, when *Hōkūle'a* and her crew returned to Kualoa, for they sum up how through the efforts of so many to re-create, demonstrate, and celebrate an ancient, life-spreading technology we have all become part of the family of the canoe:

> What began as a dream, a *mana'o* [idea] in the mind's eye of a few, has culminated in today. We have all come home with a greater understanding of the world and our place in the world. And I say "we" because we were all on that canoe, whether you strung one *lei* or a thousand, whether you looked after her as so many have throughout the Pacific, or had one thought of *aloha* for her. We voyaged together, and we are changed. *Hōkūle'a* was built to answer questions about her past. We went out as Hawaiians and scientists, and came home as Polynesian brothers and sisters.

APPENDIX A
CREW MEMBERS FOR THE VOYAGE OF REDISCOVERY
Marlene Among

Miloli'i, Hawai'i Island, Hawai'i to Pape'ete, Tahiti Island: 10 July 1985–11 August 1985. Milton "Shorty" Bertelmann (Captain), Clay Bertelmann, Dennis Chun, Tai Crouch, Harry Ho, Larry Magnuson, Michael "Buddy" McGuire, Mau Piailug (Satawal), Thomas Reity (Satawal), James Shizuru, Teikihe'epo "Tava" Taupu (Marquesas), Nainoa Thompson (Navigator).*

Pape'ete, Tahiti Island to Rarotonga Island, Cook Islands: 30 August 1985–14 September 1985. Abraham "Snake" Ah Hee, Patrick Aiu, Chad Baybayan, Karim Cowan (Tahiti), Bob Krauss, John Kruse, Vic Lipman, Mel Paoa, Mau Piailug (Satawal), Abraham Pi'ianai'a, Chad Pi'ianai'a, Gordon Pi'ianai'a (Captain), Nainoa Thompson (Navigator), Michael Tongg, Andrew Tutai (Cook Islands), Peter Sepelalur (Satawal), Leon Paoa Sterling, Puaniho Tauotaha (Tahiti), Clifford Watson. Bob Krauss, Karim Cowan, and Puaniho Tauotaha were crew members only from Tahiti to Ra'iatea.

Rarotonga Island, Cook Islands to Waitangi, North Island, Aotearoa: 21 November 1985–7 December 1985. Patrick Aiu, Chad Baybayan, Milton "Shorty" Bertelmann (Captain), Bruce Blankenfeld, Stanley Conrad (Aotearoa), Ben Finney, Harry Ho, Michael

---

*Unless otherwise indicated, crew members are from Hawai'i.

"Buddy" McGuire, William "Billy" Richards, James Shizuru, Leon Paoa Sterling, Teikiheʻepo "Tava" Taupu (Marquesas), Nainoa Thompson (Navigator), Michael Tongg.

Waitangi, North Island, Aotearoa to Nukuʻalofa, Tongatapu Island, Tonga: 1 May 1986–11 May 1986. Abraham "Snake" Ah Hee, Patrick Aiu, Carlos Andrade, Chad Baybayan, Philip Ikeda, John Keolanui, James Lyman, Mau Piailug (Satawal), Scott Sullivan, Leon Paoa Sterling (Captain), Nainoa Thompson (Navigator), Michael Tongg, Sione Uaine Ula (Tonga).

Nukuʻalofa, Tongatapu Island, Tonga to Pagapago, Tutuila Island, Samoa: 23 May 1986–25 May 1986. Patrick Aiu, Gilbert Ane, Carlos Andrade, Gail Evenari (California), Chad Baybayan, Hector Busby (Aotearoa), Sione Taupeamuhu (Tonga), Philip Ikeda, Sam Kaʻai, John Keolanui, James "Kimo" Lyman, Mau Piailug (Satawal), Leon Paoa Sterling (Captain), Joanne Kahanamoku Sterling, Scott Sullivan, Nainoa Thompson (Navigator), Michael Tongg, Sione Uaine Ula (Tonga).

Ofu Island, Samoa to Aitutaki Island, Cook Islands: 7 July 1986–16 July 1986. Milton "Shorty" Bertelmann (Captain), Clay Bertelmann, Harry Ho, Pauahi Ioane, Bernard Kilonsky, Ben Lindsey, Mel Paoa, Mau Piailug (Satawal), Tua Pittman (Cook Islands), Teikiheʻepo "Tava" Taupu (Marquesas), Nainoa Thompson (Navigator).

Aitutaki to Rarotonga Island, Cook Islands: 10 August 1986–11 August 1986. Pat Aiu, Chad Baybayan, Dede Bertelmann, Bruce Blankenfeld, Wallace Froiseth, Pauahi Ioane, Jerome Muller, Mau Piailug (Satawal), Tua Pittman (Rarotonga), Nainoa Thompson (Captain and Navigator), Reo Tuiravakai (Aitutaki), Raukete Tuiravakai (Aitutaki).

Rarotonga Island, Cook Islands to Tautira, Tahiti: 12 August 1986–21 August 1986. Abraham "Snake" Ah Hee, Patrick Aiu, Chad Baybayan, Bruce Blankenfeld, Wallace Froiseth, Harry Ho, Glen Oshiro, Mau Piailug (Satawal), Richard Rhodes, Nainoa Thompson (Captain and Navigator), Michael Tongg, Aaron Young.

Tautira, Tahiti to Pape'ete, Tahiti to Tautira, Tahiti: 27 March 1986–29 March 1986. Daniel Akaka, Chad Baybayan, Wallace Froiseth, Harry Ho, Kilo Kaina, Michele Kapana, Will Kyselka, Russell Mau, Arnold Morgado, Abraham Pi'ianai'a, Tutaha Salmon (Tahiti), Cary Sneider (California), Teikihe'epo "Tava" Taupu (Marquesas), Nainoa Thompson (Navigator and Captain), Michael Tongg, Aaron Young. U.S. Congressman (now Senator) Daniel Akaka and Honolulu City Councilman Arnold Morgado joined the crew in Pape'ete.

Tautira, Tahiti to Rangiroa Island: 2 April 1986–4 April 1986. Chad Baybayan, Clay Bertelmann, Wallace Froiseth, Rey Jonsson, Solomon Kaho'ohalahala, Will Kyselka, Charles Larson, Mel Paoa, Cary Sneider (California), Teikihe'epo "Tava" Taupu (Marquesas), Nainoa Thompson (Navigator and Captain), Michael Tongg, Clifford Watson, Nathan Wong, Elisa Yadao, Aaron Young.

Rangiroa Island to Kualoa, O'ahu Island, Hawai'i: 24 April 1986–23 May 1987. Abraham "Snake" Ah Hee, Patrick Aiu, Chad Baybayan, Milton "Shorty" Bertelmann (Captain), Bruce Blankenfeld, Stanley Conrad (Aotearoa), Eni Hunkin (Samoa), Tua Pittman (Cook Islands), Dixon Stroup, Puaniho Tauotaha (Tahiti), Sione Taupeamuhu (Tonga), Teikihe'epo "Tava" Taupu (Marquesas), Nainoa Thompson (Navigator), Michael Tongg, Clifford Watson, Elisa Yadao.

Escort Vessel *Dorcas*. Owners: Dan and Peggy Wright and their sons, Denny and Robin. Crew members: Steve Albert, Walter Benavitz, John Eddy, Jim Heumann, Bill Kepner, Charles Larson, Jerry Muller, Bill Pulaski, Allison Warren, Gary Yuen.

APPENDIX B

POLYNESIAN VOYAGING SOCIETY OFFICERS, BOARD MEMBERS, AND VOLUNTEERS DURING THE VOYAGE OF REDISCOVERY

Marlene Among

Board of Directors. Myron Thompson (President), Cecilia Kapua Lindo (Vice President), Lee Kyselka (Secretary), Virginia Elliott (Treasurer), Patrick Aiu, Tai Crouch, Keali'ipuaimoku Froiseth, Rey Jonsson, Ray Lanterman, Jerome Muller, Michael McGuire, Laura Thompson, Michael Tongg, Nathan Wong, Robert Worthington, August Yee.

Resource Persons. Marlene Among (Project Coordinator and Assistant to President Myron Thompson), Robert Worthington (Protocol Officer), Will Kyselka, Ben Finney, Dixon Stroup (Research Committee); Ruth Pratt, Will Kyselka, Marlene Among (Community Relations Committee); Keali'ipuaimoku Froiseth (Chair, Welcome Home Committee); Marlene Among, Gilbert Ane, Paige Barber, Lurline Yuen Degagne, Randy Fong, Samuel Ka'ahanui, Jr., Cecilia Kapua Lindo, Ruth E. Pratt, Claire Pruet, Billy Richards, Pee Wee Ryan, Vanessa Van Dyken, Clifford Watson, Ka'upena Wong, Robert Worthington, Elisa Yadao (Welcome Home Committee).

Arrival Ceremony at Kualoa. George Kawelo and sons, Keola and Kaulana; David Kawela and sons, Lukela and Ko'olau; Eugene Kawelo and son, Kekoa; Bert Barber and son, Kolomona; Eugene Carrero (Sentinals); Bert Barber, Ka'upena Wong (Ceremonial Foods); Bert Barber, Paige Barber (Chair and Co-Chair,

Luʻau Committee); Marlene Among, Alex Auna, Arthur Beaver, Eugene Carrero, Lurline Yuen Degagne, Lei Fernandez, Bob Froesch, Bill and Jan Gonzales, Francis Keneakua, David and Rochelle Kawelo, Eugene and Stephanie Kawelo, Gege Kawelo, George and Gloria Kawelo, Sam Keliʻikuli, Bobbie and Obe Villamor, Robert Worthington, William and Mel Worthington (Luʻau Committee); Skylark, Brickwood Galeteria, Wayne Chang, Robert Worthington, Frank Shaner, Krash Kealoha (Masters of Ceremony); Reverend William Kaina, Reverend Kawika Kaupu (Blessing); Kamuela Chun, Kalani Akana, Manu Boyd, Cy Bridges, Darryl Keola Cabacungan, Sam Kaʻai, Kamuela Chun, Kihei de Silva, Mapuana de Silva, Ellen Kekeuiaoke de la Rosa, Leinaʻala Heine, Larry Kimura, Pualani Kanahele, Pualani Kanakaʻole, Hoakalei Kamauʻu, Edith Mckinzie, Puakea Nogelmeier, Kalena Silva, Keliʻi Taua, Kaʻupena Wong, Reverend Kaupu, Malia Craver, Nalani Kanakaʻole Zane, Punahele Lerma, Keliʻi Reichel, Owen Kahaʻi Ho, Frank Kahala (Chants); Na Kamalei, Na Pualei, Carlos Andrade Trio, Hokuleʻa, Loyal Garner, Makaha Sons of Niʻihau, I Kona (Dances and Songs).

APPENDIX C
ACKNOWLEDGMENTS: TRADITIONAL AND ELECTED LEADERS, GOVERNMENT OFFICIALS, AND COMMUNITY SUPPORTERS FROM FRENCH POLYNESIA, COOK ISLANDS, AOTEAROA, TONGA, AND AMERICAN SAMOA

Robert Worthington

French Polynesia. Pierre Angeli (High Commissioner), Yves Dassonville (Deputy General Secretary-High Commissioner), Gaston Flosse (President of French Polynesia), Jacques Teheiura (Minister of Education and Culture), Geoffry Salmon (Minister of Transport), Claude Autillier (Assistant to the Director of Customs Administration), Tutaha Salmon (Mayor of Tautira), Frances Stein (Secretary General of OTAC), Jean-Yves Berroche (Director of Maritime Affairs), Christian Vernaudon (Director of Tourism Promotion Office), Philippe Guesdon (Chief of Press Service), William Ahnne (Pape'ete Harbor Master), Gerard Cowan (Chief of Events and Festivities, OTAC), Emile Buillard (Quarantine Service), Maco Tevane (Director of the Tahitian Academy, Member of Pape'ete City Council), Al Prince (*Tahiti Sun Press*), Djeen Cheou (Quarantine Service), Monique Carlmark (Translation).

Cook Islands. Honorable Tangaroa Tangaroa (Queen's Representative, Head of State), Sir Thomas Davis KBE (Prime Minister), Geoffrey Henry (Deputy Prime Minister), Dr. Teariki Matenga (Minister of Internal Affairs), Dr. Pupuke Robati (Minister of Trade, Labor, Transport, Marine Resources, and Information), Dr. Terepai Maoate (Minister of Agriculture and Health), Inatio Akaruru (Minister of Post & Telecommunication, Immigration, and Electricity), Pa Tepaeru Ariki (President, Paramount Ariki of Takitumu), Makea Nui Teremoana Ariki (Te Au O Tonga), Makea Karika Margaret Ariki (Te Au O Tonga), Makea Vakatini Ina Ariki (Te Au O Tonga), Kainuku Taupuru Ariki (Takitumu), Tinomana Napa Ariki (Puaikura), Tamatoa Purua Ariki (Aitutaki), Temaeu O Te Rangi Ariki (Mitiaro), Harold Browne (Chief Administrative Officer of Aitutaki), Tikaka Henry (Mayor of Aitutaki), Tamatoa Ariki (Traditional Leader of Aitutaki), Jon Jonassen (Secretary, Ministry of Foreign Affairs), Rohea Tongaroa (Chief Administrative Officer of Mitiaro), Bill Hosking (Secretary of Agriculture), Joseph Herman (Cultural Council), Meau Kave (Comptroller of Customs), Tutai Toru (Secretary of Immigration), Motu Kora (Outer Island Affairs), Joseph Caffery (Secretary of Trade, Labour and Transport), Iro Ioane (Waterfront Commission), Tai Herman (Harbor Master of Aitutaki), Stuart and Tereapi'i Kingan (Peacesat Terminal), Ron Powell (Drydocking), Tony Utanga (Resources), Paul Frost (Meteorological Service).

Aotearoa. The Right Honorable David Lange (Prime Minister of New Zealand), Margaret Shields (Minister of Customs), Dr. Bruce Gregory (Māori Member of Parliament for the North), Sir James Henare (Tai Tokerau), Sir Graham and Lady Lattimar (Tai Tokerau), Gary Posz (U.S. Consul General), Tom Parore (Director of Māori Affairs, Whangarei), Tupi Puriri (Waitangi Marae), Hector and Hilda Busby (*Nga Toki Matawhaorua* Canoe, Tai Tokerau), Ioane Sefulu (Director–Pacific Islanders' Educational Resource Center), Barry Skinner (Manager of Waitangi Trust), John Rangihau (University of Waikato), Eileen Parore (Representative of Māori Cultural Groups), Stewart Long (Waitangi Resort Hotel and Motel), Monty Miller (Waitangi Radio).

Tonga. His Majesty, King Taufa'ahau Tupou IV, Her Majesty, Queen Halaevalu Mata'aho, His Royal Highness, The Crown Prince Tupouto'a (Minister of Foreign Affairs), His Royal Highness Prince Lavaka-Ata (Royal New Zealand Navy), Prince Fatafehi Tu'ipelehake (Prime Minister), Honorable Baron Vaea (Minister of Commerce, Labor, Industry, and Tourism), Honorable Langi Kavaliku (Minister of Works, Education, and Civil Aviation), Honorable Ve'ahala (Retired Governor of Ha'apai), Taniela Tufui (Secretary to Government and Cabinet, Prime Minister's Office), Tu'a Taumoepeau (Secretary, Ministry of Foreign Affairs), Semisi Taumoepeau (Director of Tonga Visitors Bureau),

Sakopo Lolohea (Tonga Visitors Bureau), Tavake Fusimalohi (General Manager of Tonga Broadcasting), Sioeli Fotu (Harbor Master), Merv McGuire (Wharf Administrator), Laitia Fefeitua (Weather Office), Pasa Havea (Meteorologist).

American Samoa. A. P. Lutali (Governor of American Samoa), Eni and Hina-nui Hunkin (Lt. Governor of American Samoa and wife), Letuli Ioloa (Senate of American Samoa), Matautia Tuiafuno (Speaker of the House), Honorable Tauese Sunia (Director, Department of Education), Honorable Galea'i Poumele (Secretary of Samoan Affairs), Minnie Mann (Director, Office of Tourism), Bill Wallace (Deputy Attorney General), Gretchen Makaiwi (Office of Samoan Affairs, Protocol), Tom Tatakawa (Weather Station, NOAA), John Reid (Harbor Master), Titi and Al Lolotai (Arts Council), Tony Meredith (Director of Port Administration), Paulette Samia (Hawaiian Airlines), Jim McGuire (President, Samoan Canoe Association), Theresa Makaiwa Tau'a, Mel Makaiwi.

ABOUT THE DRAWINGS

The drawings of canoes, artifacts, and crew members have been derived from a number of sources: engravings from the journals of early European explorers, photographs, and the experiences and imagination of Richard Rhodes, who has long been involved in the project as a graphic illustrator and as a crew member. A brief description of each is given below.

Chapter One

Page 1. A Tongan double canoe of the Tongiaki type as seen in 1616 during the Dutch expedition under the command of Lemaire and Schouten.

Page 27. Lapita potsherds excavated in the Santa Cruz islands of Melanesia by Roger Green.

Page 29. A branch from a Tahitian breadfruit tree originally drawn during Cook's first expedition.

Chapter Two

Page 35. *Hōkūle'a* seen from above, but stripped of sail rig, sleeping shelters, and other deck gear to capture the feeling of its twin hulls cutting through the sea.

Page 38. *Nālehia* sailing in light airs in Kāne'ohe Bay on the northeast shore of O'ahu.

Page 49. Tahitian stone adz collected during Cook's first voyage.

Page 211. Reading: a favorite fair-weather pastime when off watch.

Page 220. Scanning the horizon ahead.

Page 228. *Hōkūle'a* anchored at Vaitepiha Bay, Tautira, Tahiti.

Page 231. Puaniho Tauotaha, Tahitian crew member and champion racing paddler.

Page 254. A Tahitian trolling lure, made from mother of pearl shell, a hook of bone, and dog hairs, collected during Cook's first voyage.

Chapter Eight

Page 255. Running before the wind, sailing "wing on wing."

Page 281. Prow piece from the reconstructed Māori canoe *Te Aurere*, modeled on a pre-classic Māori prow piece found buried in a swamp and now on display in the Auckland Museum.

Page 306. A painted Māori paddle collected on the first Cook expedition.

Chapter Nine

Page 307. Coming home to Kualoa; *Hōkūle'a* and her escorts.

NOTES

Preface

1. Baybayan et al. (1987); Finney et al. (1989).

Chapter One

1. Maximilian Transylvanus, in a letter to the Cardinal-Archbishop of Salzburg written in 1522 (Beaglehole 1974, 109n).
2. Quiros (1904, 2:152); Kelly (1966, 2:309).
3. Roggeveen (1970, 101, 153–154).
4. Quoted in Goetzmann (1986, 1).
5. Cook (1955, 169, 286–288); Banks (1962, 2:37).
6. Cook (1961, 320–327).
7. Forster (1778, 1:557); Cook (1961, 339n, 354).
8. Cook (1961, 303–304, 529–530, 537, 541).
9. King in Cook (1967, 2:262n); Cook (1967, 1:263–264).
10. De Brosses (1756, 1:80); Dumont-d'Urville (1830, 2:614–616).
11. Cook (1967, 1:279).
12. Cook (1955, 154). Although Andia y Varela, the Spanish navigator who visited Tahiti three years after Cook, apparently did not have available to him the comparative linguistic data that Cook and Banks had carried, he espoused a similar theory of the ultimate Southeast Asian origin of the Tahitians, proposing that their ancestors must "have passed from island to island from the West towards the East" (Corney 1914, 2:256–257).
13. Crozet (1783, 48, 153–154).
14. Cook (1955, 154n).
15. Relandi [Reeland] (1708); Ray (1926, 19–21).
16. Forster (1778, 353–360); Blumenbach (1795).

17. Hale (1846, 118).
18. Martínez de Zúñiga (1966, 16–19).
19. Lang (1834, 59; 1877, 97).
20. Smith (1898; 1907; 1913–1915); Fornander (1969); Howe (1988).
21. Best (1923:6); Barrère (1969); Simmons and Biggs (1970); Simmons (1976); Sorrenson (1979).
22. Handy (1930).
23. Buck (1938).
24. Heyerdahl (1950, 297).
25. Heyerdahl (1953).
26. Heyerdahl (1941; 1947, 348; 1953, 601).
27. Sharp (1956a; 1957).
28. Sharp (1957, 11–31); Cook (1967, pt. 1:87).
29. Beaglehole in Cook (1967, pt. 1:87n); (Anderson in Cook 1967, pt. 2:960); Durrans (1979).
30. The many archaeological reports that have directly refuted Heyerdahl's theory include: Suggs (1960b); Emory and Sinoto (1965); Golson (1965); and Bellwood (1979). For a sampling of the growing literature on Lapita, see: Ambrose and Green (1972); Green (1974a; 1979; 1981; 1987b); Kirch (1988a; 1988b); Kirch and Hunt (1988a; 1988b); Bellwood and Koon (1989); and Gosden et al. (1989).
31. Allen et al. (1977); Wickler and Spriggs (1988); Allen et al. (1989).
32. Allen (1984a); Spriggs (1984); Kirch and Hunt (1988a); White et al. (1988); Gosden et al. (1989); Kirch et al. (1991); Yen (1991).
33. Sharp (1963a); letter from Andrew Sharp to Ben Finney, 30 January 1971.
34. For early discussion for and against the Sharp hypothesis, see: Jones (1957); Dening (1958; 1963); Luomala (1958); Sharp (1958; 1961a; 1961b; 1963b; 1964; 1965; 1966b); Suggs (1961b); Bechtol (1963); Frankel (1963); Golson (1963); Heyen (1963); Hilder (1963); Nelson (1963); Parsonson (1963); Lewis (1964a; 1964b); Riesenberg (1965); Mason (1966); Howard (1967); Åkerblom (1968).
35. Dening (1963, 132–136); Lewthwaite (1970). The directional distortions in Cook's rendering of Tupaia's map apparently stemmed from mistakes in judging whether, when Tupaia referred to a direction, he meant to that direction or from it. Because those "traditional" Tahitian references to Aotearoa and Hawai'i only show up in lists and traditions gathered after some years of European contact, they may reflect the incorporation of new geographical knowledge rather than ancient memories of these distant places.
36. Sharp (1957, 22–30). Lewis (1972, 244) argues, however, that drift voyagers pushed here and there by wind and current could not have kept track of the bearing and distance back to their home island.

Chapter Two

1. Lewis (1966).
2. Lewis (1966, 94); Sharp (1966a).

3. Paris (1841, plate 127).

4. Extensive sailing trials conducted in 1975 with calibrated instruments confirmed this figure (Finney 1977).

5. Holmes (1981, 105).

6. Lewis (1972, 269) notes that although deep-V hull canoes of the Caroline Islands can be made to point fairly high into the wind, the islanders typically sail them "full and by" at 75°–80° off the true wind in order to maintain good speed with only a moderate amount of leeway. Gladwin (1970, 13) makes a similar observation. See Doran (1981) for an extensive analysis of sailing canoe performance. The so-called "flying proas," as Europeans called the fast sailing canoes of the Marshall and Marianas islands, may have pointed slightly higher into the wind than their Polynesian counterparts, particularly in calm waters. Sea trials with modern reconstructions should be undertaken to get a precise idea of both their speed and pointing ability.

7. Sharp (1963, 52); Finney (1967).

8. Coles (1979).

9. Olsen and Crumlin-Pedersen (1967); Crumlin-Pedersen (1970); McGrail (1974); Coles (1979, 75–77); Binns (1980).

10. Bass (1972); Katsev et al. (1987).

11. Sinoto (1979; 1983).

12. Thilenius (1901); Neyret (1950); Parsonson (1963); Lewis (1972, 254); Holmes (1981, 116–117). Fornander (1919, 3d series, vol. 6, pt. 2:249) also reports that "the favorite war canoe, or admiral's ship, 'Kaneaaiai,' of Peleioholani of O'ahu carried on board from one hundred and twenty to one hundred and forty men, besides their provisions, water, etc."

13. McGrail (1975); Coles (1979).

14. Since *le'a* can mean specifically sexual joy or orgasm, the star's name might indeed have had a special meaning for homebound sailors. *Hōkūle'a* was originally suggested as the name for the canoe by Sandra Maile while serving as secretary of the Polynesian Voyaging Society before going on to law school.

15. Lewis (1972).

16. Carolinian methods have been extensively documented by Goodenough (1953); Gladwin (1970); Lewis (1972); Riesenberg (1976); and Thomas (1987).

17. Andia y Varela in Corney (1914, 2:286); cf. Cook (1955, 154); Banks (1962, 1:368).

18. Kamakau (1890); Johnson and Mahelona (1975, 70–73).

19. Gill (1876, 319–322). The Hawaiians also apparently had some sort of a wind gourd, although the famous "wind gourd of La'amaomao" referred to in Nakuina (1990) seems to have been used for controlling local winds around the islands.

20. Kemp (1976, 942).

21. Alkire (1970, 53); Lewis (1972, 135–136). There is also the "*etak* of sighting," the segment during which the departure or target island can be seen, and the "*etak* of birds," during which land birds fishing out to sea can be seen. Although these *etak* and the first two *etak* determined by the

reference island–horizon star intersections do not always coincide, Thomas (1987, 79) illustrates a course between Satawal and Pigale where they do.

22. Kamakau (1890); Pukui and Elbert (1957, 72).

23. Keauokalani (1932, 82–83); Lewis (1972, 235–244).

24. In 1000 A.D. Arcturus would have had a declination of 24° 39′ North and thus would have passed overhead north of Kaua'i (Lewis 1972, 239).

25. Finney (1977; 1979a; 1979b).

26. Johnson and Mahelona (1975, 17).

27. Lewis (1977).

28. Sharp (1966a); Finney (1967; 1976); letter from Andrew Sharp to Ben Finney, 29 January 1971.

Chapter Three

1. Finney (1979b, 280–281).

2. Kanahele (1982).

3. See Finney et al. (1986) for a summary of Nainoa's navigation methods and how he employed them to sail from Hawai'i to Tahiti and return in 1980, and see Kyselka (1987) for a more detailed account.

4. Lewis (1972, 242) reports that some Carolinians measure the height of a star above the horizon by their outstretched hand, though, of course, without expressing that height in degrees.

5. Where currents flow against the wind direction, it is sometimes possible to gain an idea of current direction and strength from observing the exaggerated steepness of the surface waves (Lewis 1972, 100; Thomas 1987, 29, 91).

6. Stroup et al. (1981).

Chapter Four

1. It was fortunate that we had redundant systems of satellite tracking; during part of the voyage the ARGOS transmitter aboard the canoe malfunctioned because of a faulty connection.

2. Miller and Thompson (1970, 130–133).

3. Kemp (1976, 882).

4. See chapter 8 for a more detailed treatment of the sequence and timing of Polynesian dispersion and the sources for this brief outline.

5. The other interarchipelago roundtrip encompassed within the voyage, that between the Society and Cook islands (Tahiti to Rarotonga in 1985; Rarotonga to Tahiti in 1986), also retraced a legendary two-way voyaging route (Henry 1928, 121–127). Although that roundtrip will not be analyzed as such, part of chapter 5 deals with the crossing from Rarotonga to Tahiti.

6. Along with the log of the canoe and interviews with Nainoa, written narratives by Victor Lipman (1986), Will Kyselka (1988), and Jo-anne

Kahanamoku Sterling (1991) were used to prepare this summary of the Tahiti to Rarotonga leg.

Chapter Five

1. Cf. Keegan and Diamond (1987).
2. Heyerdahl (1978, 332; 1981, 35); Finney (1979b).
3. Finney (1985, 10).
4. Siers (1977; 1978).
5. Steiner (1980); Hessel (1981); Revell (1981a); Thompson (1986a, 1986b).
6. Firth (1936, 30).
7. See, for example: Cook (1955, 137, 154); Banks (1962, 1:368); La Perouse (1799, 3:66); Beechey (1831, 1:251–252); Williams (1838, 504–510); Armstrong (1839); Hale (1846, 118–119); Wilkes (1849, 1:327–328); as well as later discussions of this issue in Heine-Geldern (1952); and Höver (1961).
8. Finney (1977, 1283; 1985).
9. In an article published after Nainoa Thompson formulated his voyaging strategy, Feinberg (1986) reports that the sailors of Anuta, a tiny Polynesian outlier located midway between Fiji and New Guinea, do not like to chance the stormy seas of the westerly season. Instead, when they want to visit Patutaka, a neighboring island to the southeast, they sail during the trade wind season, waiting for the trades to drop and for brief spells of northerly and westerly winds that would enable them to sail easily to the island. Once they have reached Patutaka, they are then in a good position to return home before the wind when the trades resume blowing.
10. Corney (1915, 2:286–287).
11. Trenberth and Mo (1985).

Chapter Six

1. Smith (1898); Buck (1929; 1950, 9–64).
2. Piddington (1956, 202); Simmons and Biggs (1970); Orbell (1974; 1985, 13–19); Simmons (1976).
3. Green (1975a, 601); Davidson (1984, 256–260); Kirch (1986a, 34).
4. Green (1966, 28–29); Biggs (1978, 692); Harlow (1979, 134).
5. Ngata (1950); Kelly (1955); Sharp (1956b, 158).
6. Best (1925, 274), who also cited directions for sailing toward the setting points of Venus and the moon, as well as that of the sun. Although these bearings are more difficult to calculate than the sun's, they could well have been within the angular range of the wide target presented by Aotearoa to voyagers approaching from the east. Åkerblom (1968, 82–83) discusses the various star and planet courses to Aotearoa found in the traditional literature but muddies the question of accuracy by falsely assuming that only bodies with the same declination as the target can be employed for course setting and steering. Buck (1926, 195) points out that attempts to derive a more exact sailing date than October or November

from the Māori lunar date—such as citing the Takitumu tradition of sailing in the month of Tatau-uru-ora on the night of Orongonui as an indication of a departure on 27 or 28 November—may be specious, for a precise
correlation between Māori lunar calendar dates and our solar calendar cannot be made without first knowing the exact year of sailing.

7. Brierly (1985, 18; fig. 1).

8. Revell (1981*b*).

9. Brierly (1985, 94).

10. Smith (1907, 205); Duff (1968); Anderson (1980); Leach et al. (1986).

11. Although Alpha Centauri (also called Rigil Kent) appears to the naked eye as a single star, it is actually a triple-star system.

12. Other factors, such as *Hawaiki-Nui* taking a more southerly course,
and troubles with the canoe's sailing rig (a modern Marconi rig employing
a bamboo mast), may have contributed to the slower sailing time of the
Hawaiki-Nui. Despite a general policy against raising nontraditional sails
on *Hōkūle'a*, during the voyage some bored crew members played around
with hoisting makeshift jibs on the forestay of the forward mast to try to
make the canoe sail faster in periods of light winds. We doubt, however,
that these unauthorized "experiments" made the canoe reach Aotearoa
significantly earlier than it would have had they not been conducted.

13. Irwin (1989, 186) has recently proposed that voyages to Aotearoa
could have been made throughout the year by exploiting strong northerlies
generated along the leading edge of a front immediately following a high. It
seems doubtful, however, that such northerlies would last long enough for
a canoe to sail very far to the west before encountering the westerlies that
would inevitably follow the passage of the front.

14. Taylor (1870, 266); Buck (1926, 196; 1938, 270); Kelly (1949, 48);
Houston (1965, 20).

15. Neal (1965, 637–638). Closely related species of *Metrosideros* also
grow on Rarotonga and Raoul (Wilder 1931, 82; Sykes 1977, 119; Merlin
1985, 94–95).

16. Douglas Yen (1986) points out that the coincidence of the right
wind conditions for reaching Aotearoa from tropical Polynesia with the
warm growing conditions needed for the successful transference to this
temperate region of such tropical plants as the sweet potato, yam, taro,
paper mulberry (for making tapa cloth), and the *tī* plant may also have
been crucial to successful colonization. An arrival during November and
December would have given them a chance to acclimatize themselves during the warm summer months in order to survive the cold season to follow, whereas had the transporting canoe or canoes landed during the winter it would probably have been too cold for these tropical plants to have
taken root and grown.

Chapter Seven

1. For documentation of the 1976 voyage see Finney (1977; 1979*a*;
1979*b*) and Lewis (1977). For the 1980 voyage see Finney et al. (1986);
Kyselka (1987).

2. For the purpose of plotting Nainoa's dead reckoning on a chart, we have transformed his verbal estimates of deviation to one side or other of his reference course line and of latitude into a series of latitude-longitude intersections. This does not mean, however, that Nainoa thinks of the changing position of the canoe in such terms. To avoid the wrong impression about Nainoa's dead reckoning, we do not specify his dead reckoning estimates in terms of exact latitude-longitude intersections. Instead, when comparing where Nainoa thought the canoe was at a particular time with the satellite-derived position, we indicate approximately how many miles and in what direction the dead reckoning position bears to or from the actual position of the canoe at the time.

3. Because the new large after sail disturbed the steering balance of the canoe by moving the center of effort of the sails so far back of the center of lateral resistance of the hulls that much effort would have been required to keep the canoe on course, it was necessary to move the mast step forward to bring the center of effort closer to the center of lateral resistance.

4. This account of the sail to Rangiroa is in part based on crew member Cary Sneider's manuscript (Sneider 1987).

5. Climate Analysis Center (1987).

6. Sadler (1984).

7. During their years of sailing *Hōkūle'a*, Nainoa and the crew had learned much about trimming the sails for maximum windward performance. Although the crab-claw rig may appear clumsy to modern sailors, in reality it is well adapted for trimming and shaping the sail to enhance windward performance. By attaching sheets at various points along the boom, you can exploit the flexibility of that long, curving spar and the fact that it borders so much of the perimeter of the sail to achieve a high degree of control of both the flatness and the twist of the sail.

8. Dixon Stroup is deeply grateful for the excellent, efficient, and caring treatment he received during the swift transfer back to Honolulu. This was not the first time *Hōkūle'a* had been helped in an emergency. The U.S. Navy and Coast Guard uphold the finest traditions of the sea in rendering aid unhesitatingly to anyone in distress, and we join with all seamen in our appreciation.

9. Climate Analysis Center (1987).

10. Sadler (1967).

Chapter Eight

1. Adams et al. (1978); Kirch (1985, 52–53; 1986*b*); Dunnell (1986); Trigger (1989, 330–336); Anthony (1990).

2. Goldman (1955); Sahlins (1958).

3. Golson and Gathercole (1962).

4. Levison, Fenner, et al. (1969); Levison, Ward, et al. (1973).

5. Gladwin (1970); Lewis (1972).

6. Bloomfield (1933, 311); Biggs (1972).

7. Suggs (1960*a*; 1961*b*); Garanger (1972*a*); Yen (1973, 75); Davidson (1974); Bellwood (1978*b*).

8. Ambrose and Green (1972); Green (1974a).

9. Pawley and Green (1975); Green (1978; 1981); Irwin (1981; 1989); Kirch and Yen (1984); Kirch (1986a; 1986b); Sutton (1987a; 1987b); Spriggs (1988); Dye (1989); Irwin et al. (1990); Walter (1990); Anderson (1991, 790); Rolett (in press); Weisler (in press).

10. Coles (1979, 66–69); Green (1981); Davidson (1984, 27–28); Kirch (1984, 83); Rouse (1986, 41); Terrell (1986, 73); Bellwood (1987, 43–44; 1989, 19); Keegan and Diamond (1987); Kirch and Green (1987, 440); Sutton (1987a, 144); Irwin (1989, 168; 1992, 51–52, 60, 97, 105–106, 219); Thorne and Raymond (1989, 259); Irwin et al. (1990, 39).

11. Buck (1938, 62).

12. Biggs and Biggs (1975, 46–50).

13. Wyrtki (1975); Philander (1989). These events are often referred to as El Niño–Southern Oscillation (ENSO) events, in recognition of both their oceanic and atmospheric components.

14. Rasmussen, Arkin, Carpenter, et al. (1983); Rasmussen, Arkin, Krueger, et al. (1983); Sadler and Kilonsky (1983); Finney (1985).

15. Analysis of the sand tempers of potsherds found in Marquesan excavations indicate that they are from a pot or pots made from minerals found in Fiji (Dickenson and Shutler 1974).

16. Lawson (1875, n.d.); cf. Porter (1822, 2:30). Alternatively, since Havai'i and Vavau were the ancient names for, respectively, Ra'iatea and Borabora, these tales could relate to colonization from the Societies.

17. Dickenson and Shutler (1974). Suggs's (1961a, 180–181) early dates for the Marquesas of 2080 ± 150 years B.P. (Before Present) and 1910 ± 180 B.P. have been corrected to 405 B.C.–220 A.D. and 385 B.C.–450 A.D. (Kirch 1986a, 24). Another early Marquesan date from a cave site on Ua Pou island Ottino (1985), has recently been questioned on the basis of faunal analysis (Leach et al. 1990). Sinoto (1970) dates the settlement phase in Marquesan prehistory from 300 A.D.

18. Keegan and Diamond (1987); Kirch (1988a); Irwin (1989; 1992); Irwin et al. (1990).

19. Frankel (1962; 1963); Finney (1967, 151); Irwin (1989, 174–175).

20. Morrison (1971, 34); Needham (1971, 511).

21. Buck (1932).

22. Irwin (1981); Terrell (1986); Kirch and Hunt (1988a); Kirch et al. (1990).

23. Kirch and Hunt (1988a, 158–159); Kirch and Ellison (1993). The fortuitous discovery of a submerged site offshore Upolu Island, Western Samoa occurred when pottery shards were found beneath coral when a new boat channel was being opened in the reef (Green 1974b; Jennings 1974).

24. Steadman and Kirch (1990); Kirch and Ellison (1993); Spriggs and Anderson (1993). The 300–200 B.C. radiocarbon dates from the atoll of Pukapuka may indicate the frontier of settlement in the Northern Cooks, although they need more documentation to be fully accepted at present (Chicamori 1987, 111; Chicamori and Yoshida 1988).

25. Van Tilburg (in press).

26. Métraux (1940, 416); Finney (1985, 18–19); Bierbach and Cain (1988); Caviedes and Waylen (1993).

27. Cf. Langdon and Tryon (1983, 53–55); Green (1988, 55); Ward (1988); Irwin et al. (1990).

28. Labrosse (1874).

29. De Bisschop (1958).

30. Barthel (1978).

31. Mulloy (1979, 111).

32. Emory (1963; 1978); Green (1966); Elbert (1982). Hunt (1991), drawing on recent work on contact-induced linguistic change by Thomason and Kaufman (1988), suggests that the postsettlement impact of the repeated arrival of canoes from the Marquesas might better account for the linguistic tie between the two languages than initial settlement from the Marquesas.

33. Levison et al. (1973, 53).

34. Porter (1822, 2:54–55); Dening (1974, 62).

35. Kane (1976); Pi'ianai'a (1990).

36. Johnson et al. (1989, 156–157); Bruner (1990).

37. Von den Steinen (1988, 30).

38. Walsh (1905); Smith (1907, 172); Dening (1963, 115).

39. Thilenius (1902); Churchill (1911); Woodford (1916); Firth (1961); Davidson (1974); Kirch and Yen (1974); Bayard (1976); Ward et al. (1976); Feinberg (1989).

40. Friederici (1929); Thorpe (1929); Imbelloni (1930); Skinner (1931); Dixon (1933); Robinson (1942); Hornell (1945); Bryan (1963, 83–85); Ramirez (1990–1991).

41. Dixon (1932); Buck (1938); Yen (1974). The earliest direct archaeological evidence of the sweet potato in Polynesia comes from recent excavations on Mangaia in the Southern Cooks that indicates the plant was being cultivated there by about 1000 A.D. (Hather and Kirch 1991). Whistler (1990; 1991, 48–49) adds the bottle gourd (*Lagenaria siceraria*) to the sweet potato as a cultigen introduced into Polynesia from South America; Ward and Brookfield (1992) suggest that the coconut, which they consider has a Southeast Asia-Melanesia origin, may have been carried across the Pacific to Panama in pre-Columbian times.

42. De Bisschop (1958); Danielsson (1960).

43. Fast (1983).

44. Emory (1928); Cleghorn (1988).

45. Finney (1985, 20); Caviedes and Waylen (1993).

46. Specht (1984); Meredith et al. (1985).

47. Quiros (1904, 2:152); Audran (1927); Beaglehole and Beaglehole (1938, 352).

48. Forster (1778, 511); Cook (1955, 155–157); Banks (1962, 1:329); Dening (1963, 127–128); Lewthwaite (1967; 1970, 17–18); Lewis (1972, 196–198). On Tupaia's chart Cook transcribed the phrase in Tahitian as *"toi miti no terara te rietea,"* although he confused the issue by apparently misunderstanding Tahitian directional terminology and placing Ra'ivavae

to the northwest of Tahiti when in reality it is south of Tahiti (Skelton 1955, viii, chart 11). Intricately carved Tahitian fly-whisks provide another indication of a Tahitian-Austral Island connection; Rose (1979) considers that they were either imports from the Australs or were copied from Austral Island models.

49. Williams (1838, 64, 165–169); Gill (1856; 1876, 23–28; 1880, 189); Corney (1913, 1:306); Henry (1928, 121–127); Buck (1934, 37–43); Crocombe and Crocombe (1968, 140–142); Von Den Steinen (1988, 11–31).

50. Piddington (1956); Cordy (1974); Orbell (1974; 1985); Simmons (1976).

51. Green (1975b; 1981); Davidson (1978); Hunt (1987); Best et al. (1991); Leach (1991).

52. Green and Davidson (1974, 261); Bellwood (1978b, 80, 201); Walter and Dickenson (1989). Katayama (in press) argues for a linkage between Tonga and the Southern Cooks on the basis of his analysis of skeletal remains.

53. Leach et al. (1986); Anderson and McFadgen (1990); Anderson (1991).

54. Bury (1920); Hopper (1991). The concern expressed by W. H. R. Rivers (1926) in his essay on "The Disappearance of Useful Arts," such as voyaging canoes and other seemingly essential technologies from various Pacific islands, reflects this assumption of the universality of progress.

55. Malinowski (1922); Davenport (1962; 1964); Harding (1967); Green (1974a, 253; 1987a); Egloff (1979); Allen (1984b, 429–432); Irwin (1985); Kirch (1988a; 1990, 128–130; 1991).

56. Kirch et al. (1992, 178); Rolett (in press); Walter (in press).

57. Haddon and Hornell (1936–1938).

58. Buck (1942).

59. Moerenhout (1837, 1:158–159); Haddon and Hornell (1936, 1:79–80).

60. Alkire (1978, 112–131).

61. Dillon (1829, 112); Firth (1961); Biggs (1971, 491); Kaeppler (1973, 24); Kirch (1984, 237–242; 1988c, 8); Kirch and Yen (1984); Feinberg (1989).

62. Haddon and Hornell (1936, 1:79–91, 265–272; 1938, 3:48–51).

63. Buck (1942, 199); Weisler (in press).

64. Bingham (1847, 333); Doyle (1945, 40).

65. Ellis (1829, 1:177–178).

66. Siers (1978).

67. Winkler (1901, 507–508).

68. Beechey (1831, 1:220–237).

69. Buck (1938, 96).

70. Kirch (1988a; 1990); Hunt (1989).

71. Helms (1988).

72. Firth (1936, 415); Jacquier (1948); Laguesse (1954); Nègres (1956); McCall (1976; 1981); Feinberg (1988; 1991).

73. Firth (1936, 32, 415).

74. Green (1975b); Davidson (1978).

75. Bellwood (1970); Kirch (1986a).

76. Pawley and Green (1984, 138–139).

77. Langdon and Tryon (1983); Elbert and Kaiser (1992).

Chapter Nine

1. Hobsbawm and Ranger (1983); Handler and Linnekin (1984).
2. Malo (1898, 4–6); Barrère (1969).
3. Cartwright (1933, 8); Beckwith (1940, 352). Sources for the Moʻikeha cycle include: Emerson (1893, 14–24); Malo (1898, 7); Fornander (1916, 1st series, vol. 4, pt. 1:112–173; 1969, 2:48–57); Beckwith (1940, 352–362).
4. Sources for the Paʻao cycle include: Emerson (1893, 5–13); Malo (1898, 6–7); Beckwith (1940, 371–375); Fornander (1969, 2:33–38).
5. Emerson (1893, 9).
6. Beckwith (1940, 373); Fornander (1969, 2:22).
7. Alexander (1893, 160); Malo (1898, 10); Kamakau (1976, 5).
8. Stokes (1928).
9. Buck (1926; 1938, 239–258); Beckwith (1940); Luomala (1979).
10. Luomala (1979).
11. Sharp (1956b); Groube (1970); Cordy (1974); Simmons (1976); Tuggle (1979, 189).
12. Sahlins (1985, 74); Valeri (1985, 8).
13. Buck (1938, 22–23); Daniel (1955, 2); Vansina (1985, 190).
14. Vansina (1985, 196).
15. Mitchell (1979).
16. Garanger (1972a; 1972b, 83–100).
17. Firth (1961); Leach (1962); Hooper (1981).
18. Kirch and Yen (1984, 335); Kirch (1986b).
19. Emory (1928); Dye (1989, 4–7).
20. Emory and Sinoto (1965); Cordy (1974); Green (1974c); Cachola-Abad (1993).
21. Stokes (1928); Emory (1946; 1978; 1979); Rose (1978); Johnson (1979); Kirch (1984, 66); Spriggs (1988); Dye (1989); Cachola-Abad (1993).
22. Johansen (1958, 7–8, 116–173; 1954, 35–39, 163); Finney (1991).
23. Sahlins (1981); Kameʻeleihiwa (1986, 28–29); Lucas (1989, 107).
24. Handy and Pukui (1958, 3).

REFERENCES

Adams, William Y., Dennis P. Van Gerven, and Richard S. Levy, 1978. The Retreat from Migrationism. In *Annual Review of Anthropology* (Bernard J. Siegel, ed.) 7:483–532.

Åkerblom, Kjell, 1968. *Astronomy and Navigation in Polynesia and Micronesia.* Monograph Series, No. 14. Stockholm, Ethnografiska Museet.

Alexander, William D., 1893. The Song of Kualii, of Hawaii, Sandwich Islands. *Journal of the Polynesian Society* 2:160–178.

Alkire, William, 1970. Systems of Measurement on Woleai Atoll, Caroline Islands. *Anthropos* 65:1–73.

———, 1978. *Coral Islanders.* Arlington Heights, Ill., AHM Publishing.

Allen, James, 1984a. In Search of the Lapita Homeland. *Journal of Pacific History* 19:186–201.

———, 1984b. Pots and Poor Princes: A Multidimensional Approach to the Role of Pottery Trading in Coastal Papua. In *The Many Dimensions of Pottery: Ceramics in Archaeology and Anthropology*, ed. S. E. van der Leeuw and A. C. Pritchard. Amsterdam, Institute for Pre- and Proto-history, University of Amsterdam, 409–473.

Allen, Jim, Jack Golson, and Rhys Jones, 1977. *Sunda and Sahul: Prehistoric Studies in Southeast Asia, Melanesia and Australia.* London, Academic Press.

Allen, Jim, Chris Gosden, and J. Peter White, 1989. Human Pleistocene Adaptations in the Tropical Island Pacific: Recent Evidence from New Ireland, a Greater Australian Outlier. *Antiquity* 63:548–561.

Ambrose, Wallace R., and Robert C. Green, 1972. First Millennium B.C. Transport of Obsidian from New Britain to the Solomon Islands. *Nature* 237:31.

Anderson, Atholl, 1991. The Chronology of Colonization in New Zealand. *Antiquity* 65:767–795.

——, 1990. The Archaeology of Raoul Island (Kermadecs) and Its Place in the Settlement History of Polynesia. *Archaeology and Physical Anthropology in Oceania* 15:131–141.

Anderson, Atholl, and Bruce MacFadgen, 1990. Prehistoric Two-Way Voyaging between New Zealand and East Polynesia: Mayor Island Obsidian on Raoul Island, and Possible Raoul Island Obsidian in New Zealand. *Archaeology in Oceania* 25:37–42.

Anthony, David W., 1990. Migration in Archaeology: The Baby and the Bathwater. *American Anthropologist* 92:895–914.

Armstrong, Richard, 1839. Review of *View of the Origins and Migration of the Polynesian Nation* by John D. Lang. *Hawaiian Spectator* 1:181–208.

Audran, R. P. Hervé, 1927. Les Hiva. *Bulletin de la Société des Etudes Océaniennes* 22:317–318.

Banks, Joseph, 1962. *The Endeavour Journal of Joseph Banks, 1768–1771,* ed. John C. Beaglehole. 2 vols. Sydney, Angus and Robertson.

Barrère, Dorothy B., 1969. *The Kumuhonua Legends.* Pacific Anthropological Records, No. 3. Honolulu, Department of Anthropology, Bernice P. Bishop Museum.

Barthel, Thomas S., 1978. *The Eighth Land: The Polynesian Discovery and Settlement of Easter Island,* trans. A. Martin. Honolulu, University of Hawai'i Press.

Bass, George, 1972. *A History of Seafaring Based on Underwater Archaeology.* London, Thames and Hudson.

Bayard, Donn, 1976. *The Cultural Relationships of the Polynesian Outliers.* Otago University Studies in Prehistoric Archaeology, Vol. 9. Dunedin, New Zealand, Department of Anthropology, University of Otago.

Baybayan, Chad, Ben Finney, Bernard Kilonsky, and Nainoa Thompson, 1987. Voyage to Aotearoa. *Journal of the Polynesian Society* 96:161–200.

Beaglehole, Ernest, and Pearl Beaglehole, 1938. *Ethnology of Pukapuka.* Bishop Museum Bulletin, No. 150. Honolulu, Bernice P. Bishop Museum.

Beaglehole, John C., 1974. *The Life of Captain James Cook.* London, Hakluyt Society.

Bechtol, Charles, 1963. Sailing Characteristics of Oceanic Canoes. In *Polynesian Navigation: A Symposium on Andrew Sharp's Theory of Accidental Voyaging,* ed. Jack Golson. Polynesian Society Memoir, No. 34. Wellington, The Polynesian Society, 98–101.

Beckwith, Martha, 1940. *Hawaiian Mythology.* New Haven, Yale University Press.

Beechey, Frederick William, 1831. *Narrative of a Voyage to the Pacific and Beering's Strait, to Co-operate with Polar Expeditions.* 2 Vols. London, Henry Colburn and Richard Bentley.

Bellwood, Peter, 1970. Dispersal Centres in East Polynesia, with Special Reference to the Society and Marquesas Islands. In *Studies in Oceanic*

Culture History, Vol. 1, ed. Roger C. Green and Marion Kelly. Pacific Anthropological Records, No. 11. Honolulu, Department of Anthropology, Bernice P. Bishop Museum, 93–104.

———, 1978*a*. *The Polynesians: Prehistory of an Island People*. London, Thames and Hudson.

———, 1978*b*. *Archaeological Research in the Cook Islands*. Pacific Anthropological Records, No. 27. Honolulu, Department of Anthropology, Bernice P. Bishop Museum.

———, 1979. *Man's Conquest of the Pacific*. New York, Oxford University Press.

———, 1987. *The Polynesians: Prehistory of an Island People*. Rev. ed. London, Thames and Hudson.

———, 1989. The Colonization of the Pacific: Some Current Hypotheses. In *The Colonization of the Pacific: A Genetic Trail*, ed. Adrian V. S. Hill and Susan W. Searjeantson. Oxford, Clarendon Press, 1–59.

Bellwood, Peter, and Peter Koon, 1989. 'Lapita Colonists Leave Boats Unburned!' The Question of Lapita Links with Island Southeast Asia. *Antiquity* 63:613–622.

Best, Elsdon, 1923. *Polynesian Voyagers: The Maori as a Deep-sea Navigator, Explorer, and Colonizer*. Dominion Museum Monograph, No. 5. Wellington, Dominion Museum.

———, 1925. *The Maori Canoe*. Dominion Museum Bulletin No. 7. Wellington, Dominion Museum.

Best, Simon, Peter Sheppard, Roger Green, and Robin Parker, 1991. Necromancing the Stone: Archaeologists and Adzes in Samoa. *Journal of the Polynesian Society* 101:45–85.

Bierbach, Annette, and Horst Cain, 1988. Makemake from Hiva to Rapa Nui. *Baessler-Archiv* n.s. 36:399–454.

Biggs, Bruce G., 1971. The Languages of Polynesia. In *Current Trends in Linguistics*. Vol. 8, Pt. 1, ed. T. A. Sebeok. The Hague, Mouton, 466–505.

———, 1972. Implications of Linguistic Subgrouping with Special Reference to Polynesia. In *Studies in Oceanic Culture History*, Vol. 3, ed. Roger C. Green and Marion Kelly. Pacific Anthropological Records, No. 13. Honolulu, Department of Anthropology, Bernice P. Bishop Museum, 143–152.

———, 1978. The History of Polynesian Phonology. In *Second International Conference on Austronesian Linguistics: Proceedings, Fascicle 2, Eastern Austronesian*, ed. S. A. Wurm and Lois Carrington. Pacific Linguistics, Series C, No. 61. Canberra, Australian National University, 691–716.

Biggs, Bruce G., and Mary Veremaluma Biggs, 1975. *Na Ciri Kalia*. Working Papers in Anthropology, Archaeology, Linguistics and Maori Studies, No. 42. Auckland, Department of Anthropology, University of Auckland.

Bingham, Hiram, 1847. *A Residence of Twenty-one Years in the Sandwich Islands*. New York, Sherman Converse.

Binns, Alan, 1980. *Viking Voyagers*. London, Heinemann.

Bloomfield, Leonard, 1933. *Language*. New York, Henry Holt.

Blumenbach, Johann Friedrich, 1795. *De Generis Humani Varietate Nativa*. 3d ed. Goettingen, Vandenhoek and Ruprecht.

Brierly, Kenneth, 1985. *Weather for New Zealand Sailors*. Auckland, Endeavour Press.

Bruner, Philip L., 1990. Personal communication, 14 November 1990.

Bryan, Alan Lyle, 1963. *Archaeological Survey of Northern Puget Sound*. Occasional Papers of the Idaho State University Museum, No. 11. Moscow, Idaho, Idaho State University Museum.

Buck, Peter H., 1926. The Value of Tradition in Polynesian Research. *Journal of the Polynesian Society* 35:181–203.

——, 1929. *The Coming of the Maori, Cawthorn Institute Lecture of 1925*. New Plymouth, New Zealand, Avery.

——, 1932. *Ethnology of Manihiki-Rakahanga*. Bishop Museum Bulletin, No. 99. Honolulu, Bernice P. Bishop Museum.

——, 1934. *Mangaian Society*. Bishop Museum Bulletin, No. 122. Honolulu, Bernice P. Bishop Museum.

——, 1938. *Vikings of the Sunrise*. Philadelphia, Lippincott.

——, 1942. The Disappearance of Canoes in Polynesia. *Journal of the Polynesian Society* 51:191–199.

——, 1950. *The Coming of the Maori*. Rev. ed. Wellington, Whitcombe and Tombs.

Bury, J. B., 1920. *The Idea of Progress*. London, Macmillan.

Cachola-Abad, C. K., 1993. Evaluating the Orthodox Dual Settlement Model for the Hawaiian Islands: An Analysis of Artifact Distributions and Hawaiian Oral Traditions. In *The Evolution and Organization of Prehistoric Social Systems in Polynesia*, ed. Michael Graves and Roger Green. Auckland, New Zealand Archaeological Association, 13–32.

Cartwright, Bruce, 1933. Some Aliis of the Migratory Period. *Bishop Museum Occasional Papers* 10 (7):1–11.

Caviedes, César N., and Peter R. Wayland, 1993. Anomalous Westerly Winds during El Niño Events: The Discovery and Colonization of Easter Island. *Applied Geography* 13:123–134.

Chikamori, Masashi, 1987. Archaeology on Pukapuka Atoll. *Man and Culture in Oceania* 3:105–119.

Chikamori, Masashi, and S. Yoshida, 1988. An Archaeological Survey of Pukapuka Atoll, 1985 (Preliminary Report). Unpublished manuscript in the possession of the authors.

Churchill, William, 1911. *The Polynesian Wanderings*. Washington, D.C., Carnegie Institution of Washington.

Cleghorn, Paul L., 1988. The Settlement and Abandonment of Two Hawaiian Outposts: Nihoa and Necker Islands. *Bishop Museum Occasional Papers* 28:35–49.

Climate Analysis Center, 1987. *Climate Diagnostics Bulletin*. Nos. 87/3 and 87/4. Boulder, Colorado, Climate Analysis Center, National Oceanic and Atmospheric Administration.

Coles, John M., 1979. *Experimental Archaeology.* New York, Academic Press.

Cook, James, 1955. *The Voyage of the Endeavour, 1768–1771,* ed. John C. Beaglehole. Cambridge, Hakluyt Society.

———, 1961. *The Voyage of the Resolution and Adventure,* ed. John C. Beaglehole. Cambridge, Hakluyt Society.

———, 1967. *The Voyage of the Resolution and Discovery, 1776–1780,* ed. John C. Beaglehole. 2 pts. Cambridge, Hakluyt Society.

Cordy, Ross, 1974. The Tahitian Migration to Hawai'i ca. 1100–1300 A.D.: An Argument Against Its Occurrence. *New Zealand Archaeological Association Newsletter* 17:65–76.

Corney, Bolton G., 1913–1918. *The Quest and Occupation of Tahiti by the Emissaries of Spain during the Years 1772–1776.* 3 vols. London, Hakluyt Society.

Crocombe, Ronald G., and Marjorie Crocombe, 1968. *The Works of Ta'unga.* Canberra, Australian National University Press.

Crozet, Julien, 1783. *Nouveau Voyage à la Mer Du Sud,* ed. A. M. Rochon. Paris, Barrois.

Crumlin-Pedersen, P., 1970. The Viking Ships of Roskilde. In *Aspects of the History of Wooden Shipbuilding.* Maritime Monographs and Reports, No. 1. Greenwich, National Maritime Museum, 7–11.

Daniel, Glyn E., 1955. *Myth or Legend.* London, G. Bell.

Danielsson, Bengt, 1960. *From Raft to Raft,* trans. F. H. Lyon. London, George Allen and Unwin.

Davenport, William H., 1962. Red Feather Money. *Scientific American* 206:94–103.

———, 1964. Notes on Santa Cruz Voyaging. *Journal of the Polynesian Society* 73:134–142.

Davidson, Janet, 1974. Cultural Replacement on Small Islands: New Evidence from Polynesian Outliers. *Mankind* 9:273–277.

———, 1978. Western Polynesia and Fiji: The Archaeological Evidence. *Mankind* 11:383–390.

———, 1984. *The Prehistory of New Zealand.* Wellington, Longman Paul.

De Brosses, Charles, 1756. *Histoire des Navigations aux Terres Australes.* 2 vols. Paris, Durand.

De Bisschop, Eric, 1958. *Cap à l'Est.* Paris, Librarie Plon.

Dening, Gregory M., 1958. Review Article: *Ancient Voyagers in the Pacific* by Andrew Sharp. *Historical Studies: Australia and New Zealand* 8:322–328.

———, 1963. The Geographical Knowledge of the Polynesians and the Nature of Inter-Island Contact. In *Polynesian Navigation: A Symposium on Andrew Sharp's Theory of Accidental Voyaging,* ed. Jack Golson. Polynesian Society Memoir, No. 34. Wellington, The Polynesian Society, 102–153.

———, 1974. *The Marquesan Journal of Edward Robarts 1797–1824.* Canberra, Australian National University Press.

Dickenson, William R., and Richard Shutler, Jr., 1974. Probable Fijian Origin of Quartzose Temper Sands in Prehistoric Pottery from Tonga and the Marquesas. *Science* 185:454–457.

Dillon, Peter, 1829. *Narrative of a Voyage in the South Seas . . . to Ascertain the Actual Fate of the La Perouse Expedition.* London, Hurst, Chance & Co.

Dixon, Roland B., 1932. The Problem of the Sweet Potato in Polynesia. *American Anthropologist* 34:40–66.

———, 1933. Contacts with America Across the Southern Pacific. In *The American Aborigines: Their Origin and Antiquity*, ed. Diamond Jenness. Toronto, University of Toronto Press, 315–353.

Doran, Edwin, Jr., 1981. *Wangka: Austronesian Canoe Origins.* College Station, Tex., Texas A & M University Press.

Doyle, Emma Lyons, 1945. *Makua Laiana.* Honolulu, Star-Bulletin.

Duff, Roger, 1968. Stone Adzes from Raoul, Kermadec Islands. *Journal of the Polynesian Society* 77:386–401.

Dumont-D'Urville, Jules-Sébastien-César, 1830. *Voyage de la Corvette L'Astrolabe . . . Pendant les années 1826, 1827, 1828, 1829.* 5 vols. Paris, J. Tastu.

Dunnell, Robert C., 1986. Five Decades of American Archaeology. In *American Archaeology Past and Future 1935–1985*, ed. David J. Meltzer, Don D. Fowler, and Jeremy A. Sabloff. Washington, Smithsonian Institution Press, 23–49.

Durrans, Brian, 1979. Ancient Pacific Voyaging: Cook's Views and the Development of Interpretation. In *Captain Cook and the South Pacific.* London, British Museum Publications, 137–166.

Dye, Tom, 1989. Tales of Two Cultures: Traditional Historical and Archaeological Interpretations of Hawaiian Prehistory. *Bishop Museum Occasional Papers* 29:3–22.

Egloff, Brian, 1979. *Recent Prehistory in Southeast Papua.* Terra Australis, No. 4. Canberra, Department of Prehistory, Australian National University.

Elbert, Samuel H., 1982. Lexical Diffusion in Polynesia and the Marquesan-Hawaiian Relationship. *Journal of the Polynesian Society* 91:499–517.

Elbert, Samuel, and Michael Kaiser, 1992. The Ancestors of Easter Island. Unpublished manuscript in the possession of the authors. Department of Linguistics, University of Hawai'i, Honolulu.

Ellis, William, 1829. *Polynesian Researches.* 2 vols. London, Fisher, Son and Jackson.

Emerson, Nathaniel B., 1893. The Long Voyages of the Ancient Hawaiians. *Papers of the Hawaiian Historical Society*, No. 5. Honolulu, Hawaiian Historical Society.

Emory, Kenneth P., 1928. *Archaeology of Nihoa and Necker Islands.* Bishop Museum Bulletin 53. Honolulu, Bernice P. Bishop Museum.

———, 1946. Eastern Polynesia: Its Cultural Relationships. Ph.D. diss., Department of Anthropology, Yale University, New Haven.

———, 1963. East Polynesian Relationships: Settlement Pattern and Time

Involved as Indicated by Vocabulary Agreements. *Journal of the Polynesian Society* 72:78–100.

———, 1978. Do Consonant Shifts Prove or Indicate that Hawai'i was Settled First from the Marquesas and Late from Tahiti? Unpublished paper presented at the Archaeology and Linguistics Colloquium, October 1978. Honolulu, University of Hawai'i.

———, 1979. The Society Islands. In *The Prehistory of Polynesia*, ed. Jesse D. Jennings. Cambridge, Harvard University Press.

Emory, Kenneth P., and Y. H. Sinoto, 1965. *Preliminary Report on the Archaeological Excavations in Polynesia*. Mimeographed report prepared for the National Science Foundation on file in the Bernice P. Bishop Museum Library.

Fast, Arlo, 1983. The Hawaiian Circuit. *Cruising World* January: 27–30.

Feinberg, Richard, 1986. On "Anomalous Westerlies, El Niño, and the Colonization of Polynesia" by Ben R. Finney. *American Anthropologist* 88:454–455.

———, 1988. *Polynesian Seafaring and Navigation: Ocean Travel in Anutan Culture and Society*. Kent, Ohio, Kent State University Press.

———, 1989. Possible Prehistoric Contacts Between Tonga and Anuta. *Journal of the Polynesian Society* 98:303–317.

———, 1991. A Long-distance Voyage in Contemporary Polynesia. *Journal of the Polynesian Society* 100:25–44.

Finney, Ben, 1967. New Perspectives on Polynesian Voyaging. In *Polynesian Culture History: Essays in Honor of Kenneth P. Emory*, ed. Genevieve A. Highland, Roland W. Force, Alan Howard, Marion Kelly, and Yosihiko Sinoto. Honolulu, Bernice P. Bishop Museum Press, 141–166.

———, 1976. *Pacific Navigation and Voyaging*. Polynesian Society Memoir, No. 39. The Polynesian Society, Wellington.

———, 1977. Voyaging Canoes and the Settlement of Polynesia. *Science* 196:1277–1285.

———, 1979a. Voyaging. In *The Prehistory of Polynesia*, ed. Jesse Jennings. Harvard University Press, Cambridge, 323–351.

———, 1979b. *Hōkūle'a, the Way to Tahiti*. New York, Dodd, Mead.

———, 1985. Anomalous Westerlies, El Niño, and the Colonization of Polynesia. *American Anthropologist* 87:9–26.

———, 1991. Myth, Experiment and the Re-invention of Polynesian Voyaging. *American Anthropologist* 92:383–404.

Finney, Ben, Bernard J. Kilonsky, Stephen Somsen, and Edward D. Stroup, 1986. Re-Learning a Vanishing Art. *Journal of the Polynesian Society* 95:41–90.

Finney, Ben, Paul Frost, Richard Rhodes, and Nainoa Thompson, 1989. Wait for the West Wind. *Journal of the Polynesian Society* 98:261–302.

Firth, Raymond, 1936. *We, the Tikopia*. London, George Allen and Unwin.

———, 1961. *The History and Traditions of Tikopia*. Polynesian Society Memoir, No. 33. Wellington, The Polynesian Society.

Fornander, Abraham, 1916–1919. *Fornander Collection of Hawaiian Antiq-*

uities and Folklore. Memoirs of the Bernice P. Bishop Museum. 3 series. 6 vols. Honolulu, Bernice P. Bishop Museum.

———, 1969. *An Account of the Polynesian Race its Origin and Migrations.* Rutland, Vermont, Tuttle. (Originally published in 3 vols., all under the same title in 1878, 1880, and 1885, London, Trübner.)

Forster, Johann Reinhold, 1778. *Observations Made during a Voyage Round the World.* London, Robinson.

Frankel, J. P., 1962. Polynesian Navigation. *Navigation: Journal of the Institute of Navigation* 9:35–47.

———, 1963. Polynesian Migration Voyages: Accidental or Purposeful? *American Anthropologist* 65:1125–1127.

Friederici, Georg, 1929. Zu der Vorkolomb: Verbindungen des Südsee mit Amerika. *Anthropos* 24:441–487.

Garanger, José, 1972a. Mythes et Archéologie en Océanie. *La Recherche* 3(21):233–242.

———, 1972b. *Archéologie des Nouvelles-Hébrides: Contribution à la Connaissance des Iles du Centre.* Paris, Publications de la Société des Océanistes, No. 30.

Gill, William Wyatt, 1856. *Gems from the Coral Islands.* London, Ward.

———, 1876. *Myths and Songs from the South Pacific.* London, King.

———, 1880. *Historical Sketches of Savage Life in Polynesia.* Wellington, G. Didsbury, Government Printer.

Gladwin, Thomas, 1970. *East Is a Big Bird.* Cambridge, Harvard University Press.

Goetzmann, William H., 1986. *New Men, New Lands.* New York, Viking.

Goldman, Irving, 1955. Status Rivalry and Cultural Evolution in Polynesia. *American Anthropologist* 57:680–697.

Golson, Jack, 1963. *Polynesian Navigation: A Symposium on Andrew Sharp's Theory of Accidental Voyages.* Polynesian Society Memoir, No. 34. Wellington, The Polynesian Society.

———, 1965. Thor Heyerdahl and the Prehistory of Easter Island. *Oceania* 36:38–83.

Golson, Jack, and Peter W. Gathercole, 1962. The Last Decade in New Zealand Archaeology (Pts. I and II). *Antiquity* 36:168–174, 271–278.

Goodenough, Ward H., 1953. *Native Astronomy in the Central Caroline Islands.* Museum Monographs, Philadelphia, The University Museum, University of Pennsylvania.

Gosden, Chris, Jim Allen, Wallace R. Ambrose, D. Anson, Jack Golson, Roger C. Green, Patrick V. Kirch, Ian Lilley, James Specht, and Matthew Spriggs, 1989. Lapita Sites of the Bismarck Archipelago. *Antiquity* 63: 561–586.

Green, Roger C., 1966. Linguistic Subgrouping within Polynesia: The Implications for Prehistoric Settlement. *Journal of the Polynesian Society* 75:6–38.

———, 1967. The Immediate Origin of the Polynesians. In *Polynesian Culture History*, ed. Genevieve A. Highland, Roland W. Force, Alan

Howard, Marion Kelly, and Yosihiko Sinoto. Honolulu, Bernice P. Bishop Museum Press, 215–240.

———, 1974*a*. Sites with Lapita Pottery: Importing and Voyaging. *Mankind* 9:253–259.

———, 1974*b*. Pottery from the Lagoon at Mulifanua, Upolu. In *Archaeology in Western Samoa*, 2 vols., ed. R. C. Green and J. Davidson. Auckland, Auckland Institute and Museum, 2:150–155.

———, 1974*c*. Tahiti—Hawai'i, A.D. 1100–1300: Further Comments. *New Zealand Archaeological Association Newsletter* 17:206–210.

———, 1975*a*. Adaptation and Change in Maori Culture. In *Biogeography and Ecology in New Zealand*, ed. G. Kuschel. The Hague, W. Junk, 591–641.

———, 1975*b*. Polynesian Voyaging. *Science* 187:274.

———, 1978. *New Sites with Lapita Pottery and Their Implications for an Understanding of the Settlement of the Western Pacific.* Working Papers in Anthropology, Archaeology, Linguistics and Maori Studies, No. 51. Auckland, Department of Anthropology, University of Auckland.

———, 1979. Lapita. In *The Prehistory of Polynesia*, ed. Jesse D. Jennings. Cambridge, Harvard University Press, 27–60.

———, 1981. Location of the Polynesian Homeland: A Continuing Problem. In *Studies in Pacific Languages and Cultures, in Honour of Bruce Biggs*, ed. J. Hollyman and A. Pawley. Auckland, Linguistic Society of New Zealand, 133–158.

———, 1987*a*. Obsidian Results from the Lapita Sites of the Reef/Santa Cruz Islands. In *Archaeometry: Further Australasian Studies*, ed. W. R. Ambrose and J. M. J. Mummery. Canberra, Department of Prehistory, Australian National University, 239–249.

———, 1987*b*. *Peopling of the Pacific: A Series of Adaptive Steps, or Punctuated Evolution.* Paper presented at Section H, 57th Annual Meeting of Australian and New Zealand Association for the Advancement of Science, 24 August 1987.

———, 1988. Subgrouping of Rapa Nui Language of Easter Island in Polynesia and Its Implications for East Polynesian Prehistory. In *First International Congress, Easter Island and East Polynesia, Hanga Roa, Easter Island, 1984*, Vol. 1, *Archaeology*, ed. Claudio F. Christino, Patricia G. Vargas, Roberto S. Isaurieta, and Reginald P. Budd. Santiago, Chile, Facultad de Arquitectura y Urbanismo, Instituto de Estudios, Isla de Pascua, Universidad de Chile, 37–58.

Green, Roger C., and Janet M. Davidson, 1974. *Archaeology in Western Samoa.* 2 vols. Auckland Institute and Museum Bulletin, No. 7. Auckland, Auckland Institute and Museum.

Groube, L. M., 1970. The Origin and Development of Earthwork Fortification in the Pacific. In *Studies in Oceanic Culture History*, Vol. 1, ed. Roger C. Green and Marion Kelly. Pacific Anthropological Records, No. 11. Honolulu, Department of Anthropology, Bernice P. Bishop Museum, 133–164.

Haddon, A. C., and James Hornell, 1936–1938. *Canoes of Oceania.* Bernice P. Bishop Museum Special Publications 27–29. Honolulu, Bernice P. Bishop Museum.

Hale, Horatio, 1846. *United States Exploring Expedition during the Years 1838, 1839, 1840, 1841, 1842, Ethnography and Philology.* Philadelphia, Lea and Blanchard.

Handler, Richard, and Jocelyn S. Linnekin, 1984. Tradition, Genuine or Spurious. *Journal of American Folklore* 97:273–290.

Handy, E. S. Craighill, 1930. The Problem of Polynesian Origins. *Bishop Museum Occasional Papers* 9(8):1–27.

Handy, E. S. Craighill, and Mary Kawena Pukui, 1958. *The Polynesian Family System of Ka-'u, Hawaii.* Wellington, The Polynesian Society.

Harding, Thomas G., 1967. *Voyagers of the Vitiaz Straits.* Seattle, University of Washington Press.

Harlow, Ray B., 1979. Regional Variation in Maori. *New Zealand Journal of Archaeology* 1:123–138.

Harvey, John G., 1976. *Atmosphere and Ocean: Our Fluid Environments.* Sussex, England, Artemus.

Hather, Jon, and Patrick V. Kirch, 1991. Prehistoric Sweet Potato (*Ipomoea batatas*) from Mangaia Island, Central Polynesia. *Antiquity* 65:887–893.

Heine-Geldern, Robert, 1952. Some Problems of Migration in the Pacific. *Wiener Beitrage zur Kulturgeschichte und Linguistic* 3:314–362.

Helms, Mary W., 1988. *Ulysses' Sail.* Princeton, New Jersey, Princeton University Press.

Henry, Teuira, 1928. *Ancient Tahiti.* Bishop Museum Bulletin, No. 48. Honolulu, Bernice P. Bishop Museum.

Heyen, G. H., 1963. Primitive Navigation in the Pacific—I. In *Polynesian Navigation: A Symposium on Andrew Sharp's Theory of Accidental Voyaging,* ed. Jack Golson. Polynesian Society Memoir, No. 34. Wellington, The Polynesian Society, 64–79.

Hessell, J. W. D., 1981. Climatology of the South-west Pacific Islands. 2. Climatological Statistics. In *Pacific Islands Water Resources,* ed. W. R. Dale. South Pacific Technical Inventory, No. 2. Wellington, Department of Scientific and Industrial Research, 35–43.

Heyerdahl, Thor, 1941. Did Polynesian Culture Originate in America? *International Science* 1:15–26.

———, 1947. Le "Kon-Tiki" à Papeete. *Bulletin de la Société d'Etudes Océaniennes* 7:345–355.

———, 1950. *Kon-Tiki: Across the Pacific by Raft.* Chicago, Rand McNally.

———, 1953. *American Indians in the Pacific.* Chicago, Rand McNally.

———, 1978. *Early Man and the Ocean.* London, Allen and Unwin.

———, 1981. With Stars and Waves in the Pacific. *Archaeoastronomy* 4:32–38.

Hilder, Brett, 1963. Primitive Navigation in the Pacific—II. In *Polynesian Navigation: A Symposium on Andrew Sharp's Theory of Accidental*

Voyaging, ed. Jack Golson. Polynesian Society Memoir, No. 34. Wellington, The Polynesian Society, 81–97.

Hobsbawm, Eric, and Terence Ranger, 1983. *The Invention of Tradition.* Cambridge, Cambridge University Press.

Holmes, Tommy, 1981. *The Hawaiian Canoe.* Hanalei, Kaua'i, Hawai'i, Editions Limited.

Hooper, Antony, 1981. *Why the Tikopia Has Four Clans.* Royal Anthropological Institute of Great Britain and Ireland Occasional Paper, No. 38. London, Royal Anthropological Institute of Great Britain and Ireland.

Hopper, David H., 1991. *Technology, Theology, and the Idea of Progress.* Louisville, Kentucky, Westminster/John Knox Press.

Hornell, James, 1945. Was There Pre-Columbian Contact between the Peoples of Oceania and South America? *Journal of the Polynesian Society* 54:167–191.

Houston, John, 1965. *Maori Life in Old Taranaki.* Wellington, A. H. and A. W. Reed.

Höver, Otto, 1961. *Alt-Asiaten Segel in Indischen und Pazifischen Ocean durch Monsune und Passate.* Braunschweig, Albert Limbach.

Howard, Alan, 1967. Polynesian Origins and Migrations: A Review of Two Centuries of Speculation and Theory. In *Polynesian Culture History: Essays in Honor of Kenneth P. Emory*, ed. Genevieve A. Highland, Roland W. Force, Alan Howard, Marion Kelly, and Yosihiko Sinoto. Honolulu, Bernice P. Bishop Museum Press, 45–101.

Howe, Kerry R., 1988. Some Origins and Migrations of Ideas Leading to the Aryan Polynesian Theories of Abraham Fornander and Edward Tregear. *Pacific Studies* 11:67–81.

Hunt, Terry L., 1987. Patterns of Human Interaction and Evolutionary Divergence in the Fiji Islands. *Journal of the Polynesian Society* 96:299–334.

———, 1989. Lapita Ceramic Exchange in the Mussau Islands, Papua New Guinea. Ph.D. diss., Department of Anthropology, University of Washington, Seattle.

———, 1991. Personal communication, 25 February 1991.

Imbelloni, J., 1930. On the Diffusion in America of Patu Onewa, Orewa, Patu Paraoa, Miti, and Other Relatives of the Mere Family. *Journal of the Polynesian Society* 39:322–344.

Irwin, Geoffrey, 1981. How Lapita Lost Its Pots: The Question of Continuity in the Colonization of Polynesia. *Journal of the Polynesian Society* 90:481–494.

———, 1985. *The Emergence of Mailu.* Terra Australis, No. 10. Canberra, Department of Prehistory, Australian National University.

———, 1989. Against, Across and Down the Wind: A Case for the Systematic Exploration of the Remote Pacific Islands. *Journal of the Polynesian Society* 98:167–196.

———, 1992. *The Prehistoric Exploration and Colonization of the Pacific.* Cambridge, Cambridge University Press.

Irwin, Geoffrey, Simone Biskler, and Philip Quirke, 1990. Voyaging by Canoe and Computer: Experiments in the Settlement of the Pacific Ocean. *Antiquity* 64:34–50.

Jacquier, Henri, 1948. A la Dérive de lîle de Pâque aux Tuamotus. *Bulletin de la Société des Etudes Océaniennes* 7(83):495–498.

Jennings, Jesse, 1974. The Ferry Berth Site, Mulifanua District, Upolu. In *Archaeology in Western Samoa*, ed. Roger C. Green and Janet Davidson. Auckland, Bulletin of the Auckland Institute and Museum. No. 7, Vol. 2: 176–178.

———, 1979. *The Prehistory of Polynesia*. Cambridge, Harvard University Press.

Johansen, J. Pritz, 1954. *The Maori and His Religion in Its Non-ritualistic Aspects*. Copenhagen, Munksgaard.

———, 1958. *Studies in Maori Rite and Myths*. Copenhagen, Munksgaard.

Johnson, Rubellite Kawena, 1979. From the Gills of the Fish: The Tahitian Homeland of Hawai'i's Chief Mo'ikeha. *Pacific Studies* 3:51–67.

Johnson, Rubellite Kawena, and John Mahelona, 1975. *Na Inoa Hoku*. Honolulu, Topgallant.

Johnson, Oscar W., Martin L. Morton, Philip L. Bruner, Patricia M. Johnson, 1989. Fat Cyclicity, Predicted Migratory Flight Ranges, and Features of Wintering Behavior in Pacific Golden-Plovers. *The Condor* 91: 156–177.

Jones, Pei Te Hurinui, 1957. A Maori Comment on Andrew Sharp's Ancient Voyagers in the Pacific. *Journal of the Polynesian Society* 66: 131–134.

Kaeppler, Adrienne L., 1973. A Comparative Note on Anutan Social Organization. In *Anuta: A Polynesian Outlier in the Solomon Islands*, ed. Douglas E. Yen and Janet Gordon. Pacific Anthropological Records, No. 21. Honolulu, Department of Anthropology, Bernice P. Bishop Museum, 21–24.

Kamakau, Samuel Manaiakalani, 1890. Instructions in Ancient Hawaiian Astronomy as Taught by Kaneakahoowaha, One of the Councellors of Kamehameha I., According to S. M. Kamakau. Trans. W. D. Alexander, in *Hawaiian Almanac and Annual for 1891*. Honolulu, Press Publishing, 142–143.

———, 1976. *The Works of the People of Old: Na Hana a ka Po'e Kahiko*. Trans. from the newspaper *Ke Au 'Oko'a* by Mary Kawena Pukui; ed. Dorothy B. Barrère. Bishop Museum Special Publication, No. 61. Honolulu, Bernice P. Bishop Museum.

Kame'eleihiwa, Lilikalā, 1986. Land and the Promise of Capitalism. Ph.D. diss., Honolulu, Department of History, University of Hawai'i.

Kanahele, George, 1982. *Hawaiian Renaissance*. Honolulu, Project Waiaha.

Kane, Herb Kawainui, 1976. *Voyage, The Discovery of Hawai'i*. Honolulu, Island Heritage.

Katayama, Kazumichi, in press. Biological Affinity between the Southern Cook Islanders and the New Zealand Maoris, and Its Implications for the Settlement of New Zealand. In *The Origin of the First New Zealanders*, ed. D. G. Sutton. Auckland University Press, Auckland.

Katsev, Michael L., Susan W. Katsev, Harry E. Tzalas, 1987. *Kyrenia II, An Ancient Ship Sails Again*. Piraeus, Hellenic Institute for the Preservation of Nautical Tradition.

Keauokalani, Kepelino, 1932. *Traditions of Hawaii*, ed. Martha Beckwith. Bishop Museum Bulletin, No. 95. Honolulu, Bernice P. Bishop Museum.

Keegan, William F., and Jared M. Diamond, 1987. Colonization of Islands by Humans: A Biogeographical Perspective. In *Advances in Archaeological Method and Theory*, Vol. 10, ed. Michael B. Schiffer. New York, Academic Press, 49–91.

Kelly, Celsus, 1966. *La Australia del Expiritu Santo*. 2 vols. Cambridge, Hakluyt Society.

Kelly, Leslie G. (Te Putu), 1949. *Tainui: The Story of Hoturoa and His Descendants*. Polynesian Society Memoir, No. 25. Wellington, The Polynesian Society.

———, 1955. Cook Island Origin of the Maori. *Journal of the Polynesian Society* 64:181–196.

Kemp, Peter, 1976. *The Oxford Companion to Ships & the Sea*. Oxford, Oxford University Press.

Kirch, Patrick V., 1984. *The Evolution of Polynesian Chiefdoms*. Cambridge, Cambridge University Press.

———, 1985. *Feathered Gods and Fishhooks*. Honolulu, University of Hawai'i Press.

———, 1986a. Rethinking East Polynesian Prehistory. *Journal of the Polynesian Society* 95:9–40.

———, 1986b. Exchange Systems and Inter-island Contact in the Transformation of an Island Society: The Tikopia Case. In *Island Societies: Archaeological Approaches to Evolution and Transformation*, ed. Patrick V. Kirch. Cambridge, Cambridge University Press, 33–41.

———, 1988a. Long Distance Exchange and Island Colonization. *Norwegian Archaeological Review* 21:103–117.

———, 1988b. Problems and Issues in Lapita Archaeology. In *Archaeology of the Lapita Cultural Complex: A Critical Review*, ed. P. V. Kirch and Terry Hunt. Burke Museum Research Report, No. 5. Seattle, Thomas Burke Memorial Washington State Museum, 157–165.

———, 1988c. *Niuatoputapu: The Prehistory of a Polynesian Chiefdom*. Burke Museum Monograph, No. 5. Seattle, Thomas Burke Memorial Washington State Museum.

———, 1990. Specialization and Exchange in the Lapita Complex of Oceania (1600–500 B.C.). *Asian Perspectives* 29:117–133.

———, 1991. Prehistoric Exchange in Western Melanesia. *Annual Review of Anthropology* 20:141–165.

Kirch, Patrick V., and Douglas E. Yen, 1984. *Tikopia: The Prehistory and Ecology of a Polynesian Outlier*. Bishop Museum Bulletin, No. 238. Honolulu, Bernice P. Bishop Museum.

Kirch, Patrick V., and Roger C. Green, 1987. History, Phylogeny, and Evolution in Polynesia. *Current Anthropology* 28:431–456.

Kirch, Patrick V., and Terry Hunt, 1988*a*. *Archaeology of the Lapita Cultural Complex: A Critical Review.* Burke Museum Research Report, No. 5. Seattle, Thomas Burke Memorial Washington State Museum.

Kirch, Patrick V., and Terry Hunt, 1988*b*. Radiocarbon Dates from the Mussau Islands and the Lapita Colonization of the Southwestern Pacific. *Radiocarbon* 30:161–169.

Kirch, Patrick V., Terry L. Hunt, Lisa Nagaoka, and Jason Tyler, 1990. An Ancestral Polynesian Occupation Site at To'aga, Ofu Island, American Samoa. *Archaeology in Oceania* 25:1–15.

Kirch, Patrick V., Terry L. Hunt, Marshall Weisler, Virginia Butler, and Melinda Allen, 1991. Mussau Islands Prehistory: Results of the 1985–86 Excavations. In *Report of the Lapita Homelands Project*, ed. Jim Allen and Chris Gosden. Occasional Papers in Prehistory, No. 20. Department of Prehistory, Australian National University, Canberra, 144–163.

Kirch, Patrick V., John R. Flenley, David W. Steadman, Frances Lamont, and Stewart Dawson, 1992. Ancient Environmental Degradation. *National Geographic Research and Exploration* 8:166–179.

Kirch, Patrick V., and Joanna Ellison, 1993. Paleoenvironmental Evidence for Human Colonization of Remote Oceanic Islands. Unpublished manuscript in the possession of the authors.

Kyselka, Will, 1987. *An Ocean in Mind.* Honolulu, University of Hawai'i Press.

———, 1988. Finding Islands—Tahiti to the Cooks. Unpublished typescript in the possession of the author.

Labrosse, F., 1874. *Indicateur des Routes Maritimes de l'Ocean Pacifique.* Paris, n. p.

Laguesse, Janine, 1954. Migration Polynésienne Moderne. *Bulletin de la Société des Etudes Océaniennes* 9(9):354–357.

La Perouse, Jean-François de Galaup, 1799. *A Voyage Round the World in the Years 1785, 1786, 1787, and 1788.* 3 vols. Ed. M. L. A. Milet-Mureau. London, J. Johnson.

Lang, John Dunmore, 1834. *View of the Origin and Migrations of the Polynesian Nation: Demonstrating Their Ancient Discovery and Progressive Settlement of the Continent of America.* London, James Cochrane.

———, 1877. *View of the Origin and Migrations of the Polynesian Nation.* Rev. ed. London, Sampson Low, Marston, Low and Searle.

Langdon, Robert, and Darrell Tryon, 1983. *The Language of Easter Island: Its Development and Eastern Polynesian Relationships.* Institute for Polynesian Studies Monograph Series, No. 4, Laie, Hawai'i, Institute for Polynesian Studies, Brigham Young University-Hawai'i Campus.

Lawson, Thomas, 1875. The Origin of the Marquesas Race. *The Islander* 1(13):65–67.

———, n.d. Polynesian Migrations. Unpublished manuscript in the Bernice P. Bishop Museum Library, Honolulu.

Leach, Edmond R., 1962. Review of History and Traditions in Tikopia by R. Firth. *Journal of the Polynesian Society* 71:273–276.

Leach, B. F., M. Horwood, R. McGovern-Wilson, I. W. G. Smith, P. and M-N Ottino, 1990. Analysis of Faunal Materials from Te Ana Pua, Ua Pou, Marquesas Islands. Unpublished report, National Museum of New Zealand, Wellington.

Leach, Foss, Atholl Anderson, Doug Sutton, Roger Bird, and Eric Clayton, 1986. The Origin of Prehistoric Obsidian from the Chatham and Kermadec Islands. *New Zealand Journal of Archaeology* 8:143–170.

Leach, Helen M., 1991. *Quarry Production and Social Organization in Polynesia.* Paper delivered at the 17th Pacific Science Congress, 29 May 1991. Honolulu.

Levison, Michael, T. I. Fenner, W. A. Sentance, R. Gerard Ward, and John W. Webb, 1969. A Model of Accidental Drift Voyaging in the Pacific Ocean with Applications to the Polynesia Colonization Problem. *Information Processing* 68:1521–1526.

Levison, Michael, R. Gerard Ward, and John W. Webb, 1973. *The Settlement of Polynesia: A Computer Simulation.* Minneapolis, University of Minnesota Press.

Lewis, David, 1964a. Ara Moana: Stars of the Sea Road. *Navigation: The Journal of the Institute of Navigation (London)* 17:278–288.

———, 1964b. Polynesian Navigational Methods. *Journal of the Polynesian Society* 73:364–373.

———, 1966. Stars of the Sea Road. *Journal of the Polynesian Society* 75:85–94.

———, 1972. *We The Navigators.* Honolulu, University of Hawai'i Press.

———, 1977. Mau Piailug's Navigation of Hokule'a from Hawaii to Tahiti. *Topics in Cultural Learning*, Vol. 5. Honolulu, Culture Learning Institute, East-West Center, 1–23.

Lewthwaite, Gordon R., 1967. Geographical Knowledge of the Pacific Peoples. In *The Pacific Basin: A History of Its Geographical Exploration*, ed. Herman R. Fris. American Cartographical Society Special Publication, No. 38. New York, American Cartographical Society, 57–86.

———, 1970. The Puzzle of Tupaia's Map. *New Zealand Geographer* 26:1–19.

Lipman, Victor, 1986. The Way to Rarotonga. *Honolulu*, February:4–15.

Lucas, Wilfrid, 1989. L'identité Culturelle du Peuple Polynésien et sa Renaissance Contemporaine. In *Renaissance du Pacifique*, ed. Murray Chapman and Jean-François Dupon. Special edition of *Ethnies, Droits de l'Homme et Peuples Autochtones* 4(8–10):104–108.

Luomala, Katharine, 1958. Review of *Ancient Voyagers in the Pacific* by Andrew Sharp. *American Anthropologist* 60:776–778.

———, 1979. Tradition as Evidence of Cultural Contact with Other Polynesians. Unpublished paper delivered at the Moanalua Gardens Foundation's Seminar on Hawaiian Migration and Settlement, 28 April 1979.

Malinowski, Bronislaw, 1922. *Argonauts of the Western Pacific.* London, George Routledge and Sons.

Malo, David, 1898. *Hawaiian Antiquities (Moolelo Hawaii)*, trans. Nathaniel B. Emerson. Bishop Museum Special Publication, No. 2. Honolulu, Bernice P. Bishop Museum Press.

McCall, Grant, 1976. Reaction to Disaster: Continuity and Change in Rapanui Social Organization. Ph.D. diss., Department of Social Anthropology, Research School of Pacific Studies, Australian National University, Canberra.

———, 1981. *Rapanui: Tradition and Survival on Easter Island*. Honolulu, University of Hawai'i Press.

McGrail, Sean, 1974. *The Building and Trials of the Replica of an Ancient Boat: The Gokstad Faering*. Maritime Monographs and Reports, No. 11. Greenwich, National Maritime Museum.

———, 1975. Models, Replicas and Experiments in Nautical Archaeology. *Mariner's Mirror* 61:3–8.

Mason, Leonard, 1966. Early Micronesian Voyages: A Comment. *Oceania* 37:155.

Martínez de Zúñiga, Joaquin, 1966. *An Historical View of the Philippine Islands*, trans. John Maver from *Historia de las Islas Philipinas*. Sampaloc, Philippines, Fr. Pedro Argüellos, 1803. Manila, Filipiniana Book Guild.

Meredith, Charles W., Jim R. Specht, and Pat V. Rich, 1985. A Minimum Date for Polynesian Visitation to Norfolk Island, Southwest Pacific, from Faunal Evidence. *Search* 16:304–306.

Merlin, Mark D., 1985. Woody Vegetation in the Upland Region of Rarotonga, Cook Islands. *Pacific Science* 39:81–99.

Métraux, Alfred, 1940. *Ethnology of Easter Island*. Bishop Museum Bulletin, No. 160. Honolulu, Bernice P. Bishop Museum.

Miller, Albert, and Jack C. Thompson, 1970. *Elements of Meteorology*. Columbus, Ohio, Charles E. Merrill.

Mitchell, Rudolph Leikaimana, 1979. *From God to God: Hawai'i's Seven Centuries of Religious Influence from Pa'ao to Hewahewa*. Honolulu, privately printed.

Moerenhout, J. A., 1837. *Voyages aux Iles du Grand Ocean*. 2 vols. Paris, Bertrand.

Morrison, Samuel Eliot, 1971. *The European Discovery of America: The Northern Voyages A.D. 500–1600*. New York, Oxford University Press.

Mulloy, William, 1979. A Preliminary Culture-Historical Research Model for Easter Island. In *Las Islas Oceanicas de Chile*, ed. Gloria Echevarria Duco and Patricio Arana Espina. Santiago, Chile, Instituto de Estudios Internacionales de la Universidad de Chile, 105–151.

Nakuina, Moses K., 1990. *The Wind Gourd of La'amaomao*, trans. Esther T. Mo'okini and Sarah Nākoa. Honolulu, Kalamaku Press.

Neal, Marie C., 1965. *In Gardens Hawaii*. Bishop Museum Special Publication, No. 50. Honolulu, Bernice P. Bishop Museum.

Needham, Joseph, 1971. *Science and Civilization in China*. Vol. 4, *Physics and Physical Technology*, Part 3: Civil Engineering and Nautics. Cambridge, Cambridge University Press.

Nègre, André, 1956. *L'Odysée du "San Pedro" de l'île de Pâques à Tahiti.* Paris, Editions A. Sorel de Neufchatel.

Nelson, J. G., 1963. Drift Voyages in the Pacific. *American Neptune* 23: 113–130.

Neyret, Jean, 1950. Notes sur la Navigation indigène aux îles Fidji. *Journal de la Société des Océanistes* 6:5–31.

Ngata, Apirana T., 1950. The Io Cult—Early Migration-Puzzle of the Canoes. *Journal of the Polynesian Society* 59:335–348.

Olsen, O., and O. Crumline-Pederson, 1967. The Skuldelev Ships. *Acta Archaeologica* 38:73–174.

Orbell, Margaret, 1974. The Religious Significance of Maori Migration Traditions. *Journal of the Polynesian Society* 84:341–347.

———, 1985. *Hawaiki: A New Approach to Maori Tradition.* Christchurch, New Zealand, University of Canterbury.

Ottino, Pierre, 1985. Un Site Ancien aux îles Marquises: l'Abri Sous-roche d'Anapua, à Ua Pou. *Journal de la Société des Océanistes* 41(80):33–37.

Paris, François Edmond, 1841. *Essai sur la Construction Navale des Peuples Extra-Européens.* Paris, n. p.

Parsonson, G. S., 1963. The Settlement of Oceania: An Examination of the Accidental Voyage Theory. In *Polynesian Navigation: A Symposium on Andrew Sharp's Theory of Accidental Voyaging,* ed. Jack Golson. Polynesian Society Memoir, No. 34. Wellington, The Polynesian Society, 11–63.

Pawley, Andrew, and Roger C. Green, 1975. Dating the Dispersal of the Oceanic Languages. *Oceanic Linguistics* 12:1–67.

———, 1984. The Proto-Oceanic Language Community. *Journal of Pacific History* 19:123–146.

Philander, S. George, 1989. *El Niño, La Niña, and the Southern Oscillation.* San Diego, California, Academic Press.

Pi'ana'ia, Abraham, 1990. Personal communication, 20 July 1990.

Piddington, Ralph, 1956. A Note on the Validity and Significance of Oral Traditions. *Journal of the Polynesian Society* 65:200–204.

Porter, David, 1822. *Journal of a Cruise Made to the Pacific Ocean by Captain David Porter in the United States Frigate Essex.* 2 vols. New York, Wiley and Halsted.

Pukui, Mary Kawena, and Samuel H. Elbert, 1957. *Hawaiian-English Dictionary.* Honolulu, University of Hawai'i Press.

Quiros, Pedro Fernandez de, 1904. *The Voyages of Pedro Fernandez de Quiros, 1595–1606,* trans. and ed. Clements Markham. 2 vols. London, Hakluyt Society.

Ramirez, José Miguel, 1990–1991. Trans Pacific Contacts: The Mapuche Connection. *Rapa Nui Journal* 4:53–55.

Rasmussen, William H., Philip A. Arkin, Thomas H. Carpenter, John Koopman, Arthur F. Krueger, and Richard W. Reynolds, 1983. A Warm Episode in the Eastern Equatorial Pacific Ocean. *Tropical Ocean-Atmosphere Newsletter* 16:1–3.

Rasmussen, William H., Philip A. Arkin, Arthur F. Krueger, Roderick S.

Quiroz, and Richard W. Reynolds, 1983. Equatorial Pacific Atmosphere Climate during 1982–1983. *Tropical Ocean-Atmosphere Newsletter* 21: 2–3.

Ray, Sidney Herbert, 1926. *A Comparative Study of the Melanesian Island Languages*. Cambridge, Cambridge University Press.

Relandi, Hadriani, 1708. *Dissertationum Misscelanaearum, Pars Tertia et Ultima*. n. p., Guliemi Broedelet.

Revell, C. G., 1981a. Climatology of the South-west Pacific Islands, Part 1. Circulation Systems. In *Pacific Islands Water Resources*, ed. W. R. Dale. South Pacific Technical Inventory 2. Wellington, Department of Scientific and Industrial Research, 27–34.

———, 1981b. *Tropical Cyclones in the Southwest Pacific November 1969 to April 1979*. New Zealand Meteorological Service Miscellaneous Publication, No. 170. Wellington, New Zealand Meteorological Service.

Riesenberg, Saul H., 1965. Table of Voyages Affecting Micronesian Islands. *Oceania* 36:155–170.

———, 1976. The Organization of Navigational Knowledge on Puluwat. In *Pacific Navigation and Voyaging*, ed. Ben Finney. Polynesian Society Memoir, No. 39. Wellington, The Polynesian Society, 91–128.

Rivers, W. H. R., 1926. *Psychology and Ethnology*. London, Kegan, Paul, Trench, and Trubner.

Robinson, E., 1942. Shell Fishhooks of the California Coast. *Bishop Museum Occasional Papers* 17(4):57–65.

Roggeveen, Jacob, 1970. *The Journal of Jacob Roggeveen*, ed. Andrew Sharp. Oxford, Clarendon Press.

Rolett, Barry, in press. Marquesas Prehistory and the Origins of East Polynesian Culture. *Journal de la Société des Océanistes*.

Rose, Roger, 1978. *Symbols of Sovereignty: Feather Girdles of Tahiti and Hawai'i*. Pacific Anthropological Records, No. 28. Honolulu, Department of Anthropology, Bernice P. Bishop Museum.

———, 1979. On the Origin and Diversity of "Tahitian" Janiform Fly Whisks. In *Exploring the Visual Art of Oceania, Australia, Melanesia, Micronesia, and Polynesia*, ed. Sydney M. Mead. University of Hawai'i Press, Honolulu, 202–213.

Rouse, Irving, 1986. *Migrations in Prehistory*. New Haven, Yale University Press.

Sadler, James C., 1967. *The Tropical Upper Tropospheric Trough as a Secondary Source of Typhoons and a Primary Source of Tradewind Disturbances*. Hawai'i Institute of Geophysics Report, No. HIG-67-12. Honolulu, Hawai'i Institute of Geophysics, University of Hawai'i.

———, 1984. *The Anomalous Tropical Cyclones in the Pacific during the 1982–1983 El Niño*. Postprints, 19th Conference on Hurricanes and Tropical Meteorology, American Meteorological Society, Miami, Florida, 51–55.

Sadler, James C., and Bernard Kilonsky, 1983. Meteorological Events in the

Central Pacific during 1983. *Tropical Ocean-Atmosphere Newsletter* 21:2–3.

Sahlins, Marshall, 1958. *Social Stratification in Polynesia.* Seattle, University of Washington Press.

———, 1981. *Historical Metaphors and Mythical Realities: Structure in the Early History of the Sandwich Islands Kingdom.* Association for the Study of Anthropology in Oceania, Special Publication, No. 1. Ann Arbor, University of Michigan Press.

———, 1985. *Islands of History.* Chicago, University of Chicago Press.

Sharp, Andrew, 1956a. *Ancient Voyagers in the Pacific.* Polynesian Society Memoir, No. 32. Wellington, The Polynesian Society.

———, 1956b. The Prehistory of the New Zealand Maoris: Some Possibilities. *Journal of the Polynesian Society* 65:55–60.

———, 1957. *Ancient Voyagers in the Pacific.* 2d ed. Harmondsworth, Middlesex, Great Britain, Penguin.

———, 1958. Maori Genealogies and Canoe Traditions. *Journal of the Polynesian Society* 67:37–38.

———, 1961a. Interpreting Eastern Polynesian Prehistory. *Journal of the Polynesian Society* 70:349–351.

———, 1961b. Polynesian Navigation to Distant Islands. *Journal of the Polynesian Society* 70:219–226.

———, 1962. Fact and Fancy in the Marquesas Group. *Journal of the Polynesian Society* 71:122–124.

———, 1963a. *Ancient Voyagers in Polynesia.* Berkeley, University of California Press.

———, 1963b. Polynesian Navigation: Some Comments. *Journal of the Polynesian Society* 72:384–396.

———, 1964. Polynesian Navigation. *Navigation: Journal of the Institute of Navigation* 11:75–76.

———, 1965. Polynesian Navigation and Logic. *Navigation: The Journal of the Institute of Navigation (London)* 18:244.

———, 1966a. David Lewis's Experimental Voyage. *Journal of the Polynesian Society* 72:231–233.

———, 1966b. Early Micronesian Voyaging. *Oceania* 37:64–65.

———, 1969. Prehistoric Voyagers and Modern Experimenters. *Oceania* 39:231–233.

Siers, James, 1977. *Taratai, A Pacific Adventure.* Wellington, Millwood.

———, 1978. *Taratai II, A Continuing Pacific Adventure.* Wellington, Millwood.

Simmons, David R., 1976. *The Great New Zealand Myth.* Wellington, A. H. and A. W. Reed.

Simmons, David R., and Bruce Biggs, 1970. The Sources of the Lore of the Whare-Wananga. *Journal of the Polynesian Society* 79:22–42.

Sinoto, Yoshihiko, 1970. An Archaeologically Based Assessment of the Marquesas Islands as a Dispersal Center in East Polynesia. In *Studies in*

Oceanic Culture History, Vol. 1, ed. Roger C. Green and Marion Kelly. Pacific Anthropological Records, No. 11. Honolulu, Department of Anthropology, Bernice P. Bishop Museum, 105–132.

———, 1979. Excavations on Huahine, French Polynesia. *Pacific Studies* 3:1–40.

———, 1983. Huahine: Heritage of the Great Navigators. *Museum* 35: 70–73.

Skeleton, R. A., 1955. *Charts & Views Drawn by Cook and his Officers and Reproduced from the Original Manuscripts*. Cambridge, Cambridge University Press.

Skinner, H. D., 1931. On the Patu Family and Its Occurrence beyond New Zealand. *Journal of the Polynesian Society* 40:183–196.

Smith, S. Percy, 1898. *Hawaiki: The Whence of the Maori*. Wellington, Whitcombe and Tombs.

———, 1907. History and Traditions of the Taranaki Coast. *Journal of the Polynesian Society* 16:120–219.

———, 1913–1915. *The Lore of the Whare Wananga*. 2 vols. Polynesian Society Memoirs, Nos. 3–4. Wellington, The Polynesian Society.

Sneider, Cary, 1987. Tahiti to Rangiroa in a Polynesian Voyaging Canoe. Unpublished manuscript in the possession of the author.

Sorrenson, M. P. K., 1979. *Maori Origin and Migrations*. Auckland, Auckland University Press and Oxford University Press.

Specht, Jim R., 1984. *The Prehistoric Archaeology of Norfolk Island*. Pacific Anthropological Records, No. 34. Honolulu, Bernice P. Bishop Museum.

Spriggs, Matthew, 1984. The Lapita Cultural Complex: Origins, Distribution, Contemporaries, and Successors. *Journal of Pacific History* 19: 202–223.

———, 1988. The Hawaiian Transformation of Ancestral Polynesian Society: Conceptualizing Chiefly States. In *State and Society*, ed. John Gledhill, Barbara Bender, and Mogens T. Larsen. London, Unwin and Hyman, 57–73.

Spriggs, Matthew, and Atholl Anderson, 1993. Late Colonization of East Polynesia. *Antiquity* 67:200–217.

Steadman, David W., and Patrick V. Kirch, 1990. Prehistoric Extinction of Birds on Mangaia, Cook Islands, Polynesia. *Proceedings of the National Academy of Sciences* 87:9605–9609.

Steiner, J. T., 1980. *The Climate of the South-West Pacific Region*. New Zealand Meteorological Service Miscellaneous Publication, No. 166. Wellington, New Zealand Meteorological Service.

Sterling, Jo-anne Kahanamoku, 1991. Pape'ete to Mo'orea. Unpublished typescript in possession of the author.

Stokes, John F. G., 1928. Whence Paao? *Papers of the Hawaiian Historical Society*, No. 15. Honolulu, Hawaiian Historical Society.

Stroup, Edward D., Bernard Kilonsky, and Klaus Wyrtki, 1981. *AXBT Observations During the Hawai'i/Tahiti Shuttle Experiment*. Hawai'i Institute of Geophysics Report, No. HIG-81-1. Honolulu, Hawai'i Institute of Geophysics, University of Hawai'i.

Suggs, Robert C., 1960a. Historical Traditions and Archaeology in Polynesia. *American Anthropologist* 62:764–773.

———, 1960b. *The Islands Civilizations of Polynesia*. New York, New American Library.

———, 1961a. *The Archaeology of Nukuhiva, Marquesas Islands, French Polynesia*. Anthropological Papers of the American Museum of Natural History, No. 49, Part 1. New York, American Museum of Natural History.

———, 1961b. Methodological Problems for Accidental Voyagers. *Journal of the Polynesian Society* 70:474–476.

Sutton, Douglas G., 1987a. A Paradigmatic Shift in Polynesian Prehistory: Implications for New Zealand. *New Zealand Journal of Archaeology* 9:133–155.

———, 1987b. Time-Place Systematics in New Zealand Archaeology: The Case for a Fundamental Revision. *Journal de la Société des Océanistes* no. 84:23–29.

Sykes, W. R., 1977. *Kermadec Islands Flora*. New Zealand Department of Scientific and Industrial Research Bulletin, No. 219. Wellington, New Zealand Department of Scientific and Industrial Research.

Taylor, Richard, 1870. *Te Ika a Maui*. London, William Macintosh.

Terrell, John, 1986. *Prehistory in the Pacific Islands*. Cambridge, Cambridge University Press.

Thilenius, Georg, 1901. Die Fahrzeuge der Somoaner. *Globus* 80:167–172.

———, 1902. *Ethnographische Ergebnisse aus Melanesien*. Abhandlungen der Kaiserlichen Leopoldinisch-Carolnischen Deutschen Akademie der Naturforscher, Nova Acta. Vol. 80, Part 2 (Die Polyneisichen Inseln an der Ostgrenze Melanesians). Halle, Erhard Kallas.

Thomas, Stephen D., 1987. *The Last Navigator*. New York, Henry Holt.

Thomason, Sarah Grey, and Terrence Kaufman, 1988. *Language Contact, Creolization, and Genetic Linguistics*. Berkeley, Los Angeles, London, University of California Press.

Thompson, C. S., 1986a. *The Climate and Weather of the Southern Cook Islands*. New Zealand Meteorological Service Miscellaneous Publication, No. 188 (2). Wellington, New Zealand Meteorological Service.

———, 1986b. *The Climate and Weather of the Northern Cook Islands*. New Zealand Meteorological Service Miscellaneous Publication, No. 188 (3). Wellington, New Zealand Meteorological Service.

Thorne, Alan, and Robert Raymond. *Man on the Rim: The Peopling of the Pacific*. Angus and Robertson, North Ryde, Australia.

Thorpe, W. W., 1929. Evidence of Polynesian Culture in Australia and Norfolk Island. *Journal of the Polynesian Society* 38:123–126.

Trenberth, Kevin E., and Kingtse C. Mo, 1985. Blocking in the Southern Hemisphere. *Monthly Weather Review* 113:3–21.

Trigger, Bruce G., 1989. *A History of Archaeological Thought*. Cambridge, Cambridge University Press.

Tuggle, David H., 1979. Hawaii. In *The Prehistory of Polynesia*, ed. Jesse D. Jennings. Cambridge, Harvard University Press, 167–199.

Valeri, Valerio, 1985. *Kinship and Sacrifice*. Chicago, University of Chicago Press.

Van Tilburg, Joanne (in press). *Easter Island: Archaeology, Ecology, and Culture*. London, British Museum Press, and Washington, Smithsonian Institution Press.

Vansina, Jan, 1985. *Oral Tradition as History*. Madison, University of Wisconsin Press.

Von Den Steinen, Karl, 1988. *Von Den Steinen's Marquesan Myths*. Trans. Marta Langridge from *Zeitschrift für Ethnologie*, 1933–1934, 65:325–373; 1934–1935, 66:191–240; ed. Jennifer Terrell. Canberra, Target Oceania and the Journal of Pacific History.

Walter, Richard, 1990. The Southern Cook Islands in Eastern Polynesian Prehistory. Unpublished Ph.D. diss., Auckland, Department of Anthropology, University of Auckland.

Walter, Richard, and William R. Dickenson, 1989. A Ceramic Sherd from Ma'uke in the Southern Cook Islands. *Journal of the Polynesian Society* 98:465–470.

Walsh, Archdeacon, 1905. The Winged Pilot of Hawaiki. *Transactions and Proceedings of the New Zealand Institute* 38:127–130.

Ward, R. Gerard, 1987. Notes on Simulated Voyages. Unpublished manuscript in the possession of the author.

Ward, R. Gerard, and Muriel Brookfield, 1992. The Dispersal of the Coconut: Did It Float or Was It Carried to Panama? *Journal of Biogeography* 19:467–480.

Ward, R. Gerard, John W. Webb, and M. Levison, 1976. The Settlement of the Polynesian Outliers: A Computer Simulation. In *Polynesian Navigation and Voyaging*, ed. Ben Finney. Polynesian Society Memoir, No. 39. Wellington, The Polynesian Society, 57–68.

Weisler, Marshall (in press). The Settlement of Marginal Polynesia: New Evidence from Henderson Island. *Journal of Field Archaeology*.

Whistler, W. Arthur, 1990. The Other Polynesian Gourd. *Pacific Science* 44:115–122.

———, 1991. Polynesian Plant Introductions. In *Islands, Plants, and Polynesians: An Introduction to Polynesian Ethnobotany*, ed. Paul Alan Cox and Sandra Anne Banack. Portland, Oregon, Dioscorides Press, 41–66.

Wilder, G. P., 1931. *Flora of Rarotonga*. Bishop Museum Bulletin, No. 86. Honolulu, Bernice P. Bishop Museum.

Wilkes, Charles, 1849. *The Narrative of the United States Exploring Expedition During the Years 1838, 1839, 1840, 1841, 1842*. 5 vols. Philadelphia, n.p.

Williams, John, 1838. *A Narrative of Missionary Enterprises in the South Sea Islands*. London, John Snow.

Winkler, Captain, 1901. On Sea Charts Formerly Used in the Marshall Islands, with Notices on the Navigation of These Islanders in General.

Annual Report of the Smithsonian Institution, 1899. Washington, D.C., The Smithsonian Institution, 487–509.

Woodford, Charles M., 1916. On Some Little-known Polynesian Islands in the Neighbourhood of the Solomon Islands. *Journal of the Royal Geographical Society* 48:26–54.

Wyrtki, Klaus, 1975. El Niño—The Dynamic Response of the Equatorial Pacific Ocean to Atmospheric Forcing. *Journal of Physical Oceanography* 5:572–584.

Wyrtki, Klaus, and Gary Myers, 1975. *The Trade Wind Field over the Pacific Ocean, Part I: The Mean Field and the Mean Annual Variation.* Hawai'i Institute of Geophysics Report, No. HIG-75-1. Honolulu, Hawai'i Institute of Geophysics, University of Hawai'i.

Yen, Douglas E., 1973. The Origins of Oceanic Agriculture. *Archaeology and Physical Anthropology in Oceania* 8:68–85.

———, 1974. *The Sweet Potato and Oceania: An Essay in Ethnobotany.* Bishop Museum Bulletin, No. 236. Honolulu, Bernice P. Bishop Museum.

———, 1986. Personal communication, 14 May 1986.

———, 1991. Polynesian Cultigens and Cultivars: The Question of Origin. In *Islands, Plants, and Polynesians: An Introduction to Polynesian Ethnobotany*, ed. Paul Allen Cox and Sandra Anne Banack. Portland, Oregon, Dioscorides Press, 67–95.

INDEX

Designer: U.C. Press Staff
Compositor: Prestige Typography
Text: 10.5/12.5 Trump Mediaeval
Display: Trump Mediaeval
Printer: Haddon Craftsmen
Binder: Haddon Craftsmen